THE MOSSI OF BURKINA FASO

THE MOSSI OF BURKINA FASO
Chiefs, Politicians and Soldiers

ELLIOTT P. SKINNER
Columbia University in the City of New York

Prospect Heights, Illinois

For information about this book, write or call:
Waveland Press, Inc.
P.O. Box 400
Prospect Heights, Illinois 60070
(312) 634-0081

Cover: Youths in Ouagadougou, Burkina Faso parading with picture of Capt. Thomas Sankara. Photo: Janet Milhomme/AFRICA REPORT. Used with permission.

Copyright © 1989, 1964 by Elliott P. Skinner. The 1964 version of this book was entitled *The Mossi of the Upper Volta: The Political Development of a Sudanese People*.

ISBN 0-88133-398-0

All rights reserved. No part of this book may be reproduced, stored in a retrieval system, or transmitted in any form or by any means without permission in writing from the publisher.

Printed in the United States of America

7   6   5   4   3   2   1

In honor of my children and grandchildren.

PREFACE

THIS BOOK ATTEMPTS to contribute to our understanding of Mossi society, about which relatively little is known even within the continent of Africa. Many of the data were collected in the Upper Volta Republic between November 1955 and January 1957, a period when the Voltaics were preparing for important political changes. I did most of my field work in the area formerly included within the kingdom of Ouagadougou. I stayed only one week in the Yatenga and paid but brief visits to Tenkodogo and the Boussouma region. Thus, my basic data hold chiefly for Ouagadougou. My methods of research were the conventional anthropological ones: I recorded local oral histories, conducted personal interviews, attended court and important rituals, participated in the life of the people whenever possible, and collected genealogical and biographical data.

In addition, I read all the important documents I could find on the political history of the Mossi people in the files of the Institut Français d'Afrique Noire, in local administrative offices, and in the Archives of the Governor General of French West Africa in Dakar, Senegal. I also read published works on the Mossi by such scholars as Maurice Delafosse, A. A. Dim Delobson, Georges Cheron, Eugene Mangin, Lucien Marc, and Louis Tauxier. Their works were invaluable to me, and I owe them a debt of gratitude. My hope is that what I have added to the store of knowledge about the Mossi may be of service to Mossi scholars, whose studies will ultimately bring to light aspects of their own culture that we have missed.

The ethnographer working in contemporary Africa is faced with the problem of the time dimension. In reporting his findings, he may use the "ethnographic present" and describe the cultural system he studied as though all elements, even those dredged up from the memories of old men, were still viable in the society. Or he may use the past tense and thus underscore the fact that the society is changing, even though cultural traits from the past may be present and viable. I have elected the latter course primarily because, even though many of the aspects of Mossi culture described here are still in existence, Mossi society is changing ever more rapidly. Many old culture traits that I found there as late as 1955 had all but disappeared when I returned in 1960. Not to recognize this fact in preparing this study would have laid the ground for the criticism that anthropologists ignore the changes taking place around them in order to concentrate upon the past.

My own interest in the Mossi grew out of an early curiosity about the cultures and societies of Africa. It was born of my parents' concern over Ethiopia's struggle to remain free and nurtured by the writings of Mr. Marcus A. Garvey, Dr. W. E. B. Dubois, and Professors Melville J. Herskovits and E. Franklin Frazier. These factors, together with the help and encouragement of my relatives and friends, ultimately led me to choose a career in anthropology and African studies. I am grateful to Professor John L. Landgraf of New York University, who first taught me the elements of anthropology and thus provided me with the basic tools for understanding human societies. To Dr. Gene Weltfish and Professor Joseph H. Greenberg of Columbia University I owe a further debt of gratitude for having directed my first studies of African cultures. To them, and to Professors Conrad M. Arensberg, Morton H. Fried, and Charles Wagley, also of Columbia University, I owe whatever skill and competence in social-science research I may possess. I am grateful to the Ford Foundation for financing the field work on which this study is based, and to the Arts and Science Research Fund Committee of New York University for help in defraying the cost of preparing the manuscript for publication.

I am deeply indebted to the Mossi people for having permitted me to live among them for fourteen months. M. François Bouda, district chief of Manga, and Naba Boulga, district chief of Nobere, not only welcomed me but kindly consented to answer my innumerable questions about the nature of their political and other institutions. The Djiba Naba, who subsequently became Mogho Naba Kougri, also encouraged me in my task, and so did Dr. Joseph Conombo. Without the help of M. Beta Nyissa, my friend and interpreter, field work would have been difficult. He not only explained many aspects of Mossi culture to me, but put me in touch with persons who could answer my questions, and taught me the rudiments of the Mossi language.

I must also thank my good friend Mme. Ouennam Pousde for helping me to understand the point of view of the Mossi women. This kind lady never ceased to be amused at the attempts of this *yagenga* (brother's son) to participate as fully as possible in Mossi life. M. Frederic Guierma encouraged me to prepare this work for publication, and M. Albert Salfo Balima not only read a draft of the manuscript, but kindly made available to me his own notes on Mossi society. Other Mossi and Voltaics, far too numerous to mention, gave freely of their time and friendship.

I am indebted to M. Le Moal, Director of the Institut Français d'Afrique Noire at Ouagadougou, and to his assistant, M. Savonnet, for their hospitality. MM. Pujol and Mathieu, the French administrators in charge of the Mossi areas where I conducted my field work, were especially courteous and helpful. By introducing me to other administrators, they made it possible for me to visit other areas of Mossi country.

I should like to thank Mrs. Doby Gilletti and Dr. Shirley Gorenstein for their helpful criticism of parts of this manuscript, and the Service Information Haute-Volta for permission to use the photographs that appear between pp. 178 and 179. I am also deeply indebted to Miss Ariane Brunel for her editorial assistance.

PREFACE, 1989

THIS BOOK FIRST appeared at a time when there was a dearth of monographs dealing with the emerging independent states of contemporary Africa. This was especially true in the United States, where the only extant monographs available for students, scholars, and the general public were the theoretically dated works of primarily European scholars. The task of producing new monographs fell to the first generation of American anthropologists who had worked in Africa—those who were either trained by Professor Melville J. Herskovits or by his students. Again, it was difficult to obtain monographs on those African peoples living in non-English-speaking areas in Africa because most American scholars preferred to work in areas where the lingua franca was English. *The Mossi of the Upper Volta* was one of the few monographs written in English about one of the historically important populations of the western Sudan. Not only did the Mossi have relations with the long-vanished Sudanese empires of Mali and Songhai, but they were also important because their society still retained many features from the past. Moreover, during the colonial period that was then ending, the Mossi people had made important labor contributions to the economies of the Gold Coast (Ghana) and of French West Africa. They were—people that needed to be known.

In retrospect, it is clear that, in addition to what I wrote in the original 1964 Preface to this book, the opportunity that I had to study the Mossi was valuable to me both as a young anthropologist and in my later career. I had earlier studied ethnic relations and acculturation in what was then called British Guiana; but having grown up in the Caribbean area, which shared many aspects of culture with British Guiana, and being able to use English while doing fieldwork, I did not have the cultural baptism that is so important to the developing anthropologist. In my work among the Mossi, not only did I have to use French, (which I had learned in school and had improved while serving in Europe with the United States Army during World

War II); but also I found it impossible to work without attempting to learn the Mossi language, Moré. I also discovered the realities of the distinctions between race, language, and culture. Although I shared many biological traits with the Mossi, their language was initially alien to me, and so were many aspects of their culture. It was humbling, but instructive, to be socialized in the ways of the Mossi by very small and patient Mossi children.

Fortuitously, the growing importance of Africa to the United States and the publication of the earlier version of this book attracted the attention of the government and people of the United States, who were eager to understand the peoples of Africa. The opportunity to give two courses on CBS's "Sunrise Semester" impressed upon me the need for anthropologists who write about Africa to make their work meaningful to the public beyond the student audience in universities. Again, the opportunity to give lectures on the peoples and cultures of Africa to officials of the Foreign Service of the United States advanced my understanding of how the fieldwork of anthropologists can contribute to the mutual understanding between peoples. When President Lyndon B. Johnson invited me to be his ambassador to the Upper Volta in 1966, I was pleased to place my knowledge at the disposal of my own country in the hope that this would contribute to improved relations between ourselves and the Voltaics, most of whom were Mossi.

Over the years, *The Mossi of the Upper Volta* has been reprinted several times. In that time, the Mossi and their society have experienced independence, have felt the ravages of drought, have had their chiefs and politicians tested by repetitive coups, have experienced the rule of a charismatic soldier who changed the name of their society to Burkina Faso, and have watched that soldier later fall victim to yet another coup. I have attempted to chronicle these changes in articles for scholarly journals, but I have welcomed the further opportunity given to me by Waveland Press to publish an expanded version of the original book, now *The Mossi of Burkina Faso*.

I owe much to the generation of students, including many Mossi, who have read this book, raised interesting questions about the issues treated in it, and who have lamented that there was not a more up-to-date version of it. These students have my admiration and respect. I would also like to thank the people of Upper Volta/Burkina Faso who, over the years, have continued to welcome me in their midst, and, much to my embarrassment, assert that I have learned to understand them—a little. I am delighted to find that the hope that I evinced in the 1964 Preface, that Mossi scholars would assume the responsibility of explaining their own society to the world, has come to fruition. I thank them for their kindness to my work as they did so. Finally

I would like to express my love and respect to my wife, our children, and our grandchildren, with the hope that the reissuing of this book will compensate somewhat for their understanding during my preoccupation with scholarship.

CONTENTS

I	Introduction, 1989	1
II	Sovereignty, Kinship, and Community	15
III	Kingship and Chiefship	33
IV	Administration	62
V	Law and the Judicial Process	80
VI	Warfare	95
VII	The Economic Foundation	109
VIII	Religion and Government	128
IX	European Contact and the Conquest of the Mossi	141
X	Mossi Government during the Colonial Period	156
XI	Chiefs and Politicians	181
XII	Epilogue, 1989	206
	Notes	239
	Glossary	259
	Bibliography	263
	Index	269

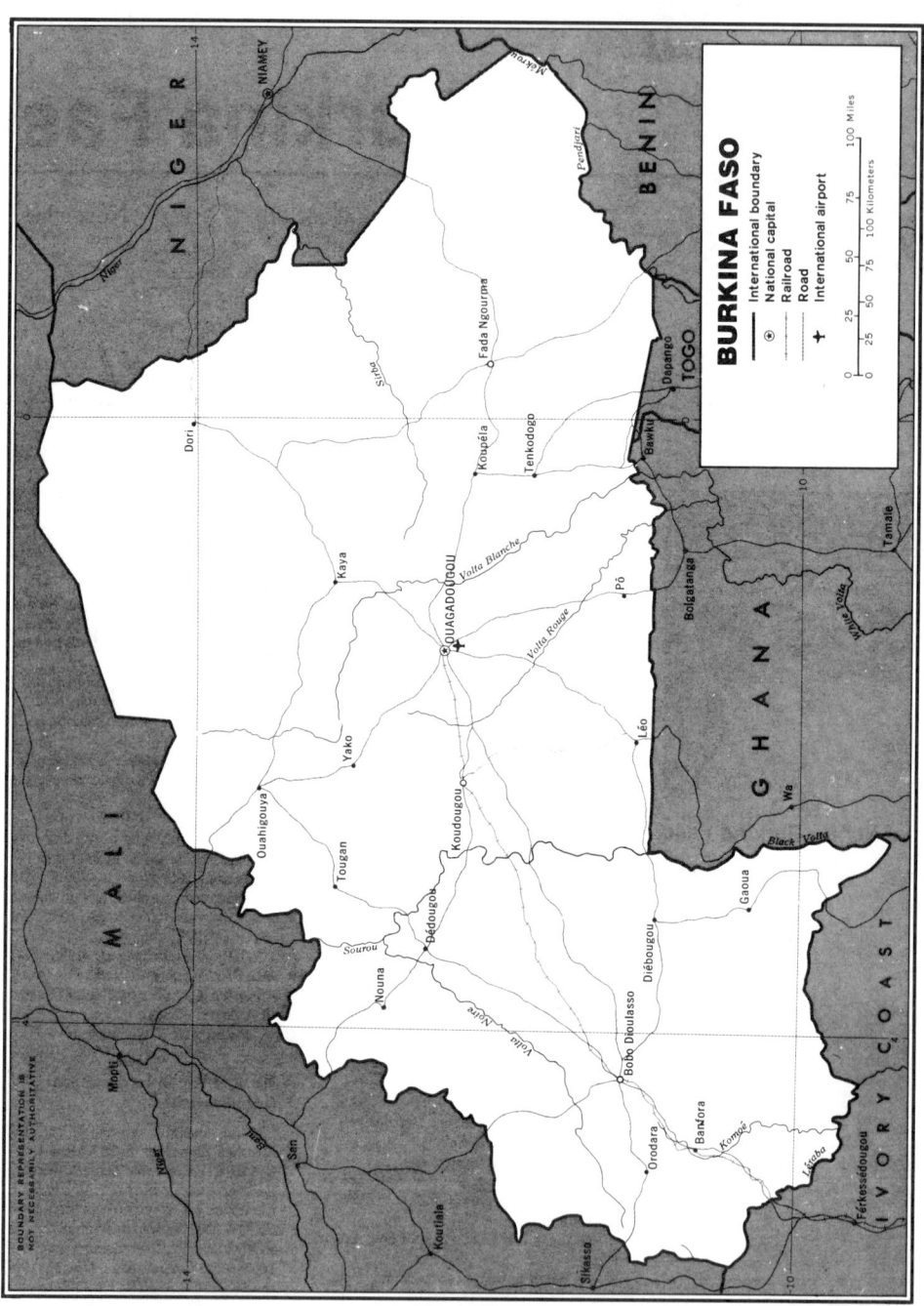

I

INTRODUCTION, 1989

THE MEDIEVAL SOCIETIES of the western Sudan are today better known than when this book was published more than twenty years ago. Then it was quite accurate to state that despite a growing interest in Africa since the start of decolonization in the late 1950s, scholars still knew very little about most of the African societies that had once flourished in various parts of the continent. With few exceptions, these societies either disappeared altogether or declined and changed their structure long before they had been adequately described. Thanks to the recent work of African and non-African scholars who pored over ancient Arabic documents and local chronicles, we know more about the origins, evolution, and nature of such ancient empires and kingdoms as Ghana, Mali, Songhai, Bornu, Kanem, the Mossi, and Hausa than might ever have been expected. Had more archeological investigations been conducted in the area, the task would have been easier. Unfortunately, the generalization still holds that for every ton of archeological materials sifted in Egypt and parts of the Middle East, only one teaspoonful has been examined in the western Sudan.

The ethnologists who started to study the societies that existed during the colonial period did provide valuable data about them, but by then most of the societies mentioned by early chroniclers had changed radically. Of course, many of their features which survived from the past were often embedded within different institutional structures. Again, many of the paradigms used by the early ethnologists to describe these societies, while valid and useful during their time, were later found to have been quite inadequate for the task. But it is the nature of all human knowledge and understanding to shift and expand. This will be true of the paradigms used in this study.

Mossi society attracted me and previous scholars because, in contrast to many of its neighbors in space and time, that society appeared to have maintained much of its ancient structure, as described by earlier chroniclers of the western Sudan. The Mossi shared many traditional African culture traits with ancient Mali and Songhai empires and later came under the shadow of these core societies, which had expanded under the impact of

Islamic civilization. The Mossi survived the rise and fall of such later Sudanese conquerors as El Hadj Omar and Samory Touré, but not without being influenced by them. Mossi society retained most of the traditional characteristics of its institutions throughout French rule. Only on the eve of independence did the traditional Mossi political organization experience radical pressures strong enough to threaten its continuity. Some analysts suggested that it was even on the point of collapse. But like many human institutions, the Mossi political system appears to be working out all of its possibilities before it, too, passes into the abyss of time.

It would have been tempting to claim, as many scholars have done, that the governmental system of the Mossi mirrored faithfully that of the early Sudanese kingdoms.[1] As will be noted below, Mossi society, especially in the Kingdom of Ouagadougou, did possess in many details, many of the political institutions described for ancient Mali. Yet it would be incorrect to extrapolate from the contemporary scene to the early Sudan, for Mossi society undoubtedly changed over the centuries. It was, however, my intention to determine in what ways a study of Mossi government could contribute to the understanding of the development, structure, and functioning of early Sudanese societies. My work was also an attempt to demonstrate how European conquest affected the political organization of the Mossi and contributed to its decline. This revised edition while retaining the original text, which used the standard ethnographic present, adds new data on the evolution of the Mossi political system during several times which followed, namely, those periods when Mossi society became part of an independent Upper Volta Republic; when the politicians who assumed power after independence rose and fell; and the spate of military coups occurred during which the name of the Upper Volta was changed to Burkina Faso.

The kingdom of Ouagadougou was selected as the main object of study, primarily because it emerged as the most important Mossi polity and retained this position through the greater part of Mossi history. Attention will be given to the other Mossi polities and the three other Mossi kingdoms—Yatenga, Tenkodogo, and the more remote Fada-N'Gourma, all of which resemble Ouagadougou—only insofar as they affect the history of Ouagadougou or highlight the basic nature of Mossi government.

The Mossi are a Sudanese Negroid population in the new Republic of the Upper Volta.[2] Today they number more than 5,000,000, or approximately half of the country's total population. Their ancestral territory, which they call Mogho (land of the Mossi), covers some 30,000 square miles in the southern part of the republic. It is a huge plateau, lying from 1,000 to 1,600 feet above sea level, and broken by three low mountain ranges and numerous small hills. The Kipirsi range in the northeast has an average height of about 2,000 feet and includes the sacred mountain of the Mossi, known as Plimpikou. The Boussouma range to the east reaches a height of some 1,500 feet, and the Naouri range in the southeast is almost as high.

The climate of Mossi country is typical of the Sudanic zone. There are two main sources, one cold and dry, the other hot and wet. The first begins in November with the coming of the harmattan, the dust-laden wind that ends in January, the coolest month, when the average temperature is about 70 degrees Fahrenheit and the humidity about 12 percent. The hot season extends from March to October. In July, the warmest month, the temperature reaches a high of 88 degrees Fahrenheit and the humidity is 78 percent. Violent dust storms herald the rains, which begin late in May and end in September. The rain falls almost entirely in heavy showers and thunderstorms, and the average annual fall is between 30 and 40 inches. In those years when the rainfall is about 40 inches and is regularly spaced, the Mossi can look forward to a good harvest. When the rainfall is below 30 inches and is spaced irregularly during the planting season, the threat of famine is serious. So narrow is the margin of rainfall or agriculture that in 1956 the people of one Mossi district anxiously awaited "two rains" (two showers), without which they feared that in 1957 there would be a difficult "hungry period" (the time between the exhaustion of one year's crops and the maturing of the next).

Mossi country is drained by only three rivers: the Black Volta, with its two chief tributaries, the Sourou and the Debere; and the Red and White Voltas, with their numerous small tributaries. Only the Black Volta flows all year round. The Red and White Voltas are important only as drainage systems during the short rainy periods, for they dwindle to a string of small stagnant pools in the dry seasons. In some low-lying areas near the main watercourses, trapped waters provide the moisture for dank riverine vegetation.

The soils of Mossi country, which are typical of the Sudanic and Sahel areas, were formed chiefly by the weathering of Precambrian rocks. Ferruginous soils of varying depths, red argils, and pure silicates of aluminum predominate in the northern regions. In the south are found thin, sandy soils formed by the decomposition of crystalline rocks and sandstones. Most of these soils are eroded by torrential rains, the scouring action of the harmattan, and the incendiary action of man and nature. Even where the soils are reasonably fertile, the nature of the underlying rocks precludes important deposits of ground water. In the western sandstone region, rain filters down with such rapidity that water can be obtained only from deep wells. In the remainder of the territory, the presence of Precambrian rocks induces a rapid runoff, with the result that wells yield very little water at any depth. Rainfall collects only in riverbed pools or along dams constructed for that purpose in hollow places. The building of dams was relatively unknown in aboriginal times, and the Mossi did not practice irrigation farming.

During the dry season, Mossi country presents a picture of such utter aridity that one wonders whether it is possible for such parched red soils to produce plant life. After the first drops of rain, however, the entire plain is quickly covered with grasses that sometimes reach heights of five or six feet. The most characteristic and valuable trees in the region are the baobab (*Adansonia digitata*), the locust-bean (*Parkia biglobosa*), and the kapok (*Bombax costatum*). The sole and unimportant representative of the palm family is the *Borassus aethiopium*. There are several kinds of acacias, including the *Kenyaya senegalensis*, and a wide variety of silk-cotton trees, the most important of which is *Eryodendron anfractuosum*.

The cultivated plants of the region include numerous varieties of cereals, roots, and legumes. Several varieties of sorghum (*Sorghum vulgare*) and millet (*Pennisetum typhoides*) constitute the staple crops of the Mossi, but maize (*Zea mays*) is extremely important because it is one of the first crops to be harvested after the difficult hungry period. Peanuts, onions, rice, beans, okra, fonio (a regional crabgrass whose seeds are a cereal), and sweet potatoes form the bulk of the other cultivated crops. Manioc (cassava) is grown only in small quantities because it requires moist soil for optimum development. The Mossi grow tobacco in fields around their homesteads, where they also cultivate their most important cash crops, cotton and indigo, which are used in the manufacture and dyeing of cotton cloth.

The wild fauna of Mossi country include several species of antelope, deer, monkeys, rabbits, snakes, and wild pigs. Elephants roam the beds of rivers and streams and often destroy cultivated fields, while lions and hyenas distress the people by attacking livestock. The pools and rivers of Mossi country are inhabited by turtles, crocodiles, and various species of scaled and scaleless fish. Chickens, Muscovy ducks, and half-domesticated guinea fowl are the most valuable species of birds.

The Mossi have long been famous for their splendid donkeys and horses. Donkeys are sometimes ridden, but they are used primarily as beasts of burden. Horses are important for military and ceremonial purposes and for export to the tsetse-fly zones to the south. The Mossi raise two main types of cattle: a zebu-like animal in the northern regions and a dwarf variety in the south. These animals are raised primarily for their milk and for export; they are seldom killed for meat until they are fairly old. Goats and sheep provide the main source of meat. Hog raising, never widespread, seems to be declining in importance with the increased importance of Islamic food taboos, which are increasingly observed, even among people who are still animists.

The subsoil of Mossi country is not well known, but so far there have been no major discoveries of mineral deposits. The only known goldfield remained unworked in aboriginal times. The Mossi prefer jewelry worked from imported copper and silver. The northern Mossi worked their local iron in aboriginal times, but those in the south obtained this metal from caravan traders. The nineteenth-century reports of Henry Barth and other European travelers indicate that the Mossi conducted a rather extensive foreign trade. At least six caravan routes passed through their territory, and traders such as the Hausa and Mandingo visited the important Mossi trading centers at Yako, Pouitenga, and Ouagadougou, where they exchanged Saharan and forest products for Mossi livestock and cloth.[3]

The Mossi belong to the Voltaic culture area, a name given by Maurice Delafosse to the regions drained by the Black, Red, and White Voltas and their tributaries. The area embraces parts of Mali, the Ivory Coast, Dahomey, the Upper Volta, and northern Ghana.[4] Its vast congeries of peoples include the Dagomba, Mamprusi, Dagari, Birifo, Senufo, Gurmanche, Gurunsi, Lobi, Bobo, Tallensi, Konkomba, Dogon, Somba, Fulse, and Ninisi, all of whom speak languages belonging to the Gur or Moshi-Grunshi group of the Niger-Congo family of African languages.[5] Like the Mossi, these groups are primarily horticultural; cereals are their main crops, and they cultivate yams where conditions permit. Their social organization takes both patrilineal and matrilineal forms. The veneration of ancestors lies at the core of their religious beliefs, but the existence of an otiose high god whose name contains the root *We* (Ouennam, Win, Wene, etc.) is also recognized. There are also tutelary spirits, the chief one being a female earth deity associated with We and called *Tenga* (also occurring as Teng, Tena, and Ten). The Tengsobadamba, who are priests or custodians of the earth shrines, are found among all the groups in the Voltaic family; and they often share leadership with more secular chiefs called Naba, Na, or Nab, which to the Mossi means "that force of God which permits a mere man to govern other men." Most of the ruling clans of the Voltaic groups claim common ancestry and acknowledge the same totems.[6]

The only glaring dissimilarity between these Voltaic peoples and the one with which this study is primarily concerned lies in the realm of political organization. Some are united into large kingdoms, while others form small acephalous (that is, having very weak chiefs or no chiefs at all) groups. Delafosse made the following generalizations about the smaller groups:

> It may be said of these people that, as a whole, they have remained quite primitive. With a few exceptions, they have not reached any significant level of political development; as a rule, they have not progressed beyond family unity. Although they neighbor on well-organized and powerful states such as the Mossi empires and the kingdoms of the Gourma and Bergo, which are inhabited by populations of the same ethnic group, they have derived little benefit from this proximity; some of them have been absorbed as subjects or vassals by these states, while others have remained on the outside, and seem to have but one purpose, the forceful preservation of their fierce but sterile independence.... Attachment to the land seems to be the only solid and fecund institution in their chaotic society.[7]

Robert Sutherland Rattray believed that the development of such highly organized political systems as those of the Mossi, Dagomba, and Mamprusi may be traced to "small bands of strangers." He thinks that the outsiders were better armed, better clothed, and familiar with the rudiments of Islam; he further believes that since they know about the institution of kingship, they were able to "superimpose upon the primitive tribes among whom they settled a new and unheard-of political conception, namely the idea of territorial and secular leadership in place of the immemorial institution of a ruler who was the high priest of a totemic clan and dealt only in spiritual sanctions." Nevertheless, Rattray is not certain that the Voltaic groups would not have evolved complex political systems if they had been left to themselves. He makes the significant statement that if the subjugation by the bands of strangers had not taken place, the local earth-priest or priest-king "undoubtedly would have evolved into the type of native ruler.... who was not only high priest and custodian of the land of his tribe and of the ancestral spirits but one who was a chief or king on a territorial basis, whose sanctions were secular and physical rather than spiritual; in other words, what the average European implies when he uses the word 'king' or 'chief.'"[8] Since pristine state development has occurred so seldom, it is difficult to evaluate Rattray's speculations about the possible local development of complex political forms. Nevertheless, his view that bands of strangers were responsible for state formation in the area is supported by most of the local traditions.

The relationship between the Voltaic peoples and the bands of strangers has not received the attention it deserves. In fact, the implications of such a relationship have often been underrated. As a result, groups that may once have been part of larger political entities created by these strangers have been regarded as acephalous. In his studies of the Tallensi of northern Ghana, for example, Meyer Fortes constantly referred to a group of lineages called *Namoos*, whose members claimed to be descended from the Mamprusi ruling group. He stated that a Tallensi chief from the Tongo area claimed to be "the ruler of all the Tallensi." In another context Fortes discussed the status of a chief called Kuna'aba, who, he told us, was regarded by the other Tallensi chiefs as their "father," to whom they owed "loyalty, respect, and ceremonial deference." Moreover, Fortes indicated that ceremonial investiture by Kuna'aba was "the crucial act conferring chiefship" on a Tale, even if the latter was actually selected by an administrative officer.[9] These facts should have indicated to Fortes that he was dealing with a rather complex historical problem that required further investigation.

Instead of carrying the investigation further, however, he dismissed the Tongo chief's claim of control over all Taleland with the assertion that "it is a distortion in terms of the modern privileges of chiefship, of a status which is merely that of *primus inter pares* in the native system." Similarly, he doubted the historical status and role of Kuna'aba: "Kuna'aba's modern judicial and administrative authority rests solely on the sanction of force represented by the [British] Administration." Interestingly enough, Fortes told us that "the Administration has always regarded Taleland as part of the 'Mamprusi State,' under the ultimate rule of the chief of Mampurugu, through his subchief and deputy, the Kuna'aba, who was considered to have full jurisdiction over the 'Kurugu Division.'"[10]

Rattray, whose study of the Tallensi predated Fortes's, declared that the Tallensi chiefs and the Namoos clans were descended from the noble lineages of the Mamprusi kingdom, which at one time controlled Tallensi country. The chief of one of the Namoos clans reportedly told him, "We came from Mampurugu.... We have now become Talense; we no longer circumcise, because the local people would not marry us. The chief of Kurugu, our 'father,' still speaks Mampelle, but we no longer do so." The chief referred to, is of course, Fortes's Kuna'aba. Rattray added that the Tallensi chief of the Namoos clans told him that they had to be sanctioned in office by the ruler of the Mamprusi at Naleregu.[11]

These data certainly suggest that prior to the arrival of the British, the Mamprusi were either incorporating Tale country into their kingdoms or losing their hold on the Tallensi. Fortes's insistence on the acephalous nature of Tallensi society stemmed from his failure to consider that these people had been defeated and dispersed by the British at the turn of the century and had probably lost a great deal of their organization. The society he described can be compared to a modern community arbitrarily divorced from its nation state. Such a community would have many of the truncated institutions and personnel of the state, but they would appear bizarre because they would lack the power normally derived from their national context. Moreover, to an investigator, the strictly local institutions would seem just as important as the truncated state institutions. His study would no doubt give a good synchronic picture of the community, but it would be incomplete because the diachronic dimension would be lacking. Fortes unfortunately gave us no idea of the relationship of the Tallensi to the Mamprusi, or of the cultural, historical, and especially the political processes in the region.

The origin of Mossi society lies buried in myths that not only sanction the power of the ruling families but support the political system with rich traditions of migrations and conquest. Traditional beliefs in the Voltaic area and among the Mossi themselves give a common origin for the Dagomba, Mamprusi, and Mossi peoples.[12] According to the most widespread Mossi belief, some forty generations ago a ruler called Naba Nedega (also known as Toese or Koulougbagha), who lived at Gambaga in present-day Ghana, reigned over the Dagomba, Mamprusi, and Nankana.[13] He had a daughter called Nyennega, whose warring skills he valued so highly that he would not grant her permission to marry. As a result, she fled Gambaga and rode toward the north, where she met and married a man called Rialle, who according to some traditions was the son of the Mali chief and according to others was a Busansi hunter. The couple had a son, whom they named Ouedraogo (Stallion) in honor of the horse that had carried Nyennega in her flight to the north.[14] A few years later, Nyennega sent Ouedraogo to Gambaga to visit her father, give him news of her marriage and of her family, and seek his aid.[15] Nedega welcomed the child and cared for him until he was ready to return to Busansi territory. As a farewell present, he gave Ouedraogo four horses and fifty cows. When he left Gambaga, the young man was accompanied by Dagomba horsemen who had seized the opportunity to leave their crowded homeland. With his troop of warriors, Ouedraogo skirted his father's village and invaded Tankourou (present-day Tenkodogo), from which the indigenous Busansi fled at his approach.

The Mossi bards relate that Ouedraogo and the Dagomba horsemen intermarried with the Busansi women and that these unions gave rise to a new group of people called the Mossi. Ouedraogo himself married a woman named Pouriketa, who bore him three sons, Rawa, Diaba Lompo, and Zoungourana. Ouedraogo thus became known as the progenitor of the Mossi, and his mother, Nyennega, as their progenitrix. Other Dagomba horsemen subsequently arrived from Gambaga to swell the Mossi group. The Mossi then undertook to subdue neighboring peoples such as the Gurunsi (a large group including the Kasena, Sisala, and Nunuma), who lived to the east; the Ninisi, who were thinly scattered to the northwest in the vicinity of Ouagadougou; other large Ninisi, Foulse, and Habe (Tombo or Dogon) populations further north in Ouahigouya and extending northwestward to the Bandiagara cliffs; large Kipirsi populations northeast of Ouahigouya; and scattered Ninisi groups in Fada-N'Gourma east of Tenkodogo. Ouedraogo sent his son Diaba Lompo to conquer and rule over the Ninisi populations of Fada-N'Gourma.[16] Rawa, another son, was sent to subdue the region called Zandoma, northwest of Tenkodogo. The Ninisi of this region quickly accepted his authority. He acknowledged their claim to the land by calling them Tinguimbissi, "sons of the earth," and allowed their earth-priests, the Tengsobadamba, to retain ritual control of the earth shrines. However, the Habe (Dogon) refused to submit to Rawa and fled to the safety of the Bandiagara cliffs. Ouedraogo did not wish his youngest son, Zoungourana, to leave Tenkodogo, and the young man remained with him.

According to Ouagadougou tradition, the successful exploits of the Mossi warriors soon came to the attention of the Ninisi chief of Guilingou village, near Ouagadougou. He and the chief of Ziri village sent a wife to Ouedraogo and requested that he join them in an alliance against their Ninisi enemies. Ouedraogo accepted the invitation and gave the woman, who was called Poughtoenga, to Zoungourana as his wife. She gave birth to a son called Oubri. Soon afterward, the Ninisi returned to Tenkodogo and asked Ouedraogo to aid them in a war against their enemies. Ouedraogo did so and in the process continued his conquest of the Ouagadougou region, though he died before completing it.

After Ouedraogo's death his elder sons refused to leave their kingdoms to succeed their father at Tenkodogo, and the territory fell to Zoungourana. He declined to continue Ouedraogo's wars against the dissident Ninisi elements of Ouagadougou but accepted the demands of the Guilingou Ninisi that Oubri, their daughter's son, be sent to rule their territory. Tradition recounts that the youthful Oubri settled with his retinue at Oubritenga near Ziri until he was old enough to continue the Mossi wars of expansion. Later he conquered Gangado, Lumbila, Boulsa, and Boussouma northeast of Ouagadougou before turning west and conquering Ninisi and Kibisi groups at La and Yako and chasing many Kibisi under a chief called Waregoumga into the Bandiagara cliffs. He then returned and conquered the Ouagadougou area itself after a bitter fight. He finally met his death in the Kipirsi region after having conquered Koudougou and chased defiant groups across the Black Volta River. By the time of his death the kingdom of Ouagadougou was firmly established. Along with Ouedraogo, he thus became known as one of the two founders of the Ouagadougou dynasty and the first Mogho Naba (chief of Mossi country). The Ouagadougou kingdom now eclipsed all of the kingdoms founded by Ouedraogo's other sons. It retained its ascendancy through the centuries, although this is denied by the other Mossi kingdoms.

As Ouagadougou developed, Tenkodogo declined; when Zoungourana's son, Sere, inherited Tenkodogo, his rule extended only over the neighboring Busansi. In time, Tenkodogo declined further, losing all control over the southern Busansi populations, which finally came under the tutelage of Ouagadougou and which have retained much of their language and many of their customs to this day. The kingdom at Fada-N'Gourma founded by Diaba Lompo gradually lost contact with the other Mossi groups and became a separate group known as the Gurmanche, or Gourma. Although these people occasionally waged war on the Mossi kingdoms, they maintained ritual ties with them.

Rawa enlarged his kingdom of Zandoma by expelling the Habe and absorbing the Ninisi population of Ouahigouya. However, his descendants ultimately lost Zandoma to Yadega, a prince of the Ouagadougou dynasty. This prince, a grandson of Naba Oubri, allegedly lost his rightful claim to power because he was away at war on the death of his father, and his younger brother Koudoumie bribed the electors.[17] When Yadega learned that Koudoumie had been elected, he led an army against him but found him too firmly entrenched to be deposed. He then returned north to a place called Gourcy in Ouahigouya. There he was joined by his sister, Pabre, who brought him the royal amulets of Rialle (Ouedraogo's father), which she is said to have stolen from Koudoumie and which were believed to sanction the power of the Ouagadougou ruler. Koudoumie gathered his army and pursued Pabre in an attempt to recover the amulets, but he met so much opposition at Yako that he returned without them.

The struggle for supremacy between Koudoumie and Yadega led many of the princely descendants of Ouedraogo to carve out their own principalities from their patrimony and declare themselves independent of Ouagadougou. Faced with the dissolution of his realm, Koudoumie dispatched his sons to different parts of the kingdom to halt the process. There came into existence such principalities as Boulsa, Boussouma, Conquizitenga, Mane, Riziam, Tema, and Yako.[18] However, some of these princes joined the ranks of the rebels, who by this time had taken for themselves the title of *Dim*, meaning "submit only to God." The ruler of Ouagadougou later recognized the autonomy of these princes, but not their independence from Ouagadougou.[19]

After Koudoumie's death his descendants at Ouagadougou continued to rule and to consolidate their territory. Each ruler resided wherever control of the population was most necessary, and the graves of the first fourteen rulers of the Ouagadougou dynasty are markers along the road to that dynasty's complete domination of the country. It was only during the reign of the fifteenth ruler, Mogho Naba Sana (ca. 1430-1450), that Ouagadougou became the permanent capital of the dynasty. Meanwhile, the northern Mossi, under Yadega (who had claimed the title of Mogho Naba and complete independence from Ouagadougou on the strength of the amulets brought by Pabre), were also extending and consolidating their territory. They had absorbed into the kingdom of Yatenga (country of Yadega) all the lands in the kingdom of Zandoma, which had belonged to Rawa, the son of Ouedraogo. Under their rulers (the Yatenga Nanamse), these Mossi moved into the bend of the Niger, a region they called Ghanata, and sacked such towns as Djenne, Sarafere, Timbuktu, and Walata.

What these Mossi traditions of origin demonstrate is that the role of women in the evolution of the state is more important than has been recognized and analyzed.[20] Whether as rulers in their own right or as consorts, mothers, sisters or daughters, women played important roles in the polities of the continent — from classical Egypt in the north, to the royal women of Baganda in the east, to the queens of the Lovedu and the Swazi in the south, and to formidable queen mothers, warriors, and state founders in the west.[21] That these African societies were secondary states is undisputed, given Morton H. Fried's well-founded observation that pristine state development took place quite long ago.[22] However, the evolution toward the full centralization of the secondary state provides fascinating examples of Fried's thesis of the emergence of greater ranking and stratification as political society develops. Noteworthy is that Fried said little about women in his classic work "On the Evolution of Social Stratification and the State"; he is equally reticent in *The Evolution of Political Society*. His references to women dealt with the issue of the sexual division of labor within egalitarian and ranked societies.[23]

Fried's major theoretical point, of course, was that the state developed in order to maintain a system of stratification and that in the final analysis it is to be viewed as "complex of institutions by means of which the power of society is organized on a basis superior to that of kinship"; more succinctly, "the emergent state . . . is the organization of society on a supra-kin basis." Had Fried pursued the issue of kinship with respect to the transition leading to full statehood, it is possible that he would have discovered the importance of the role of women. What the Mossi data suggest is that women emerged as political actors primarily because of their statuses and roles *within* kinship groups, whether based on descent or affinity. While this obviously appears to be related to the importance of the kinship idiom in justifying the right of the elite to govern, the Mossi and other African examples show that kinship was manipulated in important ways when women played important roles in the creation, consolidation, expansion, and legitimization of the state. Moreover, it was probably also because of kinship factors that women were often prevented from ruling in their own right and from passing on the power to rule to their offspring and lineal descendants.[24]

Fried's distinction between pristine and secondary types of early states is generally recognized as a brilliant depiction of the processes of state formation.[25] He did not, however, recognize the truism that many complex organizations retain within them earlier and surviving cultural, economic, political, and social characteristics. One such characteristic is what Ronald Cohen and Henri J.M. Claessen[26] have called a "duality" or a "balance of power policy," which was found in many early African states. Claessen not only considered the roles and positions of the African "royal women" as rather "complex" but also suggested that the institutionalization of these roles implies that royal women contributed to the very survival of ancient African polities.

What the Mossi data and data from other African states indicate quite clearly is the multiplicity of roles that women played in these organizations. As state-building warriors, they assumed what was normally a male role; but even in such situations their gender was limiting. They were invariably eclipsed from power, since they normally got married and produced sons who took power in these states. In the second important role, the women consolidated the states, since their marriages often linked the conquerors and the conquered. Third, in such societies as Ashanti, they performed the role of kingmaker by selecting the new king. Last, royal women performed important rituals to strengthen the power of kings, served as ritual representatives of the ruler and, most important, in all of these functions, royal women seldom acted on their own behalf but invariably acted on behalf of their kin and the corporate groups to which they were affiliated. Their institutionalized roles were vital to maintaining the power of the state.[27]

While it is clear, as Fried suggests, that the emerging state attempted to eschew kinship in favor of ranking and achieved or appointed positions, this process was undoubtedly often complicated by the surviving importance of kinship ties. The complications that arose in states that embraced primarily patrilineal populations must have differed considerably from those in states with dominant matrilineal populations.[28] But central to this issue was the continuity of sovereignty and the related issue of who was qualified to exercise that sovereignty. Most secondary African states, unlike many of their European counterparts, never reached the stage in evolution when sovereignty was so secure that males did not fear competition from royal females or their offspring.

What it is important to note is that in many African societies, women played important roles in the initial or critical phases of the secondary state. However, it was always difficult for them to maintain these roles as the states consolidated. In patrilineal societies, these royal women were quickly eclipsed, since any progeny they may have had were deemed as threats to the sovereign rights of their mothers' patrilineages. In matrilineal societies, such as the Ashanti, women remained at the core of structural descent and tended to remain queen mothers and, therefore, involved as kingmakers. Even so, the centralizing state often eclipsed these royal women by the creation of parallel patrifilial structures, within which power increasingly lies. And while women were often eclipsed from positions which threatened the role of men as sovereigns of the state, they did retain the ritual power to bolster the state at critical junctures. Thus, symbolically, women were not only "present at the creation" of the state, but they were pragmatically utilized to sustain the state throughout its existence.

While it is true that the processes giving rise to the pristine state are buried deep in time, it is suggested here that *kinship*, which in the case of the African states did permit women to play an important role in secondary state building, may have well played a more crucial role in the evolution of the primary state than is usually recognized. By emphasizing certain bonds of kinship, the builders of the emerging state may well have been able to restrict the number of persons who had access to what Fried had termed the strategic resources at hand. Obviously, this encouraged increased ranking and stratification, and one way to ensure that these processes took place was to exclude certain categories of persons with rights to these resources from access to them.[29] The structure of secondary states demonstrates the desire, not always successful, to eliminate both kinship and women from the sphere of power.[30]

What the experience of Mossi also demonstrates is that, from the beginning, they were associated with the imperial systems that arose in the western Sudan as a result of large-scale consolidations that accompanied the penetration of Islam and were used by the French to incorporate this area into the modern world system[31] And although their myths of origin indicate a southern provenance for Nynnenga, her marriage to Rialle, referred to either as a Busansi hunter or "prince of Mali," demonstrates a "northern factor" in their development.[32] In fact, there is really little contradiction between the "Busansi" hunter and the "prince of Mali," because the Busansi, although they are an acephalous population, represent an outpost of the Mande-speaking peoples who created the Mali empire. Later migrations allegedly carried the Mossi northward, where they were in contact with the Malians, who at that period were themselves in contact with North Africa, the Mediterranean, Egypt, and Mecca.

One aspect of the relations between the Mossi and their northern neighbors was well described by al-Sa'di, the author of the *Tarikh es-Sudan*, a seventeenth-century chronicle, who had based his work on earlier sources. He described the attack on Timbuktu by a Mossi ruler:

> It was in the reign of one of the princes of [sultan Kankan Moussa's] dynasty that the sultan of the Mossi at the head of a strong army made an expedition against that city. Seized with fright, the people of Mali fled and abandoned the city to its assailants. The Mossi ruler entered the city, and after killing all the people he found there and seizing all the goods he could find, he burned the city and returned to his own country. The peoples of Mali returned afterwards to Timbuktu and remained there for the next hundred years.[33]

The Yatenga Mossi subsequently warred upon and defended themselves against the Songhai, who had tried to force Islam upon them. The Mossi were among the strongest peoples in the Niger bend area when the Moroccans arrived in 1591, and there were no wars between these two groups.

There has been a great deal of discussion among scholars of Sudanese history about the relationship between the Mossi expeditions into the Niger area and the power of early Mossi kingdoms. Lucien Marc believed that the Mossi reached their zenith late in the fifteenth century, when they attacked Walata and Timbuktu for the second time. He wrote, "It was undoubtedly during this period that they extended their influence over all the territories where their language is spoken at the present day."[34]

On the other hand, Louis Tauxier believes that the Mossi reached their apogee much earlier, toward the end of the fourteenth century. He notes that this was the period when the Mossi were "propelled by a powerful drive of expanding conquest," which carried them to Timbuktu and its neighboring regions.[35] With the recapture of Timbuktu by Mansa Souliman, however, they turned back and firmly established themselves in Gourma and Yange to the east of Ouagadougou, and among non-Mossi populations in Ouahigouya and Ouagadougou. Tauxier believes that this southern drive made the Mossi sufficiently powerful to reinvade the Niger area and thus control a territory extending from Gambaga in the south up to Timbuktu and Djenne in the north. This second period of success came to a close when the Mossi were defeated by Askia the Great of Songhai in 1497 and by Askia Daoud in 1549 and 1561. After these defeats, the Mossi not only abandoned their territories north of Ouahigouya but also withdrew into their present boundaries. Tauxier concludes that from this time onward, the bonds between the different Mossi kingdoms grew weaker, and the power of Ouagadougou waned.

At the same time, the Mossi kingdoms, principalities, and districts developed their internal structure and continued to absorb the Ninisi population. They also welcomed the Moslem Yarse merchants and refugees who settled in their country and adopted most aspects of their culture.[36] These Yarse refugees were joined by Mandingo-Dioula and Soninke Moslem refugees, who entered Mossi country as the result of wars or rebellions in such places as Djenne, Segou, and Timbuktu. The sheltering of these refugees by the Mossi eventually led to a series of wars between them and the Bambara in the mid-eighteenth century.[37] In the course of these wars and up into modern times, many Fulani (Peulh or Fulbe) entered Mossi territory. The circumstances surrounding their first coming are not fully known, but many of them claim to have come originally from Fouta-Djalon and Fouta-Toro. They gained the good will of most of the Mossi rulers and spread throughout the territory.[38] Many of them married Mossi women, giving rise to a new group known as Silimi-Mossi, who continued to raise cattle but also practiced agriculture and adopted many of the cultural traits of their hosts.[39]

There are some reports that Europeans had heard about the Mossi exploits at least from the time of King John II of Portugal, who reigned from 1481 to 1495. Marc states that the Portuguese ambassadors to Mali and Timbuktu convinced their king that the Mossi were Christians and that he attempted to enter into relations with them. According to Barth, these attempts were made as late as 1533.[40] Unfortunately, we have no way of knowing whether the Mossi even knew about the existence of the Portuguese. After this period, there is no evidence of European interest in the Mossi until the end of the nineteenth century. As we shall see in a later chapter, the Mossi received more than their share of attention when the scramble for Africa began. They were not only conquered but colonized and brought into the orbit of the modern world economy. The colonial situation subjected their traditional culture to severe strains as it was integrated into the emerging world civilization.

II

SOVEREIGNTY, KINSHIP, AND COMMUNITY

THE MOSSI restricted all important positions within the traditional political organization to persons who claimed lineal descent from Ouedraogo and Oubri, the ancient founders of the Mossi nation. Thus all the *Mogho Nanamse, Dimdamba, Kombemba,* and *Tense Nanamse*—the heads of kingdoms, principalities, districts, and villages, respectively—claimed descent in the royal line. The bond of kinship among all important Mossi rulers was symbolized by membership in the lion clan (*Gegema*) and affiliated clans or *boodoo* founded by ancient members of the ruling families. Although the Mossi respected clan totems, they did not stress clan organization. They were more interested in membership in the segmentary lineages within the clans.[1] Yet not all Mossi groups stressed lineage affiliation. This was of supreme importance only for nobles whose membership in particular segments of ruling lineages gave them access to the *nam*—the power first possessed by the ancient founders, which is described by the Mossi as "that force of God which enables one man to control another." So important was the corporate possession of the nam by a ruling lineage that with few exceptions, membership in such a lineage gave a Moaga noble status.[2] Lineage segmentation gave some segments easier access to the nam, however, and resulting conflicts over sovereignty gave rise to the various Mossi kingdoms, principalities, and even districts.

Every Mossi ruling line attempted to legitimize its position by claiming the most direct descent from Ouedraogo and Oubri. The descendants of the founder of a local ruling lineage would claim that he had been an elder son deprived of his patrimony by unscrupulous younger brothers, or an elder son disqualified by a physical handicap from receiving the nam. Some ruling lineages even claimed that their founders had been elder sons who had voluntarily forsaken the problems of government and established new districts for themselves. Whenever tradition recounted that a younger son had indeed founded a kingdom or district, it was invariably said that he had done so with full permission of his father and in place of an unadventurous elder brother.

For example, the ruling family of the Boulsa province claimed that its ancestor, Naba Namende, was the eldest son of Mogho Naba Oubri and chose to become his father's *Kourita* (a young son of a deceased Mogho Naba chosen as his father's personal representative on earth) and go into exile rather than subject his younger brother to the ordeal. At the same time, Namende sought to retain royal power equal to that of his brother, the new Mogho Naba, by taking Oubri's royal amulets with him.[3]

Mane province, too, was founded by one Nyaseme, a son of Koudoumie, who felt that he should have been given the nam. When routed in battle by his elder brother Kouda, he moved into the region of Mane, where he defeated the indigenous Ninisi and ruled over them. The princes who broke away from Ouagadougou during Koudoumie's reign considered themselves theoretically equal to the supreme ruler. Thus, they took the title of Dim. By so doing, they dramatized their claim to equality of status, if not of power, with the Mogho Naba, and their determination to "submit only to God."[4]

The Mossi insist that the relationship between the Mogho Naba and the Dimdamba was similar to that between father and sons, since the Dimdamba were "really the sons of the Mogho Naba" and are said to have acted as such. This analogy is interesting in view of the Mossi traditional pattern of avoidance—combined with love and tolerance—between fathers and elder sons.[5] The Dimdamba were often allowed to act at variance with the Mogho Naba. Some of them shifted allegiance from kingdom to kingdom; others usurped the power of the Mogho Naba over smaller districts, or claimed that they had been given this power; and most of them regulated their own affairs with little interference from their sovereign. He, as "father," interfered on occasion in their internal affairs, demanding help from them and often chastising them if they failed to comply.

The Mogho Naba and the Dimdamba often appointed their younger sons or brothers as rulers (Kombemba) of the districts that made up their kingdoms and principalities. In this way, power and authority were kept within the royal clan and its lineages. Nevertheless, in keeping with the concept of corporate access to the nam, the rulers of these dependencies had traditions that served to reconcile their claims to kingly or princely status with their actual subordinate position. District founders, too, were often portrayed as eldest sons who had been cheated out of their patrimony or had voluntarily left it to establish new districts. In some cases, the legendary heroes were granted miraculous births as well.

The people of Nobere district have a legend that its founder, Naba Biligo, was sired by a spirit who impregnated the wife of Mogho Naba Oubri. She carried him in her womb for more than a year, and noticed that although her belly was extended during the daytime, it was always flat at night. She became concerned and confided her worries to the ruler's first wife, who asked the other co-wives to keep vigil for the child. When they arrived in the evening, they noticed that the woman's belly was flat. They awakened her and kept watch until dawn. At cock's crow, the child Biligo returned from his nocturnal wanderings. Seeing the women, he fell from the top of the hut into his mother's lap and began to cry as though he had just been born. When Biligo grew to manhood, he went hunting in the Nobere area. He found the region so fertile that when he returned to Ouagadougou, he told his father, Mogho Naba Oubri, that he did not want the nam but preferred to conquer the Ninisi of Nobere and become their chief.

The people of Doulougou give a slightly different account of the founding of their district. Their founder, a man called Moumde, was also said to be a son of Mogho Naba Oubri. He did not like the capital, and rode all over the kingdom until he came to Doulougou. He liked this region so much that he asked his father to name him chief over its indigenous population. Oubri then sent down an army, defeated the Ninisi, and appointed Moumde as Doulougou Naba.

According to some traditions, Mogho Nanamse appointed their sons as chiefs of conquered districts. A more common tradition, represented by the Biligo legend, is that the founders of local districts conquered their territories with or without the permission of the Mogho Naba. Biligo, the founder of Nobere district, is said to have found the area sparsely inhabited by Ninisi, most of whom fled before him. A person of gigantic proportions, he easily defeated those Ninisi who elected to give him battle. He then went into the woods, where he invited the Ninisi leader, an earth-priest (Tengsoba) called Tedego, to return to the district. Biligo promised him and the other refugees safe conduct and good treatment if they agreed to return. Tedego refused, whereupon Biligo captured him and installed him in a special quarter, with the injunction that he and his family should make sacrifices to the local earth shrines (*Tengkouga*) in the name of the new ruling lineage. Naba Biligo went back into the woods, captured the other refugees, and resettled them in their villages. He allowed the local Tengsobadamba to retain their religious duties, but sent his sons to take political control of the villages. Not satisfied with the number of people under his command, Naba Biligo then raided Gurunsi country and captured slaves, whom he settled behind his compound and in separate villages under their own chiefs. He also welcomed refugees from wars in other territories and established them in special villages under their own chiefs.

The Dimdamba followed a similar practice in establishing power and control. According to Cheron, when Mogho Naba Koudoumie sent his son Tiraongo to conquer the Ninisi of Boussouma, the Ninisi defended themselves fiercely. Tiraongo's advance was thus very slow until he found a Ninisi named Wine, dressed in a panther's skin and hiding in a hole, "who on the promise that his life would be saved, consented to serve as guide to Tiraongo and to make propitiatory sacrifices to the divinities of the country. Thanks to him, the Mossi were able to progress to Somtongande."[6] Boulsa tradition recounts that when Naba Namende left Ouagadougou as the Kourita of Mogho Naba Oubri and took possession of their province, he placed his sons at the head of the principal villages "in order to control it [Boulsa] better."[7] One son was even sent to rule over a village at the request of the local Tengsoba.

The villages that made up a Mossi district were usually ruled by chiefs who belonged to sub-lineages of the local ruling lineage. These village chiefs and the members of their lineage formed a noble class, the *nakomce* ("children of the Naba"). As long as a lineage held the nam of a district, all of its sub-lineages had all the privileges of the noble class, regardless of whether they had charge of villages. But if the Mogho Naba deprived a ruling lineage of the nam by deposing the district chief, all its members were reduced to commoner status. Such people still traced their descent from the Mogho Naba who was the ancestor of their lineage founder, but this relationship ceased to be important unless the lineage recovered the nam of the district. If it did not, the former ruling lineage officially lost its ancient link with the royal clan within a few generations and became a nondescript local group.

The place of a deposed royal lineage was usually taken by the relatives of the nobles who subsequently acquired the nam of the district. These newcomers were genealogically closer to the ruling Mogho Naba, and formed the new nakomce of the district. The new district chief sometimes sent his sons to rule over the villages under his command. But if the village chiefs did not suffer the same fate as their lineage head at the hands of the Mogho Naba, the new district chief often permitted them to retain their posts. Thus they retained possession of the nam but lost their noble status. They served the new district chief in a political sense much as the Tengsoba served him in a ritual sense.

The plight of deposed district nakomce shows quite clearly the distinction made by the Mossi between kinship and sovereignty within their governmental system. Kinship was the basis on which the ruling class was formed. However, sovereignty itself, although associated with kinship, was not unalterably linked with it. When a ruling Mossi kin group held the nam, its subgroups were linked by bonds of prestige. But once this group lost the nam or access to the nam, its component subgroups began to drift away. That this situation could exist shows the true nature of the relationship between sovereignty and kinship within the Mossi political system.

There were other chiefs in Mossi districts who had never had either a lineal or a collateral relationship with any lineage of the ancient royal clan.[8] These men were the descendants of provincial ministers. They became chiefs for the same reasons that the sons of ruling sovereigns became chiefs. When a Mogho Naba sent his sons to replace deposed district chiefs, the young men were usually accompanied by a full complement of administrators. These administrators, mostly younger sons of administrators at Ouagadougou who would not normally succeed their fathers, often automatically replaced the administrators of the former chiefs. But if, for reasons of administrative efficiency, the new chiefs elected to retain the administrators of their predecessors, they assigned village chieftainships to the newcomers. They might also settle them in independent hamlets and furnish them with wives and slaves. For chiefs in this category, kinship did play an initial role in the accession to power; but since they were not related to the district chief, they never gained noble status. Socially, they were comparable to chiefs who were former nobles; as in the latter's case, their kinship ties with the administrators at Ouagadougou gradually lost their significance.

There were yet other kinds of chiefs or men who rated the title Naba in Mossi districts. They included: the descendants of aboriginal chiefs, the chiefs of alien groups, and the chiefs of the Mossi refugee groups that had left other districts because of disputes over the nam. In districts where there were large groups of the autochthonous Ninisi, there were Ninisi "chiefs"; in most cases, however, these "chiefs" were really the senior Tengsobadamba of the villages. In most other districts, the sole Ninisi "chief" was the official Tengsoba of the district chief. This man had ritual power but no political power. Yet he was called Naba, because the Mossi thought that all persons in positions of command or prominence must be named chiefs. Villages made up of aliens (Busansi, Gurunsi, Yarse, and occasionally Fulani) had chiefs in the true sense of the word. These men were granted access to the nam by the district chiefs, and their power and authority were inherited by their families in the same manner as among Mossi lineages.

The last important category of Mossi chiefs included men who ruled over slave and serf villages. These men were themselves the descendants of slaves and serfs, for no free-born Mossi were placed in such posts. Needless to say, these chiefs were never lineally or collaterally related to the district chiefs, and therefore were never nobles. However, they might be affinally related to district chiefs, and in such cases the relationship was often of some political value.

It must be emphasized that once a man was made chief, he was respected, if not honored, by all the people of the district. In some districts, the Dapore Naba and the Baglere Naba, chiefs of two categories of serfs, were among the most valued assistants of the Kombere Naba. The only people who sometimes refused to honor the village chiefs were the nakomce, who were the holders of the district nam. Nevertheless, they were censored by the Kombere if they were disrespectful to his subordinates. No district chief could allow his government to be jeopardized by the maltreatment of persons who served it. In any conflict between the nam and the kin group, the supremacy of the nam was always maintained.

Every Mossi ruler, whether he held the nam of a kingdom, principality, district, or village, was *ipso facto* also *Boodkasma* (literally, "family head") of the local segment of his boodoo. The word boodoo refers to patrilineal groups that anthropologists would normally call clans, maximal lineages, major lineages, or minor lineages. The Mossi do not make any terminological distinction between these levels of their segmentary lineage system. Nevertheless, they recognize and use the status differences between these units to limit the access of each unit to the corporate assets of the boodoo. Their major social distinction is drawn between the minor lineage, which is also called boodoo, and its component minimal lineages. Each minimal-lineage unit is called a *babissi* (literally, "father's brother"), and is really a large extended family composed of relatives who had a common ancestor, three, four, or at most five generations ago.

The Mogho Naba, for example, was head of his babissi as well as ex officio head of the entire royal clan. Those rulers who claimed equality with him claimed that they, not he, were the true heads of the royal clan and the "direct" descendants of Ouedraogo and Oubri. As a function of their political position, the many princes and district chiefs were heads of their own babissi and of the maximal lineage to which their babissi belonged. Like the Mogho Naba, they were the ex officio heads of all members of their boodoo who lived in their territory and who claimed descent from the same royal ancestors. A Mossi village chief was likewise the head of his babissi and ex officio head of all the other babissi in his village that belonged to his boodoo. As the official Boodkasma of his village's ruling lineage, the village chief held junior or senior status in relation to other village chiefs of the same boodoo who were also the Boodkasemdamba of their respective lineage segments.

Possession of the nam influenced the pattern of seniority within lineages and lineage segments. In most cases, seniority was based on age and generation. Thus, the oldest man of the oldest generation was the Boodkasma, and his office devolved upon the next oldest man when he died. But within the ruling lineages and their segments, the man who held the nam, whether young or old, was automatically senior to all others. This does not mean that these ruling lineages did not recognize age and generational seniority. For example, whenever a chief died and sovereignty returned to the lineage as a corporate group, the senior noble of the senior generation became the acting Boodkasma and lineage head. Like all Boodkasemdamba, he managed the affairs of his group, but only until a new chief was elected. The new Boodkasma, however, sometimes delegated some of his social rights and ritual obligations to this elder, who was often regarded as the unofficial or semi-official Boodkasma of his lineage. Similarly, the senior nobles of all segments of the ruling lineage were also regarded as Boodkasemdamba. Because they were so regarded and because of the role they played, these men seldom came into conflict with the district chief. He gave them a certain amount of leeway in dealing with the everyday affairs of their group. It was understood by all, however, that nothing should jeopardize the most important asset of the lineage—the nam. Therefore, the chief was obeyed in all important matters involving the noble lineage of the district. In such matters he listened to no one; for, as one district chief said, "Once I have received the nam from the Mogho Naba, no man in this district stands above me!"

This dominance of political relations over social relations was made clear by the behavior of commoners toward ruling nobles on the one hand, and of nobles among themselves on the other. Commoners showed greater respect and deference toward members of the ruling babissi than toward persons belonging to other noble babissi. Thus, they were more respectful to the district chief's father's brothers, his siblings, and his children than to his more distant relatives. Within the noble lineage itself, everyone had to respect the chief as the holder of the nam, but otherwise the generational principle of respect and deference was maintained. The eldest nobleman of the eldest generation received deference from all others (excluding the chief), and the hierarchy of respect descended to the youngest nobleman of the youngest generation. Very often, the full-grown son and presumed heir of the district chief had to kneel in respect to a distantly related younger man of an elder generation. Of course, this deference ceased if and when he became chief. If he did not receive the nam, he continued to show deference to all his lineage elders. This distinction between nam and boodoo was a source of potential conflict within the ruling lineages. The people usually accepted the implications of both principles, but when they did not, there were dynastic quarrels and territorial secessions.

The age and generational principles also operated within non-noble ruling lineages, but here too they were often complicated by the possession of the nam. Those village chiefs who had lost their noble status but retained the nam acted as official Boodkasemdamba of their local lineage segments and had considerable influence over their lineage although they did not control all its segments. Each lineage segment had its own Boodkasma, who normally ran its affairs. But because of the importance of the nam in Mossi life, the Boodkasemdamba deferred to the village chief in important matters pertaining to their own boodoo. However, the generational principle was followed within the local boodoo. Almost no one deferred to the children of the village chief, who, after all, were not nakomce.

The situation within commoner lineages that did not hold the nam was quite different. The age and generational principles obtained within the lineage segments of these boodoo, but never *across* the segments, as they did across the babissi. These segments were more autonomous. Each had its own Boodkasma, who looked after it without deferring to anyone. This autonomy was all the more pronounced since the segments of non-noble lineages tended to be scattered throughout a district. They interacted socially and politically only when they were physically close. In any case, in the absence of the nam, the segments of non-noble lineages had no reason to remain together; they tended to lose their hierarchical quality and to become equal and separate.

As would be expected in such circumstances, not all Mossi lineages paid the same attention to their genealogies. Noble lineages kept track of their actual or putative ancestors, whereas non-noble lineages tended to ignore them and to let geographical proximity determine meaningful kinship ties. This loss of interest in exact genealogies was found even among lineages that had lost the nam of a district and with it their nobility, but still retained the nam of a village. Members of the minimal units in such lineages competed actively for the village nam and were interested in fairly recent ancestors. They did not remember how they were related unless they happened to have a common grandfather or great-grandfather who had held the nam. The differential value thus placed on genealogies by the noble and non-noble lineages was due in most cases to the differential access of these lineages to the strategic resources of Mossi society. People who held the nam and belonged to noble lineages enjoyed special claims to goods and services. Those whose lineages did not hold the nam had no such privileges.

Because Mossi society was basically patrilineal, a man shared in the status and the corporate assets of his patrilineage. Conversely, a man had no access to the status or resources of his mother's patrilineage except for some ritual rights and duties that accrued to him as a *yagenga* (a sister's or daughter's son). These rights and duties included residence in the home of a maternal patrilineage during childhood, attendance at sacrifices to the mother's patrilineal ancestors, the settling of quarrels between maternal kinsmen, and ritual license to seize specific items of property from these relatives. This license dramatized the *lack* of access rather than *freedom* of access to the property of maternal relatives.

When a man's maternal relatives controlled the nam of the territory in which he lived, he could improve his social and economic position. In many cases, a young man who had gone to live as a "stranger" with a noble uncle or grandfather remained with these relatives. His privilege to remain was sanctioned by the Mossi belief that a boy's maternal ancestors would wreak vengeance on any person who tried to evict him from the village from which his mother had been "sent into the bush" (given away as a wife). By using various strategies and subterfuges, the "stranger" obtained wives through his maternal relatives and used their land and other resources. After several generations the lineal descendants of the "stranger" frequently became indistinguishable from their maternal relatives, although such cases were not often formally acknowledged. Whether these "sisters' children" ever managed to obtain the nam of their mother's patrilineage is a moot point, because in theory they could not. Yet, also by Mossi definition, a man could never inherit rights and duties in his mother's patrilineage; however, it is known that this did happen. It is possible that the close check kept by the ruling lineage on its genealogy made usurpation impossible. Yet I know of several cases in which candidates for chiefship feared competition from men whose descent actually barred them from the nam.

The son of a nobleman and a commoner woman seldom attached himself permanently to his maternal patrilineage, although he retained all of his customary rights, privileges, and duties in it. Occasionally, noblemen did attach themselves to their maternal relatives, but those who did had usually been banished from their patrilineage for some illegal act or had voluntarily left home after a dispute over inheritance of the nam, goods, or women.

The fact that noble lineages often absorbed sisters' sons was only one of the reasons why such lineages survived and expanded, even if only at the expense of other lineages within the local society. Another reason for this growth was that the nobles, possessing the nam and its prerogatives, received more wives than the commoners. They had more children and thus multiplied more rapidly. Mossi lineages were generally exogamous through their whole depth, but exogamy became increasingly mandatory as the segments became smaller. Marriage within a maximal lineage was permitted only when some of its members had moved so far away from its original locality that the original ties were either forgotten or ignored. The Mossi have myths in which the lineage founder gives his overly numerous descendants permission to marry certain of their relatives. Even so, if a marriage was actually found to have occurred between distant relatives, appropriate sacrifices had to be made to the ancestors.

Marriage was also forbidden between persons who could trace a common maternal ancestor. But because the time depth here was very shallow, total bilateral exogamy was practiced to a depth of only four or five generations. Of course, the differential concern with genealogies between those who had access to the nam and those who did not, had an effect on the extent to which exogamy was practiced.

Most Mossi marriages were based on an exchange of women between two lineages linked by a long-term series of reciprocal exchanges of goods and services. Women were regarded as the most valuable part of this system. In theory, only the Boodkasma of a babissi had the right to give a woman as a wife to another lineage. However, the initiators of the reciprocal relations between lineage segments were often babissi heads, Yirisobadamba (heads of nuclear families), or individual lineage members. When a man from one lineage "made friends" with a member of another and rendered him a service or received a favor from him, their respective lineages were considered to be involved. The corporate nature of the lineage segment was acknowledged by all persons engaged in reciprocal relations, and the relations between two individuals were seen as relations between their lineages.

When a man wished to give a daughter to a friend as a wife, he had to consult his Boodkasma, who then gave the woman to the friend's Boodkasma. The latter accepted the woman as a wife for the lineage rather than for the man involved. The lineage retained its rights *in gene-*

tricem over the woman and turned over the rights *in uxorem* to the man. This point is very important, because, by accepting the woman as a wife for his lineage segment, the Boodkasma accepted the responsibility of giving a woman in return to the other lineage. The stress placed on the lineage in wife-exchange was due to the corporate nature of this kinship group, as well as to the prohibition against a man's exchanging his own sisters or daughters as wives. He had to use other women in the lineage. It was believed that if this rule were violated, the women exchanged would also "exchange lives"—i.e., the fate of one would automatically reflect the fate of the other.

The Mossi marriage system worked to the advantage of both the elder males of the lineage segment and the nobles of the ruling lineage. Since the older men of the various groups controlled the resources of their kinsmen, they usually initiated "friendship" relations and obtained wives for their group. The more impartial elders distributed the women equitably among their fellow kinsmen, but occasionally older men kept the wives for themselves, knowing that in time these wives would be inherited by their younger kinsmen. Younger men had to wait until their elders died, do without wives, or establish "friendly" relations with older men. Some young men and newcomers to the district appealed to the chief for *pughsiudse* (from *pugho*, the diminutive of *pagha*, "woman," and *siubo*, "to give with the hope of profitable return"). These pughsiudse were women whom the chief received from his subjects and whom he subsequently gave out as wives on condition that their husbands give him their eldest daughters as future pughsiudse.[9]

The nobility benefited by the Mossi marriage system because, as a group, they received more women than they gave out in the exchange of wives. Furthermore, this enabled them to make more marriage arrangements. This does not mean that a differential value was placed on women of different status groups. The Mossi tended to regard all women as equally valuable, but commoners tended to be more generous to noble friends than vice versa.

The nobles also received wives from their "brother," the district chief. He received women as presents and signs of fealty and homage from most of the groups in his district, and also from groups outside his district. He kept some of these women as wives; others he used as pughsiudse; and still others he gave to his lineage segments. Some nobles had another method of obtaining wives, namely, by abduction. A nobleman who saw the daughter or wife of a commoner in the market place often encouraged her to desert her father or husband and come to him. Her relatives usually appealed to the district chief, and occasionally the woman was sent back. A nobleman set on having a certain girl as a wife usually had small bracelets like those worn by all noble wives placed on her ankles. Once this was done, the chief could not be compelled to send her back to her parents, and any man who tried to retrieve her was guilty of interfering with a nobleman's wife and could be killed for it. In fact, only the male relatives of noblemen's wives could converse with them without running the risk of being apprehended and executed.

The district was the most important unit in the Mossi principalities and kingdoms. It was on this level that the Mossi nobility came into direct contact with the various social and ethnic groups of the society. Here, kinship and affinal ties linked the conquerors and the conquered, the ancient and recent nobility, the refugees from conflicts over the nam and the resident aliens, in a network of social, ritual, economic, and political relationships. It was also on this level that myths and traditions legitimized most effectively the Mossi socio-economic and political system as well as the relationships between the various social and ethnic groups.

The number and size of the Mossi districts varied greatly from one principality or kingdom to another. Some districts were large and wealthy, with a number of large villages; smaller districts had a larger proportion of small villages and hamlets. The average number of these small units was probably between fifty and sixty-five per district. The population of the districts ranged from 10,000 to 35,000 persons. Some *tense* (villages) had as many as 5,000 inhabitants and some as few as 50. The average village had about 500 inhabitants. But regardless of size, all Mossi districts and component villages had basically the same structure and fulfilled the same functions. The structure of Nobere district is representative. Nobere covered approximately 200 square miles. It was bounded on the east by a district called Manga, on the north by the districts of Toece and Djiba, and on the west and south by the Red Volta River. A census taken in 1905, just nine years after the European conquest, showed the Nobere population to be about 13,200.[10] In 1955 approximately 10,000 persons inhabited 24 villages and hamlets scattered through the more inhabitable part of the district.

The number of villages and hamlets in Nobere district apparently fluctuated. Villages were occasionally abandoned, while small hamlets grew into prominent settlements. The people of Nobere always tried to establish their villages as close to the Red Volta as possible in order to utilize the more fertile lands. But they were repeatedly driven back by disease and marauding animals. Just twenty years ago, the six villages that lay closest to the river were gradually abandoned and their populations absorbed by other villages. As of 1955, three of these populations were still paying allegiance to their former chiefs—a fact that bears out the Mossi axiom that chiefs govern people rather than land. The three other chiefs had lost control over their followers, who had placed themselves under the protection of the chiefs of their host villages. On occasion, Nobere also lost villages to other districts. One such village, Rissoma, was taken away from Nobere and given to Djiba when one of the Nobere district chiefs had a dispute with the Mogho Naba.

The hub or center of Nobere district, like that of all Mossi districts, was Nab'tenga (also called Nobere Naba Tenga, or Na-tenga), the village of the district chief. This village was rather large and in many respects a replica in miniature of the capital of Ouagadougou. Like most Mossi villages, Nab'tenga was divided into sections, quarters, or neighborhoods called *saghse* (sing. *saka*), which included a number of compounds (*yiya,* sing. *yiri*; or *zaghse,* sing. *zaka*). The district chief's compound was called Nab'yiri. He lived there surrounded by his wives, unmarried daughters, younger children, and pages. His older male children lived in separate compounds within the same saka. The saghse of Nab'tenga included Ouidi, the saka of the Ouidi Naba; Balbalse, the saka of the Baloum Naba; Tansoba, the saka of the local war minister (Tansoba or Tampsobo); Baglere, the saka of the chief's serfs; Bendere, the saka of the chief's musicians; Ouedrange, the saka of the chief's grooms; and Pwese, the saka of the guardians of the chief's wives. Scattered among them were the saghse of noble families, smiths, the Moslem Imam, and other persons. The most important market place in the district was located about four hundred yards from the chief's compound.

The number and types of social and ethnic groups within the district and its villages reflected Nobere's history. When the French arrived, the district chief was Kaglere, a descendant of Ngado, who was a son of Mogho Naba Sagha I (ca. 1787–1803). Ngado had been sent to Nobere at the end of the eighteenth century to replace Naba Peka (a descendant of Naba Biligo), who had been deposed and killed by Mogho Naba Sagha during a civil war. The other chiefly descendants of Biligo, however, were not deposed by Ngado; they remained in charge of all but five or six of the major villages in the district. The chiefs of such villages as Ronse, Barkago, Tewarka, and Pinse are *yagense* (descendants) of Naba Biligo. The village called Passintenga was ruled by the descendants of a Busanga from Lenga called Passentre, who allegedly had been given a wife by Biligo. It is not known, however, whether this woman was Biligo's daughter or one of his pughsiudse. The people of Passintenga claimed descent from Biligo's daughter, but the other groups in the district questioned this ancestry. The village called Bourougna had two chiefs. One, the Tang Naba, was descended from a son of a Ouidi Naba of Ouagadougou who had settled in Nobere; the other, the Yang Naba, claimed descent from an aboriginal Ninisi man and woman of Biligo's lineage. The Yang Naba was thus another of Biligo's yagense in the district. The chief of Nimpwe village was a descendant of the aboriginal Ninisi people and was the principal Tengsoba in the district. He had more ritual power than political power, however. The nam of Basbedo village was held by a man descended from Busansi refugees. Living in this village was a man with the honorific title of Soulougre Naba, who claimed descent from the most important Ninisi family who had lived in the district prior to the arrival of Biligo.

Most of the nobles of the local ruling lineage lived either in the saghse of the district villages or in isolated hamlets. Local tradition holds that one of the conditions set by Naba Ngado for allowing Biligo's descendants to remain as village chiefs was the right to settle nineteen of his sons in many of the villages. He allegedly sent *mabissi* (sons of the same mother) to the same village. By so doing, he took advantage of the normal lines of fission that are created after the death of a Mossi father and prevented undue rivalries. Yet there was no driving necessity for him to do so, because there were more villages than chief's sons available. In fact, there are still many villages without nobles in Nobere district. The people of Passintenga, for instance, allegedly refused to have nobles live among them, while the people of Nimpwe allegedly killed by sorcery all the nobles who ever tried to live there. The actual reason for the absence of nobles in these villages may have been that the district chief did not wish to send his sons to villages into which his daughters had married or where there lived earth priests who were thought to be powerful sorcerers. Nobles were often unwelcome, feared, and resisted, because they tended to exploit the village people and to take advantage of the commoners.

The villages of Nobere district, like those of other Mossi districts, were populated in part by refugees and strangers. Several saghse in Togese village were inhabited by Mossi refugees who had fled a district called Guiergo after a fight over the nam of that district. Scattered throughout the district's villages were people of unknown origin called Siamse. The Siamse found in the villages of Tewaka and Nabadogo claimed that their ancestors had "followed" Naba Biligo when he came down from Ouagadougou to found the district. Several saghse in Bourougna village were inhabited by Yarse, people of Mandingo origin who had been assimilated by the Mossi. There were no Fulani in Nobere, even though some lived in nearby districts. But in Pinse village there lived people called Silimi-Mossi, who claimed descent from Fulani herdsmen and Mossi women. Basbedo village was inhabited and ruled by people of Busansi origin. They claimed that their ancestors had fled from famine and other hardships in Busansi country and had been granted haven by Naba Biligo. The people who lived in the two saghse of Nab'tenga called Dapore (Dapobi) and Baglere (Bangare) were serfs of diverse non-Mossi origin. Saghse or compounds of Gurunsi slaves were found close to the dwellings of nobles and village chiefs throughout the district.

The number of saghse in the villages of Nobere district varied according to the size of the village and the pattern of nam inheritance within the major lineage segment that ruled the village. The saka itself housed a minor-lineage segment. The larger the village's minor lineage segment and the greater this group's genealogical depth, the more numerous were its component segments and thus its saghse. The proliferation of saghse and minor-lineage segments within the ruling lineage of a village was dependent primarily on possession of the nam. As soon as a man received the nam, he obtained control over a large amount of goods and services. He was then in a position to obtain many wives for himself and his immediate relatives, and as a result his minimal lineage grew rapidly. In time this group became so large that it split from its brother babissi within the saka, and formed a new saka of its own. Finally, this babissi became a minor lineage in its own saka, in segmental opposition to the other babissi and minor lineages within the other saghse. If the descendants of one man retained the nam for about three generations, their lineage segment and saka grew larger and in time cast off its own junior segments. However, if the segment lost the nam to a man of another babissi and saka, it ceased to proliferate. Some such groups even declined and disappeared by fusing with other local segments of the same lineage. Here is how the system worked in Barkago village of Nobere district.

Barkago itself was founded sometime in the dim past by a son of Naba Biligo. It had an area of eight or ten square miles and a population of about 650 when the French arrived in 1896. Its boundaries were set by such natural phenomena as clumps of trees, hills, and ravines. The village itself included five distinct saghse separated by footpaths, hills, rocks, and ravines, and an area of wasteland (*weogho*). Three of the saghse, Natenga ("chief's land"), Godin, and Kedpalago, were inhabited by the minor segments of the boodoo of Naba Biligo. Here is how this came about. After the original segment of the ruling Biligo lineage had lived in Barkago for some time, it divided into two minor lineages and settled in two saghse, Natenga and Godin. A noble from Godin possessed the nam, but it eventually passed to a noble from Natenga. The new chief then founded a new saka called Kedpalago because he wanted more living space for his own children. As a result, the minor lineage of Natenga now had two babissi living in two saghse. The minor lineage of Godin subsequently declined in size and prestige. The only evidence of its former importance was that its eldest male continued to make separate sacrifices to his own chiefly ancestors, even though the more recent holders of the nam made sacrifices to all former chiefs. These independent sacrifices were made in spite of the fact that this minor lineage kept growing smaller because its male members left to live elsewhere or to join maternal patrilineages with higher status. The sacrifices were expected to cease only if and when the minor lineage were to disappear with the incorporation of the widows and orphans of its last surviving males into the other Biligo groups of the village and district. Of course, if the Godin minor lineage had regained the nam, it undoubtedly would have experienced a rebirth and renewal of strength. It might have attracted its daughter's sons, and even aliens who would have lived in its saghse as they did in those of the ruling lineage segments.

A fourth saka, Nakomgo ("we hunger after the nam"), was inhabited by the noble descendants of Naba Ngado, the district chief who had replaced the descendant of Naba Biligo of Nobere. Since these nobles traced their descent from two full brothers, Kouliga and Kongo, they formed two related minor lineages with five component minimal lineages. The compounds of the two babissi of the Kouliga minor lineage were separate but contiguous. Near them were the compounds of the three babissi of the Kongo minor lineage. Scattered about in the Nakomgo saka were compounds of sisters' sons, strangers, and nobles' slaves.

The people of Narila, the fifth saka of Barkago, were members of the aboriginal Ninisi population, and thus furnished the village's earth-priest. He made sacrifices to the earth shrines in the village, gave ritual permission for building compounds and digging graves, and took control of the village during the period between the death of a chief and the accession of another. Scattered throughout the various saghse were compounds inhabited by people of serf, slave, or refugee origin.

Of all the groups within the village, the Ngado people kept the most exact genealogies. They did so because one of the segments of their maximal lineage held the district nam, and as nobles they had theoretical access to it. Once they had lost the nam of the district, the descendants of Biligo also lost much of their interest in preserving their genealogies. Their local lineage segment, which controlled the village nam, still showed interest in its genealogy, but the people of Godin did not quite remember how they were related to the ruling lineage segment. Several times in the recent history of Barkago (and other villages), the men who were given the village nam had to be recalled from distant villages where they were living with maternal patrilineages. So relatively unimportant was possession of the village nam without concomitant noble status that after Naba Ngado took over, the local Biligo people began to ignore all local genealogical records except descent from Biligo. The Ninisi people had the least reason to be interested in their genealogy, and they simply ignored it. They had been separated from the other Ninisi groups in the district for so long that they did not even forbid marriage into those groups.

In villages such as Barkago, the existence of several lineage groupings and families of strangers facilitated local marriages. But in villages with fewer lineage groups, the time came when all groups were so closely linked by marriage and affinal alliances that for all practical purposes the village became an exogamous unit. By 1956, this process had reached such an advanced stage in Barkago that hardly any marriages took place between the Ninisi and Biligo local lineage segments. Both groups were permitted to marry the local descendants of Ngado, because the latter were more recent arrivals in the village. These marriages were of great significance to all villagers because they linked the nobles and the commoners in a series of exchanges. Moreover, because the groups were linked through sisters' sons with special privileges in both groups, problems deriving from status differences were more easily solved. Even the most arrogant noble was often constrained by ancestral sanctions to maintain amicable relations with his in-laws.

The Biligo lineage of Barkago contracted marriages with the other, non-related groups within and without the district. The Ngado people did likewise. Whether these nobles were able to marry noble women of other districts is a moot point. Owing to distance and politics, no such marriages are known to have occurred, and no one seems to know whether they were permissible. The Ninisi, who had always been commoners, had the largest marriage circle of all the village groups. They were able to marry nobles, commoners, and the Ninisi of the district and other districts.

The inhabitants of a Mossi village built their houses and cultivated their crops on land the village chief had granted to their respective lineages. Since the royal lineage, by right of conquest, controlled all of Mossi country, the rights of usufruct of a lineage depended ultimately on the Mogho

Naba. This did not mean, however, that either the Mogho Naba or any of his chiefs owned the land of Mossi country. The Mossi chiefs and their ruling lineage controlled the Mossi people and thus were able to decide who should use the land. However, there is no evidence that Mossi chiefs ever thought of controlling people by controlling land. The land appears to have been a public good, the utilization of which was in the rulers' interests. Rulers tried to attract more people, but they hardly ever tried to get more land. The people within a Mossi community who might have been said to "own" the land were the Ninisi, whose rights were derived from first occupancy and from their special association with the soil in which their ancestors were buried. When they were conquered, they did not lose their "ritual" rights over the land of their communities, but they were persuaded or forced to "care for" them in the name of the ruling group.

III

KINGSHIP AND CHIEFSHIP

MOSSI TRADITIONAL government revolved around the Nanamse, as all Mossi rulers were called. Sometimes the title was also given on an honorific basis to commoners, serfs, or slaves who performed specific duties for a Mogho Naba or a district chief; but the only true Nanamse were persons who traced their descent from Ouedraogo and Oubri.

The heads of the four Mossi kingdoms—the Mogho Naba of Ouagadougou, the Yatenga Naba, the Tenkodogo Naba, and the Fada-N'Gourma Naba—were supreme in their own realms, but there was considerable rivalry among them throughout Mossi history.[1] In terms of closeness of descent from the nation's founders, the Tenkodogo Naba came first, the Mogho Naba of Ouagadougou second, and the Yatenga Naba third. The Naba of Fada-N'Gourma was outside the hierarchy. As time passed, the Mogho Naba of Ouagadougou gradually became more powerful than the other rulers, even though he recognized the seniority of Tenkodogo and, as we shall see, had difficulty exercising his seniority and supremacy over the Yatenga. Because he was the pre-eminent Mossi ruler, the Mogho Naba of Ouagadougou set the general pattern of kingship and chiefship. The heads of the other kingdoms, principalities, districts, and villages tried to approximate the pomp and ceremony of the Ouagadougou court as closely as their resources and etiquette permitted. The pattern of chiefship among the Mossi in general thus differed little from that of the Ouagadougou kingdom.

The Mossi of Ouagadougou believed that their Mogho Naba was superior to all other kings. They believed that his realm was the largest in the world, and that no other king was so rich and powerful. He was so awe-inspiring, so "like the sun," that no one dared to look upon his face. It was forbidden to touch his hand, or speak to him from any but a kneeling position with the forehead touching the ground. People were expected to hesitate before pronouncing his name, and no other person was allowed to bear the name of the current ruler. When Crozat asked one of his Mossi bearers why Boukary Koutou had chosen a title that means "elephant," the man declared, "He is an elephant; he is king of all kings as the elephant is king of all animals; a great elephant-king he is."[2] Another Moaga, meeting Crozat on the road to Ouagadougou, told him to be prepared to meet a monarch "whose riches are inexhaustible and whose splendor is marvelous. He and his family wear only the most admirable European clothes; a thousand horses stand before his door, and there are more than a thousand women in his house. He is served by one hundred eunuchs; he commands as master 333 chiefs; and when he speaks to them it is as though God himself had spoken; everyone bows down before him and obeys."[3] Crozat, looking at the Mogho Naba through European eyes, did not find the "great king" he had expected. Yet he and later European visitors to the Mossi capital did affirm that all Mossi officials and district chiefs prostrated themselves in obeisance to their sovereign, even if they did not subsequently follow his instructions.[4]

Many rituals associated with the person and court of the Mogho Naba served to emphasize the high esteem in which he was held by his subjects. For example, the sovereign showed himself every morning at a ceremony called "Ouend pous yan" (literally, "God rises," or "the sun rises") that survives to this day. The name of this ceremony has led many scholars and travelers to assert that traditionally the Mogho Naba was considered a divine king. Dim Delobson states that this ceremony "shows the regard which the Mossi have for their chief, since they compare him to the sun, and thus to a 'god.' "[5] However, the Mossi do not now and probably never did regard their monarchs either as gods or as divine kings. There is a great deal of difference between regarding a man as "powerful and brilliant" like the sun and regarding him as divine. As a matter of fact, the Mossi very often dramatize in humorous fashion the all-too-human frailties of their rulers, without ever considering it sacrilegious to do so. On the other hand, the Mogho Naba, as the supreme ruler, was expected to follow faithfully the strict etiquette demanded by his exalted position.

The morning ceremony was opened by the ruler's chief page, the *soghone-kasanga*, who sprinkled a phylacteric solution around a throne (*guere*) in the courtyard in front of a reception room called the *zongo*. Other pages (*soghondamba*) brought out a large cushion (*naghpure*), the ruler's sword, and other personal accouterments, and placed them on the throne. Still other pages aided the Mogho Naba in his toilet. He was clothed in a large red robe, which symbolized the rising sun; he wore a bonnet surmounted by silver streamers (*wazourfou sebere*), which represented the sun itself. The toilet was performed in complete silence, for no one was allowed to speak to the monarch until after the ceremony. Meanwhile, in the courtyard, the court dignitaries, visitors, and the musicians and minstrels (*bendere*) took their places. The provincial ministers sat on their respective stones (*coganaramse*), and the visitors sat by their hosts. The pages at the door of the zongo awaited the moment when the Mogho Naba and his escort would emerge from the zongo. On seeing the two pages who preceded the monarch, they snapped their fingers as a signal to the still silent bendere.

On seeing the monarch, the chief musician, the Bendere Naba, rubbed his fingers across the top of his drum to produce the sound of a lion's growl, and the other drummers and violinists played the royal air, "Ouend pous yan." The head guard, the Kambo Naba, and his men, carrying guns, walked up from the side and knelt down facing the assembly. And the *samande-kamba,* the "servants of the courtyard," came with heavy batons to guard against crimes of lese majesty. From the wings came a groom with a partly saddled ceremonial horse. As soon as the monarch was seated on his throne, his two pages moved to the front and knelt down facing the courtyard. The salutations now began. The first group of ministers, led by the Baloum Naba and including the Samande Naba, the Samande Nabila, the Ouedrange Naba, the Kamsaogho Naba, and the Zusoaba Kasanga, left their stones and came to the throne with slow steps and bowed heads. A few yards from the monarch, they knelt on the ground, and with their fingers folded and their thumbs in the air, leaned forward, struck the ground with both hands three times, and then rubbed the palms of their left hands with the fingers of their right. Then they arose, and with heads still bowed walked backwards to their places.[6] With the music still playing, another group of ministers, led by the Ouidi Naba and including such men as the Gounga Naba, the Larhalle Naba, and the Pwe Naba, saluted the ruler in the same manner. On Fridays and other Islamic holy days, the Moslem Imam representing the Ouagadougou congregation read aloud from the Koran. This part of the ceremony ended when the Mogho Naba rose, and, with the measured steps and swaying gait that signified royalty, retired to the zongo, preceded by his two pages.[7]

A few minutes later, the monarch returned to the courtyard without his red robe and glittering headdress. There was a second round of salutations comparable to the first, but this time the Ouidi Naba and his group did not appear unless it was an important occasion or important guests were present. When this part of the ceremony was over, the monarch called for his half-saddled horse and announced that he wished to go to

La, a village near Koudougou district. His eldest wife, the *Pughtiema*, appeared carrying her household utensils in order to accompany her husband. However, all the ministers, led by the Kamsaogho Naba, implored the monarch to have his horse unsaddled and to postpone the trip until the following day. Feigning anger, the Mogho Naba reluctantly agreed to remain in the capital, ordered his horse unsaddled, dismissed his wife, and re-entered the palace.[8]

The tradition about the origin of this ritual reveals something of the Mossi attitude toward the human frailties of their rulers. It appears that Poko, the favorite wife of Mogho Naba Waraga (ca. 1660–80), asked permission to visit her father at La, and that he refused to grant her request because of his love and admiration for her. Nevertheless, she continued to ask him for permission, and after her third request he granted her wish and sent a page and a small girl with her as chaperons. When Poko did not return to the palace on the third day, Naba Waraga sent two pages to her father's compound to fetch her, and here they discovered that she had died. Fearing the king's wrath toward persons who brought bad tidings, the pages did not report back to him but notified the ministers of Poko's death. When subsequent messengers also failed to return, the king decided to go to La. The following day, after the morning ceremonies, he ordered his horse saddled and commanded the Pughtiema to get ready to accompany him on his journey. But the ministers, anxious to protect him from grief, told him that a great king never followed a mere woman under any circumstances and persuaded him not to depart. The monarch went back into the palace, and the dignitaries ordered the horse unsaddled and sent it away. Shortly afterwards, the king changed his mind and decided to go to La, but he was beseeched not to do so. He swore that he would leave the following morning, and that if he were prevented from doing so, he would advise all his descendants to try to go to La every morning until one of them succeeded.[9]

At the end of this ceremony, a page gave the ministers an ample supply of beer and kola nuts. The Moslems were given presents of kola nuts and millet water (*zom ƙom*) sweetened with honey, since they were forbidden to drink millet beer. Later in the morning, the Mogho Naba left the palace and entered the zongo, where he greeted his visitors, accepted gifts from visiting chiefs and subjects, dispensed gifts in turn, and presided over the court of justice. Anyone who went to see the ruler had to be accompanied by his provincial minister or his host—regardless of whether it was his purpose to pay a courtesy visit, to pledge allegiance, to plead for aid, or to give testimony in a lawsuit. Pages moved back and forth between the palace and the courtyard, dispensing kola nuts and beer or millet water prepared by the sovereign's wives. Other pages waited upon the monarch, and accompanied him when he moved about the courtyard. When the ruler drank any liquid, the pages rubbed the palm of one hand with the fingers of the other; when he sneezed, everyone clapped; and when he stepped out to urinate, a page accompanied him, turned his back to him, knelt down, and saluted by rubbing his palm.

When the Mogho Naba had finished his morning audiences, he entered his palace for a solitary meal. This meal was prepared by one of his young wives, who tasted it in his presence before giving it to the page who served him.[10] After eating, the monarch rested for a few hours; then he emerged into the courtyard to grant audiences and hear court cases until sunset. At that time he retired to his palace, and those courtiers who were not connected with the evening ceremonies returned to their homes.

The ceremony that closed the day at the monarch's court was called "Kwaga Basgha" (literally, "final meal"). This ceremony still survives. As soon as the sun began to set, the samande-kamba took their heavy batons and stood guard to prevent unauthorized persons from coming near the *namtibo* (royal amulets). The Baloum Naba and the Bendere Naba entered the palace courtyard and knelt before the zongo. The chief page then brought out the *kwaga*, a pottery vessel containing a fire ritually associated with the namtibo.[11] The vessel was placed on the ground, and the page blew on the fire to make it burn brightly. Meanwhile, the Bendere Naba rubbed his fingers across his drum to make the growl of a lion. When the fire finally died out, the Zusoaba Kasanga and the Baloum Naba closed the ceremony by rising, coming together, and saluting the namtibo in the traditional Mossi manner. (The Mogho Naba did not attend this ceremony.) Before the officials left for the night, the pages gave them pots of beer prepared by the royal wives. Sometimes these officials visited the Mogho Naba before they retired to their compounds. Once these men had departed, the pages served the ruler his evening meal, which again had been prepared by one of his young wives.

During the hours of darkness the Mogho Naba conducted many secret affairs of state and conversed with the members of his household. Persons seeking the nam of a deceased relative were often granted audience at night, as were litigants in court cases. When there were no pressing matters of state, the ruler gathered some of the royal wives around him and discussed family affairs, which protocol forbade him to discuss during the day. Some rulers reportedly disguised themselves and visited the wards of the town in the company of a young man from the palace, in an effort to learn things that did not ordinarily come to a ruler's attention.

The Mogho Naba slept in a grass hut in the palace compound. Two reasons are given for the choice of a grass hut over a brick building: first, the grass hut was considered better protection against sorcerers, who were believed to induce storms that destroy buildings and their occupants; second, it was believed that the ruler's ancestors preferred to visit grass huts because it was easier for them to enter through the interstices in the walls. When the monarch retired for the night, one of his pages stood guard at the door. The Mogho Naba usually slept all night, but he occasionally made the rounds with a page to check on the palace guards or the safety (and virtue) of his wives.

The routine of the Mogho Naba seldom varied. Only in times of danger or on great ceremonial occasions did protocol permit any major changes in court procedure. Normally, pages, ministers, and other court officials adhered very strictly to their traditional tasks.

The Mossi considered the king's office to be such a difficult one that even today they say, *Mogho Naba toumde ya yida fa* ("The Mogho Naba's task is the most difficult of all"). Nevertheless, the Mogho Naba's office was always eagerly sought, and considerable care had to be exercised to ensure that the right person was chosen. As soon as the incumbent Mogho Naba died, and even before he was buried, the Ouidi Naba, as prime minister, began the consultations leading to the selection of a new monarch. Mossi custom decreed that the eldest son of a previous ruler be chosen as the new Mogho Naba. This choice was not automatic, however, in view of the primary consideration that the person selected should have the skill to "keep" the country. Other qualifications for office were membership in the royal minimal lineage, soundness of body and mind, and sufficient age to command universal respect. Given these requirements and the lack of any provisions for a regency, it is not surprising that a dead ruler's sons, brothers, uncles, and even grandchildren—that is, his entire babissi—should have competed to "eat the nam" (accede to power).[12] Of the thirty-four kings who have ruled since Oubri, the founder of the Ouagadougou dynasty, twelve succeeded their brothers and twenty-two their fathers. Interestingly enough, there is some indication that at the beginning of the Ouagadougou dynasty, the successor of a king was usually chosen from among his brothers before the nam was passed on to the next generation.[13] For example, Oubri's four sons all reigned in turn before the kingship descended to the son of the last brother in office. Then, two of this brother's sons reigned before the nam descended to a new generation. Initially, then, seniority within the royal lineage, like seniority within the local ruling lineages, may have been determined by generation. On the other hand, accidental factors may have governed: a weak state organization may have required mature rulers, or an uncle may have vanquished a nephew by physical prowess or force of character.

The pretenders to the Mossi nam began to press their claims as soon as propriety allowed. They presented gifts to the Ouidi Naba and to the other ministers in an attempt to sway the issue. The Ouidi Naba finally called a secret council composed of the Gounga Naba, the Larhalle Naba, the Kamsaogho Naba, and the Tansoba, and recited to them the following formula: "The country does not have a chief, and it needs one. Among all the people who wish to be elected [*di nam,* "eat the nam"], it is for you to choose the most worthy."[14] To this the councillors responded: "Naba! You are our superior, and the right to make the choice rests upon you alone." Thus given a free hand, the Ouidi Naba chose the most capable candidate. However, before announcing his choice, he said to the Tansoba, "My heart is heavy because I fear that those persons whose hopes have not been fulfilled will resort to violence to get their way." The Tansoba responded, "That will be against tradition and justice. Do not fear. I am here with my army to see that your decision is respected." Having received the support of the Tansoba, the Ouidi Naba announced his choice to the other councillors. They said to him, "Naba! You have expressed our will, and that of all the people." It is not to be understood from these formulas that the other councillors had no voice in selecting the candidate. They did in fact advise the Ouidi Naba concerning the best candidate, but these formulas emphasized that it was the Ouidi Naba, as prime minister, who was responsible for the choice.

The Ouidi Naba's choice of a new Mogho Naba was kept secret until the successful candidate was summoned for investiture. This occurred on the second night of the late Mogho Naba's funeral ceremony. Toward nightfall, the Ouidi Naba secretly dispatched a messenger to summon the successful candidate. The need for secrecy was demonstrated in 1890, when Boukary Koutou forced the committee to name him Mogho Naba. The circumstances were as follows: Mogho Naba Sanum died without male issue, and all his brothers vied for the nam. One of them, Boukary Koutou, was felt to be ineligible because he had been exiled for leading a civil war against Sanum, but like his brothers he hastened to Ouagadougou. Boukary feared that the electors would not look favorably upon his claim, and when he failed to ascertain their intentions he decided upon a *coup d'état.* He gathered an army composed of his supporters and his Gurunsi slaves, and surrounded the compound in which the electors were gathered. One of the electors discovered the army during a break in the deliberations and reported his findings to the Ouidi Naba. The chief minister and his aides knew that Boukary Koutou was the only person capable of such a conspiracy. Fearing for their lives if they did not nominate him, they immediately sent a messenger to summon him as the successful candidate.[15] Under normal circumstances, however, there was no coercion of the ministers and the nominee was quietly brought to the councillors.

Wearing a pair of trousers and a sheepskin mantle and carrying a spear in each hand, the nominee entered the courtyard of the compound through the women's door.[16] He was preceded by the Samande Nabila, who sprinkled the earth with water. He came up to the councillors and saluted them, and the Ouidi Naba addressed him as follows: "Before your father [brother] died, did he designate you to be his successor?" The nominee replied, "No, Sire! My father has left you free to choose whom you wish, be he a blind man or a leper!" This question was asked three times, and the nominee responded three times. The Ouidi Naba then made the following declaration: "I am giving you the nam of your father and grandfathers. You must try to conduct yourself as they did when they had the nam." The Ouidi Naba then listed the names of the territories over which the ruler had absolute power and authority. The new monarch raised his two spears in the air, made a speech in which he announced three guiding principles by which he vowed to reign, and "named a name," that is, suggested the title by which he wished to be known. For example, Mogho Naba Sagha II (1942–57) said in his inaugural speech: "Without rain, there is no life. I will be like rain for the country." He then became known as Mogho Naba Sagha ("Rain"), a rather fitting title for a ruler in a country with uncertain rainfall. The present Mogho Naba stressed in his inaugural speech (in 1957) that he was "solid as a rock." His official title is now Mogho Naba Kougri ("Rock").[17]

The taking of a new name was only the first step in the elaborate process through which a man became Mogho Naba. Next, the Ouidi Naba took the two spears from the new monarch and removed his sheepskin mantle. Then he gave him his new white clothes, which included a pair of trousers, a bonnet, and a sleeveless robe, all made for him by the people of the Soulougou ward in the capital. Next, he was given a cushion made by the people of Baramimi. The Baloum Naba then took the closely guarded namtibo, the sacred amulets of the dynasty, and used them in the preparation of a potion of millet beer mixed with millet-flour water, part of which was poured as a libation to the earth goddess, Tenga.[18] The ruler and the assembled ministers all partook of the potion in a kind of communion. The ministers then shook the ruler's hand, an act thereafter forbidden, and departed for their own compounds. The newly elected monarch secreted himself either at the Samande Nabila's home or elsewhere in the capital until daybreak. Tradition holds that if he were killed before being officially proclaimed before his subjects as the new ruler, the assassin could become Mogho Naba.[19]

The public ceremonies marking the official proclamation of the new ruler's accession to power took place on the following day. Early that morning, the monarch left his secret sleeping quarters and proceeded to the Koumbi Naba's house. Here he dressed in his white garments and mounted an old, unsaddled horse. The Baloum Naba then gave him a sack containing the namtibo, which he placed over his shoulder, and the Kalzi Naba led him out of the courtyard by the women's door. As the ruler's horse passed through the gate, his sister, the *Napoko* ("female ruler"), cried, "The sun has reappeared! The fire is relighted! The earth lives again!" A large crowd of musicians and warriors who had been alerted by the ministers shouted and danced as they accompanied the monarch, who circled the compound three times.[20] The ruler then reentered the compound, and this time he came out through the men's door as a sign of his full status. Here he was greeted by the Ouidi Naba, who proclaimed in a loud voice, "Mossi people, here is the Mogho Naba!" The warriors shouted and fired their muskets, and the musicians played. Then all the dignitaries and their followers solemnly prostrated themselves and paid homage and swore allegiance to their monarch. He, in turn, listened attentively when his ministers and some of the elder chiefs gave him advice about how the affairs of state should be conducted. After each declaration of loyalty or word of counsel, the people shouted in praise of their ruler. The Bendere Naba, accompanied by his musicians, then recited the ruler's genealogy, announced the pledges the new monarch had made to his people, and acclaimed him by his royal title, "Mogho Naba [X]." From this moment on, no child born during his reign could bear the ruler's name, and those persons who already bore it called themselves *Nab'yure* ("king's name").

As the next stage in the ceremony the Mogho Naba, accompanied by his retinue, visited the various wards in the capital. In each he was proclaimed ruler and received the allegiance of both Mossi and non-Mossi ward chiefs. He visited the wards controlled by such men as the Loumbila Naba, the Sapone Naba, and the Ouagadougou Naba, and at each stop the ward chief declared, "People of [X], here is your new sovereign." Having been acknowledged by the leading chiefs of the capital, the new ruler then returned to his host's house. He emerged later in the day to visit the compound of a palace attendant, the Samande Nabila, where he sat under a tree and again received oaths of allegiance from his chief ministers and other dignitaries. He then proceeded to the house of the Ouagadougou Naba (a direct descendant of the aboriginal Ninisi population), where he spent the night. The following morning, his host made sacrifices to his Ninisi ancestors in the name of the new ruler. Once again, the principal ministers and dignitaries appeared and joined in a ceremony of allegiance to their king, but this time they drank a potion prepared with the namtibo and swore that they hoped their ancestors would kill them if they should prove disloyal to the Mogho Naba.

The monarch then left the Ouagadougou Naba's compound, accompanied by the Tansoba and his warriors, and went to Paspanga (a ward in the capital whose name means "to add strength or power") to receive homage and allegiance from his assembled district chiefs. Along the way, he met symbolic opposition from the candidates he had defeated. However, these "hostile" forces were quickly routed by the Tansoba and his army. According to one Mossi tradition, when Sagha I (ca. 1787–1803) was elected Mogho Naba, his father's brother, Kaoko, tried to kill him during this mock battle. A vigorous civil war ensued, in which some district chiefs joined Kaoko. Sagha defeated and killed Kaoko and many of his supporters, and then swept through the country, executing rebellious district chiefs and placing his own sons in power.

At Paspanga the sovereign sat under a tree, surrounded by his ministers, warriors, and musicians. The onlookers formed two facing ranks in front of the sovereign, between which the district chiefs and their retinues walked up to pledge their allegiance. Those members of the royal sub-lineage who had been put to flight by the Tansoba's army returned and rendered homage to the monarch. Emissaries from the autonomous Mossi princes also greeted him.

When this ceremony was over, the Mogho Naba instructed his retainers to provide food and drink for his subjects and guests, and retired for the night. He remained at Paspanga for a week, during which time he greeted those persons who had not arrived in time for the first day's ceremony. On the seventh day, the monarch and a few courtiers and retainers retired to Dimvousse ("king's resting place"), where the district chiefs who had come to Ouagadougou for the installation brought him presents before returning home. The Mogho Naba remained at Dimvousse for a period ranging from several weeks to three years, depending on whether the earth-priests advised him to inhabit his predecessor's palace or build a new one.[21] When at last he ended his retreat, a large crowd of horsemen, warriors, and musicians accompanied him to his palace, where he set up his permanent court.

The Mogho Naba had an elaborate court composed of many officials, relatives, and servants. The most important courtiers were the five ministers, who appeared daily at court and took part in all important ceremonies in addition to administering their own provinces. Aside from these men, the Mogho Naba had a number of other officials called Naba whose responsibilities covered the full range of duties in the palace and in the capital. One of the most interesting was the Pwe Naba, a royal diviner and court chaperon. His chief duty was to guard the morals of the pages and the royal wives; he also administered the ordeal to persons accused of treason. The pages were required to be chaste until they were discharged from the palace, lest their amorous adventures lead them to compromise the virtue of the royal wives, with whom they were constantly in contact. A wife and a page suspected of adultery were tested by the Pwe Naba. He forced them to look into a mirror or a calabash of water, and declared them guilty or innocent according to the way their faces were reflected. If they were found guilty, the wife was executed and the page was either executed or discharged in disgrace. The Pwe Naba also saw to it that strangers did not address the ruler's wives either on the street or in the market. Offenders were executed.

The Dapore Naba served as the court's chief executioner and as head of a group of the Mogho Naba's hereditary serfs. Members of the royal clan were executed by strangulation, since royal blood could not be shed; all other persons were executed either with a sword, by hanging, or with heavy clubs. Another palace official was the Ouedrango Naba, the head groom. It was he who saddled and presented the king's ceremonial horse to him at the morning ceremony. The Kambo Naba commanded the palace guard; only he and his guards were permitted to carry guns. The Samande Naba and the Samande Nabila supervised the work of the samande-kamba, young men who worked around the palace courtyard and kept watch with heavy batons to enforce order during ceremonies. A lesser palace official was the Zusoaba Kasanga, who, as chief of the palace eunuchs, ruled over the guardians of the royal harem. The Gande Naba made sacrifices for the ruler and also distributed gifts from the king to the royal officials and the royal household.

Another courtier, and one who played an important role during the installation of the new ruler, was the Ouagadougou Naba. As a direct descendant of the Ninisi, he was all but indispensable at sacrifices propitiating or honoring his ancestors. The Bendere Naba was the chief musician and court historian; according to some reports, a Bendere Naba was killed instantly if he made a mistake while reciting the ruler's genealogy. The Raga Naba was chief of the markets in the capital. Under him were the Kos Naba, who levied taxes on general merchandise sold in the markets, and the Nemdo Naba, who collected taxes on meat sold in the markets and was responsible for distributing meat within the royal household. Most of these positions were hereditary, but here primogeniture was not as important as in the ruling and administrative lineages.

The various foreign groups in the capital also sent representatives to the court. Among them were the Zangweoto Naba for the Hausa, a Naba for the Songhai, and an Imam for the Ouagadougou Moslems. Even total strangers such as the early European visitors were placed under the care of a special chief.

The most ubiquitous persons at the Mogho Naba's court were the pages, who were boys between the ages of ten and twenty. These boys were regarded as comparable to the ruler's wives, since they served him in the same manner as ordinary Mossi women serve their husbands at home. They wore women's bracelets and women's clothes, and dressed their hair in the same style as the royal wives. As we have seen, they were forbidden sexual intercourse until they were released from the royal household.[22]

The institution of pages is said to have originated sometime in the seventeenth century, during the reign of Mogho Naba Waraga. Before his reign, the wives of the Mogho Naba attended him at court. The change came during a lengthy civil war between Waraga and the chief of Riziam territory, who had refused to pay allegiance to him. During five "dry seasons" (five years) of fighting, the Mogho Naba was attended only by a small boy. He found him so efficient that at the end of the war he resolved to employ only page boys and prohibit his wives from attending him at court. This origin is conjectural. However, the use of pages effectively segregated the royal wives from court intrigues, and, once instituted, the practice spread throughout the country.

The Mogho Naba had little difficulty recruiting pages. Many of them were the sons of pughsiudse whom he had given to his subjects as wives. In theory, the Mogho Naba could select boys at will, but in practice the pages were usually selected by the ministers and sent to the palace. Most boys willingly accepted service, but some, often with the support of their parents, resisted confinement to the palace. Some ten-year-olds even ran away to escape their impending fate, but they were soon caught and braceleted with the insignia of their new status. Once this had been done, their lineages encouraged them to remain at the palace. Their period of service terminated when they began to "push beards," usually at about eighteen years of age. One district chief claims that ancient Mogho Nanamse used to take the sons of district chiefs as pages and release them only when their fathers died. In this way the rulers not only retained the allegiance of the boys' fathers but had a unique opportunity to determine whether these boys were qualified to succeed to the nam.

The life of a page was confining, even if sometimes very rewarding. Pages were bound by the demands of the ruler, whose every wish had to be satisfied immediately. A quarrelsome ruler was a terror to his pages, who had to bear silently his insults and blows. On the other hand, a considerate monarch permitted or encouraged his pages to profit from the small political intrigues in which they were invariably involved. Prospective district chiefs "made friends" with pages to find out whether their suits were progressing, or to whom they might usefully offer gifts. The pages used any money they might procure to buy clothes for themselves, to supplement the clothing and presents they received from their relatives. Every page was "adopted" by one of the royal wives, who prepared his meals and took care of him. In return, he helped this woman cultivate her field when his presence was not required by the monarch. When a page completed his service satisfactorily, he received a pughsiudga as a wife. If his work had not been satisfactory, he was simply dismissed.

The only woman who played any significant role at the court of the Mogho Naba was the Pughtiema, his head wife. She was the only wife to whom he presented his friends, and whom he allowed his subjects to visit. This woman, who was commonly the widow of the former Mogho Naba, was often chosen because she was past childbearing age: she was thus older and wiser than the other wives, less preoccupied with children, and above the sexual jealousies that may often develop in polygynous households. She arbitrated among the wives and stood *in loco parentis* to the younger ones, whom she instructed and advised. She served also as official hostess to the ancestors during the annual propitiatory rituals. It was her duty to prepare the millet beer and millet water for the sacrifices to the ancestors, who were believed to feast at her hut before they visited the rest of the household. In addition, it was she who prepared to accompany the Mogho Naba to La each day. Lastly, it was her duty to introduce any new royal wife to the ancestors, and to ask them to watch over this potential mother of their descendants.

The ruler inherited some of his wives from his father; some he received from his many friends and vassals; and others he selected from among his pughsiudse. Crozat reports that Mogho Naba Wobogo (1890-96) allegedly had a hundred wives. Crozat did not see this many women at Wobogo's court, understandably, since most of a ruler's wives lived in villages, where they were guarded by eunuchs.[23] Of the substantial number of royal wives who did live at the palace, only a small minority prepared the ruler's meals and shared his bed. Dim Delobson reports that Mogho Naba Kom II (1905-42) had thirty-seven wives. His son, Mogho Naba Sagha II (1942-57), had twenty.[24] The present Mogho Naba, Kougri, recently married according to Western tradition and is officially monogamous.[25] There seems to be a general trend toward fewer wives among Mossi chiefs.

Mossi rulers never married for the purpose of forming state alliances, and their marriages had no political significance. The Mogho Naba's marriages were exogamous with regard to the royal lineage and to his mother's minimal lineage. Aside from these restrictions, however, the Mogho Naba could marry women from any Mossi lineage or group, including serfs, slaves, and foreign populations. It is said that when Mogho Naba Sanum (1850-90) despaired of having an heir by a Mossi woman, he took a Fulani wife.[26]

The Mogho Naba had no formal wedding ceremony. The task of introducing a new wife to the royal harem fell to the Pughtiema. She and her assistants welcomed the wife in a prescribed fashion. First they shaved all the hair from her body. They then bathed her in warm water to which shea butter and ritual herbs had been added, and during the bath they recited the ruler's genealogy to impress her with her new status.[27] The Pughtiema advised her on the need for proper deportment, and warned her that adultery was punished by death. To close the ceremony, a smith fastened to the girl's wrists and ankles the silver or brass bracelets that identified her as a wife of the Mogho Naba. If the bride was still a child, she was often allowed to return to her father's house until she reached childbearing age. If she was past the age of puberty, her marriage was consummated without further ceremony, and she joined the ranks of the ruler's wives.

The wives who lived in the palace were divided into three groups. The first group included the wives who lived with the Pughtiema in a section of the palace harem called the *zaka sanga* ("large courtyard"). These women were all past childbearing age and no longer received nocturnal visits from the Mogho Naba. They had their own fields in the vicinity of the palace and cultivated them with the aid of the samande-kamba, the pages they had adopted, and their own children. The women of the second group, those of the *zagbilin* ("small courtyard"), were mostly in their thirties or forties and still sexually active. They received occasional visits from the Mogho Naba, but fewer than his younger wives. These women also cultivated their fields with the help of the young men of the court.

The third group of wives, the *dogunba* ("keepers of the household"), was the most important. The dogunba prepared the ruler's meals and satisfied his sexual desires. Since these women were in the monarch's favor, they were better dressed than the other wives and received more attention from him. The dogunba generally cultivated a large field in common with the aid of the palace retainers, but some insisted on cultivating their own fields instead. Like the other wives, the dogunba usually lived in huts of their own. Childless women sometimes shared the same hut until one of them became pregnant and had to set up a hut for herself and her child.

Those wives who lived in special villages under the supervision of eunuchs rarely went to the palace. Usually, they were past childbearing age or had lost favor with the monarch. They cultivated plots of land, spun cotton, and prepared locust-bean flour, locust-bean "balls," and shea butter. They kept a part of the produce for their own use and sent the remainder to the palace stores; the same arrangement obtained for all three categories of palace wives.

The Mogho Naba's heir was usually born while his father was still Crown Prince. He was never born in his father's compound because, unlike other Mossi women, the wife of a Mogho Naba or Crown Prince returned to her father's house for confinement. As soon as she announced her pregnancy, the Pughtiema or one of the older wives held a ceremony to notify the ancestors. Once the rite had been completed, the wife was sent to her relatives for fear that she might be harmed by her less fortunate co-wives. If the child was a boy, the ruler or Crown Prince was notified immediately, because the important privileges of a first-born hinged upon this notification. Since several wives of the Mogho Naba might be pregnant at the same time and errors might be made about the onset and duration of pregnancy, primogeniture had to be established immediately to forestall dynastic conflicts. For example, it is commonly believed that the present Doulougou Naba was born several days before Mogho Naba Sagha II (1942–57) but was deprived of the nam because the messenger who brought news of his birth reached Mogho Naba Kom after the messenger who announced Sagha's birth. Undoubtedly, such allegations were sometimes used to foster and support dynastic rebellions.

So strong was the fear that the most likely heir to the nam would be harmed by jealous co-wives that the child and his mother never returned to the palace except for brief visits on ceremonial occasions. The young prince remained with his mother's relatives and was guarded and educated by servants sent from the palace. If his father was on the throne at Ouagadougou when the boy reached the age of ten, he was formally installed as chief of Djiba district, the traditional seat of the Crown Prince. If his father was not on the throne, the boy remained with his mother's relatives and went to Djiba when his grandfather died and his father was installed as Mogho Naba.

The origin of Djiba's status as the seat of the Crown Prince is rather obscure. The people of the neighboring district of Nobere say that Djiba was founded by a "companion" of their own founder, Naba Biligo, one of the numerous "eldest" sons of Mogho Naba Oubri, the implication being that Djiba was supervised by Nobere. However, no one seems to know when Djiba's status changed or what happened to the ancient family who used to govern it. The consensus is that in earlier times the heir presumptive to Ouagadougou did not necessarily become chief of Djiba, but was given any district whose chieftainship was vacant when he came of age. Dim Delobson reports that Djiba became the district of the Crown Prince sometime during the seventeenth century, when Mogho Naba Zombere, who had reigned for sixty years, found it necessary to establish a permanent seat for his heir.[28] However, Dim Delobson does not report under what conditions Djiba was chosen, nor does he say what happened to the local ruling lineage when this transfer took place. That the transfer was carried out in the manner reported by Dim Delobson is not doubted, because each new Mogho Naba obtained districts for his relatives in this way. Through this process, the people of the ancient ruling lineages were usually reduced to the level of commoners, and this is apparently what happened to the rulers of Djiba.

The first public sign that the young prince was being prepared for the nam came in the form of a summons commanding him to go to Ouagadougou to be installed as Djiba Naba. On his way to the capital, he visited several villages where the local Tengsobadamba made sacrifices to the earth goddess in his name. He took this opportunity to meet with the district chiefs and their assembled village chiefs; he was entertained by them; and in turn he distributed gifts to the old women, whose praises were considered especially effective in bringing health and long life. When the boy finally arrived at the capital, he lodged at the compound of the Kambo Naba, head of the palace guard, until the Mogho Naba and his ministers installed him as chief of Djiba.

The installation rites for the Crown Prince were very similar to those already described for the Mogho Naba, and identical to those for the district chiefs. During the ceremony, no mention was made of the fact that the prince was the son of the Mogho Naba. The only special feature was that when the prince went into the courtyard after the ceremony to render homage to the Mogho Naba, he sat in an area assigned to him by custom. When the ruler appeared, the prince followed the Gounga Naba, who was provincial minister for Djiba, and rendered homage to the sovereign. After this reception the prince went to the Gounga Naba's compound, which henceforth was his headquarters whenever he visited Ouagadougou; for, like other district chiefs, he had to consult with this minister before seeing the monarch. Everyone in the kingdom had to follow the political hierarchy, even the ruler's heir.

The young prince remained at his host's house and from there visited the other important officials, in the order of their rank, receiving from each presents of sheep, millet beer, kola nuts, and sometimes wives. He then visited the Imam of the Ouagadougou Moslem community, where he received a blessing in the name of Allah and was given kola nuts and millet water sweetened with honey. On the fourth or fifth day the prince went to a small village called Zoangha, where he made a sacrifice to his ancestors and requested their protection against all enemies.[29] He returned to Ouagadougou on the same day and was given a palace escort to accompany him to his district.

During his journey, the royal heir had the opportunity to establish or re-establish friendly relations with district chiefs who were now his peers, but who might someday become his subjects. He visited in turn the war leader at Tansobatenga, the Koubri Naba, the Ipelse Naba, and the Kondrin Naba. Each of these chiefs offered him livestock, slaves, and wives. He, in turn, distributed salt (a valuable commodity) to the old women and gave kola nuts and other commodities to the chiefs' head wives. The Baganmini Naba presented the prince with a special quiver of arrows, and the chief of the Fulani at Bedego gave him a pretty maiden and one of his best bulls. The prince spent a few days with each of his hosts, but stayed for seven days in Bere, a district bordering on his own. The Bere Naba gave him a wife, a robe, and a cow, and sent messengers to the village chiefs of Djiba to announce that their chief had arrived in Bere. The chiefs then journeyed to Bere, pledged allegiance to their ruler, and presented gifts to him. On the seventh night there was a ritual (whose main features are unclear), in the course of which the prince entered Djiba secretly on horseback, accompanied only by one servant, one groom, and the nobles and chiefs of Djiba.[30] Most members of the escort who had accompanied him from the capital were left behind at Bere, and followed only when the prince had established himself in his district. When the prince's band entered Djiba under cover of darkness, it was met by the local Ouidi Naba, who ruled the district in the absence of a Crown Prince. The Ouidi Naba now became the prince's protector if the boy were still young, or his most trusted adviser if he were old enough to rule by himself.

As soon as the prince arrived, the Ouidi Naba made preparations to receive the chiefs of such local districts as Manga, Nobere, and Basgana, who visited the prince and brought him wives, livestock, and money. During a seven-day period, other chiefs and well-wishers visited the new chief and offered him gifts. When this period was over, the new Djiba Naba gave wives to the noble members of his escort and livestock, money, and kola nuts to the commoners and serfs, and sent the group back to Ouagadougou. Then he settled down to the life of a typical district chief, governing his villages in the name of the Mogho Naba, paying him tribute, and settling disputes among his villagers. Dim Delobson reports that the other district chiefs and the heads of such principalities as Boussouma and Conquizitenga formerly sent presents to the Djiba Naba when they sent their annual tribute to the Mogho Naba.[31] But this contradicts all that I heard and saw of the relationship between the royal heir and the other district chiefs. They treated him as an equal and showed no deference to him either in private or on ceremonial occasions. As a matter of fact, in the presence of the Mogho Naba, the royal heir actually effaced himself before the other district chiefs. This behavior served to preserve the concept of equal access of all members of the ruling clan to the ancestral nam. The Mogho Naba was head of the ruling group as well as political leader of the Mossi. His son, on the other hand, was often a junior in terms of age and generation within the ruling group, but politically he was on the same level as the other district chiefs. The sovereign could not show by his behavior that his son was either actually or potentially superior to the other Nanamse; nor could the prince presume to be haughty because of his strategic but accidental relationship to the actual possessor of the nam. Had he tried to do so, he might have ruined his chances of being selected to take over the "house" of his father and his father's fathers.

The relations between the Mogho Naba and his children, including his heir, were characterized by formality—at least in public. Nevertheless, the ruler took a vital interest in the training and welfare of the youthful Djiba Naba. Mogho Naba Wobogo (1890–96) reportedly had the Ouidi Naba and the Baloum Naba of Djiba executed because the Crown Prince died under strange circumstances while under their care. Yet the Mogho Naba was not expected to enjoy seeing his son and heir, because of the Mossi father's traditional anxiety regarding those individuals who would profit most from his death. At the assemblies of district chiefs called by the Mogho Naba, the royal heir was not even greeted by his father; moreover, the heir usually stood at the edge of the assembly and left without attending the customary feast. However, there is considerable evidence that the Mogho

Naba regularly saw his son in private, and that the prince often interceded successfully with his father for the lives of rebels or criminals.

The Mogho Naba seldom saw his younger sons, who usually remained with their mothers' patrilineages until they were old enough to be assigned district chieftainships or sent to live in villages controlled by the Baloum Naba. He was rather suspicious of these boys, who, if certain traditions are believed, were not averse to plotting the death of the Djiba Naba in order to succeed to the nam. The district chiefs also feared these younger sons, in whose favor they were often deposed by the Mogho Naba. Almost all of the dynastic changes that occurred in the Mossi districts seem to have stemmed from a ruler's attempt to find districts for his brothers or his younger sons.

The ruler was less concerned with the welfare of his daughters and female relatives. Their marriages seldom benefited the political system. As a matter of fact, the behavior of a royal princess usually strained the relations between her husband and the ruling lineage. The reason for this was a status conflict: as wives, they had low prestige in Mossi society; but as relatives of the Mogho Naba, they enjoyed high status. This contradiction made it difficult for them to accept the low estate of wives. Consequently, they clashed with their husband and often dominated the women and co-wives in his compound. Since few Mossi men tolerate strife within their household, these noble wives often withdrew from their husband's home and established one of their own. The one exception to this pattern was the ruler's eldest daughter, the Napoko, whose ceremonial duties at his death and during the interregnum compelled her to remain loyal to the husband chosen for her by the king. Like her brother, the Crown Prince, if she violated any of the traditions and thus became ineligible to fulfill her duties to her father and to the state, she endangered the country at its weakest moment, when the government was being transferred from the deceased Mogho Naba to his successor.

The death of a Mogho Naba was usually attributed to foul play or supernatural forces. When Mogho Naba Sagha II died in 1957, a report from Ouagadougou stated that the Governor of the Upper Volta had felt constrained to have an autopsy performed to quell rumors that the monarch had died of poisoning.[32] The obvious function of such rumors was to dramatize the gravity of the situation during the interregnum.

Because the Mogho Naba was usually accompanied by a page, it was often this boy who witnessed his death. It was the page's responsibility to notify the Baloum Naba, who notified, in order, the Ouidi Naba, the Larhalle Naba, the Kamsaogho Naba, the Gounga Naba, the ruler's children, the Tansoba, the members of the royal sub-lineage, and the district chiefs. The Tengsoba of the Ouagadougou area was also notified. Because he was a descendant of the aboriginal Ninisi population that "owned" the land, he supervised the burial ceremony.

The Mogho Naba's death was kept secret, and no mourning was allowed until the Crown Prince had arrived at the capital and the Tansoba had recruited an army to protect the realm against would-be usurpers of power. Then the cry was raised in the palace, to reverberate throughout the land, that "the fire had gone out." Once the ruler's death had been announced, the country was plunged into an interregnum, which was characterized by ritual and often by actual anarchy. The people in the towns immediately looted the markets and stole their neighbors' goods; the prisoners and captives in stocks were released by their guards; the nakomce in all the territories, districts, and villages subjected the local populations to robbery and pillage; and the members of the monarch's babissi began their intrigues for power. The traditional sanction for this anarchy was that only when people suffer during the breakdown of political control do they really appreciate the sovereign's role. The Mossi declare (with some truth) that no one was safe during the interregnum. However, as we shall see, the ruler was symbolically kept alive, and the country was never without effective political leadership.

When the Tengsoba arrived at the palace, he was joined by five hereditary funeral chiefs: the Pazany'tengsoba, the Tampouy Naba, the Benghin Naba, the Toghin Naba, and the Tanghin Naba. In the ceremony that followed, he gave permission for the royal grave to be dug. Meanwhile, the ruler's body was prepared for burial in the traditional manner by his female relatives and laid in state in the zongo. These women kept vigil over the body, shouting and weeping. Only the five ministers of the realm and the male members of the ruler's babissi were allowed to pay homage to the corpse within the zongo. All other mourners had to pay their respects to the monarch's eldest daughter, who, as Napoko, was dressed in the dead sovereign's clothes and sat in his place before the zongo. As her father's symbolic representative, she held daily court and received greetings and homage from all visitors until a new ruler was chosen. The drummer who sat by her side declared to all visitors, "You say that the Mogho Naba is dead! Well, who is that sitting there? Tell me! Is that not the Mogho Naba?"

The ruler was buried the day after he died, at the end of an elaborate ceremony. Libations were poured out to the ancient rulers, and sacrifices made to them. All the important officials and members of the royal minimal lineage segment except the pretenders to the throne shaved their heads as a sign of mourning. The royal pretenders donned sheepskin mantles to signify that they were willing to "eat the nam." Once the ruler had been buried, the country settled down to an uneasy peace until the eighth day, when the funeral ceremonies took place. In the meantime, the Napoko symbolically held daily court, and the Tansoba's army acted as a check against the attempts of ambitious princes to seize power by force of arms.

Two days before the funeral, the Kamsaogho Naba selected the Kourita, who was to replace the Napoko as the living symbolic representative of the dead Mogho Naba. The person chosen to be Kourita was usually a young son of the deceased king, but since this person was banished from the capital, most of the royal wives hid their young children or fled the palace with them.[33] Once the Kourita had been chosen, the Kamsaogho Naba performed a ceremony (similar to those connected with the divine kings of the Near East) during which the youth was given one of his father's horses, dressed in his father's clothes, and given his father's youngest widow as a wife. He was then paid the homage due the Mogho Naba, and after receiving many gifts from the dignitaries, he was banished from Ouagadougou forever. As he went through the country, he was treated like the Mogho Naba and given many wives and presents. If he should chance to return to Ouagadougou or see the new Mogho Naba, either or both of them would be killed by the ancestors. Many Mossi districts seem to have been founded by exiled Kouritadamba. These men were undoubtedly among the numerous "elder" sons of past kings who are said to have "refused" the nam and gone to live in the districts now governed by their descendants.

The choice and banishment of the Kourita heralded the funeral rites, which were characterized by numerous animal sacrifices to the ancestors in the name of the deceased ruler. On the afternoon of the first day of the funeral, the Crown Prince mounted a horse and left the palace by the women's door. The Napoko then took the bridle of her brother's horse and led him and an immense crowd of cavalry, armed warriors, and musicians around the palace walls three times. After the third round, the Napoko demanded that her brother give her a personal servant as a present; he hesitated, but finally granted her request. The Napoko was then lifted up by the warriors, who shouted as they carried her home. The funeral thus came to an end.

All Mossi potentates tried to emulate the Mogho Naba of Ouagadougou in matters of pomp, ceremony, and government.[34] Their courts were inferior to his, but only because they were less powerful and less wealthy.

Some of the more important rulers, such as the heads of the Yatenga, Fada-N'Gourma, and Tenkodogo kingdoms, were chosen by local electoral colleges, which did not have to seek the approval of the Mogho Naba of Ouagadougou or notify him of the choices made. Their authority, as we have seen, was supported by claims of equality with Ouagadougou. But, with the exception of the Tenkodogo ruler, they were actually farther removed from the main line of royal descent than the Mogho Naba of Ouagadougou. The autonomous Dimdamba had their own electoral colleges, which in some cases were made up of men related to the electoral-college members of the Mogho Naba of Ouagadougou. (For example, the Ouidi Naba of Boulsa was descended from the Ouidi Naba of Ouagadougou.) These local colleges were usually free to nominate and elect the Dimdamba without consulting the Mogho Naba, even though he ratified many nominations.[35] According to Cheron, "The nomination of the Dim of Boulsa did not become definitive until ratified by the Mogho Naba, who was always consulted by the electors and who could impose his own candidate."[36] This was not always true; nor did every Mogho Naba refrain from interfering in the internal affairs of autonomous provinces. Whether he did or not often depended on his strength relative to that of the Dimdamba. Once the Dimdamba had been chosen, however, they were installed with ceremonies similar to those for the Ouagadougou ruler.

Like their superiors, the Dimdamba had the authority to delegate power to the Kombemba and Tense Nanamse. Some of them also had the right to grant the nam to a fellow Dim. The Boussouma Naba, for instance, could grant it to the Mane Naba.[37] Mogho Nanamse granted such rights to Dimdamba for various reasons. They might do so on the basis of their relative strength vis-à-vis a particular Dim at a particular time, or because they admired him or were closely related to him. However, a Dim exercised sovereignty in his own name, regardless of whether he was subordinate to the Mogho Naba or to another Dim. In contrast, the district chiefs and the village chiefs exercised sovereignty on behalf of the Mogho Naba or of the Dim in whose territory they resided.

The installation ceremonies for the two lower orders of chiefs were not too different from those for the Mogho Nanamse and Dimdamba. For example, when the Nobere district chief died, the provincial minister for Nobere—in this case the Gounga Naba—reported his death to the Mogho Naba. The ruler then summoned one of the deceased chief's officials to the capital to report on the qualifications of all potential candidates for the nam. The provincial minister, in turn, dispatched one of his own representatives to the district to verify the reports he had received. It was only when this man had returned to the capital that all the nobles in the local ruling lineage were invited to Ouagadougou to press their claims. Only the dead chief's babissi went to Ouagadougou, even though all nobles subscribed to the traditional concept that "the nam does not belong to any one sub-lineage; it can be given to any nobleman." Unlike the others, these nobles did not shave their heads in mourning, thus indicating their candidacy for the nam. When they donned sheepskin cloaks and carried spears on their shoulders, they indicated that they were interested in the nam of the district.

Before a candidate for the district chieftainship left for Ouagadougou, he collected livestock, money, clothing, and grain from his friends to give as gifts or bribes to important officials in the capital. When he arrived there, he lived with friends and conducted his campaign from their home. He and the other candidates visited their provincial minister and his colleagues, the Mogho Naba, and other courtiers, giving presents ostensibly as a sign of friendship but actually with the ultimate aim of impressing these people with their generosity. These activities were often very costly; for if the Ouagadougou officials suspected that the candidates were wealthy, they made every effort to obtain as many presents as possible. It was not unusual for candidates for the district chieftainship to remain at the capital as long as "thirty-three" or "sixty-six" days before the officials were satisfied with their generosity and made preparations for the election.

The evening before the election, the Baloum Naba asked each candidate to provide a chicken and a sheep for the evening sacrifices to the namtibo.[38] After the morning ceremony on the following day, the Ouidi Naba reminded the sovereign that a new chief had to be chosen for Nobere district. The Mogho Naba summoned the Gounga Naba and asked him which candidate had the best character and was most capable of taking care of the district—a question which shows that the Mossi never placed primogeniture above the ability to rule.[39] The Gounga Naba had already consulted his friends about the matter, but he recounted both the good and the bad qualities of each candidate. At the same time, he hinted which one would make the best chief. He finally told the Mogho Naba that all of the candidates were worthy men, adding, "You can give the nam to any of them." The Mogho Naba then looked around to ascertain whether the other ministers had concurred in the Gounga Naba's implied choice before declaring, "I will give the nam to X, because when his [father, grandfather, or brother, used in the generic or classificatory sense] was alive, he was good to me. The ancestors would be angry if I did not give his [son, grandson, or brother] the nam." With these words the selection was made, and the ministers now prepared to install the successful candidate.

A man usually heard about his nomination through his "friends" (usually pages) long before the Baloum Naba had received instructions from the Ouidi Naba to summon him to the palace. Nevertheless, protocol demanded that he show proper humility and surprise at receiving the news, and that he be tardy in arriving at court. When he arrived, he was taken before the Ouidi Naba, who asked him three times, "Did your [father] say who should be his successor?" To this the nominee replied each time, "No, Naba! My [father] did not say who should replace him. You may appoint anyone you wish, even if he is a blind man or a leper." The Ouidi Naba then asked the candidate, "Which of the nakomce do the district people prefer?" The candidate's standard reply was, "That is the affair of the Mogho Naba. The people will accept anyone, even a blind man or a leper." This question was asked three times, and each time the candidate gave the same answer. The Ouidi Naba then declared, "The Mogho Naba has given you the nam of your [father]." Upon hearing these words, the Samande Kasma (head servant of the palace) came up to the new chief and removed his sheepskin mantle, while the samande-kamba took their heavy batons and chased away the other pretenders who, having heard about the election, had come to the palace. The samande-kamba then bore the new chief on their shoulders to the *tomboko* (a circle filled with sand in the courtyard). To the accompaniment of the royal airs played by musicians under the direction of the Bendere Naba, he took sand and poured it on his head as a sign of submission to the Mogho Naba. The ruler's wives and the courtiers surrounded the new chief, raised their hands over his head, and shouted their praises to the Mogho Naba. Then the new chief showed his respect for all the ministers and important men, in order of rank, by falling on his knees before them in the traditional Mossi salute. He then went to the Bendere Naba's shed, where he stood in the middle of the musicians and made a speech, the leitmotiv of which became his ruling title. The present chief of Nobere, whose name is Naba Boulga ("Well"), says that he made the following speech when he was nominated: "I am like a well; he who opens me will profit greatly." After the new chief had thus "taken a name," he came to the zongo to "drink the namtibo."

The drinking of the namtibo was the highlight of the election ceremony because it strengthened the link between the new chief and his ancestors and provided the ritual sanction for loyalty, obedience, and service to the Mogho Naba.[40] After the new chief had drunk the namtibo, he called upon the ancestors to kill him if he should ever betray the Mogho Naba or fail to render him homage and faithful service. This oath was the sign for the unsuccessful candidates to pledge their allegiance to the new chief. Then they hoisted him on their shoulders and proceeded to his host's house with loud acclaim.

The next morning, the new chief went to the palace to pay homage to the Mogho Naba and receive from him the traditional cowries, three kola nuts, and a small jar of millet water. In the days that followed, he celebrated his good fortune at the house of the important ministers and court officials. About a week later he returned to the palace, and the Baloum Naba's chief assistant invested him with the insignia of office: a white gown, a cushion, a pair of slippers, and, most important, a bonnet—the true symbol of chieftainship. Soon afterward, the new chief asked the Mogho Naba and his provincial minister for permission to return home. He was then provided with an escort to accompany him to his district.

The journey of a new chief to his district was marked by pomp and ceremony. The Nobere Naba stopped at such districts as Toudou and Twili, where he was entertained by the chiefs and presented with wives and other gifts. Some districts he would never be allowed to visit again, and others he had to bypass during his joyful journey. The reasons for these restrictions and prohibitions have long since been forgotten, but they were probably instituted to prevent conflicts among Kombemba and to prevent the new chief from coming into contact with the descendants of the Kouritadamba of former Mogho Nanamse.

As the new Nobere Naba neared his district, he was met by a welcoming committee of village chiefs, nobles, and commoners, who pledged allegiance to him and gave him wives, goods, clothing, money, grain, and livestock. He was then taken to the Soulougre Naba, a descendant of the aboriginal Ninisi, at whose hands he had to undergo another series of rites before he could set up his new compound and begin his rule. These ceremonies were rather simple in comparison with those at Ouagadougou, but they represented a ritual re-enactment of the Mossi conquest of the district, and reinforced the status relationship between the Mossi and the aboriginal population. At the end of seven days, the Kombere Naba gave the Soulougre Naba a black cow to be sacrificed at a pool called Yarega, a shrine of the ancient Ninisi on a tributary of the White Volta River. When this final rite was over, an enthusiastic crowd fetched the chief, and the young people of Soulougre village bore him aloft to his compound. A period of celebration now began during which all the heads of villages, lineages, and compounds paid homage and swore allegiance to their ruler. This ended when the chief summoned his escort from Ouagadougou and gave presents to those who wished to return there and wives and land to those who wished to settle in his district.

The Kombere Naba, as the person who had "eaten the nam" of the district, was infused with some of the power and authority of the Mogho Naba and had the right to use force to maintain this power and authority. He was respected, and people uncovered their heads and removed their slippers in his presence. Unlike the Mogho Naba, the Kombere Naba was permitted to eat with his peers. But whenever he drank the musicians made a roar-like sound with their instruments, and when he sneezed his attendants clapped. These rituals were rigidly adhered to because the Kombere Naba was readily accessible to the populace and might easily have lost their respect if he behaved in an undignified manner. He emphasized his social distance from them by never visiting the market place, and he did not go anywhere without a large entourage.

The Kombere Naba performed ceremonies and duties that were similar to but simpler than those of the Mogho Naba, and he was surrounded by officers bearing the same titles as those in the capital. But, as will be shown later, these officials had fewer and sometimes different duties than the courtiers at Ouagadougou. Some district chiefs had as many pages and wives as the Mogho Naba, but this was as much a result of their own desires as of their popularity with the local people. The death and funeral rites of a district chief were not as elaborate as those of a Mogho Naba. They included the circumambulation of the chief's compound by the principal heir and heiress, the symbolic reign of the Napoko, and the banishment of the Kourita.[41]

Every district chief, whether a Mogho Naba's vassal or a Dim's subordinate, was empowered to bestow the nam on his own subordinates. These might be other district chiefs, but most often they were village chiefs. The circumstances under which a Kombere Naba received the authority to grant the nam to another Kombere Naba were usually complex and sprang from rebellions and dynastic changes. Once granted, this authority was seldom revoked, but the district chief had to report to his immediate superior, a Mogho Naba or Dim, whenever he wished to confer the nam upon another district chief.

In some cases the Mogho Naba invested a district chief himself, and afterward placed him under the control of a neighboring district chief. For example, the chiefs of two districts, Vooko and Nobila, were always installed by the Mogho Naba of Ouagadougou, but were supervised by the Nobere district chief. This practice dates back to the civil war involving Mogho Naba Sagha I (ca. 1787–1803), in which chiefs of Vooko and Nobere sided with the loser. The Mogho Naba executed the local rebels and placed one of his sons in Nobere. He then divided Vooko into two districts, placing a younger son in the one he called Nobila (little Nobere) and subjecting him to the control of his brother at Nobere. The other district, still called Vooko but now half its former size, was given to a descendant of its deposed ruler. The relationship between these two rulers and the Nobere Naba was that of vassals and lord. They did not stand up in the presence of the Nobere Naba, but knelt or sat on the ground and uncovered their heads in respect to him. The Nobere Naba traditionally appointed the village chiefs in the Vooko and Nobila districts; however, he sometimes granted that right to the two district chiefs. Furthermore, the traditional provincial administrator could not transmit any orders to those two district chiefs without first notifying the Nobere Naba. In their everyday affairs the two chiefs were autonomous, but the Nobere Naba could challenge and countermand all their actions. Actually, he did seem to exercise greater control over Vooko than over Nobila. One may even say that the relationship between the Nobere district chief and the Vooko chief was like that between the Mogho Naba and his district chiefs, and that the relationship between the Nobere Naba and the Nobila Naba was comparable to the one between the Mogho Naba and the Dimdamba. We have seen that the Dimdamba claimed equality with the Mogho Naba because of their alleged descent from a putative common ancestor. The Nobere Naba was actually more closely related to the Nobila Naba than to the Vooko Naba, and his behavior toward them reflected this fact. In both cases, the relationships involved were determined by the concept of joint possession of the nam by the ruling family.

A district chief was not required to notify his superior when he wished to confer the nam upon a village chief. In this choice he was completely autonomous and subject only to tradition. The fact is that on the district and village levels, traditions were more frequently modified in the face of practical political and socio-economic considerations. This occurred primarily because the district chief had closer relations with persons who possessed goods and services or who controlled them directly than did the chiefs on higher levels. Secondly, he was often under great temptation to allow presents or bribes to affect his choice of subordinate chiefs.

When a Tenga Naba died, the district chief permitted control of the village to revert to its Tengsoba. If there was none, the village was "given" to the eldest man among the aboriginal Ninisi lineages or to the eldest member of the ruling lineage segment. However, none of these persons was considered anything but a trustee of the village, and even when the trustee was a potential candidate for the nam, the Mossi did not feel that this man had any advantage over his competitors. Whoever held control of the village was held responsible for its affairs by the district administrator until the new chief was elected.

Competition for chieftainship on this level was very keen because of the greater number of lineage members eligible for the nam and the shallow genealogical depth. Every man who had the ability or desire to rule was encouraged to seek the post. Many candidates tried to impress the district chief and his advisers with their good qualities; most tried to bribe them. Since the candidates could not openly seek the post during the day, they visited the important officials of the district at night, taking money and cattle as presents. Some candidates even promised wives. The intrigues on this level, such as seeking the friendship of pages to find out about the activities of rivals, paralleled those at Ouagadougou. The more gifts a candidate gave the district chief, the more his rivals tried to surpass him. Consequently, the district chief often kept the office vacant for months or even as long as two or three years in order to enjoy these lucrative gifts. Neither the caretakers of the village, who complained about the administrative problems of a village without a chief, nor the Tengsobadamba, who declared that without the permission of a chief they could not make sacrifices to help the people avoid illness, drought, and sterility, could force the Kombere Naba to name a new village chief. Only when the candidates had exhausted most of their wealth was the process to elect the chief set in motion.

The district chief had a better knowledge of the character of candidates for the village chieftainship than the Dimdamba or Mogho Nanamse had about the men whom they selected. The district chiefs were better able than other Mossi rulers to obey the dictum that only those men capable of "keeping" the country should rule. Nevertheless, before making a choice, the Kombere Naba called in the local minister responsible for the village in question and discussed with him the character and capabilities of the various candidates.[42] As on higher levels, the eldest son of the former chief was usually favored, especially if he had sent a large *fado* (death tax) to the district chief and had been generous to him during the interregnum. But it was also possible that one of the dead chief's younger sons or one of his brothers or uncles might be chosen. In some cases, the district chiefs chose men from related sub-lineages that had not held the nam for generations. One district chief chose a man who had lived away from the village for thirty years. He had gone to live in his mother's brother's village as a young man and did not return until he was named chief. Admittedly, such cases were exceptional, but they kept alive in the minds of the local people the concept of the Mossi lineage's corporate possession of the nam.

On the day chosen for the election of a village chief, all the candidates with their unshaved heads and sheepskin mantles reported to the village administrator's house along with all the other men of their lineage. They gave him presents, and he led them to the compound of the district chief.

The entire assembly saluted the district chief, and the official declared the reason for his visit. Then the district chief sent a page for a chief's bonnet, which he gave to a samande. This youth took the bonnet, came up to the kneeling candidates, and jokingly attempted to place it on the head of each one in turn while asking, "Whom did the *keema* ["dead person"; in this case, the dead chief] say should be chief?" When no one answered he gave up the game, ran to the successful candidate, and placed the bonnet on his head. As soon as this happened, all the unsuccessful candidates and men of the lineage ran away, followed by other samande-kamba, who waved big clubs and feigned violence if they should catch them. The men of the lineage soon returned while the new chief did homage and pledged allegiance to the Kombere Naba by prostrating himself on the ground and by putting sand from the tomboko on his head. By this act the Tenga Naba became the district chief's subordinate and the lowest elected official in a ruling hierarchy that extended from the Mogho Naba down to the least village chief.

Once the oath-taking ceremony was over, the new chief's followers saluted the district chief, lifted their new leader onto their shoulders, and bore him triumphantly back to his village, shouting for joy. Here, in imitation of his superiors, the new chief made a speech in which he ridiculed his competitors, reviewed his background, and made known his chiefly intentions. Here, too, the people seized upon some significant point in his speech as an indication of the name "he had named." However, this name was seldom used, since people referred to him as the Naba of such-and-such village, e.g., Barkago Naba, and addressed him simply as "Naba." The village Tengsoba then performed propitiatory sacrifices to the Ninisi ancestors and to the local earth deity in the chief's name, and "gave him back the village" of which he had been the temporary caretaker. Only after these rites had been performed could the chief assume command of the village without incurring supernatural sanctions of the ancient Ninisi.

The typical village chief had no court. His compound was only slightly larger than that of a village family. He had no officials, but some of his companions who assumed special duties similar to those of the Ouidi Naba and the Tansoba were sometimes jokingly referred to by these honorific titles. The village chief had neither soghondamba nor samande-kamba, and he permitted his wives to serve refreshments to his visitors. In general, everything was on a smaller scale than on the district level, including all ceremonies even to the burial of the village chief.

IV

ADMINISTRATION

THE MOSSI always looked to their rulers, especially to the Mogho Nanamse, the Dimdamba, and the Kombemba, to determine administrative policies and to pronounce on all relevant issues. All foreigners who requested information were told, "You must talk to the chief."[1] The Mossi believed that men cannot live without chiefs, and insisted that even animals have chiefs. Mossi rulers were therefore expected to ensure internal tranquillity in times of peace and to protect their subjects and territories in times of war. The expectation that they would also provide impartial judgment is best expressed by a dictum of the Ouagadougou people: "The truth is at Ouagadougou." Finally, Mossi chiefs were held responsible for inducing the ancestors to bring health and prosperity to their subjects. To this end, they supervised and participated in rituals to their ancestors and encouraged the people in every territory, district, village, and compound to do likewise. In return, the people paid homage and allegiance to their chiefs and provided them with the goods and services they needed to support the administrative process.

The nature of the administrative relationship between the Mogho Naba of Ouagadougou, the rulers of Yatenga, Fada-N'Gourma, and Tenkodogo, and the autonomous Dimdamba was not clear to the early visitors to Mossi country, and remains a matter of controversy. Two conflicting principles were always at work: seniority with respect to the nam and claims of close descent from Ouedraogo and Oubri on the one hand, and relative political strength or military power on the other. The stronger a ruler, the less he deferred to his lineal seniors. He might even claim a supremacy over them that came close to a claim of seniority. When Barth visited the Sudan in 1853, he was told that the Mossi country was "split into a number of small principalities, almost totally independent of each other, and paying only slight homage to the principality of Woghododogo." Barth reports, however, that the Dim of Boussouma was "probably the most powerful of the Mossi chiefs at the . . . time, especially with regard to cavalry." Similarly,

Binger reports that the Mossi were divided into "a number of confederacies, more or less independent of each other, whose chiefs were vassals of Naba Sanum, the Mogho Naba of Ouagadougou." He found, nevertheless, that although the Mogho Naba of Ouagadougou claimed suzerainty over the Yatenga, he could not grant travelers permission to enter that territory.[2]

Crozat, who visited the Mossi in 1890, just two years after Binger, was told repeatedly that the Mogho Naba of Ouagadougou had the right to control the destinies of all chiefs who claimed descent from Ouedraogo and Oubri. But he, too, found that the principalities were self-governing and mutually independent, and were united only by the weak bond that attached them all to Ouagadougou. Noting the claims of the people he encountered that Ouagadougou was still supreme, Crozat suggests that "time and circumstances have weakened this sovereignty. The ruler of Ouagadougou is regarded by the other chiefs merely as their senior and the head of their family. They seldom obey him, yet they recognize that in certain cases he has the right to give them orders." Like many Frenchmen who came after him, Crozat concludes, "One will be struck, as I have been, by this political organization in which the waning of the central authority has led to a true feudal system closely reminiscent of a certain period in our own history."[3]

Delafosse tells us that "the authority of the emperor [of Ouagadougou] does not seem to have been ignored within his borders except in very rare instances. The vassal kings, who were brothers, sons, or nephews of the emperor, usually obeyed him. In any case, the emperor did not interfere with the administration [of their territories], and required nothing from them except the payment of taxes and the raising of contingents for any expeditions he might have to organize against outside enemies (the emperors of Mali, Gao, or Segou; Moroccan pashas; etc.). In return, the emperor granted his support to those of his vassals who were unable to command the obedience of their subjects or tributaries."[4]

It appears, then, that although the independent rulers and autonomous princes sometimes recognized the supremacy (if not the seniority) of the Mogho Naba of Ouagadougou, they were relatively free to rule as they wished. As possessors of the nam, they claimed and exercised the right to administer the peoples of their realms. It appears, furthermore, that the rulers of Ouagadougou seldom challenged the independence of their confreres in Yatenga, although the latter often disturbed them. For example, when Yatenga Naba Kango (ca. 1754–89) sacked and burned the Ouagadougou district of Yako for sheltering refugees from a civil war, the Mogho Naba did not come to the aid of the Yako Naba. Nor did he take offense when this chief, in order to regain his seat, was compelled to switch his allegiance to the Yatenga. The situation lasted throughout Kango's reign, "but as soon as he died, the Yako chiefs ceased to pay allegiance to his successors and paid homage, as before, to the court of Ouagadougou."[5] About fifty years later, Yako district was again captured by a Yatenga ruler, Naba Tougouri (ca. 1806–22), who deposed the reigning chief and installed his own. The deposed chief fled to his sovereign at Ouagadougou for aid and safety. He did receive sanctuary and eventually reconquered his principality, but there is no evidence that the Mogho Naba gave him any active support. Similarly, when another Yatenga ruler, Naba Totebaldbo (ca. 1834–50), once more conquered Yako as well as Riziam, another dependency of Ouagadougou, the Mogho Naba took no action. It was only after Totebaldbo's death that Riziam seceded from Yatenga and returned its allegiance to Ouagadougou. Yako did not submit to Ouagadougou's rule until some time later, when it revolted against Totebaldbo's son.[6] Similarly, both Mogho Naba Sanum and Mogho Naba Wobogo had difficulty in controlling a civil war between Yatenga and Yako which they felt would cause European travelers to think ill of the Mossi. During Crozat's visit to Ouagadougou, Mogho Naba Wobogo asked the combatants to cease fighting, but his efforts failed because "Yako would have liked to obey, but Yatenga refused."[7]

The Ouagadougou rulers experienced less difficulty with the weaker Tenkodogo kingdom, which seldom attacked their vassals or territories. Instead, the rulers of Tenkodogo often sought the aid of the Mogho Naba of Ouagadougou against their enemies or rebellious subjects. For example, when the Busansi subjects of the Tenkodogo Naba rebelled against him in the fifteenth century, Mogho Naba Dawoema of Ouagadougou went to his aid and defeated them.[8] However, when Korongo, the Tenkodogo Naba, asked Mogho Naba Wobogo to help him defeat a contestant for the nam in 1894, the Ouagadougou ruler refused and said he would acknowledge the victor.[9] In this case, personal considerations seem to have dictated the Mogho Naba's reply.

The rulers of Ouagadougou appear to have taken greater interest in the affairs of the Dimdamba. Here again, however, intervention was conditioned by personal considerations, and especially by relative strength. Failure to be prudent in this respect often resulted in disaster. Mogho Naba Doulougou's insistence on punishing Naba Piga (1806–23), a ruler of the Boussouma principality, resulted in his own death. One of Piga's subjects had fled to Ouagadougou to evade punishment, and the Mogho Naba had returned him with the injunction that he should be imprisoned but not killed. Nevertheless, Piga had the prisoner executed. Moreover, he sent a disrespectful message to the Mogho Naba asking that a horse which a Fulani had stolen from him and presented to the ruler be returned. Doulougou sent an army to chastise Piga, who quickly fled and later appealed to the Mogho Naba for pardon. No sooner had this pardon been granted than Piga again offended the Mogho Naba by granting refuge to his wayward son, who had been expelled from Ouagadougou. The Mogho Naba subsequently forgave his son, but he decided to punish the recalcitrant Piga once and for all. Piga fled at the approach of the royal army, but Doulougou, who had accompanied his troops, was wounded by an enemy arrow and died shortly after his return to Ouagadougou.[10]

A later Mogho Naba, Sanum (ca. 1861), fought, defeated, and executed Naba Zande of Boulsa for taxing the Boulsa people so heavily that they rebelled. After Zande was succeeded by his brother Yemde (ca. 1863–72), the Mogho Naba continued to intervene in Boulsa's affairs and eventually had Yemde executed. Yemde's undoing was the result of his inability or unwillingness to implement the Mogho Naba's desire—which was contrary to Mossi custom—to elect a ten-year-old boy to the chieftainship of Koupela district. The Koupela chief's brother ignored his young nephew and seized the nam; Yemde sent an army to depose him, but his men were routed. Suspecting treachery on Yemde's part, Mogho Naba Sanum sent an army to defeat and depose him and to place his father's brother in command of Boulsa. Yemde defeated the Mogho Naba's army. His victory was short-lived, however, because the Mogho Naba sent a larger army and routed his forces. Yemde fled to the territory of the Boussouma Dim and requested asylum. The Boussouma ruler, Ligidi, did not wish to incur the wrath of the Mogho Naba and dispatched Yemde to Ouagadougou. Yemde apparently convinced the Mogho Naba of his loyalty, but he was executed because he had inadvertently violated the rule that no descendant of a Kourita might see a Mogho Naba and live.[11]

Ligidi, in turn, found himself in conflict with the Mogho Naba. After surrendering Yemde to his sovereign, he had proceeded to Boulsa and seized some of the prisoner's property. At first the Mogho Naba paid no attention, but when he had made peace with Yemde's son, Kiba, he ordered Ligidi to return the property. Ligidi refused to do so and consequently became involved in a series of wars against Kiba and the Mogho Naba. Ligidi died of natural causes before peace was restored, leaving a legacy of hostility between Ouagadougou and Boussouma. Either in complicity with the ruling Mogho Naba (Wobogo) or in an attempt to gain his favor, the electors named Ligidi's brother, Kom, to the nam and ignored his son and rightful heir, Venewende. This unfortunate young man had no one to turn to, and fled to Wobogo for safety. Wishing to maintain good relations with Kom, the Mogho Naba forced Venewende to return to Boussouma, but with the injunction that he should not be killed. Nevertheless, the Boussouma ruler had the young prince executed. The angry Mogho Naba threatened reprisal and declared that "if the Boussouma chief was not careful, it would be too bad for all his people, because they would fare as badly as their chief."[12] He did not have an opportunity to carry out his threats, however, because the French arrived soon afterwards.

Whereas some Mogho Nanamse took an active interest in the affairs of their Dimdamba or even tried to control them, others hesitated to interfere with disobedient or recalcitrant subordinates, especially when they fought and quarreled among themselves. Mogho Naba Oubya did not interfere when a Boussouma ruler, Pougoula (1745–67), bragging that no one in the nation was strong enough to depose him, arrogantly annexed the Ouagadougou province of Pisila and chased its ruler into Yatenga. Pougoula then gave the chieftainship to the fugitive's son, on condition that he should henceforth recognize his sovereignty.[13] On another occasion, a recalcitrant Boussouma Dim called Zabo (ca. 1767–84) defeated and punished the people of the Mane principality for rejecting the ruler he had chosen for them. They insisted that the Mogho Naba of Ouagadougou had given Zabo the right to express his preference for a certain ruler, but not the right of choice itself. They appealed to Mogho Naba Waraga for help, but he ignored them. It may well be that Waraga was too involved in a war with the recalcitrant Riziam Naba to interfere, but there is no evidence that he ever censured Zabo. Again, Mogho Naba Sanum apparently took no part when Zende (ca. 1862–76), the ruler of Tema principality, and Totoabo, the ruler of Yako, joined forces against the ruler of La in a dispute over an abducted wife.[14] Perhaps, like other Mossi rulers, he did not care to deal with men who fought over women.

The relationship between the Mogho Naba and the Dimdamba, then, apparently varied in accordance with the persons involved and their relative strength. Sometimes they quarreled and fought; sometimes the Mogho Naba remained aloof from the Dimdamba's affairs; and sometimes the Dimdamba obeyed their sovereign and came to his aid. The one aspect of this relationship that seems to stand out, especially when the Dimdamba had no serious grievance, is their reluctance to fight against the Mogho Naba. Even Piga, the most belligerent in a long line of quarrelsome Boussouma rulers, always fled when Mogho Naba Doulougou attacked him, because "he did not wish to oppose his sovereign."[15] As we have seen, Yemde did fight against Mogho Naba Sanum, but he did so mainly because he thought Sanum had attacked him unjustly. For such acts of war, the Dimdamba involved usually lost their lives, and in at least one such case a Dim was turned over to the Mogho Naba by another Dim. We have seen that Dimdamba occasionally came to the aid of the Mogho Naba against another Dim.

A question of some importance is whether this relationship between the Mogho Naba of Ouagadougou and the rulers of independent kingdoms and autonomous principalities was characteristic of Mossi society or a rather late development. Was warfare the natural concomitant of a system in which the normally powerful Ouagadougou ruler was sometimes too weak to command allegiance from his peers and subordinates? Did the Mogho Naba resort to warfare as the only possible means of exercising his authority when his commands were challenged or ignored? Delafosse states, "Sometimes . . . , especially in very recent times, discord arose between the emperor [of Ouagadougou] and some of his vassal kings: thus Naba Sanum had to fight against the desire for independence of the kings of Boussouma and Boulsa."[16] Delafosse seems to suggest that the Mossi people were undergoing a period of stress when the Europeans arrived, and were faced with significant new administrative problems.

Here Binger appears to support Delafosse's view:

> Ever since he acceded to the throne, [Mogho Naba Sanum] has been compelled to govern the Mossi with unmitigated despotism. His fear of losing power led him to take such severe measures that he was forced to relax them. As soon as his major vassals saw this, they took these concessions as signs of fear and began to conspire secretly against him. Today, the chiefs of Mani, Boussouma, Yako, and Koupela represent forces with which Naba Sanum will have to reckon. . . . Before long, the Mossi empire will break up; the country will organize into confederacies like those of Beledougou and Yatenga.[17]

It is not completely clear, however, whether Binger really understood the intricacies of the Mossi political organization. He lists as "vassals" of the Mogho Naba such territories as Mane, Kaya, Koupela, Bonsa, Boussouma, Djitenga, Boulsa, Dakay, and Doulougou, as though they were all related to Ouagadougou in the same way. In reality, some were autonomous and some were directly dependent on the Ouagadougou ruler. It is possible that at the time of Binger's visit, the relations between the Mogho Naba and his subordinates were so fluid that the outsider had difficulty in understanding them. If this is the case, then the situation in Mossi country had indeed changed when the Europeans came in.

Crozat, who says the Mossi governmental structure was feudal in nature, offers what is probably the best analysis of power relations among the important Mossi chiefs. In commenting upon the Mogho Naba's inability to stop the war between Yako and Yatenga he asks, "How could it be otherwise? With what sanctions could this king without an army back up his orders if he ventured to give any? . . . In short, when the Ouagadougou ruler speaks, he is sometimes obeyed. If he is, all is well; if he is not, all is still well. Everything remains as before."[18] Crozat was mistaken if he believed that the Mogho Naba did not have a fighting force. What he did not have was a standing army to exercise his power whenever he wished. When he was able to summon an army, he was effective; when he was not, he had little power over any territory but his own. Crozat, like Binger, gives a strange picture of the political relationship between the Mogho Naba and the other rulers. He tells us that in the Mossi political hierarchy, "after the ruler of Ouagadougou comes the ruler of Boussouma, then the Yatenga ruler, and then the ruler of Yako."[19] Yatenga was traditionally independent of Ouagadougou, whereas Boussouma and Yako were simply autonomous principalities dependent on the Mogho Naba. It is possible that Crozat mistook the relative power of these various political entities for a hierarchical relationship. It is also possible that at the time of his visit, the Dimdamba felt sufficiently powerful to ignore the traditional hierarchy as far as their political relationship with other rulers was concerned, and were simply acknowledging relative gradations of power.

Clearly, the sovereignty of the Mogho Naba of Ouagadougou over the independent kingdoms and autonomous principalities depended chiefly on military might. The stronger a Mogho Naba was, the more actively he tried to control the internal administration of the autonomous principalities and to exercise police powers over them or on their behalf. However, most Mogho Nanamse were content to claim superiority or control over the independent kingdoms and refrained from meddling in their affairs.

Within the Mogho Naba's own kingdom, however, the situation was different. Here, like other important Mossi rulers, he directed the administrative apparatus. For administrative purposes, the kingdom of Ouagadougou was divided into five large provinces (*weto*; sing. *weogho*; or *solem,* from *so,* "command"). Together they included some three hundred districts, in which there were over four thousand villages inhabited by some 862,000 persons.[20] (Not included here were districts and villages directly administered by the Mogho Naba.) The provinces were not compact physical entities, because their component units were scattered throughout the country. To be sure, some of the districts within a province were close together or even contiguous, but many others stood alongside districts belonging to other provinces. Provinces also differed with respect to the number of districts they included and the nature and size of these districts. Some provinces were larger than others; some were wealthier; and some were more difficult to administer.

Each province was administered by a governor, who also functioned as an important minister at the court of Ouagadougou. In the order of their importance, these governors were the Ouidi Naba, the Larhalle Naba, the Gounga Naba, the Baloum Naba, and the Kamsaogho Naba. Smaller administrative units (both districts and villages) were under the direct control of the Mogho Naba himself, or under the supervision of his relatives or lesser officials. None of the governors were nobles or descendants of Ouedraogo and Oubri, but their positions were hereditary. According to one tradition, the first provincial administrators were personal slaves of the early Mossi rulers who were given the task of supervising the activities of district chiefs of noble status. Another, more romantic tradition is that the man who became the first governor or Gounga Naba was a companion of Mogho Naba Oubri during the conquest of Ouagadougou. Later, the Gounga Naba presented one of his friends to Oubri with the request that the man take precedence over him, be made chief governor, and be given the title of Ouidi Naba. Oubri allegedly acceded to this request, and later granted another request of the Gounga Naba that a friend of the Ouidi Naba be named Larhalle Naba and be made the second governor. The Gounga Naba told the Mogho Naba that he preferred to see his friends happy and that he was content to be third minister. This tradition does not state when or how the Baloum Naba and the Kamsaogho Naba were named governors.[21]

With the exception of the Kamsaogho Naba, who was a eunuch and had no heirs, the provincial governors headed administrative lineages. These lineages provided administrators not only for Ouagadougou but also for the principalities and districts. Cheron states that the Ouidi Naba of Boulsa was "a descendant of the Ouidi Naba of Ouagadougou, a great dignitary who rules a province and sits among the electors of the Mogho Naba."[22] Many administrative lineages on the district level were descended from officials sent down by the Mogho Naba with a new district chief in lieu of one deposed. When a chief was deposed, his administrators, like his relatives, lost their importance and their ties to Ouagadougou.

The Ouidi Naba, called *Moss' ba* ("father of the Mossi") and *Sida soba* ("master of the truth"), was the principal administrator and the prime minister. His titles undoubtedly sprang from his important role in the election of the Mogho Naba and from his position as caretaker of the kingdom during the interregnum.²³ The latter task was especially suited to a prime minister, since the Mossi regarded the interregnum as the most difficult period in their political life. The Ouidi Naba's administrative tasks were considered so important that he never went to war and was theoretically immune from punishment or execution by the Mogho Naba. This immunity was necessary, because the Mogho Naba had the right to execute anyone who brought him unwelcome news, and often did so. Since the Ouidi Naba announced good news as well as bad, it would have been folly to subject him to this rule. Some reports in the French colonial archives state that the Mogho Naba was expected to follow the Ouidi Naba's advice at all times, and could not veto any of his actions. These reports add, moreover, that if a Ouidi Naba considered a Mogho Naba dangerous for the welfare of the country, he could rightfully compel the ruler to kill himself. According to Lambert, one Ouidi Naba known as Baba forced Mogho Naba Karfo (ca. 1800) to commit suicide. It appears that aside from waging a long and unpopular war against Naba Djighima of Lalle, this Mogho Naba had seized the riches of his wealthy subjects for distribution among the poor. Moreover, he allegedly dispensed justice without making much distinction between nobles and commoners, which so displeased the nobles that they encouraged the Ouidi Naba to put Karfo to death. Baba sent the sovereign a poisoned arrow and a message consisting of a single word: *ki* (die). Karfo allegedly committed suicide that very night.²⁴

Thus, it appears that under certain conditions the prime minister could impeach his "all-powerful" sovereign. We cannot assume, however, that all prime ministers were sufficiently powerful to control the Mogho Naba. Many Mogho Nanamse limited their Ouidi Naba to merely giving advice on affairs of state and insisted that he concern himself solely with his own province.

The provinces administered by the five ministers were made up of smaller entities or districts. The districts in the provinces of the Ouidi Naba, the Larhalle Naba, and the Gounga Naba were ruled by the sons and other descendants of ancient Mogho Nanamse. The province controlled by the Kamsaogho Naba was more important. His districts were the wealthiest and among the most populous in the nation, and they brought the largest revenues to the Mogho Naba. The reason for this, of course, was that the Kamsaogho Naba was a eunuch and had no heirs; when he died, all his riches reverted to the Mogho Naba. The province controlled by the Baloum Naba was the most difficult to administer. Its districts were ruled by the sons of recent Mogho Nanamse who felt that as holders of the nam they were free to appropriate the goods of the population. The Baloum

Naba was responsible for checking these depredations, but he had little coercive force since these nobles were infinitely superior to him in rank.

The Mogho Naba held his five ministers responsible for the administration of the districts within their provinces. Therefore they had to function as liaison officers between him and the district chiefs. Every morning, in order of precedence, the ministers reported the news they had received from their provinces since the previous day. At this time, the Mogho Naba also gave them messages for their districts. Later in the day, the ministers presented to the ruler those persons who had come from their provinces to the capital with special grievances, requests, or gifts. Delicate affairs of state were left for the evening, when they were discussed by the Mogho Naba, his minister or ministers, and other important persons.

From all reports, these administrative affairs kept both the ministers and the Mogho Naba quite busy. Binger, who could barely conceal his displeasure with Mogho Naba Sanum, gives this critical but otherwise highly illuminating view of the Mossi ruler's administrative activities:

> The duties of Naba Sanum are not too important. They consist of receiving visits throughout the day. In the morning, at about six o'clock, the drums announce that the ruler has arisen. When he has washed and refreshed himself with a meal, his captives and his wives go to his chamber to salute him. Then comes the turn of strangers, people of the neighborhood, petitioners, and others. They squat before the reception area until the ruler deigns to appear. When a large number of people have gathered, one of the [pages] goes to notify the ruler, who then arrives, sits on his cushion, and casts an amiable glance on the gathering while all present snap their fingers. As soon as Naba Sanum is seated, the petitioners and visitors hurry toward the monarch, throw themselves face down on the earth, and cover their heads with sand. Then each of them gets up and presents a gift of greater or lesser importance, in cowries or foodstuffs, according to what he wishes to ask. Then the [pages] come and say to the ruler, "A certain man has brought a sack of cowries, or a goat, or an ox. He desires to speak to you." The ruler thanks all of them with a *nif kende* (thanks) and retires into his chamber. It is well known that not one out of fifty petitioners was given the opportunity to have his wishes heard. Those who were heard had first spoken to an attendant who, after being paid in advance, had put off their case indefinitely by stating that it would be dealt with next. . . . Since the monarch's days are so well filled, one easily understands why he finds it difficult to deal effectively with the internal and external affairs of his kingdom; in any case, Mossi country is in a period of decadence that will only be aggravated with time.[25]

The activities Binger considered frivolous were, on the contrary, important for the proper administration of the kingdom. The Mogho Naba had to receive petitions from the districts and transmit administrative orders to his people. We shall see that these orders ran the gamut from demands for soldiers, tribute, and labor, to requests for sacrifices to the ancestors or to local deities for the welfare of the country.

The provincial governors seldom visited the districts under their control more than once or twice a year. They transmitted official orders to the districts through retainers. Some ministers such as the Gounga Naba kept the sons and servants of district chiefs in the capital to be used as messengers. The district chiefs, in turn, used their sons or servants to transmit messages to their provincial governors or through them to the Mogho Naba. The use of intermediaries in the administration served another purpose: it prevented face-to-face contact, with all its potential for personal animosities, from impairing relations between those whose status depended on their political office and those whose status was derived from membership in the royal lineage.

Relations between the provincial ministers and the district chiefs were often charged with hostility and suspicion. The district chiefs regarded the provincial ministers as representatives of the Mogho Naba, and thus as persons to be obeyed. Simultaneously, however, they resented this control by social inferiors. They felt that since they were the descendants of Ouedraogo and Oubri, they should receive orders only from the Mogho Naba himself. Thus, while the district chiefs accepted orders from their provincial governors, they never permitted them to forget their social status or to interfere with the internal affairs of the districts. They felt that this was the prerogative of the royal lineage. Most provincial ministers accepted these restrictions on their activities, but nevertheless saw to it that the district chiefs surrendered the goods collected for the Mogho Naba and governed their people well. Sometime in the 1920's, a provincial administrator went to a district and insulted its chief for failing to deliver the quota of millet set by the French colonial government. The accusation of laziness and embezzlement so infuriated the district chief that he asked the provincial minister whether he had taken leave of his senses and forgotten to whom he was speaking. The person who reported this incident said that if the district chief had not been restrained, he would have killed the administrator on the spot.

Both provincial administrators and district chiefs could impose indirect sanctions on each other if the bounds of propriety were overstepped in either direction. A district chief harried by his minister could not complain directly to the Mogho Naba. But he could, and often did, show his dissatisfaction by lodging with another provincial minister when he went to the capital. He would then ask the official to accompany him when he went to render homage to the monarch. This attracted the attention of the Mogho Naba, who investigated the grievance of the district chief. If the provincial minister were found to be in serious error, he might be deposed and executed. The Ouidi Naba was theoretically exempt from such punishment, but it is doubtful that a strong monarch would have allowed even this official to cause trouble.

A provincial governor dissatisfied with a district chief under his charge could, under certain conditions, have him deposed and put to death. He achieved this by complaining to the monarch that the chief was either withholding tribute or misgoverning his people. In most cases, however, the minister could curb the district chief by hinting that his son would not receive a recommendation as successor to the nam of the district. This was usually enough to win the cooperation of the most recalcitrant chief, if only because his future status as the honored ancestor of a ruling local line would be jeopardized if he rebelled. These sanctions were thus sufficient to ensure satisfactory relations between the provincial ministers and their district chiefs, at least on the surface. This was to the advantage of both groups, since in the final analysis the failure of either to administer or rule well might result in the death penalty.

Many districts and villages in Ouagadougou were administered not by the provincial ministers but by officials directly responsible to the Mogho Naba. The districts in question were often ruled by close relatives of the Mogho Naba or by persons who had gained his good graces. The villages were often inhabited by slaves and governed by headmen who were themselves slaves. Like the other territories of the Mogho Naba, these districts and villages were not physically contiguous. The districts were mixed in with districts administered by the provincial ministers, and the villages stood within the territorial boundaries of district chiefs. Whenever the Mogho Naba wanted to communicate with a chief of such a village or district, he sent one of his retainers. The chiefs, in turn, used their own people to send messages and goods to Ouagadougou. The general administration of these districts and villages differed little from that of the territories administered by the provincial ministers. The main difference was that the Mogho Naba took a greater interest in their everyday affairs. This called for greater efficiency on the part of local officials; for they, like the other chiefs, faced the penalty of deposition and death for maladministration.

Of all Mossi officials, the district chiefs had the most difficult administrative task. They were in direct contact with the people, and thus ran a greater risk of being charged with misgovernment. Countless district chiefs were deposed and executed because they had allegedly disobeyed or rebelled against the Mogho Naba. I say "allegedly" because it was never quite clear whether the district chief was at fault or whether the Mogho Naba wanted to replace him for dynastic reasons. For example, Tanga, a district chief, was accused by Mogho Naba Sanum (1850–90) of withholding tribute and of maladministration. The Ouidi Naba who administered Tanga's district advised him to prove his innocence by making a sacrifice on Naba Oubri's tomb, and then go to Ouagadougou and ask the Mogho Naba's forgiveness. Tanga agreed to do so. But it appears that the Mogho Naba, who wished to place his own father's brother in Tanga's place, did not want a reconciliation. He waged war on Tanga, and seized his relatives, retainers, and cattle. Tanga tried to regain his losses by appealing to his provincial minister, but the minister told him that the Mogho Naba had distributed the livestock and had sold the people to Hausa traders. Moreover, he informed Tanga that he could not help him because the Mogho Naba could do as he pleased. Tanga thereupon decided to take matters into his own hands. He successfully attacked the Mogho Naba's villages, and was still a rebel when the French arrived shortly afterward.[26]

Tanga's action was unusual, for district chiefs seldom risked rebelling against the Mogho Naba when accused of maladministration. In 1895, for example, Koabga, chief of Doulougou district in the province of the Gounga Naba, took poison rather than wage war when Mogho Naba Wobogo accused him of misgovernment. Usually, a district chief who disobeyed an order of the Mogho Naba was summoned to the capital to answer the charge of lese majesty. If he was found guilty, the ruler knocked the bonnet off his head, thus deposing him, and had him strangled. The Mossi seldom spilled royal blood. A district chief who refused to go to Ouagadougou could either kill himself (traditionally by taking arsenic) or resort to civil war.[27] If he chose suicide, he was given an honorable burial as though he had died naturally. If the Mogho Naba sent down an army, however, the offending chief was invariably killed. His compound was burned, his slaves and cattle were seized, and his allies and immediate relatives were compelled to flee. The strength of this tradition is borne out by Tanga's case. He had successfully resisted the attempts of two Mogho Nanamse to bring him to heel, and was still at large when the French conquered the country. But Ouidi Naba Koabga, who had deserted his sovereign and selected Kouka Koutou as Mogho Naba under French orders, had not forgiven Tanga. When the French asked him what additional steps they should take to pacify the country, he asked them to capture Tanga. The unfortunate district chief was captured, placed on an unsaddled colt, and taken to Ouagadougou, where he was ignominiously executed.[28]

The district chief was relatively secure in the control of his territory as long as he maintained amicable relations with his immediate superiors and administered his district to their satisfaction. A less important but more constant source of concern was his relationship with neighboring chiefs. Many people who can remember the pre-conquest period say it was unsafe for a man to trespass into another district unless he was on an official mission from his chief to another chief. It appears that most of the fighting occurred over strayed cattle and stolen women, with constant raids and counter-raids. The cattle were eaten, and the women kept as wives. Captured men were sometimes sold as slaves, but more often were held for ransom. They were not kept as slaves, since the Mossi were forbidden to enslave other Mossi. Needless to say, this fighting was frowned upon by the Mogho Naba. Since all district chiefs believed in their common descent from Ouedraogo and Oubri and paid allegiance to the Mogho Naba, any fighting among them was not only a sin against the ancestors but also an act of disloyalty to the Mogho Naba. When (as was usually the case) this fighting was of short duration and few people were killed, the Mogho Naba took no official notice of it. But when it became serious, he sent the provincial administrator to stop the fighting and to summon the dissident elements to the capital for trial. The speed and severity with which the Mogho Naba dealt with quarrels within his own realm usually depended upon his strength. At some periods in Mossi history there was little internal disorder, because the rulers were strong; at other periods, under weak rulers, disorder practically amounted to internal chaos. During such periods, the Mossi were kept together only by the bonds of kinship and religion which united them against outsiders.

The district chief maintained tight control over his own territory and took an active part in its administration. In a district like Nobere, for example, the chief was aided both by an informal council and by an administrative apparatus similar to but smaller than the one at Ouagadougou. The council included men with whom the chief had grown up, members of his immediate family such as his brothers, and a few formal administrative personnel. These councillors visited him every day, brought him occasional gifts, received gifts from him in turn, and discussed informally all matters of interest. Yet, informal as this communication was, it enabled the district chief to know what was going on in his villages. Moreover, these councillors interceded for various villages and gave the chief valuable advice in administrative matters.

The formal administrative personnel of the district included a Ouidi Naba, a Baloum Naba, a Tansoba, and lesser officials with titles identical to those found at the court of Ouagadougou: Baglere Naba, Dapore Naba, Pwe Naba, Samande Naba, Ouedrange Naba, Raga Naba, etc. However, the officials who bore the same titles as the chief administrators of the Mogho Naba did not necessarily serve in the same capacity. A local historical event often determined which official held which administrative task. In Nobere, the Ouidi Naba and the Tansoba were the two principal administrators. The Ouidi Naba administered those villages north and west of Nab'tenga (the chief's village), and the Tansoba administered the villages south and east of it. The Baloum Naba and other officials had no villages under their jurisdiction, but performed many valuable services for the chief.

Administrative processes on the district level were not as formal as in the capital. Except on Fridays and on important occasions, the district administrators visited the chief's compound only when summoned or when they had an important matter to discuss. (Of course, those administrators who formed part of his unofficial council could visit him at any time.) Their problems differed little from those of the Ouagadougou officials, except that their personal problems were greater, owing to the intimacy of the smaller area. The differences in status between non-noble administrators and noble relatives of the district chief were more keenly felt and caused more difficulties. Whereas the provincial administrator seldom met the district chiefs, the district administrators regularly met nobles in the market place, at ceremonies, and in the course of their everyday work. The latent conflict between official status and royal rank often broke out openly. When it did, the nobles of a village would refuse to obey the orders the administrators had transmitted to their village chief. This compelled the district chief either to summon the nobles for an explanation of their behavior or to use his own relatives to transmit orders to them. He did not like to take either course of action, especially the latter, because both violated hierarchical procedure. Furthermore, when he sent a near relative to a village, the relative often demanded goods and services not authorized by the district chief. Of course, not all the nobles made the administrator's task difficult, but enough of them did to cause him anxiety.

The duties of the district administrators fell into several categories. First, it was their task to transmit to the village chiefs orders which the Kombere Naba had received from the Mogho Naba concerning warfare, special gifts and tribute, and nation-wide ceremonies and rituals. Second, they had similar duties toward the provincial governor and the district chief. Third, and most important from the local viewpoint, they handled those affairs concerning only the district. The administrators seldom had difficulty discharging these duties, for, nobles aside, the Mossi usually obeyed orders from their chiefs—a fact verified by most observers. At the same time, a district chief had to be temperate in his demands upon his villagers, and could not take advantage of his obligations to the Mogho Naba as a means of personal enrichment. Similarly, the district administrators could not seek personal gain either by augmenting the demands of the district chief or by withholding part of the goods and services rendered to him. District administrators who were found guilty of maladministration or embezzlement were executed, because activities of this kind could—and often did—jeopardize the life of the district chief.

The Mossi might complain among themselves about the administrative policies of their district chief, but they took no measures against him unless he was very cruel or exploitative. A district chief who by his disregard for the people's welfare was believed to have lost the ability to "command people" jeopardized not only his position but also his life. When the people were dissatisfied with a chief, they either boycotted him or deserted their villages and migrated to another district, thus "increasing the force" (nam) of the chief who gave them sanctuary. This placed the deserted chief in a rather difficult position. Mogho Nanamse are known to have ordered the execution of district chiefs and even autonomous Dimdamba who had lost their subjects through their own fault. In 1863, when Mogho Naba Sanum was informed that the ruler of Boussouma, Naba Zande, had been chased away by his subjects for administrative abuses and had fled to a Ouagadougou village, he had him captured and executed.[29] Thus, the threat that people might leave the district was often strong enough to ensure a just administration, because the district chiefs and officials depended upon the villagers not only for the economic support of the central administration but also for their livelihood and their lives.

Those district chiefs who supervised other district chiefs for the Mogho Naba did not interfere with the internal administration of the districts. The chiefs of the Vooko and Nobila districts, for instance, had administrators of their own to look after their villages. But they were responsible to the chief of Nobere district, not their respective provincial ministers, for their internal affairs. Moreover, they had to follow the Nobere chief when he went to Ouagadougou to pay homage and allegiance to the Mogho Naba. But aside from these prescriptions, the chiefs of these subordinate districts administered their territories in the same manner as the Nobere chief administered his own.

The Mossi village chief had no administrators of his own to help him with day-to-day affairs of his village. However, like the district chief, he had a group of confidants who acted as an informal council. These men included senior members of his own lineage, elders from other local lineages, and personal friends. Again, like the confidants of the district chiefs, these men visited the village chief whenever they were not busy with their own affairs to talk to him about wives, crops, and village matters. Although protocol was at a minimum on this level, the chief had to maintain a high degree of decorum. As a member of the ruling lineage of the district, he had noble status and had to be treated accordingly. The non-noble village chief was also respected as a recipient of the nam. But all chiefs, whether nobles or commoners, were expected to lead exemplary lives lest the flaws in their characters as revealed by the intimacy of village life should weaken their prestige.

The village chief received his orders from the district chief through the administrator in charge of his village or through one of this official's servants. He, in turn, used his own sons or relatives to transmit messages to the heads of the saghse. If the message was extremely important, the village chief's messenger might be accompanied by the administrator's messenger or by the district chief's personal representatives. The saksobadamba then transmitted the order to the various compound heads. This hierarchy was always followed because, by following it, the officials knew who was responsible for disobeying or frustrating the wishes of the superior chiefs. As on the district level, the orders transmitted to the village and its sections dealt with such things as collecting tribute, picking fruits from the district chief's trees, allocating labor for the district chief or his personal retainers, transferring or summoning cases to the district court, procuring sacrificial animals for the local Tengsoba, and requesting soldiers. The village chief also sent his own messages to the saghse. These messages, however, dealt with such village matters as local sacrifices, quarrels, and court cases.

Misrule and maladministration by a village chief were punished either by the district chief or by the villagers. Like other Mossi rulers, the village chief could not be deposed and allowed to live. However, he had a better chance of fleeing and finding refuge in another district. His presence in a strange district did not challenge the authority of the local chief, and he had no opportunities to seize any of his host's villages. In fact, if the refugee was accompanied by a large number of his subjects, his host might even give him land on which to erect a new village. The proviso was, of course, that he should not "spoil" the district by causing trouble. If a village chief accused of maladministration was seized by the district chief before he could flee, he was invariably executed. If he was a commoner, he was decapitated or even stoned to death; if he was a nobleman, he was taken into the bush and strangled in secret by the district police. If a district chief hesitated to punish a village chief whose followers had complained, the aggrieved lineage or the entire village simply took its movable property and left. This sanction does not seem to have been applied often, but its threat was normally sufficient to curb the excesses of the worst village chief.

V

LAW AND THE JUDICIAL PROCESS

THE MOSSI possessed a comprehensive body of rules governing human conduct. These rules were well known to the people, and violators were punished by the responsible authorities. The Mossi might be said to have had substantive law, but they had no written codes. Nevertheless, the lack of written codes does not warrant Mangin's blanket criticism of Mossi judicial processes: "Of course, there was no written code, no formal scale of penalties. Everything depended on custom and on the whim of the judge. Thus, the wealthy could obtain sentences in their favor by paying the judges, and thieves could avoid punishment by sharing their loot with the Naba."[1] Custom did dictate the penalties, just as "written custom" dictates penalties in all written legal codes. But, as we shall see, the Mossi did have a known scale of penalties. Moreover, a Mossi judge had to be careful in rendering judgment, because his decisions could be reviewed by a higher court.

The head of the Mossi extended family, the *Yirisoba,* was responsible for the everyday conduct of his charges. It was his duty to settle all family quarrels, and to punish persons guilty of theft within the compound, disrespect toward elders, and incest. Punishment for the lesser wrongs included reprimands and floggings. A person found guilty of disrespect to the elders or of incest could be banished from the group. But banishment was so severe that it was imposed only if the criminal refused to make the usual conciliatory gestures and was condemned by all the members of his boodoo. Even after this condemnation, however, he could ask a "sister's son," a yagenga, to intercede for him. This man, the son of a female lineage member, had many privileges within his mother's brother's lineage, including the right to mediate between an exile and his boodoo.

Amicable relations within the family group were most often disrupted by conjugal difficulties. A Mossi husband could occasionally flog an erring wife, but he was not allowed to maltreat her. When a man became disgusted with his wife and wished to repudiate her, he put her water pots in the compound yard. This rather serious action often led to hostile relations between the lineages concerned. If either the repudiated woman or a member of her husband's lineage wished to initiate a reconciliation, she or he had to summon a yagenga. He alone was permitted to reconcile the couple after the pots had been placed in the courtyard. When a woman felt that she was being maltreated by her husband, she usually fled to her own patrilineage and waited for her husband's patrilineage—usually his brothers—to visit her male relatives and discuss the case. If the woman was judged guilty, she was reprimanded and sometimes flogged by her own relatives for causing trouble between the two lineages, and then sent home to her husband. However, if the man was found guilty, his wife was returned to him, but he was warned that he would forfeit all rights to her if he maltreated her again. A man who lost his wife through repeated maltreatment could not take the matter to court, because chiefs usually refused to deal with purely domestic issues. His only recourse was to induce one of his lineage brothers to recall a daughter who had married into his wife's lineage. This act was usually sufficient to bring about the reconciliation of the estranged couple before innocent persons were hurt.

The Mossi made every effort to solve minor problems without recourse to the chiefs. The local Boodkasemdamba and lineage elders adjudicated quarrels and simple offenses involving members of minimal segments in the various village saghse. They even tried to resolve difficulties between lineage members of larger segments who lived in different villages. The elders often imposed punishments such as reprimands, floggings, and even banishment. The convicted person did not usually appeal to the chief, because he knew that the chief would advise him to settle his problem within the family.

Unrelated villagers also tried to settle difficulties among themselves without appealing to the chief. For example, a man who was caught stealing could be beaten or even killed by his intended victims, and the chief did not punish them for their action. In many cases, villagers simply took the thief back to his relatives, knowing they would punish him. Occasionally, a family disgraced by a thieving member forced him to kill himself. When this happened the chief held an inquest but took no other action.

The Mossi gave a fairly simple explanation for returning a thief to his relatives for punishment. They said that every family had "weak" members, and that by not harming the captured thief they were only protecting themselves against retaliation if one of their own relatives should commit a similar crime. But a more important reason seems to have been their fear of starting a feud that might result in the premeditated murder of a man and the subsequent execution of his murderer.

The one crime that invoked terrible unofficial sanctions was rape. If the offender was caught in the act, he was immediately killed. If he was merely suspected of guilt both by his own lineage and by the lineage of the wronged woman, he was banished from his lineage and from the village. So swift and sure was this punishment that a rapist always fled if he believed he would be discovered. The Mossi considered rape such a heinous crime that if the act resulted in pregnancy, an abortion was attempted; if this failed, the child was killed at birth. Furthermore, the rapist could never hope to return to his community, because even if the yagenga appealed on his behalf and his lineage forgave him, the community ban still stood.[2]

The village chief was usually aware of the torts and crimes that occurred in his village, and of how the families concerned had handled them. He seldom interfered in the internal affairs of a lineage, or in problems between lineages, unless he felt that a case was beyond their legal competence. In the case of a rapist's expulsion, community feeling usually ran so high that if the chief intervened, it was only to support the will of the community. However, when people could not settle their differences peaceably or when a major crime was committed within a village, the chief usually summoned the offender to his court for trial. His right to do so was sanctioned by his possession of the nam, but the very concept of the nam often made his task difficult. If he was a commoner, the nobles often emphasized their relationship to the holder of the royal nam, the district chief, and objected to being tried by a commoner. They usually appeared at the village court if summoned, but often attempted afterward to find some excuse for taking their case to the district chief. They felt that their local reputation would prevent them from receiving a fair hearing from anyone but their lineage brother. Furthermore, if they were judged and convicted in the lower court and the verdict was confirmed in the district court, they felt that the district chief, in concurring with the village chief, had broken the solidarity of their lineage. But if they took their case directly to the district chief, they knew they were being judged by an equal or a superior, and that an unfavorable judgment would not damage their status.

The competence of the village chief to deal with court cases was limited.[3] He did pass on all the legal infractions that occurred in his village, but he tried to adjudicate only the minor cases. Thus, he tried cases involving theft, quarrels, trespassing, adultery, indebtedness, and abuse, and tried to settle them by reprimanding the guilty ones. He sent cases involving serious injury and homicide to the district court, along with cases he was unable to resolve.

The district court was a most efficient and effective judicial organ, and the nature of the Mossi judicial process was most evident on this level. The district court did not deal with all cases referred to it. Many cases, especially those concerning the behavior of women, were referred back to the village to be resolved by the respective lineages. The district chief considered it beneath his dignity to deal with such cases, and his guards ostentatiously chased away the litigants. He consented to try such cases only when he suspected that more serious trouble would develop if he did not. Theoretically, district courts could not try cases involving the death penalty, but in practice most of them did. Higher chiefs tolerated this as long as district chiefs did not abuse their usurpation of power.[4]

When a major crime was committed in a district, the case was usually sent immediately to the district court. The chief of the village where the crime had been committed sent one of his relatives with the accused or with the litigants to the district chief's compound, and dispatched another relative to notify the village administrator. The administrator either went to the district court to await the litigants, or sent his representative to meet the court-bound party on the way and question them about the case. Such parties were often very large, because the Mossi believed that a man should not go to court alone. They felt that the criminal act of a relative reflected on all of them, and that it was important for them to appear with him. To quote a Mossi proverb, "A chicken without its feathers is a very small bird indeed." Therefore, no matter how grievous his crime might be, the accused was accompanied to court by his relatives. If his own lineage members refused to do so, his mother's patrilineage was duty-bound to come to his aid. These relatives believed that they would incur ancestral wrath if they refused to help him.

As soon as the accused or the litigants arrived at the district chief's compound, a page notified him that the people of such-and-such a village had brought him a case. If it was after dark, the chief told his police to take charge of the litigants until morning; otherwise he prepared to convene the court. When the chief was ready, the page reappeared and alerted the court party, who had been milling about in the courtyard under the watchful eyes of the chief's guards. They ranged themselves at a respectful distance on either side of the chief's chair. When he appeared they arose, and when he sat down they knelt and offered the customary salutation. The litigants and their relatives then gave the chief the customary kola nuts, cowries, and chickens.[5] He, in turn, acknowledged the gifts and inquired about the case. The relatives of the village chief who had accompanied the litigants reported what had allegedly happened; what action, if any, had been taken by the village court; and why the case had been brought to the district court (either because the crime was too serious to be judged on the village level, or because the litigants had rejected the village chief's verdict). The chief then asked the plaintiff or "the people of X village" to state their case. Someone usually spoke up, and after he had finished, the chief asked the defendant or defendants to do likewise. The litigants were then asked to produce reputable witnesses to support or refute the testimony.

Witnesses had to be male, adult (to have begun to "push a beard"), and free. Women and bondsmen had no legal personality before a Mossi court. A slave was represented at court by his master, and a woman by her husband (and, by extension, by his patrilineage). In marital quarrels or property suits, a woman was usually represented by her patrilineage. Only if she alone could give the required evidence was she allowed in court. When she was asked to testify, she knelt, and spoke in a high, thin, soft voice, thus showing extreme respect to the chief and proper deference to the court. Except for these restrictions, any person could be called in as a witness. Tempers often ran fairly high among the litigants' relatives and friends while they gave their testimony and argued the case, but their physical separation and their respect for the chief prevented abuse and fighting. Anyone who started a fight in court was liable to a beating by the samandekamba.

The Mossi believed that most people, given sufficient reason, would commit any crime. Thus they examined the litigants carefully and at great length in an attempt to "get behind" the offense. The district chief interrogated the litigants, but the dignity of the court prevented him from arguing with them. As a matter of fact, most of the cross-examination was done by the litigants themselves. From time to time, the village administrator and the chief's confidants asked brief, direct questions. When a woman was involved, the chief's Pughtiema usually listened to the proceedings from behind a wall and questioned her. When all the evidence was in, the chief either rendered his verdict without delay or retired to the zongo to confer with his confidants and the village administrator. He took the latter course whenever he felt that further discussion was necessary or that false testimony was confusing the issue. Not until he felt that he had the facts well in hand did he return to the court to render his verdict.

The Mossi did not use ordeals in court except in the "chastity trials" conducted by the Pwe Naba. Some litigants called upon the ancestors to kill them if they were not telling the truth; others went to earth shrines and drank an infusion of dust to show that they were not afraid of the spirits who wrought vengeance on the guilty. However, such acts were never carried out in court and thus were of no use to the chief.

The following case, tried in a district court in 1956, illustrates the Mossi

LAW AND THE JUDICIAL PROCESS   85

concept of justice. To reach the central market, the people of Donse village used a path that ran across the fields belonging to two of their fellow villagers, Zami and Isa. The path was normally open all year round, even during the planting season, because neither man wished to inconvenience the villagers. But one day the two men quarreled, and shortly thereafter Isa announced his decision to close his path during the planting season. He said he feared that "people would steal his growing crops" if he left it open. Moreover, he wanted to use the path to increase his planting area. Zami objected to what he considered an insult, and, believing that Isa had violated a customary rule, used the path. In doing so, he crushed several stalks of millet. Isa witnessed his action, and the men came to blows. When the village chief proved unable to reconcile them, they were brought before the district court.

The district chief ruled that according to Mossi custom, a man could close a path during the planting season to prevent people from stealing his crops. But if he closed a path, he had to provide an alternative route, for no one had the right to restrict the movements of others. The chief sympathized with Isa over the small size of his field, but insisted that he provide a path across or around it. However, he persuaded Zami to let Isa use a portion of his land in compensation for the new path.

The chief tried to reconcile the interests of Isa and Zami with those of the entire village. He apparently felt that reconciliation was more useful than judgment. He did uphold the law that the right of passage is mandatory, but also maintained that a man has the right to protect his property from potential thieves. At the same time, he made it clear that although a man may defend his own rights, he may not do so by infringing upon the rights of others.

The same principles seem to have been upheld in the following case, also recorded in 1956, which is interesting because it illustrates the flexibility of Mossi law. A man named Hammadou died, leaving fifteen cows as his legacy. Moussa, his eldest son and principal heir, distributed the cows among his father's other sons and male relatives, but did not give any to his father's daughter. Strictly speaking, he was right to exclude her, because a woman was not supposed to inherit any of her father's property unless he had no living lineal or collateral relatives. In practice, however, a daughter always received part of her father's legacy, especially if he had been wealthy. Hammadou's daughter therefore felt slighted, and when she received no redress from Moussa or her other male relatives, she had the case taken to the village chief. He could not resolve it, and referred it to the district chief.

When Moussa was called before the district chief, he explained that his father had given the woman a silver bracelet before he died, and that the babissi felt that this was sufficient, since she had a husband to provide for her. Furthermore, Moussa said that the inheritance had already been distributed, and that any redistribution would impose a hardship on all concerned.

Interpreting the inheritance law according to common practice, the chief ruled that the milk from a man's cattle was for *all* his children, regardless of sex, and that the fact that the father had formerly given the daughter a bracelet should not have influenced the distribution of the inheritance. The chief stated that the woman should receive at least one cow, and that if the defendant did not agree, he (the chief) would recall all the animals and supervise their distribution. He did not feel that he had to state the principles by which he had reached his judgment, for the consensus among the people of the district was that the heir was trying to take advantage of the law for his own selfish interests. Rather than appeal to Ouagadougou, Moussa and his babissi accepted the verdict.

On the basis of these and other cases, we are led to the conclusion that the Mossi felt that law and the judicial process should serve to reconcile people and to maintain what was commonly considered to be social justice.

Most of the cases at the district court were tried in the same manner as those cited above. Cases involving relations between men and women were the most common. This is paradoxical, because the district chief tried to avoid any involvement with such cases. For every domestic case tried by the district chief, five others were sent back to the village or lineage level. Even so, it is estimated that about 80 per cent of the cases tried by Mossi district chiefs ultimately concerned women. The most common case of this type was the alleged refusal of a woman to return to her husband.[6] If the judge found that another man had encouraged her to leave her husband, he ordered her to return to him and warned her and the man about the possibility of serious difficulty with her husband's relatives. On the other hand, if the chief found that the woman had left a cruel husband who threatened to harm her or her relatives, he warned the husband not to carry out his threats. The Mossi had no bride price; thus, a woman's family was not faced with the problem of restitution. Sometimes, an angry husband did demand that his wife's family return the gifts (*pogopossum*, "thanks for the woman") he had given them from time to time—e.g., at funerals—and they complied.

Adultery cases were next in frequency at the district court. A man convicted of adultery with another man's wife was either warned to leave her alone or fined a sheep or a goat. He was also liable to be put in stocks for several days, and when released he was warned against visiting the local markets, where he might be tempted to renew his illicit relations. A nobleman convicted of adultery was often merely warned or fined, since his movements could not be restricted. But if a man caught his wife and another man in *flagrante delicto* and killed them, his act was considered justifiable homicide (even if the slain man was a noble), and he went free. If, however, he killed the lover but spared his wife, he had to send her to the chief's household. Here she was made to perform hard work under the supervision of the palace guards until it was believed that she had reformed. A man who was experiencing difficulties with an unfaithful wife and feared he might eventually kill her or her paramour also sent her to the chief's compound for a few months.

The Mossi have always been great creditors and debtors, and cases concerning indebtedness seem to have been next in frequency at the district court. The chief usually dismissed cases of indebtedness brought against minors, because it was considered unseemly for adults to give credit or to loan valuable property to youths not yet of age. Thus, if the minor's family refused to make restitution, the creditor usually had no redress. However, if a woman borrowed property and refused to return it, her husband's lineage was held responsible. Similarly, if an adult male borrowed anything and refused to return it or to do so on time, the case was taken to the local court and eventually to the district court. The creditor was asked to supply witnesses to the loan, and if the chief was satisfied that the loan had been made under the conditions specified, the debtor was ordered to make restitution. If the debtor claimed bankruptcy, the chief ordered that his goods be seized and sold, and that restitution be made to the creditor. If the debtor was truly destitute, his relatives were compelled to pay his debts. The collective responsibility of the babissi for the debts of its members was seen most clearly in cases where men died in a state of indebtedness. The creditors were allowed to summon the debtor's babissi to court, and if proof of the debt was established, the relatives were compelled to repay. If they failed to do so, the chief's police seized and sold their goods to repay the debt.

Cases dealing with violations of civil contracts were somewhat similar. The Mossi did not believe in the axiom *caveat emptor*. If a man sold an animal that died within a week for no apparent reason, the chief ordered an investigation. If it was found that the animal had been ill when sold, the chief ordered that the buyer be reimbursed. If the investigation showed that the animal had been healthy when sold, no restitution was made. Similarly, if a man borrowed an ass or an ox to transport goods and the animal died while he was using it, the owner could not press any claims. However, the borrower was obliged to sell the animal's flesh and give the money to the owner along with the animal's skin as proof of its death. Under no circumstances would a district chief absolve a man from paying the market value of an animal if he failed to return the skin. Such failure would brand him as a thief and involve an additional fine.

The Mossi considered theft a major crime. A thief could be killed with impunity if he was caught in the act and in the presence of several witnesses. If these conditions were not met but the man killed was known to have been a thief, the killer was fined several cows. But if he was known to have been a man of good character, the killer ran the risk of being executed. In this way, the Mossi tried to prevent any abuse of an accepted practice. The theft of grain and other foodstuffs was considered especially reprehensible, because it was held to indicate that the thief was so depraved that he would not even grow his own food. During the rule of Naba Kaglere of Nobere district (1888–1906), a man called Yahiya left his own village of Donse and went to a village called Quitenga to steal sweet potatoes. The people of that village caught him in the act and shot him with a poisoned arrow as he made his escape. Yahiya died without revealing the source of his wound, and his babissi, suspecting foul play, asked Kaglere to investigate. When the Quitenga people learned of the investigation, they went forward voluntarily and reported the circumstances under which they had wounded Yahiya. Kaglere absolved them of all guilt and told the Donse people that Yahiya had deserved to die, not only because he had stolen food (which he might have received if he had asked for it), but because sweet potatoes were the easiest vegetable to cultivate.

A thief who was too clever to be caught in the act but who was apprehended afterwards was treated quite harshly by the Mossi court. Here, the penalty of double indemnity was often applied. A man who was brought to court for stealing a chicken or guinea hen was fined a goat or a sheep. Hence the Mossi proverb "Zou noaga ronda bouga"—"He who steals a chicken repays a goat." The thief who stole one cow had to return several. If a thief could not pay the fine, he was placed in stocks until his relatives paid for him. If they refused to do so, the chief's retainers seized their property, sold it, and made restitution. This often compelled the family of a recidivous thief to make him commit suicide. If the family would not resort to this, the district chief had the man seized and clubbed to death.[7] Sometimes the chief sent recidivists to the Mogho Naba, who sent them to a village called Teemetenga to be made into eunuchs.[8]

The Mossi seem to have made a distinction between theft and pillage—

a practice whereby nobles deprived commoners of their property. Those nobles who lived among commoners quite often confiscated their neighbors' property. But this was not regarded as theft and was not punishable as such, although a rapacious nobleman could be sanctioned for terrorizing and "spoiling" a village. If a nobleman was caught performing an act that *was* considered theft, or if he was accused and found guilty of theft, he was severely punished. During Kaglere's reign, the people of a small village suffered a series of livestock thefts. One day, while the friends of a village chief were sitting with him, a dog came out of the chief's compound dragging an animal skin. The men recognized the skin as that described for a stolen goat, and decided to investigate. In the chief's courtyard they discovered the hole from which the dog had unearthed the skin. They also found the skins of several other stolen animals. The villagers took the village chief to the district chief, who found him guilty and exiled him from the region. In passing judgment, the district chief told him that he had been elected "to care for the village," but that he had betrayed his trust by robbing his own people.

According to Mossi law, willful homicide or murder was punishable by execution. The Mossi did not use wergild or "blood money," but insisted on the *lex talionis,* which they interpreted as "a life for a life." They did not believe that money or any other valuables could compensate for the life of a man, nor would they allow a slave to be executed in place of the murderer. They believed that only by executing the murderer himself could they prevent his victim's relatives from resorting to vengeance and thus "spoiling" the district or village.

A man who grievously wounded another was apprehended, bound, and taken to the village chief and subsequently to the district chief. Here he was kept in stocks in the serfs' quarter without being tried until his victim either died or recovered. If his victim recovered and the judge found that the wound had been inflicted accidentally, the defendant was fined or had his goods confiscated, but he was released. If the judge found that the victim had been wounded in a fair fight, the prisoner was usually censured and dismissed. The chief often warned the wounded man that he ought to have lived up to the Mossi axiom that a grown man is always able to protect himself. If, however, the trial revealed that the prisoner had ambushed his victim with the intent to kill, he either was fined several cows or had his entire property confiscated. District chiefs are known to have executed the perpetrators of cowardly ambushes even though their victims recovered.

If a man died at the hands of another, an inquest was held immediately. If the killing had been accidental or committed in self-defense, or if it was found to have been justified—that is, if the victim was a thief or a nocturnal intruder—then the accused was acquitted or simply fined. If, however, the accused was found guilty of murder, he was sentenced to die, and the mode of execution was at the chief's pleasure. The chief surrendered the prisoner to his executioners, serfs who lived in the Baglere ward. They took him into the woods and carried out the sentence by strangulation, hanging, decapitation, clubbing, or stoning.

The perpetrator of an unusually heinous crime was often ordered to kill himself with a poisoned arrow. This form of execution was feared most, because it tested the murderer's mettle and called into play the coercive force of his lineage if he proved to be a coward. When such an execution was ordered, the district chief had a poisoned arrow prepared and brought to the murderer's father, his brother, or his father's brother's son. The relative gave the arrow to the condemned man, and, while apologizing for his painful mission, explained that the crime had to be expiated. If the murderer agreed to kill himself, his relatives prepared food and drink for him while his grave was dug. Some proud and brave men helped their relatives dig the oblong-shaped grave required for a murderer; some even insisted on digging it themselves. When both the food and the grave had been prepared, the murderer bade his relatives farewell, took the food and the poisoned arrow, and went into a hut. Here he ate the food and afterward killed himself by pushing the poisoned arrow into his leg. In some cases he had to be provided with a second arrow to hasten his death. If a cowardly murderer refused to kill himself, one of his relatives offered to die in his stead. He told the murderer that death was preferable to the knowledge that his lineage brother was a coward. What would happen, he asked the murderer, if he saw a relative being harmed? Would he choose his own safety rather than run the risk of death? The other relatives asked the same questions, and this subtle coercion was usually sufficient to induce the most cowardly man to kill himself. There are no reports of a murderer's permitting a relative to die for him; life would have been impossible for him afterward. One suspects that if ever a murderer had attempted to elude his fate, the district chief would have had him executed.

The district court also prescribed capital punishment for individuals convicted of arson, abduction, witchcraft, or lese majesty. A person convicted of willfully setting fire to someone's hut or crops was put to death even if no one was killed in the resulting fire; he was held to have jeopardized the life and livelihood of his victims. Similarly, the rare person convicted of threatening the well-being of others through the practice of witchcraft was usually tortured and killed. Conviction usually followed the testimony of witnesses or the confession of the accused.

The torture was seen as a punishment, and not as a form of ordeal to ascertain guilt or innocence. It was designed to cause the culprit as much suffering as possible before he died, and its harshness reflects the Mossi fear of witches and witchcraft. In one form of punishment called *koudgilga,* the culprit was sent to the smith, who tortured him by placing hot iron balls in both his hands. He was then beaten to death. Another type of punishment called *swengalenga* was more painful. A pottery jar from which the bottom had been removed was heated in a fire. Then it was placed over the head of the convicted witch and allowed to burn its way down onto his shoulders. The culprit was subsequently killed. Sometimes a convicted witch was not killed; instead, a man was sent to Ouagadougou to be castrated and sold as a eunuch, and a woman was sold outside the country as a slave.

Gross disrespect toward the chief and crimes of lese majesty were uncommon among the Mossi. These crimes were usually committed by persons who came into close contact with the chief—nobles and court retainers—rather than by commoners, serfs, or slaves. The most common form of lese majesty was adultery with one of the district chief's wives. The penalty for this was death for both violators. Anyone who dared insult the district chief at court was seized and executed. The same fate awaited those who talked about him maliciously in public or threatened to stir a rebellion against him. If the culprits were commoners, they were executed; if they were nobles, they were strangled in secret or were forced to commit suicide.

The district chief was caught in a dilemma whenever nobles committed major crimes or unlawful acts. They could not be imprisoned, and only the Mogho Naba had the legal prerogative to execute them. When a noble committed a major crime such as treason or rebellion, he was sent to the capital to be executed by slaves, who strangled him with a piece of cotton cloth. However, no district chief could allow the nobles to commit crimes with impunity, secure in the knowledge that they could only be punished at Ouagadougou. If a nobleman subverted the chief's rule by repeated acts of cruelty and brigandage, he was executed, although illegally. The executioners were the Baglere Naba and the Dapore Naba. These two men secretly visited the condemned noble, taking with them a bundle as a present from the chief. This bundle contained a new white robe in which were secreted a chief's bonnet and a poisoned arrow. As soon as the noble saw the gift, he knew that he was being ordered to kill himself. If he attempted to raise an alarm or run away, he was instantly strangled and his body was discarded in the bush. If he accepted the sentence, he was allowed to have food prepared, to eat, and then to kill himself. The chief ordered an elaborate funeral for his kinsman as though he had died an ordinary death. Thus, he was able to observe all the proprieties while at the same time safeguarding his position within the district and toward the Mogho Naba. For, as already pointed out, the district chief who failed to protect his subjects as well as to rule them was deposed and executed by the sovereign.

The promptness with which the lower courts dealt with litigations left little time for pre-trial bribery, and there is general agreement that the traditional courts were just. Of course, some lower chiefs were known to have been unfair and to have taken bribes. However, they were always in danger of having their verdicts appealed to Ouagadougou.

The Mossi believed in and acted on the dictum that "the truth is at Ouagadougou." They were convinced that they could obtain justice from the Mogho Naba if from no other chief. If a man was not satisfied with the ruling of a lower chief, he was free in theory to seek a higher verdict, and this influenced the kind of justice rendered on the lower level. As a rule, however, the district chiefs did not favor appeals to Ouagadougou. They felt, like most Mossi, that the less their superiors knew about their activities, the better. Thus, the district chief used all of his influence to prevent cases from being appealed to the capital. Some district chiefs were not above coercing litigants into such abstention. They even threatened them with reprisals if the verdict should be unfavorable. But the greatest deterrent against such appeals was the expenditure of time and money. The docket of the Mogho Naba's court was always crowded, and the suitors often had to remain at the capital for as long as three months before they were given a hearing.[9] During this period they often spent more money than the action was worth. Marc states that the word "Ouagadougou" means "the place where one becomes thin," a reference to the amount of money litigants had to spend while waiting for their cases to be heard.[10]

When the object of a lawsuit was the inheritance of cattle, the litigants sustained a double loss. As soon as they asked that the case be taken to the capital, the district chief impounded the cattle. While the case was pending he appropriated the cows' milk, and when the case was settled both he and the Mogho Naba received some animals. Thus, suitors were usually under a great deal of pressure to resolve their problems on the district level. However, if they were determined to go to the capital, they were permitted to do so.

The district chief always sent one of his retainers to the capital with the litigants. The group went directly to the district's provincial minister, who was empowered to hear the appeal and decide whether it should be brought before the Mogho Naba or returned to the district court. If he decided to send it to the Mogho Naba, he placed it on the docket and told the litigants when it would be heard. On the day set he took his charges to court, where they waited in the company of the litigants from other districts and from the wards of the capital itself.

The procedure of the Mogho Naba's court differed little from that of the district chief's court. When called upon, the litigant stated his case, called witnesses, and underwent cross-examination by his opponents and by ministers of the Mogho Naba. The litigants were not allowed to look at the Mogho Naba while they spoke, but had to kneel forward on the ground with their faces turned away from him. The Mogho Naba himself seldom looked at the litigants and rarely questioned them. When presented with a complex case, the Mogho Naba, like the district chief, retired with his councillors and canvassed their opinion in order "to ascertain whether or not their verdicts were similar to his own." Nevertheless, he could not follow their advice. He had to make up his own mind, and when he returned to court he rendered his verdict, which could not be appealed. If those who received an unfavorable verdict showed any displeasure, they were taken outside by the palace guards and executed.

The penalties imposed by the Ouagadougou court were usually more severe than those handed down at the district level. The main reason for this was that aside from cases involving residents of Ouagadougou, the lawsuits tried by the Mogho Naba were serious ones and often had been sent to him on appeal. Moreover, the Mogho Naba's court was alone empowered to impose the death penalty within the kingdom of Ouagadougou. It should be noted here once more that district chiefs often executed criminals. But it should also be reiterated that the Mogho Naba never surrendered his prerogative to the district chiefs. They simply usurped it, and if they used it judiciously they were not penalized.

Those nobles and commoners who were convicted for serious crimes at the monarch's court were killed by the royal executioners. Moreover, in contrast to the procedure at the district court, the criminal's property was often seized before his execution. The reason for this is not clear, but it was probably related to the lack of a personal relationship between the court and the relatives of the accused, which enabled the Mogho Naba to impose a harsher penalty. The district chief, it must be remembered, lived in close association with his people and was influenced in his behavior by social relationships. Interestingly enough, the Mogho Naba did not keep the goods seized, but allowed them to be distributed among his executioners.

Crimes against the person or office of the Mogho Naba were punished with greater severity than crimes against the district chief. Any man who was seen speaking to one of the ruler's wives and who did not happen to be related to her was tried and executed. In some cases, he was put to death without a trial. Adultery with a royal wife was considered so reprehensible that both adulterers were publicly beaten to death. Their bodies were denied burial and were thrown into the bush to be eaten by vultures. The Dapore Naba and the Baglere Naba seized and retained the man's property.

Men who committed treason against the Mogho Naba were usually killed before they could be tried. Chiefs and nobles who were suspected of treason and who consented to come to Ouagadougou for trial were deposed and executed if found guilty. Those who were found innocent were released and sent back to their chiefly duties. The sole exception on record to this general rule was the case of Naba Yemde, a Dim of Boulsa province. He had fought and defeated the forces of Mogho Naba Sanum, and when the Mogho Naba sent a larger army and routed him, he was treacherously delivered to the monarch by another Dim. Sanum found Yemde innocent of treason, but had him executed because he had violated another rule: as the descendant of a Kourita, he had come face to face with the Mogho Naba, thus jeopardizing the monarch's life. This exception is always cited by the Mossi when the inevitability of execution for treason is brought up. Actually, a person accused of treason rarely went to court. He either took poison or died in battle against the royal forces. As a posthumous punishment, his compound was burned, his property seized, and his relatives and servants sold into slavery outside the country. Thus, the supreme penalty was not merely the death of a traitor but the permanent banishment of his entire lineage.

VI

WARFARE

THE MOSSI were proud of their warrior tradition, which had earned them their several kingdoms, principalities, and districts. Even the least district chief had stories about the wars in which his ancestors had wrested their territories from aboriginal populations. These traditions of conquest legitimized to a large extent the power of the Mossi kings and chiefs, who never hesitated to use force in order to obtain tribute, to maintain their rule, and to enforce their authority. The Mossi value fighting ability so highly that even today, when fighting is no longer necessary, most Mossi males in the rural areas carry sticks and other weapons on their shoulders as symbols of manhood. In their view, every man should know how to fight and should be able to defend his village, his district, and his kingdom.

According to tradition, the northward thrust of the Mossi warriors during the fourteenth, fifteenth, and sixteenth centuries carried them into the region of the Niger River bend. Here, around A.D. 1329, the Yatenga Mossi attacked and sacked the town of Timbuktu, which belongs to the Mali. When Mali was on the decline during the early fifteenth century, the Mossi again attacked its towns. According to the *Tarikh es-Sudan*, when the Mali ruler appointed Amin-ben-Ahmad jurisconsul of Timbuktu,

> the sultan of the Mossi led an expedition against Benka. The population of that region went out to engage the enemy, and at that time left others sitting around El Hadj. He pronounced certain words on the millet which was being served and asked those around him to eat of it. All of them ate except the son-in-law of El Hadj, who did not because he was related to him. "Now go and fight," said the holy man, "and you will have nothing to fear from the weapons of the enemy." All, in effect, returned safe and sound, and only those persons who did not eat the millet died in the battle. The king of the Mossi was routed, and his troops were chased without having seized anything from the people of Benka. All this thanks to the protection of the blessed person.[1]

Later, the Mossi attacked towns of the Songhai empire whenever they felt strong enough, only to be driven away later by a stronger adversary. Sa'di describes a Mossi incursion into the Songhai empire as follows:

Sonni-Ali entered Kabara in the year 882 after the Hegira (1477); and it was during the course of the same year that the king of the Mossi entered Sama. In 884 (1479) Sonni-Ali was at Tosoko. . . .

During the month of Jumada I of that year (July 9 to August 8, 1480), the king of the Mossi entered Biro [the Songhai name for Walata] and did not leave until Jumada II (August 8 to September 7, 1480). The siege lasted one month, and during that time he demanded a woman from the inhabitants. . . . After the siege the Mossi king gave battle to the inhabitants of Biro, vanquished them, and took them and their families into captivity. But, as he was returning to his country with his booty, the inhabitants of Biro followed and fought him, and freed their families. Omar-ben-Mohammed-Nadi, who was at Biro at this time, distinguished himself by his valor and ardor during the battle; for he was the first warrior to attack the Mossi king and thus force him to give up the families which had been captured.[2]

A few years later, the Mossi again invaded the area, this time making war on Sonni-Ali himself. The chronicler writes:

Then the prince Sonni-Ali undertook the task of digging a canal leading from Ras-el-Ma to Biro. He was devoting all his effort and a great deal of energy to this task when word reached him that the king of the Mossi had decided to make war on him, and was then leading the attack at the head of his troops. Sonni-Ali was at a place called Chan-Fenech when he heard this news, and he stopped work on the canal right there. God spared the inhabitants of Biro the misfortune which threatened them; for Sonni-Ali, going out to meet the king of the Mossi, made contact with him at a place called Djiniki-To'oi, situated near the town of Kobi behind the river. The battle took place there, and the victorious Sonni-Ali put the Mossi king to flight, and pursued him into his own country. That battle took place in the year 888 (1483).[3]

This battle seems to have represented the high point in the northern expansion of the Mossi, because the next reference to them in the *Tarikh es-Sudan* tells of Askia-El-Hadj-Mohammed's holy war against them. This man, who had usurped the throne from Sonni-Ali's heir, made a pilgrimage to Mecca, and when he returned he decided to convert the pagan masses of the Sudan to Islam:

During the year 903 (August 1497 to August 1498), he undertook an expedition against Na'asira, the king of the Mossi. He took with him the mallam, Mour-Salih-Djaaura, inviting him to give the necessary indications so that the expedition would be a veritable holy war made in the name of God. Mour did not refuse this request, and explained to the prince all the rules relative to the holy war. The prince of the faithful, Askia-Mohammed, then asked the mallam to be his envoy to the Mossi king. The learned holy man accepted this mission; he went to the country of the Mossi and delivered the letter of his master which called upon the king to embrace Islam. Before replying, the Mossi ruler declared that he wished first of all to consult his ancestors who were in the other world. Accompanied by his ministers, he went to the temple of the idol of the country. The learned holy man went there also, in order to see how one went about consulting the dead. They began by making the customary offerings; then a very old man appeared. At his appearance everyone prostrated himself and then the king announced the object of his visit. Calling upon the names of the ancestors, the old man said: "I will never agree to this step for you. On the contrary, you must fight until you or they die to the last man."

Then Na'asira replied to the mallam: "Return to your master and tell him that between us there will be only war and combat." Remaining alone in the temple with the personage who appeared in the form of an old man, the mallam questioned him in these words: "In the name of God Almighty I ask you to declare who you are." "I am Iblis [Satan]," replied the deceiving old man; "I have led them astray so that they will all die in a state of unbelief."

Mour returned to prince Askia-El-Hadj-Mohammed and reported all which had come to pass. "Now," he added, "your duty is to fight them." Straightway he launched his war against them, killed a number of their men, devastated their fields, plundered their habitations, and took their children into captivity. All of the men and women who were taken away as captives were made the object of divine benediction [converted to Islam]. In the entire country, no other expedition outside of this one had the character of a holy war made in the name of God.[4]

The rulers of the Songhai appear to have kept up their attacks on the Mossi during the following hundred years. One of them, Askia Daoud, launched an expedition against the Mossi in 1549 to celebrate his accession to the throne. He attacked and defeated them again in 1561 while on his way to attack Bornou, and their ruler "abandoned the country with all his troops."[5] After this and several other crushing defeats, the Mossi refrained from attacking Songhai territory. Their ardor for external adventures apparently cooled after this period, and there are no reports of their fighting anyone else except the Bambara of Segou in the eighteenth century.[6] Of course, Mossi chiefs made local forays among smaller neighboring groups such as the Busansi, Gurunsi, and Samogo, but only to catch slaves.

During the nineteenth century—a rather chaotic period in the western Sudan—the Mossi appear to have been immune from outside attacks. Crozat, who visited them in 1890, states: "From the very first, in Mossi country, one feels that one has entered a new land, more peaceful, richer, and more populous [than other African countries he had visited].... The people one meets on the roads are workers on their way to the fields, or are carrying wares to the neighboring market. They are not like the Songhai and the Bobo, who always carry bows on their shoulders."[7] The immunity of the Mossi from attack by such intrepid nineteenth-century warriors as El Hadj Omar and Samory Touré surprised and puzzled many of their early visitors. Binger explains it as follows:

> Thanks to the primitive tribes that surrounded them like a rampart, the Mossi were spared the incursions of their powerful neighbors. This immunity cannot last much longer, because [Mogho Naba] Sanum is weak, has little spirit, and is badly counseled.[8]

Binger was partly correct in attributing the immunity of the Mossi to the presence of weaker groups on their borders. To the military adventurers of the period, the Mossi must have appeared invulnerable when compared to their weaker neighbors. Nevertheless, the Mossi declare that it was their vigilance and willingness to fight that prevented Samory Touré, among others, from invading their country.[9] They claim to have captured and executed nine of the ten spies he sent to survey their territory. The one spy who returned allegedly told Samory Touré that the Mossi were too strong to be attacked, because they banded together against all outsiders.

Crozat attributes the Mossi freedom from attack to miraculous and magical factors:

> There is widespread belief in surrounding territories that Mossi country is inviolable. Alone amid the troubled populations that surround it, it enjoys relative peace. It owes this to the very special protection of a deity, and also to the virtues of the special talismans owned by the ruler of Ouagadougou. The terror inspired by these charms is such that some years ago the leader of Gadiari's column suffered a mass desertion of his men when he tried to lead them to the conquest of Mossi country. He himself was killed, perhaps by his own *sofas* [soldiers]. This case cannot be expected to undermine belief in these presumptuous charms.[10]

This statement, like Binger's, contains an element of truth, but not in the way that Crozat believed. The Ouagadougou kingdom did have a series of ritual pacts with neighboring Mossi and non-Mossi groups. Crozat found that Mogho Naba Sanum was on "good terms" with the people of Fada-N'Gourma. He tells us that this friendship was maintained by a "curious custom" whereby the Ouagadougou ruler sent wives, captives, and horses from his predecessor's estate to the ruler of the Gurmanche.[11] Similarly, Pinchon, a British officer stationed in the Gold Coast at the beginning of the century, reports that there existed an ancient pact between the Mossi and the Mamprusi. This pact kept the ruler of each country from attacking the other on pain of death by the ancestors. Like the pact between the Mossi and the Gurmanche, this agreement was sanctioned by an annual gift of a horse, slaves, and cloth from the Mossi to the Mamprusi. Pinchon speculates that it was the existence of this pact that induced the Mamprusi ruler to grant asylum to Mogho Naba Wobogo in 1897. He adds that it was probably the injunction in the pact that they should never meet which prevented the ruler from personally receiving Wobogo.[12]

A ritual pact also bound the Mogho Naba of Ouagadougou to the ruler of Dagomba. He sent him goods from the estate of the previous Mogho Naba as well as gifts for yearly sacrifices on the grave of Nyennega, the Mossi progenitrix. There are reports that the Ouagadougou ruler also exchanged annual presents with the Ashanti ruler, but it is not known whether these were courtesy gifts or goods sanctioning ritual pacts.

The ritual pacts among Mossi kingdoms and between them and their neighbors appear to have derived from actual or putative kinship ties. This seems to be supported not only by the traditions of the Mossi but also by those of the surrounding peoples. Whatever their origin, these pacts seem to have afforded their beneficiaries a remarkable degree of freedom from external aggression. It is possible that the Mossi and their neighbors really believed in the efficacy of supernatural sanctions, for purposes of mutual protection. But one suspects that it was the relative weakness of these various groups that caused them to rely on supernatural agencies rather than military might for protection. As will be pointed out below, the Mossi (and probably all of their important neighbors) had considerable difficulty in building and maintaining a fighting force sufficiently large to wage protracted or large-scale wars against foreign groups.

The Mossi kingdoms seldom fought among themselves, although their leaders quarreled over status and committed aggression against each other's territories. For example, the Ouagadougou rulers, who claimed suzerainty over Yatenga, often tried to impose their will on that kingdom. Yet, although they were usually rebuffed by the Yatenga Naba, they never tried to resolve the issue by force of arms. In fact, even when a Yatenga ruler appears to have given the Mogho Naba just cause for war, little fighting actually took place. Several times the Yatenga rulers seized such principalities as Riziam and Yako, which were dependent on Ouagadougou, but in no case did the Ouagadougou rulers wage war against them. In 1890, Crozat witnessed Mogho Naba Wobogo's attempt to stop a war between Yatenga and Yako. The Yako people wanted to obey their sovereign and stop the war, but the Yatenga monarch refused to do so.[13]

Crozat attributes the ineffectiveness of the Mogho Naba's authority over brother kingdoms to the fact that he had no standing army with which to enforce his rule. While relative strength may have been and probably was the main reason for the Mogho Naba's lack of aggressiveness, the ritual pact that prevented the Mogho Naba of Ouagadougou from meeting the

Yatenga Naba (and other rulers) or treading on his territory should not be overlooked. The suggestion that force was not the only consideration was lent force by later events. The French conquest later reduced the rulers of both Ouagadougou and Yatenga to impotence and obviated war between them, yet they did not meet until 1946—some fifty years after the conquest. They met then only because they had to represent their subjects at a meeting to plan the restoration of the Upper Volta and reunite all the descendants of Oubri and Ouedraogo into one territory.

Relative strength obviously played an important part in determining whether one Mossi kingdom interfered in the internal affairs of another. For example, when a Tenkodogo ruler asked a Mogho Naba to help him suppress Busansi subjects who had rebelled, the Mogho Naba readily complied.[14] But when a fratricidal struggle over the nam broke out in Tenkodogo in 1894, the Mogho Naba decided not to intervene even though he was asked to do so.[15]

The central governments of the various kingdoms found it necessary to wage war against their subordinate territories at regular intervals. In the Ouagadougou kingdom, most of these wars seem to have been administrative actions against a prince or district chief who had contravened an order from the Mogho Naba or refused to pay tribute. The Dimdamba were the Mogho Naba's most rebellious subordinates, and it was against them that he fought most of his wars. Characteristic of these wars was the series between Naba Ligidi (1866–90), Dim of Boussouma province, and Mogho Naba Sanum.[16] Ligidi had seized and turned over to the Mogho Naba the recalcitrant Naba Yemde, then Dim of Boulsa, and confiscated the rebel's property. Later on, when the Mogho Naba had made peace with Yemde's son, Naba Kiba, he asked Ligidi to surrender the seized property. Ligidi refused to do so, and the angry Mogho Naba sent the royal army into his territory. The army sacked and burned several villages and retreated. Ligidi's forces skirmished with the rear guard but abandoned pursuit near the Ouagadougou border.

Ligidi took his revenge by helping a district chief who had rebelled against Naba Kiba. While he was thus engaged, the royal army again attacked and defeated him. Four days later, it reinvaded Boussouma, engaged Ligidi's forces at a place called Goudri, and won a brilliant victory. Despite Ligidi's furious counter-attacks, the army captured his capital, Ouayougya. The ruler's army finally returned to Ouagadougou, satisfied that Ligidi was thoroughly beaten. But the Mogho Naba had underestimated Ligidi's tenacity. For the next ten years, this Dim waged war against his fellow Dimdamba. The Mogho Naba finally grew tired of his depredations and launched another expedition against Ouayougya. The expedition failed because of a lack of water, and the army was forced to return to Ouagadougou. The war would have continued had not both Mogho Naba Sanum and Ligidi died in 1890.

It appears that the Mogho Naba tolerated fighting among his immediate subordinates, and seldom intervened in local wars unless one of the combatants openly flouted his authority. For example, when the autonomous principality of Riziam attempted to wrest control of Salmetenga district from Boussouma province, Mogho Naba Doulougou did not intervene. He knew that Salmetenga owed allegiance to Boussouma, but was perfectly willing to allow its ruler to transfer allegiance to Riziam. When Boussouma was on the brink of defeat, the Salmetenga Naba fled to Ouagadougou to seek asylum. The Mogho Naba sent him back to Naba Piga, the Boussouma Dim, with the request that he be allowed to live. Piga was so angry with the chief that he ignored the Mogho Naba's request and executed him. This incurred the wrath of Mogho Naba Doulougou, and he sent an army to attack Piga. Fortunately for this disobedient Dim, the Mogho Naba died and the attack was called off.[17]

The reaction of Mogho Naba Koutou to fighting among his subordinates was more typical. He did not interfere in a long series of battles between the principalities of Riziam and Mane which culminated in 1866 when the Riziam people seized, imprisoned, and executed several Mane merchants who had gone to buy salt in Timbuktu. Mane appealed to its brother province of Boussouma for aid, and Riziam appealed to a Fulani chieftain for reinforcements. Before a battle could ensue, however, the Boussouma Dim, Naba Siguiri, died after drinking some millet beer, and the fighting was called off. Naba Kom of Mane then went off alone with his army, defeated the Fulani, and killed their chief, Sekki. When Ligidi (the chief mentioned above) succeeded his father, Naba Siguiri, he elected to continue the war against Riziam with the help of the Mane army, but the battle was inconclusive. The stalemate did not satisfy the bellicose Ligidi, who attacked Riziam once more in 1871, burning villages and seizing property. The Riziam people finally rallied and halted him. They ambushed his soldiers when they tried to retreat, and harried them so thoroughly that Ligidi had to call off the war when slaughter and thirst decimated his ranks.[18]

Similarly, Mogho Naba Sanum did not interfere when one of his own district chiefs, the Salogho Naba, was attacked and defeated by the ruler of Tema principality. Nor did he enter the fray when another of his district chiefs was attacked and defeated by the Boulsa Dim. The fighting in both cases was over women. The Tema Dim successfully defended his principality against a Zittenga district chief who not only had the effrontery to demand the return of a wife who had fled into Tema but also invaded the principality when she failed to return.[19] The Boulsa Dim attacked and defeated the Salogho Naba when he refused to repatriate a man and woman convicted of adultery who had fled into his district. It is possible that in each case the Mogho Naba refused to become involved in a squabble over women, but it is more likely that he refrained from participating in a local war that did not threaten the security of the entire country.

Many Dimdamba made it a practice to help each other in wars against common enemies. In the middle of the nineteenth century, Naba Zende of Tema and Naba Totoabo of Yako joined in a war against Naba Sebogo of La when Sebogo refused to repatriate one of Totoabo's wives, who had fled into his territory. The two victorious allies burned villages in La and forced Sebogo to flee for his life. They searched for the woman, but she was never found. The successors of the three rulers remained embittered by this war and eventually renewed the fighting. On this occasion, Naba Tanga of Tema and Naba Sagha of Yako fought against Naba Kombase of La. But this time Yako and Tema were unable to defeat La and had to withdraw. There is no evidence that the Mogho Naba of Ouagadougou took any part in these wars.[20]

The Mogho Naba appears to have taken a greater interest in wars between his Dimdamba and non-Mossi populations, and to have profited by them occasionally. When the followers of a Fulani chief named Karfo carried off some cattle belonging to the Boussouma people, the Boussouma Dim, Naba Siguiri, threatened war if the animals were not returned. Karfo not only refused to surrender the cattle but insulted Siguiri in his reply. Siguiri marched against the Fulani, killed Karfo, seized all the cattle he could find, and sent some of the "most beautiful animals" to Mogho Naba Koutou.[21]

Although the Mogho Naba tolerated wars among his Dimdamba, he apparently forbade the district chiefs under his direct command to fight among themselves. As we saw in Chapter IV, some such fighting did take place, but the Mogho Naba seems to have ignored it in most cases because of its relative unimportance. The Mossi, on the other hand, magnified this local fighting, which they called *tengkom* ("civil war"), and which consisted of mere skirmishes between villages or neighboring districts, with few casualties. In fact, the Gounga Naba once stopped a war between districts after only nineteen persons had died. But as a rule, districts seldom if ever fought among themselves. The actual combatants were villagers who fought the villagers of other districts over stray livestock, stolen goods, and runaway women, in that order of frequency.

The main reason for these inter-village wars was the lack of local mechanisms (aside from meetings of district chiefs) to deal with problems between villagers of different districts. If the district chiefs refused to meet, they could either refer the matter to the provincial level or allow the villages to resolve the problem among themselves. Many district chiefs preferred the latter course because it saved them from interference by the authorities in the capital. Besides, these problems were usually unimportant and did not pit one entire district against another. People of different districts were often bound to each other by familial and ritual ties, and did not like to fight against relatives. Only when the potential combatants were unrelated or all attempts at reconciliation failed would the people of a village (and occasionally of a district) band together, either secretly without their chiefs or under their chiefs, and go to war. In such cases, persons who had relatives in the enemy villages often remained at home.

The inhabitants of Mossi districts did band together eagerly under their chiefs to participate in slave-raiding expeditions into non-Mossi territories. This type of warfare seems to have been fairly common. Ruelle writes, "Before our [French] occupation, warfare was the chief preoccupation of the chiefs. Moreover, expeditions into Gurunsi country had as their goal pillage and the procurement of slaves for sale."[22] Similarly, Mangin states, "The Gurunsi and Busansi were frequently raided with the sole intent of obtaining slaves."[23] Binger gives the following description of a Mossi slave-catching expedition and the subsequent disposal of the slaves:

> During my second stay at Banema, Boukary [later Mogho Naba Wobogo], knowing my aversion to pillage and slavery and fearing to displease me, sent off two expeditions during the night without warning me—one to Nabouli, and the other towards the south to Baouer'a. By six o'clock in the morning of the following day, the returning horsemen were heralded by gunshots. Soon afterwards, a line of slaves of both sexes appeared, tied to each other by a cord slung around their necks. The expedition to Nabouli brought back seventeen slaves; that to Baouer'a brought only five, along with an ass laden with salt and a little cotton. As soon as these unfortunate people arrived, they were given water to drink, and mallets were used to remove the rings and copper bracelets which they wore on their arms and legs. Then they were classified into three categories:
> 1. The men formed a lot destined for immediate sale for fear that they should run away. They were led forthwith to Sakhaboutenga, to be exchanged against sorghum for the horses, millet for the personnel, and gunpowder.
> 2. A second lot, composed of women, was kept as a reserve to trade for horses.

3. Finally, a third lot, composed of young girls and young boys, was distributed among the warriors and put into their charge. The boys will be employed until further notice as grooms to the warriors; later on, those who prove themselves useful and docile will be kept. The others will be sold at the first opportunity. The girls will be given in marriage to warriors who distinguish themselves.[24]

The military campaigns of the Mossi, in contrast to their slave-raiding expeditions, appear to have been well organized. When the Mogho Naba felt that a war was necessary, he summoned his five provincial ministers and the Tansoba to a parley. If war was decided upon, the Tansoba was given full charge of all operations. This man, chosen from a hereditary clan of warriors who lived in a village called Tansob'tenga in Sapone district, was listed among the Mogho Naba's courtiers but seldom appeared at court unless war was imminent. His duties as chief warrior were considered so dangerous that he constantly sought out religious practitioners for supernatural aid. Nevertheless, a war minister who was good and brave was not expected to live very long. If he did live to become gray-haired, the other courtiers made fun of him by pretending that his graying head could only be the result of his having carried a sheep captured in warfare on his head as a present to the ruler.

Once given a mandate for war, the Tansoba collected his magico-religious apparatus and prepared the requisite sacrifices. He then asked the provincial ministers to notify the district chiefs to assemble with their warriors under the leadership of the local Tansobadamba, who were often members of the Tansoba clan. When the district chiefs received this notice, they beat their *zongagondo* (war drums), and the local administrators sent orders for men to the village chiefs. The village chiefs, in turn, beat their war drums to summon their noble cavalrymen and commoner foot soldiers, who came armed with bows and arrows, spears, swords, and clubs, with or without iron tips. The tips of the sharp weapons were often covered with a vegetable poison derived from a shrub of the Strophanthus species. Some of the men also carried guns after firearms were introduced among the Mossi from the desert region and from the coast. Many carried rawhide shields.

As soon as the village contingents had assembled and had gathered their provisions, they marched to the district centers. Then they proceeded either to the place of battle or to Ouagadougou. In the latter case, they became part of the royal army and were joined by the forces of those princes who were prepared to honor their obligation to the Mogho Naba. For example, when the French invaded Ouagadougou in 1896, the Boulsa Dim sent his prime minister "at the head of an army to aid Mogho Naba

Wobogo. However, he did not have to intervene, because while still en route he heard that Ouagadougou had fallen."[25] Thanks to this type of aid, the Mogho Naba was able to gather quite a large army, a fact that contradicts Crozat's belief that the Mogho Naba was a "king without an army."[26]

The early Mogho Nanamse used to accompany their armies into the field, but this practice was later abandoned and was revived periodically only by the more adventurous rulers. (The last ruler to die in warfare was Mogho Naba Doulougou [ca. 1800].) However, it was the Mogho Naba's duty to greet the army when it came to Ouagadougou, to beat the royal war drum, and to turn the troops over to the Tansoba. This officer served as commander in chief of the army, and was assisted by the Gounga Naba, a provincial minister, who served as his aide-de-camp. The Gounga Naba was expected to die rather than retreat in battle, especially if the Tansoba was killed. Two other ministers, the Kamsaogho Naba and the Larhalle Naba, also accompanied the army. The later Baloum Nanamse did not venture into battle, because they had to attend to the personal needs of the Mogho Naba. In early times, however, they accompanied their sovereigns into battle and fought alongside them. The Ouidi Naba never went to war, because it was his duty to look after the kingdom. He had to ensure the interests of all the people even if the royal army was defeated, the country invaded, and the ruler killed or forced to flee. The Samande Naba went to war and served as chief of the infantry.

Scouts preceded each district contingent as the army marched off to battle. Within the contingent, the younger warriors marched in front, followed by older men. It was the duty of the more experienced warriors to make sure that the younger men did not break ranks and run under the stress of battle. Behind the foot soldiers came the cavalry, composed of nobles and of the few commoners who possessed horses. Behind these came the district chief, surrounded by his own palace guard. Several heralds known as *yumba* (sing. *yuma*) accompanied the district forces to exhort them to fight. As the men marched to battle the yumba shouted:

> Men! Your ancestors were not slaves. They were men. They were stronger than anyone else. They did not bathe with water; they bathed with blood. Do you wish to return home to drink millet water and eat bread? Never! A man does not eat bread or drink millet water; a man fights. Your ancestors were not afraid of anyone; you must not be afraid of anyone. Even if you are killed today, you must march ahead, beat your enemies, and take their villages. You must not be afraid!

Mossi armies on the march used scouts to keep a sharp lookout for the enemy or for any evidence that he was aware of impending attack. The tactics these scouts used to avoid detection, such as camouflaging themselves with leaves and branches and crawling upon the ground, can be witnessed even today at Mossi funerals where men re-enact warfare practices. Whenever possible, the Mossi preferred to take the enemy by surprise, but this was seldom possible when large-scale fighting and massive preparations were involved.

When two Mossi armies drew up to each other, the heralds from both sides issued such challenges and epithets as: "If you men do not wish to die, you should run or you will never eat again. We will have your blood to wash with." In the meantime, the Tansobadamba on both sides deployed their forces in accordance with the number of men available, the spirit of the enemy, and the nature of the terrain. From the description of warfare given to me by an old Tansoba in Nobere district, it appears that the strategy most commonly used was to split the infantry in two while attacking, thus making room for the cavalry to charge through. If the initial charge was successful, the attack was maintained, but if it failed, the army usually turned about and fled. Despite their braggadocio, Mossi commanders seldom insisted that their troops fight against overwhelming odds. However, shame over impending defeat often induced such officers as the Tansoba and the Gounga Naba to fight to the death. For example, during the war between Boulsa and Fada-N'Gourma in 1897, the Boulsa army lost so many men that the Boulsa Dim wanted to commit suicide in his humiliation. However, he was prevented from doing so by one of his subordinates.[27]

Soldiers wounded by poisoned spears or arrows extracted the projectiles if possible, and kept on fighting until they died. Even if they were wounded by an unpoisoned weapon, they did not seek medical aid. Most wounded men believed that they were doomed, because their protective amulets had failed them. For the same reason, a defeated army fleeing a battlefield made no attempt to retrieve its dead and dying, but left them to the vultures. When an army was victorious, however, the Mossi either carried their dead home for burial or buried them on the battlefield, saving some item of their clothing or equipment for the funeral.

Victorious Mossi armies usually pursued the enemy, burning villages as they went. The soldiers killed all the infants and the infirm, and when they fought against non-Mossi, they captured young people to be sold as slaves. Then they collected all the available booty and departed hurriedly, fearing that the confiscated cattle and slaves would slow their return and enable the rallied enemy to catch up with them.[28] If the army could not return home before dark, camp was set up for the night near a body of water so that the Tansobadamba could offer thanksgiving sacrifices. Pickets were later posted to alert the troops in case the enemy should attempt an attack at dawn. If the war was waged against foreigners, individual soldiers were allowed to keep a slave or a cow out of the booty; the remainder was divided between the district chiefs and the central government. In victorious civil wars against the enemies of the Mogho Naba, however, the entire booty was sent to the capital.

When the Mossi had to defend their own territory, their most common tactic was to evacuate the villages. This was the technique most often employed against invading French forces.[29] Other defenses included palisaded villages, barricades of fallen trees, trenches, and hedges, some with poisoned foot traps. Mangin reports that the Boulsa were defeated in their war with Fada-N'Gourma not only because their enemies fought valiantly, but also because they "were favored by very propitious terrain covered with thorny scrub, behind which the besieged men took cover to shoot on the Mossi."[30] Mangin does not say whether the scrub was poisoned, but his data indicate that this type of defense was common in the area. The Mossi say that the use of poisoned prickly plants (*silenage*) against invading forces dates back to the early conquest of the territory. Tradition recounts that Naba Oubri was unable to conquer Ouagadougou until his Ninisi wife advised him to shoe his soldiers against the poisoned foot traps of the aborigines.

Mossi wars or raids were usually limited to the dry season and stopped at the beginning of the planting season. Commenting on the war between Boulsa and Fada-N'Gourma, Mangin tells us: "This was during the dry season. Thirst completed what the courage of the Gyekango people had begun, and many Mossi perished."[31] Tradition recounts that it took Mogho Naba Waraga five successive years of attack before he defeated Ramzi, the rebellious chief of Riziam principality. He finally defeated him when his army attacked the province before its people had been able to harvest their crops and retire into an impregnable fortress for the dry season. Judging by the reports of European visitors, this type of dry-season warfare continued as late as the 1890's. For example, Crozat could not understand why the Mogho Naba did not send an army to defeat the chief of Lalle district, who had imprudently raided a village near Ouagadougou, and he concluded that the ruler did not have an army. The fact is, however, that Crozat was in Ouagadougou between September 9 and September 30, a period when the potential soldiers of the Mogho Naba had not yet harvested their crops. Had Crozat remained in Mossi country for three or four months longer, he would have seen the ruler's army in action; for, as a matter of fact, the Lalle Naba's attack on Mogho Naba Wobogo was but the latest episode in a prolonged struggle between the two rulers.

For several years Mogho Naba Sanum had tried unsuccessfully to corner and defeat the rebellious Lalle Naba. Then one dry season the Mogho Naba called his Tansoba and said to him:

> "I want you to assemble immediately an army composed only of courageous men, to go to Lalle and bring me, alive, Tanga [also called Wobogo], chief of that district." Several thousand men, eager for glory, were gathered, and the army advanced against Lalle. It managed to burn Siguele, Tanga's residence, but did not capture the chief, who had fled to Koudougou. The royal army would have pursued him, but because the rainy season was imminent, and the men were needed to work in the fields, the army returned to Ouagadougou with a considerable amount of booty. The king received his war minister very kindly, because he foresaw the impending defeat of his obstinate enemy. The Mogho Naba then said to his warriors, "Go and cultivate your fields, but remember that as soon as the harvest has been stored, you have to capture Tanga. Regardless of the cost, I must have him, even if all of you must die."[32]

Mogho Naba Sanum died before he could capture Tanga, and the task fell to his successor, Mogho Naba Wobogo, who fared no better. One dry season, the royal army chased the rebel into Gurunsi territory but failed to catch him. They would have continued the chase, but "it was during the rainy season, and the royal army was disbanded."[33]

Mogho Naba Wobogo never succeeded in capturing Tanga, because the French came in and conquered the Mossi. Nevertheless, the rebel did not go unpunished. After the French had completed their conquest they asked the Ouidi Naba what steps should be taken to ensure peace. He told them to capture and kill the Lalle Naba. This unfortunate chief was hunted down, captured, placed on an unsaddled colt, and brought to Ouagadougou, where he was publicly humiliated and then executed.

The episode with Tanga and the limiting of warfare to the dry season indicate that the Mogho Naba did not have the resources to maintain a standing army, and, therefore, had difficulty exerting his authority by the use of force. There is no doubt that the Mogho Nanamse were able to gather very large armies at specific times against both internal and external enemies, but when the planting period came the soldiers had to attend to their crops. This lack of resources also limited the power and authority of Mogho Nanamse over their autonomous subordinates. As a result, the Mossi kingdoms remained segmentary in nature, and became highly organized only at certain periods of their history.[34] The availability of military resources thus had a significant effect on the nature of the Mossi governmental and political system.

VII

THE ECONOMIC FOUNDATION

THE REVENUE for the support of the Mossi chiefs and their governmental system came from many sources in a variety of forms. The Mossi of Ouagadougou held that "the Mogho Naba is master of everything" (*Mogh Nab n so fa*), and when they referred to the control he and his chiefs exercised over their goods and services, they said, "The commoner rears his livestock for the chief," and cited the proverb "The snake gets whatever is in the belly of the frog."

Since the Mossi were, and still are, primarily an agricultural people, the products of the soil were the main source of revenue. The Mossi chiefs did not own the land, but they controlled it and assigned land rights to their subjects. The Mossi believed that land had no value apart from people, and, conversely, that people could not exist without land. As they said, "Land is the mother; it fed the ancestors of this generation; it feeds the present generation and its children; and it provides the final resting place for all men." Therefore, a Mossi chief never hesitated to give anyone permission to use unoccupied land. It was in his interest to do so, because the more subjects he commanded, the greater were his revenue and prestige. An unpopular chief was censured not by a withholding of tribute and presents, but by a mass exodus of his subjects to another area.

Through the administrative hierarchy, the common people contributed to the support of the various levels of government. The Mogho Naba periodically received agricultural produce from all his subjects. Through the village chiefs, the village people sent part of their produce to the district chiefs, who forwarded it to the provincial ministers. They, in turn, delivered it to the central government during a ceremony appropriately called "Soretasgho" ("completion of the road"). This event occurred at the end of the harvest festival, after all the crops had been gathered in.[1]

To open the ceremony, the provincial governors' retainers began to clear the paths leading from the governors' compounds to the palace, for they had become overgrown with grass and weeds during the rainy season. This clearing was done to within a few yards of the palace, but was not completed. Early in the morning of the day chosen for the actual rendering of the agricultural tribute, the retainers placed baskets of produce along these paths. During the morning ceremony, the Ouidi Naba presented a basket of millet to the Mogho Naba. Then the Bendere Naba, acting as Sore Naba ("chief of the road"), signaled on his drum, and the men with baskets who were waiting on the uncleared portion of the paths, preceded by drummers and men with hoes, axes, and other tools, began to move forward. The men in the processions raised a din, shouting, singing, drumming, and pretending that the task of clearing was very difficult. From time to time, the more energetic among those who were not carrying bundles ran ahead of the others, turned somersaults, and then, going through the motions of warriors in battle, pranced back into the procession. All the processions came to the shed occupied by the royal drummers and deposited their burdens. These were later retrieved by the palace staff and stored for use in the royal household.

The royal household was also supplied with produce grown by the royal wives. Foodstuffs for guests and fodder for the ruler's horses were provided by the people of the Bilbalgo and Dapoya wards, which were under the general supervision of the Kam Naba. Two or three times during the agricultural season, this official recruited extra help from these wards to help cultivate the fields. In recompense for this *sosogha* (work bee), the laborers were given food, drink, and kola nuts from the royal household. At the end of the year, the harvesting and threshing of the grain from the Mogho Naba's fields was the occasion for an elaborate ceremony, "Mogh Nab' kawinre" ("threshing the ruler's grain").[2]

To begin this ceremony, the Mogho Naba summoned a local earth-priest, the Manougoudougou Tengsoba, to the court. This man, a descendant of the Ninisi, had to perform the propitiatory sacrifices to the earth deity who was symbolized by the threshing floor. After the sacrifices were completed, the Kam Naba went to the threshing floor with the young men of the Bilbalgo and Dapoya wards, who threshed the millet gathered there. The next morning they all returned to the threshing floor with the Bendere Naba and his minstrels, who recited the Mogho Naba's genealogy and sang praises to his ancestors. The drummers then beat out work rhythms and traditional drum patterns to which the workers danced while scattering the millet far and wide. Finally, the dancing stopped, and the Kam Naba drew a line on the threshing floor, dividing the pile of millet in two; the Bilbalgo people gathered one half, the Dapoya people the other. Regardless of the amount of millet harvested from the Mogho Naba's fields, there had to be one hundred baskets full of grain. If the number of baskets filled with the Mogho Naba's grain fell short of the mark, the serfs and slaves had to make up the difference with the produce of their own fields. The ceremony concluded with sacrifices to the royal ancestors, after which the Mogho Naba's wives, daughters, and sisters gave beer and kola nuts to the laborers.

As head of the central government, the Mogho Naba received revenue in the form of money and livestock which the district chiefs collected from the village people. These were given to him during an elaborate annual ceremony called the "Basgha" ("feast of the royal ancestors"). Several days before this post-harvest festival, the district chiefs and their retainers arrived in the capital and lodged with their provincial ministers. At a designated time during the ceremony, the district chiefs and nobles went to the palace. In provincial contingents and led by their ministers, they walked up to the sovereign's throne and gave the Mossi salute. After they had returned to their places, their servants gave the royal pages the presents they had brought to the palace.

The Dimdamba apparently made their annual contribution to the Mogho Naba at the time of the Basgha. There is one report that they took this opportunity to send gifts to the ruler's son, the Djiba Naba, as well. The Dimdamba customarily sent the Mogho Naba part of the goods they had seized in combat against non-Mossi peoples, as well as a tax (*fado*) out of the goods they had inherited from their predecessors.[3] There is also some evidence that the Mogho Naba solicited goods from the Dimdamba at other times. Crozat says:

> During my first visit to Yako, three envoys from Ouagadougou were at the chief's house. They were tax collectors. They had come to offer the vassal a silver bracelet sent by the sovereign. The Yako Naba responded by sending horses, captives, and cowries to Ouagadougou.[4]

Crozat could not understand this reciprocity between the Mogho Naba and his vassals, and questions whether the Mogho Naba really collected taxes from them. He concludes that the Mogho Naba did receive taxes, "but these are never given to him except in the form of presents which are reciprocated."[5] Crozat found it puzzling and disturbing that many of the Dimdamba had not given the Mogho Naba any "taxes" for several years. He indicated, moreover, that they did not wish to pay taxes to the Ouagadougou ruler even under the guise of an exchange of presents. This was especially true of the Yatenga Naba, who had not sent the Mogho Naba any presents for six or seven years prior to 1890. Crozat surmised that because of this delinquency, the Mogho Naba might hesitate to come to the aid of any of his vassals if a general war broke out. It is true that the Mogho Naba did not aid the Yatenga ruler when the French arrived. But whether this was because of his failure to pay taxes, or because the French conquest of the Yatenga coincided with a civil war there, we shall probably never know. We do know that many of the Mogho Naba's vassals came to his aid when the French finally arrived at Ouagadougou. It is my opinion that the gifts exchanged between Yatenga and Ouagadougou were not "tributary," but were more in the nature of tokens of friendship between two peers.

The Mogho Naba and his provincial ministers also received revenue as a function of their judicial roles. The nature and disposition of the fines levied against legal offenders were discussed in Chapter V. The Mogho Naba's fees came in the form of the traditional gifts the litigants gave him even before their cases were tried. These gifts were never regarded as bribes, for this would have contradicted the Mossi axiom that "the truth is at Ouagadougou."

The Mogho Naba inherited all the property of the Kamsaogho Naba, and claimed all the property of district chiefs who died without close relatives. He also received inheritance taxes (fado) from the estates of deceased district chiefs. In collecting the fado, the Mogho Naba first retained the horse on which the messenger came to announce the chief's death. He reciprocated by sending envoys with cowries and animals to be offered to their common ancestors at the chief's funeral. After the funeral, the envoys claimed the dead chief's quiver of arrows to take to Ouagadougou for deposit with those of other dead chiefs. Then they demanded the fado, and jestingly told the heirs that the Mogho Naba would be satisfied with nothing less than "a thousand of everything" (*tusri bumbu fa*) the deceased had possessed: wives, slaves, horses, cows, goats, chickens, articles of clothing, and so on. The heirs pleaded poverty and jokingly gave the envoys a few old and sickly animals, old chickens, tattered pieces of clothing, etc. Eventually, they handed out the fado, which usually consisted of livestock, clothing, food, weapons, jewelry, cowries, and even slaves. Lastly, they gave the envoys the chief's ceremonial horse and presents for themselves.

The Mogho Naba and his ministers collected a considerable amount of revenue from the traders who visited Ouagadougou and the larger market towns and village markets throughout the kingdom.[6] The Mossi (especially the assimilated Yarse) were good traders, and they benefited from their country's strategic location between the Sahara and the forest regions. According to Barth, some six caravan routes crossed the country, linking the Niger River area to the Gold Coast and Togoland. Important stops were made at such Mossi centers as Ouagadougou, Bere, Dakay, La, Mane, Yako, and Koupela.[7] At Dori, northwest of Ouagadougou, Barth found Mossi with "their fine donkeys, which are greatly sought after." He adds that in addition,

> the people of Mossi supply this market with gabaga, or "tari" [cotton bands], as Arabs near Timbuktu call them, cotton being extremely cheap in their country, so that in the great market places of that country, especially in Kulfela [Koupela, but really at Poitenga a few miles away], an indigo-colored shirt is not worth more than from 700 to 800 [cowry] shells. . . . Besides salt, cotton strips, dyed cloth, kola nuts, corn, and asses, some copper manufactured chiefly into large drinking-vessels is also brought into the market by the people of Mossi. However, I do not think they manufacture the copper vessels themselves, but bring them from Ashanti.[8]

Dubois, one of the early visitors to Timbuktu, tells us that he saw Mossi men carrying on their traditional trade in that city. Mossi traders dealt in such diverse commodities as millet, rice, manioc, peanuts, honey, kola nuts, peppers, dried onions, tobacco, dried fish, soap, iron, antimony, lead, cotton bands, straw hats, mats, jars, pots, and calabashes. They traded these articles for needles, mirrors, beads, coral, amber, tea, coffee, perfumes, carpets, fezzes, tailored robes, and salt. What impressed Dubois most was that while the merchants from Bamako, Djenne, Sansanding, and Touat enjoyed themselves at Timbuktu, "the great town of pleasures with the freest morals in the Sudan," and spent a great deal of money in gifts to beautiful women, "the Mossi did not waste their money, and left as soon as they had finished their business."[9] On the way south, Mossi and other caravaneers picked up goods from the Yatenga and other northern Ouagadougou provinces before stopping at the capital and then proceeding to the forest regions.

It is impossible to determine the exact volume of caravan trade that passed through Mossi country, and the amount of revenue it brought to the Mossi rulers. We can get some idea of this trade, however, by examining the customs reports on goods crossing the border between Mossi country and the northern territories of the Gold Coast in the few years just following European conquest.

The official figures for 1901 and 1903 are as follows:[10]

Year	Horses	Head of Cattle	Sheep and Goats	Loaded Donkeys	Bales of Cotton Cloth
1901	126	3,111	18,181	2,095	236
1903	196	6,624	30,392	4,294	269

Marc, who had the opportunity to check the volume of this trade in 1904 and 1905, estimates that about 16,000 head of cattle and 75,000 sheep and goats passed through the two customs posts in Mossi country. Furthermore, he believes that since "the Mossi also supply in part the markets of Togoland and the market at Bondoukou [Ivory Coast], one may assume a minimum annual export of 20,000 head of cattle and 100,000 sheep or goats. The import of kola nuts is at least 500 tons."[11] It is clear that this volume of trade could not have been achieved so soon after the French conquest. We can only conclude that it existed prior to the coming of the Europeans, and that it brought the Mossi rulers a considerable income.

The Mogho Naba's officials collected taxes from all caravans that passed through his capital. The caravaneers also gave the Mogho Naba important gifts, and he apparently traded with them, even if always to his own profit. Binger states that Mogho Naba Sanum forced horse traders from the Yatenga and Hausa merchants to sell him part of their commodities at one-hundredth the purchase price.[12] Crozat reports that Mogho Naba Wobogo

> appears to have had some business relations with white merchants who came to Salaga every dry season. He sent horses to them in exchange for silver. He claims that he had no reason to be pleased with their integrity, and that the silver they sent him contained plenty of copper. Some traders apparently came as far as Ouagadougou, bringing merchandise of German origin. There was one of them there during my stay. I was told that he was an important *marabout,* a shereef, perhaps an Arab or a Moor, for I was assured that he was very light in color. As was repeated to me several times, his relations with the king were limited to the solemn greetings on Fridays. He never entered the royal hut in spite of being an important marabout. He was at Ouagadougou for about three and one-half months, but he was compelled to return to the coast since the merchandise which he had brought was exhausted. He spoke no Mossi.[13]

All the caravans that passed through Mossi country were obliged to stop and give presents to the district officials. Those caravaneers who tried to elude taxation by going through the forest ran the risk of being attacked by local nobles, who usually confiscated their goods.

The Mogho Naba and the lesser chiefs had "market officials" who taxed the merchants in the markets of their territories. The officials at Ouagadougou, the Kos Naba ("sales chief") and the Raga Naba ("market chief"), were fairly rigorous in their exactions. The Kos Naba collected taxes in cowries for every cow slaughtered at the market, and also took its hump and gave it to the Nemdo Naba ("meat chief") for distribution in the royal household. He also collected taxes on every cow sold in the market, but did not usually tax goats and sheep. In lieu of this, he occasionally took one or two of these animals from each herd that passed through the market and sent them to the palace kitchens. Donkeys sold in the market were taxed at the rate of 200 cowries each. Horses sold to the nobility were not taxed, but those exported were.

The Raga Naba collected taxes on the other commodities sold at the market. Cotton weavers paid him according to the size of their bolts of cloth, and cotton growers paid taxes on the sales of their raw produce. The tailors and dyers paid no fixed amounts, but were asked to send clothing to the palace. Every donkey- and ox-load of salt entering the market place was taxed. The smiths were not taxed in cowries, but had to supply the Mogho Naba's wives with hoes and the palace personnel with arrowheads, spear points, and iron clubs. The jewelers also sent bracelets as presents to the ruler. There were no fixed taxes on the cereals, vegetables, and cooked food sold at the market, but each day the Raga Naba, accompanied by several pages or retainers carrying baskets, went from vendor to vendor taking several calabashes of their produce for use in the palace. In addition, the vendors of cooked food had to feed the Mogho Naba's young grooms, who were not normally fed by the palace household. The beer sellers were not formally taxed, but they contributed a substantial percentage of their beverage to palace and market personnel, who demanded the customary *lembgha* ("taste before buying") more frequently and freely than ordinary buyers.

There is some evidence (mainly from European travelers) that the traders occasionally found the caravan and market taxes prohibitive. Binger reports that the high taxes exacted by the Mogho Naba were "one of the reasons why Ouagadougou placed second [as a market town] and Mane was the commercial capital of Mossi country." Binger himself was caught in the institutionalized gift system and wrote sarcastically: "On market day [at Ouagadougou] the receipts are good. People bring everything to the palace, whether it be millet, hoes, or peanuts, and everything is accepted. *All this giving is left to the discretion of the donors.*"[14] The italics are Binger's.

Some of the later Mogho Nanamse appear to have obtained a great deal of revenue through the sale of slaves. Most of these slaves were captured in raids among the smaller groups surrounding Mossi territory, such as the Samo, Gurunsi, and Busansi populations. According to Mangin, Gurunsi and Busansi countries were true granaries for the Mossi, who drew upon them according to their needs.[15] In early times the Mossi chiefs utilized these slaves (*yemse*, sing. *yamba*) as agricultural workers, until Mogho

Naba Baongo (ca. 1800–30) decided that it was more profitable to sell them.[16] Subsequent rulers, especially the two Mogho Nanamse who ruled just prior to the French conquest, sold most of their captives to passing caravans or in special sections of the larger markets. When other persons sold slaves in the market, the Raga Naba collected some 1,000 cowries on each transaction—the largest tax on any market commodity.

The Mossi rulers seem to have benefited even more from the sale of eunuchs, for they had a monopoly over them. The Mogho Naba of Ouagadougou sent some captured slaves and all recidivous thieves to Teemetenga village in Koubri district, some 13 miles south of the capital, to be operated upon.[17] So successful were the Mossi surgeons that—in contrast to specialists in other areas, who lost nine lives for every successful castration—the mortality among the Mossi was only one out of ten.[18] Some of the eunuchs furnished by the Mossi were sold as far away as Constantinople, a fact which surprised the French ambassador to Turkey who saw them there in 1900.[19]

In addition to slaves and eunuchs, the Mogho Naba kept a large number of bondsmen to provide services for him. One group, the Dapore, lived in a ward of the capital called Dapoya, and had a chief, the Dapore Naba, who was himself a Dapore. The origin of these people is obscure, but they seem to have been the children of foreign captives who were brought to Ouagadougou and placed in the ruler's service. Some of them even claimed that their ancestors had come to Ouagadougou voluntarily and had placed themselves under the care and protection of the ruler. This seems unlikely, however, since the status of these people resembles that of persons captured by Sudanese rulers and installed in special wards as serfs.[20] Some of the Dapore lived in villages of their own and cultivated fields for the Mogho Naba. Others lived in a ward of Ouagadougou, served in the palace household, and provided the royal executioners. Some were selected to serve as palace eunuchs, and placed under the charge of the Kamsaogho Naba. The Dapore were hardly ever sold unless they were convicted criminals. The Mogho Naba and his chiefs refrained from selling serfs or captives who had been born in Mossi country. However, they often claimed the sons and daughters of these people as pages or pughsiudse.

The Baglere made up the second group of bondsmen providing services for the Mogho Naba. They, too, lived in a special ward and were headed by the Baglere Naba, one of their own people. Their origin is also obscure: some of them claimed to be descended from Fulani slaves who had run away from their masters and sought asylum in Mossi country; others believed that they were the descendants of foreign captives. The Baglere worked for the Mogho Naba in and around the palace courtyard, and in the fields. They also kept his herds and provided him with animals from their own herds. Like the Dapore, they were seldom sold, but they often had to give their sons and daughters to the Mogho Naba.

The last group of persons who contributed their services to the Mogho Naba were the Kamboinse. Their origin is also unclear. Most of my respondents claimed that the Kamboinse and their chief first came to Ouagadougou from the direction of the Gold Coast, that they bore guns, and that they offered their services as guards to the Mogho Naba.[21] Later on, the sovereign allegedly assigned slaves to the Kamboinse unit, with the result that the entire group eventually took on a serf-like character. The Kamboinse guarded the Mogho Naba's palace and seized for him the goods of persons whom he condemned to death.

The services performed for the Mogho Naba by his pages and other youthful retainers also contributed significantly to the support of his administration. We have already seen how these young men and boys took care of his every need and functioned as important messengers within the royal household. The Mogho Naba also had control over the daughters of his serfs, whom he used to obtain revenue from aliens and subjects alike. Periodically, the Mogho Naba gave one of these girls as pughsiudga to a man, thus obligating him to render goods and services to the court. Moreover, the man had to return the eldest daughter he had by this wife to the Mogho Naba as a future pughsiudga. In this way, the sovereign had a revolving store of women through whom he could bind men to himself in a nexus of obligations, and from whom he eventually received additional women.[22]

The provincial ministers of the Ouagadougou kingdom occupied such a strategic position within the central administration that anyone rendering gifts or tribute to the Mogho Naba always gave presents to them as well. Their main source of revenue, however, came from the villages under their direct control, and from the retainers who lived in their compounds and in their wards in the capital. The economic relations between the ministers and their villages were similar to those between the district chiefs and their villages, and will be discussed below. The retainers, serfs, and slaves who served these ministers provided them with many of the services their counterparts rendered to the Mogho Naba. They kept their houses in repair and provided them with firewood and with fodder for their horses. Many of them also cultivated fields for their masters. Whenever the ministers needed extra goods or services, they called on those persons who lived in their compounds or in their wards. For example, hundreds of persons lived in Ouidin, the ward of the Ouidi Naba. Some of them were related to him; others had been attracted by his wealth and by his ability to obtain wives for his charges. All of them benefited from being attached to him in one way or another, and in return helped him to augment his income.

All the district chiefs sent women to their provincial ministers to be kept as wives (and thus as agricultural workers), or to be given out as pughsiudse. The Kamsaogho Naba received more pughsiudse than the other ministers because he was in charge of the wealthier districts, and also of course distributed more. The Baloum Naba was especially favored in another respect. Each year, he was entitled to call several *seghse* (sing. *seka*; a corvée or convocation) of his former pages and their relatives to help cultivate his fields. The Ouidi Naba's sources of revenue were about the same as the Baloum Naba's. In addition, his position as chief minister enabled him to obtain numerous gifts from persons who visited Ouagadougou. Moreover, the Mogho Naba often gave him horses from the fado of deceased district chiefs. The Larhalle Naba had full ministerial privileges, and a few other means of obtaining revenue. He was allowed, for instance, to keep the animals that had not been sacrificed on the graves of deceased rulers.

The provincial ministers received many goods and services from the district chiefs of their provinces. Whenever one of these ministers sent a messenger to the district, the chief gave the messenger money and livestock for his master. Furthermore, the district chiefs brought presents for their minister when they paid their annual visit to Ouagadougou to render homage to the Mogho Naba. The provincial ministers used their position as confidants and advisers to obtain as many presents as possible from persons who came to Ouagadougou to ask special favors from the Mogho Naba, to participate in judicial proceedings, or to seek the nam. Moreover, they cooperated with each other in these exactions, so that a person seeking a favor from or through one minister was prudently advised to give presents to or to seek the aid of the others.

The district chief played a key role in the procurement of revenue for the central administration, and derived an income for himself in the process. The seignorial rights over the Mossi people delegated by the Mogho Naba to all nam holders were quite obvious on this level. The district chief had rights to all valuable fruit trees, such as locust-bean and shea-butter, that grew within the boundaries of his territory. He instructed the village chiefs to harvest the fruit of these trees and send it to him. The village chiefs even had to send him the wood from the fallen branches of these trees.

The district chiefs did not often exercise their rights over fruit trees in the weogho, as the wasteland in their districts was called. If a villager went into the weogho and collected fruit or wood from the chief's trees, he surrendered only part of it to the chief. On the other hand, if he received permission from a district chief to farm in the weogho, he was obliged to gather and send to the chief the fruit on any valuable trees. A district chief sometimes granted the rights over certain fruit trees in the inhabited areas to specific families or individuals, for personal reasons or as a reward for services. In such cases, the chief forfeited his rights to these trees, but retained his rights to the others.[23]

District chiefs also controlled all the resources of creeks and pools within their jurisdiction that were not sacred to certain aboriginal families, or which had not been transferred to specific persons. The aboriginal Ninisi families always notified the district chief when they planned to perform their annual fishing rite to the earth deities. He, in turn, sent representatives to the ceremony, and they were given part of the catch as his share. Persons who were granted permission to fish in the chief's water holes gave him a substantial part of their catch, and even those persons who had private control of fishing places regularly did the same.

The district chiefs also had rights to certain parts of animals caught in their territories. This applied especially to animals caught with such traditional weapons as traps, clubs, bows and arrows, and spears. Men who had obtained flint guns and other firearms from the Ashanti or elsewhere and who had bought their own powder were not obliged to give the chief a part of their game, but it was always prudent to do so. According to a long-standing tradition, the tusk and legs of a slain elephant that were not resting on the ground belonged to the chief, and those that lay on the ground belonged to the Tengsoba in whose ritual jurisdiction the animal had been slain. But the district chief's secular power was so much stronger than the Tengsoba's sacred power that he usually took both tusks, leaving the Tengsoba only two legs. The district chief also received other portions of elephants and parts of all the larger animals killed in his territory. And when hunters in the district were successful in the chase, they usually gave him entire small animals.

Every village in a district contributed to the district chief's revenue by performing special services for him. Certain villages were responsible for keeping specific huts in his compound in good condition; others, whose lands bordered on the woods, had to provide firewood for his compound; and yet others furnished grass and other fodder for his horses. Many villages had the task of cultivating special fields and crops for the district chief.

For example, the villagers of Barkago traditionally cultivated and harvested a field of millet behind his compound for the chief. The people of Pinse, Donse, Passingtenga, and Tewarka cultivated millet for him in their own villages, and those of Togose and Basbedo cultivated rice for him in their excellent lowlands.

The district chief had fields both behind his compound and in the bush, which were cultivated for him by his retainers, serfs, and slaves. More than the Mogho Naba and the provincial ministers, the district chief believed that a Moaga must perform agricultural work during the planting season; to show his interest in farming, he often personally supervised the work on his plantations. When the task of weeding or harvesting proved too much for his own people, he asked his villages for a *sosogha*. On that day, each village chief, accompanied by his men, went to the district chief's fields, where, to the accompaniment of drums and chants and with the verbal encouragement of district administrators, the villages vied with each other in their task. The district chief usually sat under a tree and watched the proceedings and occasionally visited the various contingents to observe the progress made. Toward evening, the chief's wives gave the workers large quantities of food and drink in compensation for their services.

Like the Mogho Naba, the district chief had officials who collected taxes on commodities sold in local markets. These district market officials were usually serfs, Gurunsi captives, or bondsmen from other populations. Mossi rarely served in such capacities because many of the local market places were considered ritually dangerous, and their titular deities, the Tengkouga, were believed to wreak vengeance on market officials who were tardy with sacrifices. The local Kos Naba supervised the slaughtering of every animal killed in the market, kept its skin so that its ownership could be verified if necessary, and collected taxes from the butchers in the form of meat or cowries. The Raga Naba of the district was not as strict as his counterpart in Ouagadougou, and seldom imposed formal taxes on the traders. He usually walked around the market, trailed by the chief's servants, and seized calabashes of grain and other commodities, which he placed in the servants' baskets. The Raga Naba did not tax those itinerant traders or caravaneers who visited the markets in the district, nor did he interfere with them in any other way. These merchants usually had business and personal relations with the chief, and he himself handled revenue from this source. The merchants gave him goods from the forest and Sahara regions, and he in turn often gave them wives, who were thus taken out of the district.

The Mossi district chief was always on the lookout for new sources of revenue, and thus welcomed strangers into his district because they "increased his force" and ultimately added to his income. Men who had been compelled to flee from other districts because of crimes or power struggles were granted refuge and given pughsiudse. In this manner, the district chief, like the Mogho Naba, established seignorial rights over his new subjects, incorporated them into the district, and obtained goods and services from them. The better a district chief's reputation, the greater the number of refugees who sought shelter with him and added to his wealth. Conversely, a chief who was known for his injustice, his rascality, and his excessive demands from persons seeking the village nam was shunned by potential subjects and might even be deserted by his own.

Those persons who visited the district chief's compound to settle court cases also contributed to his revenue. When the case dealt with cattle or other livestock, the chief received a few animals. In other cases, he received only the customary gifts from the litigants. He also received gifts from all the families in his district several times a year. One occasion was the "Tense," a festival in honor of the mother of Mogho Naba Oubri, the founder of the Ouagadougou dynasty; the other was the Basgha. During these two ceremonies every village chief, preceded by his district administrator and followed by his subjects, paid homage to the district chief and gave him presents. The district chief retained part of what he received for the upkeep of his household and to fulfill such obligations as hospitality to travelers, and added the remainder to his own annual tribute to the Mogho Naba.

The manner in which the district chief collected his annual tax or tribute for the Mogho Naba is the subject of controversy. Several of my respondents declared that the collection of this tribute was rather informal. The district chief allegedly notified the village chiefs that he wished to give a present to the Mogho Naba, and these chiefs sent word to the family heads, who, in turn, notified every household. The village people then collected chickens and livestock, baskets of grain, and cowries, and sent them up through the hierarchy to the district chief. The district chief's retainers checked the gifts from each village very carefully, and if some villages gave less than was expected of them, the district chief summoned their chiefs for explanations. In most cases the district chief knew exactly how much could be expected of his subjects, because his informers—usually his own pages and courtyard servants, or messengers of the local administrators—kept him informed of the wealth of each hamlet. Usually, a village chief who had withheld too much from the commodities turned over to him, or who had not demanded sufficient goods from his villagers, sought to make amends. It was in his interest to do so, since it was always dangerous to incur the district chief's wrath. Thus, there was some method in the collection of this tribute and certain expectations had to be met, even though many of the contributors may have felt that their gifts were voluntary.

In direct contrast, Dim Delobson, himself a chief, states that Mossi chiefs demanded a stipulated amount from their villagers. He adds, however, that the tribute "varied in amount according to the resources of the contributors," and that the district chief set the "amount of cowries and grain due from each village in accordance with the number of its inhabitants."[24] According to him, the rate of assessment was usually 100 cowries for a married man and 50 for an adult bachelor (apparently, this difference was an acknowledgment of the woman's contribution to her husband's wealth). In addition, each adult male was assessed 10 baskets of millet of about 100 pounds each. Dim Delobson adds that to these exactions the district chief added his own contributions to the Mogho Naba, usually in the form of cattle.

It seems that Dim Delobson rationalized and regularized a rather informal system of contributions. The present-day Mossi declare that soil differences in the villages and variations in rainfall prevented a district chief from demanding a set tribute, because no one could tell whether a crop would be good or bad. Only a ruler's informers could tell him how much he should receive each year, and the chief based his exactions on this report. Several of my respondents agreed with Dim Delobson that the district chief provided mostly cattle for the annual tribute to the Mogho Naba, and that the village people furnished cowries, small animals, and grain.

A district chief was seldom wealthy, because he always had to use his revenue to fulfill unexpected obligations toward his subjects, his superiors in the political hierarchy, and his household. He had to be generous to his subjects, providing millet water, millet beer, and the more expensive imported kola nuts for those who visited and conferred with him daily. He was expected to provide food and shelter for the countless strangers who settled in his district, until they could provide for themselves. He also lodged and fed the messengers who brought him orders from the capital, and gave them gifts to take back to the provincial ministers. And he had to provide goods for the many members of his family who depended upon him. Finally, in the event of crop failure or famine in any of his villages, he had to provide grain from his granaries to feed the hungry. "How could he do otherwise? Was he not a 'father' to his people?"

The expectation that the district chief should provide hospitality to his subjects was so strong that those chiefs or princes who were deprived of an income for any reason often resorted to banditry to fulfil their obligations. Binger, who found Boukary Koutou (the future Mogho Naba Wobogo) living in exile for having led a rebellion against his brother, Mogho Naba Sanum, tells us:

> Boukary has no resources, and does not even have the advantage of receiving periodic tribute from several large villages. In order to subsist and to maintain a certain status, he is compelled to live by pillage and even by brigandage. From time to time, his horsemen make incursions into the outskirts of some Gurunsi or Kipirsi village, and carry off by surprise the inhabitants whom they find working the fields or looking for wood. His people also hide and lie in wait along the roads to capture any persons who may pass within their range. This type of behavior has given Boukary Naba a bad reputation. However, the people who understand his position forgive him, knowing the situation in which his brother has placed him. And, in spite of all this, he has numerous partisans, and many others who would be happy to see him gain power.[25]

Those district chiefs or princes who wished to retain their power legitimately were forced to be generous or run the risk of losing the allegiance and good will of their villagers, who were their ultimate supporters.

It is very difficult to generalize about the amount of revenue collected by a village chief. He did not receive any revenue from the land used by his villagers. He treated the weogho in his village in the same manner as the district chief. If some families grew too large and wanted to establish permanent residence in the village bush, they asked the chief for permission to settle there. However, many village chiefs had special areas of waste for their own use. They had usually received them as gifts from some district chief, and therefore had the right to collect tribute on any crops, firewood, or fish obtained from these lands.

The average village chief's main source of revenue was derived from the agricultural and other labor of his wives and relatives. A village chief received a number of wives from his subjects and from aliens living in his village. These women helped cultivate his fields. If their labor was insufficient he called a sosogha, to which he often invited his wives' relatives. Some chiefs also had serfs and slaves who helped cultivate their land and kept their cattle as well.

The village chief did not have the power to tax his subjects. Instead, he functioned as a channel through which commodities and services passed up the hierarchy and on to Ouagadougou. Many villagers voluntarily helped the chief to repair his huts and compound walls and to cut thatch for his roofs. Many gave him baskets of grain and other vegetable products after the harvest. They also visited him and gave him presents during the annual rites to his ancestors. In contrast to higher chiefs, however, the village head did not derive any revenue from his judicial functions. He could not levy a fine against any malefactor. However, his intermediary position between the villagers and the district chief did permit him to obtain some revenue whenever commodities moved from one level to the other.

The officials who administered the villages for the district chief received part of their revenue from the villages under their charge. These local administrators had no courts or retainers comparable to those at the provincial level. However, they did have a large number of wives who contributed valuable agricultural labor. These administrators were permitted to ask the village chiefs for sosose on their own fields several times during the planting season, but—unlike the district chiefs—they were not permitted to have the villagers cultivate special fields for them. In return for any help received, they had to provide food and drink for the workers.

The administrator received most of his revenue as a by-product of active duty in the villages. When he visited a village or transmitted a message to a village chief, he almost invariably received a sheep, a goat, a chicken, or some millet, from the village chief. He also acquired large quantities of goods during the village interregnum: he received gifts from the chief's heirs during the chief's funeral; he received additional presents when they took the fado to the district chief; he could prolong the interregnum in order to receive as many bribes as possible from contenders for the nam; and he was handsomely rewarded when the candidate he had backed was finally installed in office.

The extended family was the basic socio-economic unit supporting the Mossi political organization. The Yirisoba received land rights in his saka from his Sakakasma, who had obtained his rights from the village chief. An extended family in need of additional land would seek help from its Sakakasma or its Boodkasma. When the family no longer needed this land, it reverted to the lineage. If all the land granted to the lineage was already occupied, the extended family, through its lineage head, asked the village chief for more land. The chief usually granted this request, unless he had no more weogho available. In this case, the needy Yirisoba sometimes tried to borrow land from his non-kin neighbors. Such a step was not undertaken lightly, however. If a man borrowed land from his own lineage members or from the chief, the land rights reverted to its donors without difficulty. However, if he borrowed land from another lineage and either he or his benefactor died without assuring the return of the land, litigation often ensued. In some cases a man would seek land from his lineage brothers in another village, who let him use some of their land with their chief's permission. Some Yirisobadamba even asked their district chief for permission to use weogho in the district, and new hamlets arose in this way. A Yirisoba who could not obtain adequate land on which to grow food for his family left the district and sought land elsewhere, especially among his mother's patrilineage. However, village and district chiefs always tried to prevent this because they did not like to lose any of their subjects.

As director of economic activities in the household, the Yirisoba supervised the agricultural labor of his charges. It was he who directed the work of his wives, his sons, and his sons' wives, and supervised the care of the family herd. He provided the cotton, which was carded and spun by the women and woven by the men. It was also his task to ensure adequate clothing for the members of his household; and he sold excess commodities in order to buy salt, kola nuts, bracelets, foreign clothes, and other products imported from the forest and desert zones. In each case, the Yirisoba had to balance judiciously the requirements of his household against his obligations to the community and to the political hierarchy. He had to prevent economic rivalry among his sons, and especially among his sons' wives. He had to make sure that every married member of the household had sufficient time to provide goods and services for his own family, and that foodstuffs were distributed equitably among the wives. Finally, he had to use the resources of the household to build and maintain the nexus of socioeconomic relationships that provided wives for the male members of the household, and to meet his obligations to the political hierarchy.

The Yirisoba also had social and economic responsibilities toward the other members of his babissi and boodoo. He furnished labor and goods to needy lineage members and to non-relatives with whom he had marriage arrangements. Since much of this help was given on the basis of ultimate reciprocity, very little loss was involved. However, the relationship between commoner and noble families was quite different. In theory, the nobles had no claims on the property of the commoners; but in practice, they did claim such rights. Furthermore, commoner lineages often gave the nobles many more wives than the nobles returned. This inequality enabled the nobles to receive more goods and services from their marriage partners among the commoners than they gave in return. The nobles thus took advantage of their power as possessors of the nam, but even membership in the royal lineage did not exempt them from supporting the governmental services at all levels. This duty was incumbent upon every Moaga.

The Mossi people could not refuse to support their political organization, but often complained about having to do so. Many Mossi felt that their rulers were greedy and avaricious and received too many gifts. Some Mossi held that if the chiefs were not placated with goods and services, they might take the lives and property of their subjects. There are many stories of avaricious chiefs who convicted wealthy commoners of spurious crimes and had them executed or banished in order to seize their wealth. There are also stories of twin tricksters, Raogo, a boy, and Poko, a girl, two *enfants terribles* who always succeeded in outwitting and killing avaricious chiefs. When I asked a district chief to explain the significance of the Raogo and Poko tales, he replied that they were "meaningless stories told by children who do not understand how difficult it is for a chief to command and protect men." This remark prompted one of his officials to add that in olden days, people gladly supported the Mogho Naba and his chiefs in order to be safe from their enemies—a statement which might have been made by a conscientious government official anywhere. However, whether commoners or chiefs, all Mossi believed that men must have government, and that without it chaos would prevail.

The Mossi political organization was subject to severe strains. For one thing, its economic basis was not very strong. True, goods and services were channeled to the capital from the smallest areas, and in time this permitted the establishment of increasingly complex governmental structures. Nevertheless, the Mossi fiscal system was not highly developed, and much of the revenue the rulers received came to them in the form of legal fees and gifts. Moreover, most of these revenues were irregular in nature.

Despite this fact, the Mossi believed that their rulers were wealthy—and there can be no doubt that they were wealthier than their subjects. Nevertheless, visiting Europeans found little difference between the standard of living of the chiefs and that of the people. Binger would have us believe that Mogho Naba Sanum bragged so much about imaginary wealth, including 10,000 horses, that he "managed to convince himself of it."[26] Binger's subsequent remarks about Sanum's resources are illuminating even if somewhat biased, because they throw light on the economic basis of the Ouagadougou kingdom. He tells us that Sanum's revenues were

> not well regulated. He lives on gifts and offerings which people have brought him with the aim of obtaining justice, or to demand something from him. He sometimes sends a band of men to capture slaves in Kipirsi country, or at least supports such ventures. But these revenues, like those of all the black chiefs, are not sufficient, because these men are prone to squander their resources. As a result, these sovereigns are compelled to use expedients in order to procure horses and other commodities. Thus, like the rulers of Tieba, Pegue, and Kong, Naba Sanum still has captives in villages devoted to agriculture, but he does not take proper care of these villages. If he does not receive enough millet in the form of gifts, he must sell his slaves in order to procure it.[27]

Binger's statement about the "squandering" to which "all the black chiefs" are prone reveals his ignorance of the nature, role, and function of West African chiefs in general and of Mossi chiefs in particular. These men were often the center of redistribution systems that embraced their entire territory. The Mossi chiefs did not necessarily squander their resources when they used them to support their household, their administrative staff, and even visitors to their realm. A rather large portion of the millet the Mogho Naba received was not even used by his own household, but was held for gifts to visiting strangers. Binger himself benefited from the generosity of Mogho Naba Sanum, and he provides us with excellent data about how Boukary Koutou distributed his resources: "I can say that never has a chief given me food, kola nuts, and beer as often as he did. I received things to eat two or three times a day."[28] No Mossi chief could have done less. This was a role that chiefs had to play, and they lost power and prestige if they proved inhospitable or parsimonious either to visiting strangers or to their own subjects.

Binger's lack of insight into the economic basis of the Mossi political organization also kept him from obtaining a clear understanding of the political system itself. For example, he saw the loose political organization of the Mossi as a sign of decadence, and felt that the Ouagadougou kingdom was too weak to survive for any length of time:

> Before long the Mossi empire will break up, and the country will be organized into a confederacy like Beledougou and Yatenga. This is an event that we Europeans can only favor. Experience has shown us that as soon as a Negro chief commands more than 2,000 people, he dreams of empire; his needs grow, and he tries to expand. Since his revenues are small, he labors under a deficit, which he must remedy with slave raids. In a confederacy the chiefs do not reach this point so rapidly. As soon as one of them begins to rise, the others can band together and nip his ambition in the bud.[29]

It is quite true that many of the political systems in the western Sudan had a loose character similar to that of a "confederacy." This was not due to the vigilance of neighboring chiefs, however. From time to time, such powerful rulers as Sundiata, Mansa Musa, Sonni-Ali, El Hadj Omar, and Samory Touré did arise and conquer vast areas, but they were unable to sustain their gains over extended periods.

The political organization of the Mossi was not decadent but structurally weak—its economic base was never strong enough to support a higher degree of centralization. Strong chiefs only tested the limits of the system; they could not change the system itself.

VIII

RELIGION AND GOVERNMENT

RELIGION AND RITUAL played an important role in supporting and preserving the Mossi political system. Religio-political ceremonies were centered around the ancestors (Keemse) and the earth deities (Tengkouga); the otiose high god (Ouennam or Naba Zid Ouende) had a very minor role.

The political importance of ancestor veneration lay in the fact that every Mossi chief claimed Nyennega of Dagomba and her descendants, Ouedraogo and Oubri, as his ancestors. Furthermore, possession of the amulets of Rialle, Nyennega's husband and Ouedraogo's father, legitimized possession of the nam. In order to rule, a Moaga had either to be a member of a royal lineage still in possession of the nam or to have received the nam from such a lineage. No Moaga ever tried to usurp the nam of a kingdom or principality without trying to steal the royal amulets at the same time; nor, if his rebellion was successful, did he ever fail to claim that he had stolen the amulets or had received them as a gift. Thus Yadega, who rebelled against his father's brother, Mogho Naba Koudoumie, and founded the Yatenga kingdom, declared that he had obtained Rialle's amulets. He claimed that they had been given to him by his sister, Pabre, who had stolen them from Ouagadougou and had thus deprived that kingdom of any legitimate sanctions for power. Thus, when the Yatenga people declare that they are equal to Ouagadougou, they add that the only "amulets" that still legitimize the nam of the Ouagadougou dynasty are the droppings left behind by Pabre's horse as she fled northward.

Similarly, all the princes who founded principalities and proclaimed their independence of Ouagadougou defended their action on the grounds that they, being as close to the main line of descent as the Mogho Naba, were also entitled to rule. The younger sons of deceased Mogho Nanamse who were banished from the capital as Kouritadamba and who subsequently became provincial Dimdamba also stressed their relationship to the royal ancestors. Even those district chiefs whose ancestors had probably been younger sons sent to rule in conquered territories claimed that their ancestors were direct descendants of Ouedraogo and Oubri. Thus, to the Mossi, the power to rule was intimately linked to closeness of descent from the royal ancestors. The supernatural power of these ancestors, and the vigilance they were believed to maintain over the affairs of their descendants, were regarded as important factors in Mossi government.

From the moment when the Mogho Naba of Ouagadougou or any other Mossi ruler "drank the namtibo" and thereby received the nam of his ancestors, he had the right—indeed, the duty—to offer sacrifices to these ancestors in the name of his subjects. Every night, throughout Mossi country, the Baloum Naba of every ruler performed an act of supplication (Kwaga Basgha) to the ancestors. He beseeched them to protect the subjects of their descendants through the night, to maintain peace in Mossi country, and to grant health, children, and prosperity to all Mossi. This nightly ceremony was climaxed yearly by an elaborate ritual in honor of the ancestors (called the Basgha in some areas, and the Pelegha, Filigha, or Kinkiriga in others) that began at the highest levels of the government and ultimately linked every Mossi chief and lineage head.

The Mogho Naba of Ouagadougou, like the other Mogho Nanamse and Dimdamba, initiated this ceremony in his own kingdom. His celebration, called "M'barengma," was held at the end of the Mossi agricultural year and after the Soretasgho. Thus, the M'barengma was a New Year's festival in thanksgiving for good crops, as well as the annual Feast of the Dead. A few weeks before the first moon of the new year (the *ki-basgha* or *ki-pelegha*), the Mogho Naba ordered his soghondamba and samande-kamba to clean up the palace buildings and courtyards—an activity intended to notify the ever-vigilant ancestors that preparations were being made to offer sacrifices in their honor. A short time later, the Mogho Naba gave grain from his fields to the Pughtiema so she could prepare millet water for the sacrifices. Present-day Mossi insist that part of the grain came from the first ears harvested that year and part from those of the previous year. This was supposed to symbolize the continuity between crops, mirroring the continuity between the ruler and his ancestors. A few days before the principal ceremony, the Mogho Naba ordered the Larhalle Naba to pour millet water and sacrifice chickens on the graves of former Mogho Nanamse.

Shortly before the ki-basgha moon appeared, the ruler had to leave his palace at night to elude the ancestors, who had been attracted by the preparations and who were expected to be angry when they discovered that the sacrifices were not yet ready. The unjust ruler feared ancestral sanctions; the just ruler that his ancestors might want him to join them. One night he went to the home of his Samande Naba, the next to the Gounghin ward, then to Baghin, and subsequently to the homes of other officials. He could not remain long at one place for fear that the ancestors might find him. Every morning, however, when the cock's crow heralded the ancestors' departure, he returned to his palace.

The principal part of the Basgha ceremony was performed on the night when the crescent moon appeared. On that night more than any other, the ruler had to seek refuge elsewhere, because the ancestors visited the palace to accept the sacrifices offered to them by the Pughtiema with the help of the Baloum Naba and the chief eunuch of the harem. The exact nature of this ceremony is unknown, but it is known that the Baloum Naba used the sacred namtibo along with animals and millet-flour water provided by the Pughtiema and the chief eunuch for propitiatory sacrifices to the ancestors. The aim of these sacrifices was to induce the ancestors to grant good crops, health, happiness, and children to their descendants, and to "increase the force of the namtibo."[1] At cock's crow the Bendere Naba sprinkled a flour infusion called *gningmassem* ("water of health") on the palace courtyard so that the ruler might walk upon it when he returned. The Mogho Naba was greeted with drumbeats and escorted to the palace gate. His entry into the antechamber marked the close of this ceremony, and the people retired until later in the day.

The elaborate public ceremony of the Basgha took place in mid-morning. The ministers and important officials, clad in ceremonial garb, arrived at the palace quite early. When the Mogho Naba appeared, the Bendere Naba recited the official genealogy, starting with Ouedraogo and Oubri and ending with elaborate praises of the current ruler. The ministers and their entourage then saluted the Mogho Naba and wished him *Ne tarbo,* which means a happy and prosperous new year for himself and the country. He, in turn, took advantage of this occasion to give many presents to his retinue, and his wives distributed huge amounts of food and drink to the assembly until everyone was satiated. Then all the officials except the Bendere Naba and his group paid homage to the Mogho Naba and departed. The musicians remained at court most of the day, beating their drums and singing praises to their sovereign and his illustrious ancestors. The royal pages kept them well supplied with food and beer, and now and again during the day the ruler sent them gifts among which robes were often included. Whenever the drummers received a gift, they slipped into a rhythmic pattern that signified: *Tompaongo, Wend'kaouss' Naba niore, Wenne wilig vinre,* or, "We bow in thanksgiving for your gift. May God give the ruler long life. May God grant us to be alive next year so that we may do this again." The climax of this gift-giving came when the ruler sent the Bendere Naba about 19,000 cowries and a slave.[2] This ceremony terminated at nightfall.

The close of the Mogho Naba's Basgha heralded the start of similar ceremonies throughout his kingdom. The heads of the other Mossi kingdoms and the Dimdamba were free to hold their own Basgha when they wished; but the Ouagadougou ruler's own subjects, including the provincial ministers, district chiefs, village chiefs, and lineage heads, apparently were not. One reason for this, aside from respect for the ruler, was that the important officials' head wives had to wait for the yeast (*dabili*) from the Mogho Naba's beer before they could prepare the sacrificial offerings for their husbands' ancestors. This dabili went from district to district or to several districts at once, depending on whether the chiefs celebrated Basgha at the same time or successively. Thus, the dabili from the capital united all the wives of the royal clan, and made for both a ritual continuity in the veneration of all ancestors and a strengthening of religious and political bonds.

The Basgha ceremonies on the district level were much less elaborate than those held at Ouagadougou, but just as important. The district chief, too, had his buildings repaired and his grain distributed for sacrifices for the ancestors. A few days before the actual ceremony, he ordered the Gande Naba to pour millet water on the graves of recently deceased chiefs and to sacrifice chickens there. As in Ouagadougou, these sacrifices were offered to induce the chiefly ancestors to grant the villagers health, food, and children. Unlike the Mogho Naba, most district chiefs did not ritually hide from their ancestors for several nights prior to the ceremony. Some of them did change their sleeping place within the compound every night, and the court people always slept indoors during this period. On the night of the Basgha itself, however, the district chiefs did not sleep in their compounds.

As in Ouagadougou, the Pughtiema performed the main ceremony by pouring millet water as a libation to the ancestors who visited her hut. She was assisted by the Baloum Naba, who had possession of the namtibo. Apparently, the district chief remained in hiding and took no part in the ceremony. But he was the main figure in the morning ceremony, which differed little from that of Ouagadougou. In some districts the Tengsoba performed a public sacrifice to the ancestors. He was given the namtibo—sacred objects that had belonged to former district chiefs—and poured libations and sacrificed chickens to all of the chief's ancestors. He also prayed both to these ancestors and to his own on the chief's behalf, and beseeched them to grant long life and happiness to the district population. He also declared that the sacred objects would seek out and kill any enemies of the local ruler, wherever they might be. Once this ritual had been completed, the remainder of the ceremony followed the pattern of the Ouagadougou ritual.

During the weeks that followed, the village chiefs and the heads of the larger lineage segments all offered sacrifices to their ancestors. The Pughtiema of each prominent local administrator, chief, or lineage head prepared and poured the millet water as a libation to the ancestors. Whenever possible, each of these personages invited musicians to sing praises to his ancestors. He dressed in his best robe and sat outside his hut to receive presents from his relatives, friends, and subjects, along with their best wishes for the new year, and for long life and prosperity. In return he gave them kola nuts, beer, and food. Thus, in celebrating the Basgha, all the Mossi were united in prayers and supplications to the ancestors, upon whom rested the future of their country and the successful reign of the descendants of Ouedraogo and Oubri.

The earth deity, Tenga, held the central place in the second major religio-political ceremony which linked all Mossi. This ritual, called *Tense* (from *tenga*, "earth") and sometimes *Naba Oubri ma koure* ("the anniversary of the funeral of Mogho Naba Oubri's mother"), was so important to Mossi cohesion that it was banned by the French, and as a result its main features are now unclear. According to tradition, Naba Oubri loved Poughtoenga, his Ninisi mother, so much, and was so pleased with the elaborate funeral he gave her, that he decided to repeat this ceremony each year in the hope that his subjects would be blessed with the bountiful crops and herds which had made the first one possible. Curiously enough, Oubri's mother was not a central figure in the Tense celebration. Instead, great stress was placed on the fructifying powers of the earth and on the importance of the royal ancestors in Mossi life. The juxtaposition and association of the earth deity with Oubri's mother has important implications for the Mossi political organization. Mossi tradition holds that a Ninisi woman was the ancestress of the Mossi of Ouagadougou. Her people probably celebrated the Tense as a fertility rite to their earth goddess, Tenga. The Mossi apparently took over the ceremony and used it both as a fertility rite and as a memorial festival, thus symbolically uniting the conquerors and the conquered.[3]

In contrast to the Basgha, no special date appears to have been set for the celebration of the Tense. It was held sometime before the crops were sowed, but according to Tauxier it was not celebrated at all in Ouagadougou when the previous year's harvest had been poor.[4] Before setting the date for the festival, the Mogho Naba summoned the Larhalle Naba and ordered him to have sacrifices made on the graves of all former rulers. This minister provided the sacrificial animals for the royal tombs in the area of the capital, and the Ouagadougou Naba, as chief Tengsoba, performed the sacrifices. The Larhalle Naba also dispatched his servants to the distant districts where royal tombs were located, with orders to obtain (by force, if necessary) the animals for the sacrifices from the local populations and give them to the special guardians of the tombs. Sacrifices were made on the grave of Naba Oubri at Koudougou and on that of his father, Zoungourana, in the village of Zomtoega in Tenkodogo. However, there is no indication that a sacrifice was made on the grave of Ouedraogo, who is believed to have died in Sagabatenga but whose burial place is unknown. Nor is it clear whether, as some Mossi claim, annual sacrifices were made on the alleged grave of Nyennega in Gambaga. As soon as these preparatory sacrifices had been completed and the Mogho Naba had been notified, preparations were made for the celebration.

The Mogho Naba met with the Larhalle Naba, and the date of the Tense was set for twenty-one days after the meeting. On the following day, the Larhalle Naba made five cords out of tree bark and tied nineteen knots in each of them. The next day, he gave each provincial minister a cord to send to the districts in his province. The provincial ministers then sent their messengers with the cords to the districts, with orders to untie one knot every day the cords were in transit. Thus a district chief, counting the number of knots in the cord on the day it reached him, knew how many days were left before the Tense. As soon as the entire kingdom had been notified of the festival, the envoys returned to Ouagadougou and returned the cords to their ministers.

On the Friday morning before the Tense, the Larhalle Naba went to the palace. Kneeling before the monarch, he untied the last knot on each cord to indicate that the ceremony would begin on the morrow. To acknowledge this fact, the Mogho Naba distributed bars of salt to his courtiers and visitors instead of the customary kola nuts, beer, and millet water. Visitors left the court early in order to provide their families with foodstuffs for the celebration.

Early on Saturday morning, royal servants brought huge quantities of beef and mutton that had been cooked without pepper (this spice being disliked by the ancestors) and other foods, and deposited them in large heaps in the courtyard. Nearby, they also placed numerous large pots of millet beer. As soon as the morning ceremony was over, the Larhalle Naba slowly approached the Mogho Naba, who presented him with a new white robe. The minister donned the robe and walked to the piles of food, from which he took three portions of millet mush, dipped them in a specially prepared sauce, and flung them in three directions to the waiting ancestral spirits. He then beseeched the royal spirits, the spirits of former provincial ministers, and the spirits of the ancient people (the Ninisi) to grant a long life to the Mogho Naba and peace to all the Mossi. He repeated the ritual with three morsels of meat and with the contents of a pot of beer. When he had finished, the Gande Naba picked up the food thrown to the ancestors and carried it away. He did not look backward for fear that he should see the ancestors and die as a result. The departure of the Gande Naba was the signal for the palace retainers to rush toward the food. They seized and ate what they could, spilling and wasting a good deal in the process.[5]

Meanwhile, chiefs and headmen held similar ceremonies in every district, village, hamlet, and compound in the Ouagadougou kingdom. District and village chiefs offered sacrifices to their ancestors in the name of their subjects. The sacrifices on the hamlet and compound level were more specific. Every grown man had to take a sheep, goat, or chicken to his elder and request that it be offered to the ancestors in his name. The elder sacrificed the animal and beseeched the ancestors to grant the petitioner good health, bountiful crops, and many children during the coming year. The women and children did not take part in the ritual, but they did participate in the general feasting that followed.

The festivities of the Tense lasted only a few days in the districts and villages, but in the capital it did not end officially until about four weeks had elapsed. At the end of this period, the Larhalle Naba gave the Mogho Naba all the cords that had been used to mark the coming of the Tense. A few days later, the chief Tengsoba of Guillingou, the native village of Oubri's mother, and the Tengsobadamba of other important ceremonial centers, visited the Mogho Naba in the palace courtyard. Here they all sacrificed white cocks and placed the blood and feathers of their victims on their ceremonial axes in order to "increase the power" of these objects. Later on, they were given cooked mutton, millet cakes, and other presents. Their departure for home later in the day marked the close of the Tense.

The religio-political function of the Tense is quite explicit, despite the statement by Dim Delobson, himself a Mossi chief (but also a convert to Catholicism), that "it is apparent that this festival has no outstanding features. Its sole aim is to make peace between the living and the dead, and, in the process, to allow everyone to enjoy the food."[6] Judging by the reports of old men who participated in the festival before it was banned, the people did have a good time and enjoyed the food. What is important, however, is that like the Basgha, the Tense served not only "to make peace between the living and the dead," but also to strengthen the political bonds between the Mogho Naba and his chiefs, down to the humblest elder of a Mossi compound.

In addition to the Basgha and Tense, the Mogho Naba of Ouagadougou appears to have offered another yearly sacrifice to Tenga. Each year, after the Basgha, the Mogho Naba, the Baloum Naba, and a large entourage reportedly visited a large earth shrine called Tantibo in the vicinity of Sabatenga to offer propitiatory sacrifices in the name of all the people. When the royal party arrived at Sabatenga, they were joined by the Sabatenga Naba and his Tengsoba. The group proceeded to the foot of the sacred hill, and here the monarch dismounted, took off his bonnet and shoes, and climbed the hill. He made the customary Mossi salute at the shrine and looked on silently while the Tengsoba sacrificed animals and poured libations of millet beer and millet water in supplication for the health and prosperity of the Mogho Naba and all his people.[7]

When evil befell Mossi country in spite of the annual sacrifices to the ancestors and to the earth deity, the Mogho Naba had to offer additional sacrifices. If the country was plagued by drought, the ruler went to an earth shrine in Ouagadougou itself, called "Kom be paspanga" (literally, "water is strong there"), for a sacrifice. Moreover, he might order all his district and village chiefs to perform similar sacrifices to the earth shrines within their territories. In Nobere district, for instance, the district chief went to the village called Barkago, where, standing barefoot and bareheaded on the hilly shrine known as Beta, he ordered the local village chief and the Tengsoba to offer sacrifices for rain and good health.

It is generally believed by the Mossi that when the French attacked Ouagadougou, the deposed Mogho Naba Wobogo made sacrifices to earth shrines. Tradition has it that he sacrificed a black cock, a black ram, a black donkey, and a black slave on a large hill near the White Volta River, beseeching the earth goddess to drive the French away and to destroy the traitor Mazi whom they had placed upon the throne. When Mazi died, the Mossi people believed that he had received his just deserts from the earth shrine for treason. The French believe that Mazi was poisoned.[8]

The district and village chiefs, like the Mogho Naba, were required to make propitiatory sacrifices to the earth shrines on behalf of their subjects. Before taking office, a district chief was ritually shown the major earth shrines in his territory, and he could not ignore their existence and their need for sacrifices. In a country with major local variations in rainfall and localized animal and human epidemics, the Tengsobadamba of stricken areas always called upon the local chiefs to help them propitiate disgruntled spirits. The chiefs could not refuse such requests, especially when the villagers were poor, because they were regarded as "fathers of their people." In some cases, however, district chiefs had to protect their subjects against unscrupulous Tengsobadamba who took advantage of local crises and tried to prey upon the villagers by refusing to perform the requisite sacrifices unless they received substantial gifts. The ensuing struggle was between the secular and the sacred; between the chief as a representative of the conquerors, and the Tengsoba as a member of the conquered group. It was always resolved in favor of the Mossi chief, who never permitted his Tengsobadamba the same privileges held by religious practitioners in neighboring societies.[9] The Mossi chiefs recognized that they needed the Tengsobadamba, and many myths recount how invading Mossi chiefs went into the woods where the Tengsobadamba were hiding to beseech and eventually force them to return to their districts so that sacrifices might be continued. On the other hand, the Mossi chiefs always insisted on the primacy of the nam over any other power. They employed the Tengsobadamba to intercede with Tenga for the welfare of their subjects, but they never allowed the priests to control them.

The coming of Moslems to the kingdom of Ouagadougou had little effect on the way in which the Mogho Nanamse used the traditional religious system to bolster their political power.[10] In fact, the Mossi rulers later used Islam and its adherents in the same manner as they had used the aboriginal religion. The Moslems first tried to subdue the Mossi in the fifteenth century by persuasion, and later by the jihad. Both attempts failed, but the Moslems finally entered Mossi country as refugees from Sudanese wars. Their fortunes waxed and waned, depending on whether they were befriended by the ruler in whose territory they lived. During certain periods, they were subjected to many restrictions and were forbidden by the Mogho Naba to recite their prayers in public places.[11] At other times, they were left free to practice their religion, and even succeeded in converting several Mogho Nanamse to Islam. Under converts such as Savadogo (ca. 1760), Islam spread into many districts and gave rise to such important local centers as Sakhaboutenga (Dakay).

The Moslems in Ouagadougou were represented at the court by their Imam. This person even received his badge of office—a white turban and white robe—from the Mogho Naba, and had to swear in the name of Allah and *Nabiyama* (the prophet Mohammed) to be faithful to him, obey him, and aid him in times of need. However, he did not have to drink the namtibo as suggested by Dim Delobson; nor did he have to observe such non-Moslem customs as drinking the millet beer the Mogho Naba provided for his guests.¹² On the contrary, when the Imam visited the ruler on Fridays or during important festivals to read from the Koran, the sovereign gave him sweetened millet water and appropriate gifts.

Most Mossi rulers at all levels had Moslems among their councillors. These men were often the only persons who had traveled extensively outside the country (on pilgrimages to Mecca), and thus could counsel a ruler about how to deal with foreign visitors. Most early European visitors to Mossi country were either helped or hindered (chiefly the latter, it seems) by these travel-wise councillors. Crozat had difficulties with the Moslems long before he arrived in Mossi country proper. When he got to Lanfiera, the Mossi who lived there were alarmed, and refused to help him proceed to Ouagadougou despite his protestations that "I come for the good of all, white and black, that we may be together like brothers, since the same God has made us all." Crozat reports that his plea was in vain because "El Hadj All-Karl declared that he would not receive me, and he will not receive me. El Hadj is wise, El Hadj is prudent, El Hadj knows all, El Hadj does not make decisions without good foresight, and once made, he keeps them."¹³

Crozat had the same difficulty when he entered Mossi country. He tells us, "At Dounse [near Yako], for example, the marabouts did not look favorably upon my arrival, and it took a great deal of insistence on the part of Moussa to convince the Imam, my unwilling host, to present me to the chief who had expressed the desire to see me."¹⁴ Crozat also found that he had to lodge with the Imam when he arrived at Ouagadougou, and he was assigned the same huts "which had served Captain Binger," who had visited the capital before him. He was disappointed with his reception and declares:

> I already knew from experience what sort of influence these men exercised over the chiefs. As a councillor of the chief, the Imam was overtly acknowledged as the second official in the village, but in reality he often commanded it. The Imam of Ouagadougou, therefore, could do much to help me or to hurt me. My decision to court him might flatter him, and that would be a move in the direction of winning his good graces, which, all things considered, was most important to me. The result was only partly in my favor. I succeeded insofar as the Imam was not hostile to me, but he did not help me as he might have.¹⁵

These Moslem councillors realized better than most other people what the visits of the Europeans implied for the independence of the country, and they tried their best to counsel the monarchs against receiving such visitors.

Beginning with Mogho Naba Doulougou (ca. 1750) Mossi sovereigns, whether Moslem or pagan, participated in the more important Moslem festivals. Being monarchs of the Mossi, they could not do otherwise. A few days before the Moslem feast of Tabaski (called *Kibsa* by the Mossi), the Mogho Naba sent the Imam of Ouagadougou cattle and sheep to be sacrificed on the holy day. On the day of the festival, the Mogho Naba and his entourage went to the mosque and joined the Imam and his flock in prayer. After the ceremony the sovereign returned to his palace and ordered that a well-washed sheep be given to the Imam for a sacrifice. This Moslem sacrifice was performed in the palace courtyard, and the Mogho Naba himself held the tail of the animal while the Imam officiated. The Mogho Naba afterward ordered his servants to provide millet water and food for his Moslem subjects. Similar ceremonies were held in all of the districts and villages where Moslems lived.

The feast at the end of the Moslem month of Ramadan was also celebrated by the Mogho Naba and most of the people within the kingdom—a fact that so surprised Binger that he wrote, "It is a most curious fact that, whether Moslem or not, all the blacks celebrate this feast."[16] The Moslems usually flattered the Mogho Naba and the other chiefs by pretending to believe that they had observed the month-long fast (which the Mossi called *no-lwere*, from *nore*, "mouth," and *lwere*, "to tie up") during Ramadan. Thus, whenever they visited the Mogho Naba or another chief during this period, they greeted him with the salutation *Ne no-lwere*, which means, "I greet you who are fasting." Similarly, the morning after the end of the fasting period, the ruler and his officials were ritually given millet water "to break their fast." The important point here is that everyone knew that the Mogho Naba's fast was a ritual fiction. Binger, who was with Boukary Naba at the end of Ramadan before this prince became Mogho Naba Wobogo, commented: "Boukary Naba is a Moslem in outward appearance only. When the prayers were about to begin, he asked me whether I was going to worship. I told him that this festival was not in accord with those of the Christians. He seemed to be delighted by the idea that the whites are not Moslems."[17]

Most Mossi chiefs celebrated the end of Ramadan in a grander manner than they did Tabaski. The members of the royal household joined the other inhabitants of the capital in their anxious vigil for the crescent moon that was to herald the start of the ceremonies. There was general rejoicing when the moon appeared, and all through the night palace guards fired shots and launched arrows into the air. The following morning, the Mogho Naba went to the mosque with his courtiers to attend prayers. Then he returned to his palace to await the Imam, who came to offer prayers of thanksgiving. The Mogho Naba gave him presents, and was visited by gift-bearing

Moslems. In return, he gave them millet water sweetened with honey, millet cakes, meat, and kola nuts.

The celebration of the festival in the districts was not as imposing as it was at Ouagadougou, but we have Binger's excellent eyewitness account of the festivities at Sakhaboutenga:

> First of all, Boukary sent word that he would like me to accompany him to Sakhaboutenga, where it is his custom to go on the day of the festival. The chief's men spent the entire day attending to preparations: they distributed powder, cleaned guns, tried on harnesses, and polished copper fittings as we would in France on the eve of a great parade. . . . It was an occasion for revelry, and they took full advantage of it. They ate as much as they could, drank a great deal of beer, and fired many rounds of ammunition. . . . In the evening there was a moment of consternation: no one had seen the crescent; however, they consoled themselves by repeating that although it had not been sighted here, it had certainly shown itself elsewhere, and they sat down to drink beer all night long.
>
> Monday, June 11. Early this morning Boukary sent a horseman to Sakhaboutenga to consult the marabouts. The messenger soon returned and assured the chief that the moon will be seen tonight. "All the marabouts have said so." The much-desired crescent appeared for a few moments this evening; shots were fired through half the night, and beer ran in floods. . . .
>
> Tuesday, June 12. From four o'clock in the morning, the tam-tams sounded everywhere, and everyone was busy; it is obvious that this is the eve of an important event. . . . Half an hour after our departure we arrived at Sakhaboutenga. We dismounted and camped under the trees at the entrance of the village. Some Moslems from the neighborhood came, greeted Boukary, and offered him some kola nuts in lots varying from five to eight. But they always held them out in a fold of their robe [it being forbidden for a commoner to hand a gift directly to a chief]. A village nearby sent twelve large jars of beer.
>
> From afar and from all directions, long files of Moslems emerged from the village on their way to the Imam's for prayers. Several onlookers arrived on donkeys from the surrounding countryside. The religious ceremony took place on a flat expanse to the east of the village. It was an impressive spectacle. The crowd was silent. The faithful, ranged in ranks about 20 feet deep, prostrated themselves and rose again in perfect harmony and with awesome slowness. From time to time the voice of the Imam was raised, and his *amina* [amen] was heard with deep reverence.
>
> There were about three thousand persons of both sexes there, almost all of them dressed in white. The *bournous* [robes], the red tarbooshes, and the multitude of black faces lent to the ceremony the grandiose character of an oriental fete. As soon as the prayers were over, Boukary Naba walked up to the Imam of Sakhaboutenga to the sound of tam-tams to receive his blessing and the good wishes of the Moslems, who wished on my illustrious host many horses and warriors. Boukary Naba ordered that the Imam be given a magnificent sheep and several sheepskins full of cowries. He presents this

gift every year to the Imam and to Karamakho Isa, for whom he has great veneration. These are old and wise men who cannot but give him excellent counsel.[18]

The relations between Boukary Koutou and the Moslems of the Sakhaboutenga district show how Mossi chiefs, though pagans, were able to establish viable political bonds with potentially hostile believers of another religion. Boukary Koutou was probably a Moslem "in outward appearance only," as Binger suggests. Nevertheless, it was by being Moslems of this kind that Mossi rulers managed to retain the allegiance of their Moslem subjects. This was their duty as "fathers of their people," and apparently they did it without much hesitation. In this manner, they effectively used religion to bolster their power and sustain their authority.

Ritual connections between the Mossi rulers and the chiefs of surrounding countries enabled them to protect their subjects from foreign attack and to maintain internal cohesion. The numerous reciprocal gifts between the Mossi and such other Voltaic groups as the Dagomba, Mamprusi, and Gurmanche were based on the belief in descent from a common ancestor or ancestress. Ritual and the supernatural thus played an extremely important role in the cohesiveness of the Mossi kingdoms and in the functioning of their governmental processes. Without these ritual factors, it is doubtful whether the Mossi rulers would have been able to maintain such a relatively high degree of control over their subjects, given the relative weakness of their economic resources, communications, and armed forces. In trying to understand why the Mossi retained their autonomy for so long, one must take into consideration the statement made by a French officer a year after the Mossi were conquered: "We must not lose sight of the fact that [the Mossi] have always presented a common front to strangers, and that a single word of command is sufficient to unite them against the invader in the name of kinship and national unity."[19]

The phase of Mossi political history that began when Nyennega left Dagomba and moved northward came to an end with the European conquest. Most French scholars believe that the Mossi were in a state of decadence at the time of conquest and might have fallen to such African conquerors as El Hadj Omar, Samory Touré, or Baba To. The fact remains, however, that these conquerors all skirted Mossi country without entering it. If these African rulers believed that the Mossi were invincible in their unity, it was because the Mossi, through mythical bonds of common descent and actual bonds of kinship, had welded themselves into a cohesive and powerful group.

IX

EUROPEAN CONTACT AND THE CONQUEST OF THE MOSSI

No one knows with any degree of certainty when the Mossi came to the attention of an expanding Western Europe. Marc reports that the ambassadors of John II of Portugal (1481–95) who visited Mali and Timbuktu heard about the Mossi and convinced the King on their return that the Mossi were Christians, and that the King attempted to establish contact with them.[1] Similarly, Barth tells us that around 1488,

> The Jolof [Wolof] Prince Bemoy came to Portugal and communicated so much information with regard to the nations of the interior of Africa, especially the Mossi, who, according to him, had much in common with the Christians, that he excited the greatest interest. It was supposed that the king of Mossi was the long-sought Prester John. Ogane is the native royal title of the king of Mossi. In consequence, from this time forward, numerous messengers were sent into the interior by King John from different quarters, and a nearer alliance seems to have been concluded with the king of the Mandingoes, although it was well understood in Portugal that the empire of the Mellians had fallen in ruin.[2]

Barth also states that as late as 1533, "The Portuguese endeavored also to open communication with the king of Mossi (el rey dos Moses), of whose power they had received reports, but from the wrong side, namely from Benin. The king of Mossi was then waging war with Mandi Mansa."[3] Unfortunately, no Mossi tradition reveals whether they had heard about the Portuguese at that time.

There are no authentic reports that Western Europeans tried to reach the Mossi until three centuries later. During the intervening period, the Europeans were so preoccupied with the gold- and slave-rich coastal African states and with their American and Asian colonies that they had little interest in the interior of the African continent. Only after the slave trade had been abolished and they were trying to find out about the interior of the Sudan in the hope of establishing trade relations there did the Europeans again hear about the Mossi.

The Mossi were probably brought to the attention of modern Europe by T. E. Bowdich, an Englishman who went to Ashanti in 1817 to sign a trade agreement with the Asantehene. While at Kumasi, Bowdich diligently sought information about the lands in the interior, but was relatively unsuccessful because his hosts pleaded ignorance. Nevertheless, he did find out that "five journies [days] from Yngwa [Yendi] is Mosee, a warlike but less visited kingdom: it consists of many states, but the superior monarch is named Billa, and the capital Kookoopella."[4] This misinformation is interesting because it shows that Bowdich's respondent had precise information only about Koupela, a town located near the great caravan center of Poitenga. Similarly, the linguistic data reported by Bowdich are for Dagomba rather than Mossi.

Another Englishman, Joseph Dupuis, led a trade mission to Kumasi in 1819, and obtained data on the Mossi that are surprisingly accurate given the reluctance of middlemen traders to reveal commercial information. He reports that Ashanti traders "sometimes travel as far as Aughoa, the Magho, and to the east of Kasogho. Aughoa is distant from Coomassie twenty-five journies by the Salgha and Yandy Roads, which would give a distance of 360 British miles. Their object in frequenting this place is to collect that vegetable substance by the name of shea butter."[5] There is no doubt that "Aughoa" is really "Ouagha," the term often used by the Mossi to refer to their capital, and the distance between Kumasi and Ouagadougou as reported by Dupuis is approximately the same as the road mileage today. The name "Magho," which appears from time to time in these early documents, seems to be none other than "Mogho," the traditional name of Mossi country. "Kasogho" probably refers to the section of Ouagadougou that was controlled by the Kamsaogho Naba.

The Hausa merchants knew a great deal about the Mossi and the resources of their territory, but only with difficulty did the English trader Hugh Clapperton persuade Sultan Mohammed Bello of Sokoto to give him the following information:

> The country of Mouchier or Mouchi is situated to the west of Ghurma. It is vast and possesses a gold mine, rivers, forests, and mountains. It is inhabited by tribes of the Sudan who possess many fast horses and large donkeys. Their king is called Wagadougou; their asses are sent down to the Gondja to carry the drums of the Army.[6]

Either Clapperton or his informant obviously confused the capital of the Mossi with their king, and included parts of Dagomba in their territory.

Barth, who traveled extensively in the Sudan between 1849 and 1855, did

THE EUROPEAN CONQUEST 143

not enter Mossi territory. Nevertheless, he obtained rather precise information on the important caravan routes leading from Timbuktu through the Mossi trade centers of Ouagadougou, Kaya, Yako, and Koupela, down to Salaga and other towns in Ghana, and even across to Sansane Mango in Togoland. His data on the Mossi are invaluable:

> The whole triangle interposed between the Niger toward the north, and the country of the Eastern Mandingoes or Wangarawa toward the south, appears to be inhabited by a single race of people whose language, although they are divided into several states and nations, nevertheless appears originally to have been the same stock. It is very probable that this race in ancient times occupied the whole upper course of the Niger, and that this tract may have been wrested from it in later times by the Songhai and the Mandingoes, especially that section of the latter which is generally called Bambara. These are the Gourma toward the N.E., the Tombo toward the N.W., and between them the Mossi. . . . The strongest among these pagan kingdoms five centuries ago, and even at the present moment, is that of the Mossi, although the country is split into a number of small principalities, almost totally independent of each other, and paying only some slight homage to the ruler of the principality of Woghodogo.[7]

Europe learned more about the Mossi from Sigismund Koelle, who visited Sierra Leone in 1854. His informant was one Andrew Dixon, who had lived in Koupela before being captured and sold into slavery. He furnished information on the location of the Mossi, their wars with the Busansi, and their important commercial and political relations with the Ashanti.[8] Koelle's report, taken in conjunction with the reports of Dupuis, Bowdich, Clapperton, and Barth, shows that the Ashanti, like the Hausa and other coastal peoples, were protecting their trade when they attempted to isolate the peoples of the interior from the Europeans. But as soon as the British defeated the Ashanti in the war of 1873–74, the Sudan was opened and adventurers poured in. In 1877 and 1878, two missionaries of the Basel Mission visited the northern regions of Ghana, and subsequently gave a good description of Mossi commerce in that area.[9] Lonsdale, who visited Salaga in 1881, found among the traders in the market "the Mossi with his cattle, sheep, and slaves—these latter, generally Gurunsi, are not exposed for sale in the street or market, but can be seen where the owner resides."[10]

The activities of the various European nations in West Africa and other regions at this time led to military and diplomatic difficulties, which the Berlin Conference of 1884–85 was convened to resolve. Agreement was reached to assign "spheres of influence" to the various European nations, to regulate trade, and to provide for arbitration between rival claimants of conquered or "protected" territories. In West Africa, this meant the end of the long Mossi isolation from European activity. In 1886, a German by the name of Krause became the first European to enter Ouagadougou. He left German-controlled Togoland and joined a caravan at Salaga in July 1886 with a load of kola nuts destined for Timbuktu. He arrived in the Mossi district of Bere sometime in August, and remained there long enough to observe that although this was the period of cultivation, there was a severe food shortage. The caravan proceeded to Ouagadougou and remained there until October, when it continued northward.[11] Krause reports that the journey through the Yatenga and Bandiagara region was uneventful, but that shortly after the caravan left Douentza, in December, he received word from the Mogho Naba to return to Ouagadougou immediately. Afraid to disobey, he returned to Ouagadougou in January 1887, tarried there for about two weeks, and then returned to the Gold Coast. Krause gives only a brief topographic description of Mossi country, and says little about the people and their society.[12] His visit might even be doubted, had Binger not visited Ouagadougou the following year and met the person at whose house Krause had lived.

In 1888 Binger left the French colony of Senegal with the sole purpose of reaching the Mossi and placing their country under the "protection" of France if this proved feasible. In many of the towns he passed through on his way to Mossi country, he encountered Mossi men trading slaves, salt, and kola nuts.[13] He also met a future Mossi ruler, Boukary Koutou, who was then in exile at Banema on the outskirts of the territory of Ouagadougou. Binger thought well of this prince, and described him as having "an honest countenance. His whole appearance denotes intelligence. He seems to be a just man, but firm in his resolutions."[14] Binger got better treatment from Boukary Koutou than he had from any other African ruler. He writes:

> Boukary Naba . . . treated me with plenty of good will, and had edibles and meat sent to me every day. . . . It is a great pity that I did not find Boukary Naba in power upon my arrival in Mossi country. It certainly would have facilitated my journey toward the Niger, and if he ever accedes to the throne, he will help with all the means at his disposal the European traveler who happens to pass through his country. This man has fine ideas; he loves progress, and will be well disposed to hear the counsel of the white man. Although his intelligence is higher than the average among blacks, he considers himself quite inferior to the European.[15]

Boukary Koutou further endeared himself to Binger by providing him with an escort so that he might reach the capital safely.

In contrast, Binger was not impressed with Mogho Naba Sanum. He lamented the fact that when Mogho Naba Koutou died in 1850, the youthful Boukary Koutou had not been able to defeat his brother in the struggle for power. He voiced his disappointment with the town of Ouagadougou:

> I expected to find something better than the ordinary royal residence in the Sudan, because everywhere I went people bragged to me about the riches of the chief and the number of his wives and eunuchs. I did not have to wait long to find out the true state of affairs, because that very evening I found that what was acknowledged as a palace and seraglio was nothing but a group of miserable huts surrounded by heaps of filth, and a group of straw huts which served as stables and lodgings for captives and *griots* [bards]. In the courtyard were cows, sheep, and donkeys, which had been brought that day as presents for the king, but which had not yet been presented to him.[16]

Binger did say that Sanum had treated him well and had allowed him to remain at Ouagadougou for over a month, but he was angered when the ruler refused to let him pass through Yatenga (which he claimed as part of his realm) to go to Timbuktu. Nor would Sanum consider his request to place the Mossi under French protection. Finally, Sanum sent him a message ordering him to leave the capital immediately. Binger asked the reason for this summary dismissal, and was informed that the Mogho Naba believed that he was an advance guard for Europeans who were coming from the south, and that he did not show sufficient respect for the ruler. Binger scoffed at the first charge, but later found out that a German column under Von François was indeed heading for the Mossi. He violently rejected the charge of disrespect. He states:

> I feel that a white man traveling in this country, whoever he may be, should not prostrate himself before a black king, however powerful the latter may be. It is necessary that a white man should inspire respect and consideration wherever he goes; for if the Europeans should ever come here, they should come as masters, as the superior class of the society, and not have to bow their heads before indigenous chiefs to whom they are definitely superior in all respects.[17]

Despite these personal sentiments, Binger was compelled to leave Ouagadougou. He stopped briefly to visit his friend Boukary Koutou, and proceeded to the Gold Coast.

For some reason, Von François and his expedition never reached Mossi country. He left Togoland in February 1888 with a sizable force, intending to establish German rule in the Niger bend area, but turned back at Surma on the Mossi border.[18] He was soon followed by numerous British missions from the Gold Coast, German missions from Togoland, and French missions from Dahomey and the Sudan. Marc states: "The three

European powers established in the vicinity realized that by controlling the markets of the Mossi, they could become masters of all the commercial routes in the interior near the bend of the Niger River."[19] The French pursued a more aggressive policy than any other power, dispatching mission after mission to the Mossi. In August 1890, Crozat was sent "to establish friendly relations between the French Sudan and the Mossi."[20] When he reached Ouagadougou in September, he found that Boukary Koutou had succeeded his brother and was reigning as Mogho Naba Wobogo.

Crozat, like Binger, was disappointed by the appearance of the Mossi capital, which he describes in the following words: "Like the smallest of Mossi hamlets, the capital is but a village surrounded by fields, and except for the absence of forest vegetation, nothing would indicate to the traveler that this is a great center and the home of the sovereign."[21] Most European travelers in the Sudan were disappointed by the capitals of African states. They could not reconcile the glowing reports of the Africans with their own ideas of royal splendor. Crozat was even more disappointed with Boukary Koutou. He states:

> The king of Ouagadougou is the same Boukary Naba who was Binger's cordial host at Banema; but what I was told about him and what I saw a little later were two different things, and the difference was to the ruler's disadvantage. Binger knew him as friendly, dignified, simple, somewhat opportunistic, and showing very little displeasure at his brother and predecessor who had exiled him from Ouagadougou. I found myself in the presence of a monarch very proud of his newly obtained but long-hoped-for dignity (Boukary, in effect, became king at Ouagadougou only because his brother died without male issue). Yet he was timid, shaky, and lived confined to his palace with his servants and wives, not daring to go out. He spent his time consulting holy men who had him under their control and who used up the resources of the realm to contrive the oddest and most expensive charms in order to allay the ruler's fear that he would be assassinated.[22]

Mogho Naba Wobogo did little to change Crozat's opinion of him. He hesitated to grant the Frenchman an interview because his councillors had advised against it. When Crozat was finally permitted to see the ruler, he told him:

> I was sent to you by the white chief who rules all the countries of the blacks from Bamako to Kayes, and from Fouta-Djallon to Kaarta. I have come in his name, and in the name of the ruler of all the French, to greet you and congratulate you on your ascension to the throne and to thank you for having received so well my countryman, the white man, who came to the Mossi two years ago. My superior has instructed me to remain with you for several days, so that you may have the opportunity to find out that whites will not harm you, and so that you may become our friend.[23]

Wobogo thanked Crozat for coming to his country, and expressed his thanks to the chiefs who had sent him to Ouagadougou. But he refused to accept the gifts Crozat had proffered publicly. Crozat states, however, that the Mogho Naba sent a messenger to him explaining that he would accept the gifts if offered in secret, but could not accept them publicly because his ministers distrusted the Europeans. Crozat says that he complied with his host's wishes, and promised him more of "the kind of gifts that will be exchanged between two rich and powerful monarchs in mutual friendship."[24] Nevertheless, the Mossi ruler and his councillors showed by their behavior that they mistrusted the Frenchman. In trying to ascertain the nature of this mistrust, Crozat asked a servant of the king whether it was thought that Europeans would come to Mossi country if they felt that the Mogho Naba did not wish them to do so. The man replied that the monarch was being advised as follows: "The white men always act in the same way. . . . One of them always comes, and if he is well received, they come in large numbers; they establish themselves in the country; and where they establish themselves there are no more black rulers. It is they who rule."[25] The servant added that the Mogho Naba had replied that he was not afraid of the whites since his ancestors had all "died in bed." Crozat was reassured by the ruler's reply.

The Mogho Naba did not grant Crozat another audience, however, until he had stated his intention to leave Mossi country. Then Wobogo sent a messenger to tell him he could come to the palace and discuss any affair he wished before he left. Crozat appeared at court, and, acknowledging the strength of the opposition, attempted to counter its charges with feigned anger and guile:

> I do not have any affairs to discuss; for all that I had to say to you I said during the first meeting. I am not a merchant come here to sell, or to buy. I am a chief, as you can see from the attendants who escort me. I was sent to greet you in the name of the white men who are in the West, and to ask you to be our friend. If you wish to be our friend, that will be good for us, and our chief will be happy to have a great king like you as a friend. I think that such an agreement will be equally good for you. Our merchants will bring you the money and the goods you lack, and you will give us in return those things which you have in excess. Such are the relations that will be established between the Mossi and the French. Our ruler will often send you as gifts the wonderful things we make, and this exchange will make us both greater, richer, and stronger.
>
> There may be some who are trying to prevent you from becoming our friend, saying that we are evil and bad. Those who speak like that are liars. Have you heard of any evil I have done, even to a child, since I came to the Mossi or during my trip? Have you heard of any maltreatment on our part

of those chiefs whom we like, in those countries on the other side of the Niger which have been given to us? Perhaps people will tell you again that everywhere we go, we change everything and wish to be the only masters. Have we changed something in Kenedougou, whose *fama* [chief] has been our friend for a long time? We have, it is true, deposed Ahmadou of Segou, but he waged war upon us, and Segou is not his. . . .

The Mogho Naba listened to Crozat in silence and later sent a servant to him with an equally diplomatic message:

The Mogho Naba is very happy that you came, and thanks the chiefs who sent you; he wishes to declare his friendship with the white men who are in the West, especially with the French. He will see them with pleasure when they come again to the Mossi. They will be well received by us. . . . The chief declares his alliance and friendship with the French. . . . He will be pleased to see other Frenchmen come here, provided that they are not too numerous. As for your black traders and French merchants, they can come and trade with the Mossi in all security: he will not maltreat them.

On his part, the chief will send his people to trade in your possessions. As for you . . . you are now free to depart whenever you wish, and by whichever route you choose. The chief will give you four men to accompany you to the border.[26]

In his report to his superiors, Crozat suggests that the widespread belief in the Mossi immunity to attack by neighboring populations is based on imperfect knowledge of their actual strength and fighting ability. He questions the Mogho Naba's riches and power, declares that "he does not have an army," and concludes by stating that the commoners are exploited by their rulers and by the Moslem holy men and "would welcome the Europeans as rulers." He thus shows quite clearly that the Mossi were correct in viewing him as an enemy.[27] Marc, who had no reason to be hostile to Crozat, commented: "It seems to us that Crozat is somewhat unfair in his notes on the indigenous culture of the Mossi. It is possible that the total failure of his mission made him rather intolerant."[28]

Crozat was followed the next year by another French emissary, Lt.-Col. P. L. Monteil. The chief of Yako detained him briefly on the advice of a Moslem who had had unpleasant experiences with Europeans. When Monteil finally reached Ouagadougou and asked for an audience with the Mogho Naba, he was informed that the ruler would not see him and had given orders for him to be expelled from the country. Monteil had no recourse but to leave, but he made this observation: "One important result of this journey augurs well for the future. We were able to travel throughout Mossi country without difficulty."[29] He made a careful survey of the country which was used to good effect by his countrymen five years later.

THE EUROPEAN CONQUEST

Meanwhile, the British were not idle. Their emissaries were traveling all through the northern section of the Gold Coast, making alliances with, and in some cases subjugating, the local rulers. One such emissary, George Ferguson, referred to as "a mulatto from Sierra Leone," worked extensively in the north from 1884 until 1897, when he was killed fighting at Wa.[30] He was at Ouagadougou in December 1894. From a Frenchman who sought to discredit him, we have this report of his activities:

> He drew up before [Ouagadougou] with several soldiers. The entry refused to several French political missions which had preceded him was accorded to him because he declared that he had come to trade. When Ferguson saw the chief before leaving Ouagadougou, he expressed his wish to aid him in a war he was fighting against the people of the district of Lale, and offered him "an object which was to ensure victory." This object was a flag to which Ferguson had pinned a roll of paper: the flag was to be shown to the rebels of Lale, and the paper to the whites who would undoubtedly arrive at Ouagadougou sooner or later. The chief found a use for these two objects right away. The diplomatic instrument was buried in the old trunk of a councillor from which it was eventually retrieved, and the flag was used as a skirt for the head wife of the ruler. . . . Such is the singular procedure whereby Ferguson "established" English influence among the Mossi.[31]

There is still some argument about whether the Mogho Naba knew that this paper was a treaty, and whether he actually signed a treaty "of friendship and freedom of commerce" with Ferguson. In any case, the document terminated with the words: "Signed at Wagadougou, the 2nd July 1894, between Her Gracious Majesty Victoria, Queen, etc., her heirs and successors, represented by her loyal subject George Ekem Ferguson, an officer in the Gold Coast civil service acting by virtue of the special instructions of His Excellency [Sir William E. Maxwell] the officer in charge of the government of the same colony; and the king, chiefs, and principal notables of the Mossi."[32] The discrepancy between the July date and Ferguson's actual visit in December shows quite plainly that the treaty had been drawn up before he left the coast for Mossi country. One must conclude, therefore, that Ferguson, like other European agents of the period, was dishonest. Nevertheless, as we shall see, the Mossi did claim that the treaty had been accepted voluntarily.

In the following year, the French again sent an envoy from Dahomey to make a treaty with the Mossi. This man, Alby, even sought the aid of the Mossi Crown Prince at Djiba, but was turned back not more than twenty-five miles from the capital.[33] During that year, the race to Mossi country was intensified. The French sent Decoeur, Band, and Vermeersh; the English, Lugard; and the Germans, Gruner, Von Karnap, and Von Zech.

None of these men reached Ouagadougou, however, and no treaties were signed.[34]

The events that eventually led to the fall of the Mossi had already occurred two years earlier in the Sudan, even before the last group of European agents tried to reach Mossi country. In 1893, the French defeated Ahmadou, the sultan of the Toucouleur, and captured Bandiagara, just north of Mossi country. Thus, when civil war broke out in Yatenga between Naba Baongo and a rebel noble, Bagare, the French were near enough to take advantage of the situation. Baongo journeyed to Bandiagara and sought the aid of France against his enemy. The French commander, Destenave, desiring to place the country under French protection and not wishing to become involved in local dynastic rivalries, tried to reconcile all the dissident elements. The Yatenga ruler rejected this offer and launched an attack against Bagare, but was killed during the ensuing battle. Bagare then became Yatenga Naba. Soon afterward, he became embroiled in a civil war with rival princes of the royal house and sought help from Destenave, who, according to Tauxier, "was awaiting an opportunity such as this to take a decisive action, which, starting with Yatenga, would have annexed all Mossi areas to our other Sudanese possessions."[35] In May 1895, the French troops accompanied Bagare to Yatenga, defeated the rebels, reinstalled him in the sacred town of Gourcy, and placed his realm under the protection of France. While still in Yatenga, Destenave allegedly sent a message to the ruler of Ouagadougou asking him to sign a treaty with France. Mogho Naba Wobogo reportedly replied:

> I had the oracles consulted a long time ago, and they all answered that if I should see a white man, I would be a dead man. I know that the whites want me to die in order to take my country. And besides, you (my friend) pretend that they are coming to help me organize my country. But I find my country very good as it is. I have absolutely no need of them; I know what is good for me, and what I need. Also, you should consider yourself fortunate that I am not having your head cut off. Away with you, then, and, above all, do not return.[36]

Destenave ignored this reply and pushed southward to the Ouagadougou territories. His small force met with such resistance at Yako that he returned to his base at Bandiagara. Shortly afterward he returned to Paris and appealed to Colonial Minister Delcassé to send a strong military force to occupy Say (on the Niger River), Mossi country, and the surrounding area, and subject them to a military administration. Before Destenave could return, however, the commander of the Sudan, Lt.-Col. Trentinian, ordered Lt. Voulet to prepare the way for the occupation of Mossi country.[37]

With his staff, African infantry, cavalry, and bearers, Voulet left Bandiagara in July 1896 to conquer the Mossi and Gurunsi territories. As the column entered Yatenga it was hailed by Bagare, who had again been chased from his capital by rebel forces. Voulet allowed him to join the invading force, and together they proceeded to Gourcy.[38] According to French sources, the Mossi army offered only token resistance, and the people deserted their villages as the column advanced.[39] In contrast, local tradition states that the Mossi fought valiantly, and that heroes entrenched themselves along the way to die at their posts. However, the French eventually routed the defenders and reinstalled Bagare at Gourcy. Voulet then proceeded to Yako, and the population fled. After capturing this town, Voulet proceeded to Ouagadougou.

The events leading to the capture of the Mossi capital are not clear, because the official sources and the information culled from the memories of witnesses differ a great deal. Noll reports that Voulet sent an emissary to Mogho Naba Wobogo demanding the surrender of the town, and that the emissary was whipped for bringing bad news to the ruler and sent back to Voulet with a rejection of his demand. In the words of Noll, "That insult was immediately punished, and that same evening the French flag flew above the walls of Ouagadougou."[40]

One Mossi version, as related by Dim Delobson, is that a man named Seddo met Voulet's column and, after acting as its guide until nightfall, ran off and notified Mogho Naba Wobogo that the column would arrive at Ouagadougou the following day. The ruler's ministers then held a conference. Some of them counseled him to await the French and show them the flags and the treaty of protection they had received from the British. Others feared that if the Mogho Naba waited for the French, they might seize him, maltreat him, humiliate him before all the people, and probably kill him. They advised him to leave the country. Wobogo decided to be prudent and fled the capital.[41]

According to another tradition, a Moslem from Bere district who had been to Mecca and who had encountered Europeans told Wobogo that it would be folly for the Mossi to try to fight the gun-bearing invaders, and that he should either surrender or flee. The Tansoba who heard this statement became so angry that he wanted to kill the speaker. He declared that no man could enter Mossi country without the ruler's permission, and he swore to die before this happened. However, the other councillors persuaded Wobogo to leave the capital.

Dim Delobson states that Voulet arrived at Ouagadougou with his column in September 1896, and sent a former Gurunsi slave of the Mossi with eight soldiers to reconnoiter the town. (This slave might be the emissary referred to by Noll.) The people who had gathered for the market day were unaware that an attack on the capital was imminent, and were frightened when they saw the soldiers. A deaf man named Wanda, who was a tax collector in the market, went home for his gun and his horse in the belief that the Mogho Naba's army was on the march. He went out to meet the French and was killed. Later that day the Mossi army, under the command of Koabga, the Kamsaogho Naba, and the Tansoba, launched an attack on the invaders. Their flint guns, spears, clubs, and poisoned arrows were powerless against superior French arms. Dim Delobson states that when the French guns began to fire, "It was a thorough stampede; all tried to save themselves and fled in all directions. Some of them, in their precipitous flight, even rode past their homes and villages." According to local tradition, one of the first persons to run was the Tansoba, who had once pledged to defend the Mogho Naba to the death. About five o'clock that afternoon, the French flag flew over Wobogo's palace.[42] The Mogho Naba and his army did not regroup until they reached a village called Bagare, some 25 miles southeast of the capital.

Three days later, Wobogo marched back toward Ouagadougou at the head of a large army in an attempt to crush the relatively few enemy soldiers. But Voulet's men chased him toward the south. It was either during this battle or after he returned from the pursuit of Wobogo that Voulet burned Ouagadougou to punish its inhabitants for helping their sovereign. Meanwhile, Wobogo had regrouped his forces, and although Voulet pursued him and burned Mane and Boussouma, where the sovereign had sought refuge, Wobogo fled rather than sign a treaty with the invaders. This attitude surprised and annoyed Voulet, who is quoted as saying:

> Although we represent peace, safety, security on the trade routes, and thus ease of communication . . . nothing could prevail against their fear that in accepting us, they would also have to accept the suppression of slavery: the principal activity around which everything revolves in this backward country. The majority of the population are kept well in hand [by their chiefs]. Although the central power (I speak of the authority of the chief of Ouagadougou vis-à-vis the other chiefs, his vassals) is *relatively* weak, each of these vassals, on the other hand, is thoroughly obeyed in his own territory. There is not one village chief who would dare to receive us if his superior forbade him to do so. We are told that if anyone permitted himself such a liberty, he would have his head cut off the moment our backs were turned.[43]

After being routed by Voulet's forces for the second time, the Mogho Naba sent requests for aid to many of the autonomous Dimdamba and to his district chiefs. The Dim of Boulsa sent an army under the command of his prime minister, Rimsekedo, and the chiefs of the districts of Bere, Djiba, Manga, Nobere, and Rissouma led their armies to join the royal forces at a rallying point near the White Volta River. Meanwhile, Voulet had expended most of his supplies in trying to bring Wobogo to terms. Having failed to do so, he tried to solve the problems of Mossi government by electing Wobogo's younger brother, Mazi, as ruler of Ouagadougou and emperor of the Mossi. Voulet then marched off to his base at Bandiagara by way of the White Volta, hoping to catch and defeat Wobogo's forces along the way. The monarch fled at Voulet's approach, so that when the forces of Rimsekedo and of the district chiefs arrived at the rendezvous, "they found only the droppings of Wobogo's horses," and angrily returned home. Naba Kaglere, chief of Nobere, was allegedly so infuriated by Wobogo's cowardice that he withdrew his support from his sovereign. However, the chiefs of Djiba and Rissouma remained faithful to their ruler, and the Dim of Mane attempted to intercept Voulet's advance toward Bandiagara, only to be defeated by the French, who burned his villages.

When Wobogo heard that the enemy had left the country, he ordered that the roof of his palace be restored, resumed his traditional duties such as appointing to office the heirs of district chiefs who had died during his absence, and prepared to return to the capital. In the interim Mazi had died (under suspicious circumstances, according to the French), thus leaving the people of Ouagadougou without a ruler and eager for Wobogo's return.[44] Unfortunately for the Mogho Naba, Voulet unexpectedly returned to Ouagadougou in December 1896, thus preventing Wobogo's return. Voulet, too, was in a predicament, for he had few allies among the Mossi, and Wobogo was firmly entrenched near Kombissiri in the south. To prevent many chiefs from coming to the aid of their sovereign, Voulet immediately launched an offensive against Wobogo. He burned several villages along the way, and received the allegiance of Wobogo's two brothers, Tarbega and Mahmadou, of two of his sons, and of two of his important vassals, the Mane Naba and the Boussouma Naba. But he failed to find the sovereign, who had fled to the region of Djiba and Nobere. Voulet then turned back to Ouagadougou, which he reached about a month later, in January 1897. On the following day, the Ouidi Naba surrendered, and two days later the Tansoba followed suit. Voulet now formally deposed Mogho Naba Wobogo. A week later, he obtained the permission and cooperation of the traditional electors and placed Wobogo's brother Mahmadou on the throne as Mogho Naba Sighiri. This sovereign then "solemnly signed a treaty which placed his kingdom under the protection of France."[45]

Voulet left Ouagadougou in February to establish French control among the Gurunsi, leaving a military commander, Captain Scal, and a Resident Officer at Ouagadougou. But he acted without taking into account the resourcefulness of Wobogo (now once more Boukary Koutou), who had gained the allegiance of chiefs in the Manga area. The Gounga Naba, who was provincial minister for that region, tried to gain the support of the Djiba and Rissouma districts for Mogho Naba Sighiri. He failed, and ordered the troops of Garanse, Nobere, Toise, and Yake districts to attack Boukary Koutou's supporters. In the ensuing battle the Gounga Naba's forces lost nine men, the rebels ten. The Gounga Naba considered these losses too high and called off the fighting.[46]

Meanwhile, Boukary Koutou had sent an appeal to Steward, the commander of a British force that was then on its march of conquest through Gambaga and that had designs on Ouagadougou, "for protection in virtue of the treaty concluded with Mr. Ferguson in 1894." Wishing to avoid conflict with the British, Voulet hastened to Tenkodogo in February 1897 to meet Steward, and the two men established boundaries between the French and British spheres of influence. Boukary Koutou was thus left to fend for himself.[47] Undaunted, he crossed the Gold Coast frontier once more and proceeded toward Ouagadougou. Scal heard about his activities and decided to launch an attack against him. He took Boukary Koutou by surprise in June 1897, and forced him to flee. Boukary passed through Bere district and arrived in the Gold Coast, where he was granted refuge by the British. About a year later, he convinced a Colonel Northcott that he had been unjustly deposed by the French, and that under the treaty of 1894 the British were his protectors and were obliged to restore him to his throne. In May 1898, a British force under Northcott and with Boukary Koutou in tow arrived at Kombissiri, some twenty-five miles from Ouagadougou, but here they were met by French emissaries who brought with them copies of the treaty of protection signed by Sighiri in January 1897. The British troops retreated, taking the dejected ruler with them into permanent exile.[48] Boukary reportedly settled at Zangoiri, a few miles from Gambaga.[49] He was forbidden to enter Gambaga because of the tradition that if he ever saw the Gambaga ruler, both of them would die. Boukary never returned to Mossi country. He died and was buried in the Gold Coast in 1904, but his funeral was held at Ouagadougou.[50]

Boukary Koutou is seen in retrospect as a tragic figure, whose main fault seems to have been that he ruled at the most difficult time in his country's history. Judging by his treatment of Binger, he appears to have been a clever politician, but his resources were of no avail against the superior might of the French. Like many other African groups, the Mossi have now evolved traditions to account for his fall and for the conquest of their country. They say that Wobogo lost his realm because he was a cruel ruler. According to the Mossi, he executed the noble retainers of Djiba in whose care his heir had died. But most important, the Mossi believe that Boukary was destined to lose his country to foreigners. According to one tradition, a holy man warned the ruler of Tenkodogo that an evil child who would bring harm to the country would be born into his house unless his birth was prevented by oblations to the ancestors. The Tenkodogo Naba made the necessary sacrifices, and the tragedy was averted. The holy man then went to Ouagadougou and gave the same warning to Mogho Naba Koutou. Koutou replied that he was the direct descendant of Ouedraogo and Oubri, and that no child of his could bring harm to the patrimony of the royal ancestors. He made no sacrifices, and a child who had "two teeth like the tusks of an elephant" was born into his house. This child, Boukary Koutou, was disrespectful of his father and made war against his brother, and was eventually defeated by the French.

X

MOSSI GOVERNMENT DURING THE COLONIAL PERIOD

IN AN EFFORT to undermine the power of the Mossi chiefs, change the traditional Mossi administration, and incorporate the Mossi territories into the colonial complex, the French attempted to weaken the structure of the Mossi political organization. They tried at first to apply their policy of *assimilation,* which was characterized by direct rule and by "giving the colonies institutions analogous to those of metropolitan Frence, [which] little by little removes the distances that separate the diverse parts of French territory and finally realizes their intimate union through the application of common legislation."[1]

The French attitude toward the Mossi political organization and its chiefs is clearly defined in the instructions Commander Destenave gave to Captain Scal for the administration of a territory that had not yet been brought completely under French control. Destenave writes:

> We have no interest in strengthening the power that is regarded as central, nor in increasing the power of the various Nabas; on the contrary, we must look for points of stress which will permit us to divide the country, and thus preclude any coalitions against us. . . . In so doing, the authority of the Mogho Naba itself will be weakened, because we can easily acknowledge the independence of these great [princes] and free them from his influence. This is an excellent measure from a political standpoint; for we must not lose sight of the fact that we have no interest in strengthening the power of the central authority. On the contrary, we must encourage as much as possible the tendency of the great chiefs (vassals) to break the last bonds that still attach them to Ouagadougou. This is the course which has been followed by the Resident Officer. It has produced excellent results, and the requested taxes have come in regularly. In future, we should seize every opportunity to weaken the authority of these vassals by declaring the independence of the villages under their command. Just recently, the chiefs of Coundiri and Tema were removed from under the command of the Yako chief, and are now under the direct command of the Resident.[2]

At first the Mossi resisted all changes in their political organization and all demands for foodstuffs, information about their territories, and laborers.³ In desperation, the French sought help from those very chiefs whose power they wished to curb, especially from the Mogho Naba of Ouagadougou, whom they regarded as the supreme ruler of the Mossi. However, they met with the same resistance:

> The king of the Mossi, Kouka Naba [Mogho Naba Sighiri], is lavish with vows of devotion and fidelity, but these vows are never translated into action. It is impossible to obtain from him any pertinent information about the country—he tries to give the impression that he knows nothing about it—or any information about Boukary Koutou [then in exile, but still a threat to the French], of whom he pretends to have no news.⁴

One cannot tell whether the Mogho Naba knew about Boukary Koutou's activities, but it is highly unlikely that he could have given the French much information about the country even if he had wished to do so. No Mogho Naba ever possessed this kind of information. The Dimdamba and the Kombemba paid allegiance and tribute to their superior ruler, but did not furnish him with specific data on their principalities and districts.

The death of Mogho Naba Sighiri in 1905 enabled the French officials to secure the election of a Mogho Naba they could control and to change the Mossi political organization. Sighiri's principal heir was his sixteen-year-old son, Saidou Congo, who in the opinion of the Mossi electoral college "could not keep the country" because of his youth. The French, keenly aware that they could more easily control a young ruler, insisted that Saidou be given the nam, and he became Mogho Naba Kom. Two years later, in 1907, the French began to reorganize the kingdom of Ouagadougou and the surrounding territories. They suppressed certain districts and principalities, enlarged some, and unified others by granting them control over the smaller political entities that lay near or within their boundaries. These changes were often made without regard for the traditional hierarchies, and many district chiefs found themselves controlling other district chiefs, while Dimdamba were reduced to the level of district chiefs.

The French also reorganized the provincial administration, replacing the five ministers with persons more favorably disposed toward their rule. The Larhalle Naba was replaced in 1908 after he had mysteriously left the capital for Koudougou. The Kamsaogho Naba was deposed by the Mogho Naba, and was replaced by a nominee of the French. As in the case of the district chiefs, the French shifted the territorial responsibilities of these ministers "without taking into consideration the hierarchy prevailing among [them]. The intention of the administration apparently was to reward certain young and capable ministers to the detriment of those who were old."⁵ One commentator concludes: "In view of the youth of the reigning king, Naba Kom, and also owing to certain difficulties, the administration was compelled to grant more authority to the five great ministers and to make them true provincial chiefs with whom it could deal and who would govern their territories directly."[6]

Some of the demoted chiefs and their followers opposed these changes. In 1910, they refused to pay taxes and fought the police. However, they were forced to accept the changes when the police burned their villages, seized their goods and animals to pay the taxes, and deposed uncooperative chiefs. These harsh measures so shocked the Mossi that they remained docile from that time onward, and thereafter the French were able to rule the country with one European administrator for every 60,000 Mossi.[7]

Once the French officials had put down the opposition to their policies of control and had succeeded in installing loyal provincial administrators, they sought to bring Mossi country into the political structure they were creating in West Africa. In 1895, they had installed a Governor-General at Dakar to represent the French Government in the territories of Senegal, the French Sudan, French Guinea, and the Ivory Coast. With the subsequent conquest of Mossi country and other areas, however, this arrangement became obsolete, and a decree was passed in October 1899, dividing the French Sudan in two. One half was attached to the coastal colonies. The other half was combined with the Voltaic region (which included Mossi country), declared a military territory, and placed under the direct control of the Governor-General. In 1900 Niger was also made into a military territory, and two years later, by a decree of October 1902, a new territory called Sénégambie-Niger was set up which included Mossi country. This new arrangement lasted only two years. It was superseded by a decree of October 1904 dismembering Sénégambie-Niger and creating, among others, a territory called Haut-Sénégal et Niger, which included Mossi country. This new colony was similar to the others in that it had its own administration (at Bamako), its own budget, and a Lieutenant-Governor responsible to the Governor-General at Dakar. The territory was divided into administrative units called *cercles,* each with a commander responsible to the Lieutenant-Governor. Each cercle commander was assisted by adjutants who served in smaller units called *subdivisions* and *postes.* Mossi country itself was divided into three cercles: Ouagadougou (including Tenkodogo), Ouahigouya (including Yatenga), and Fada-N'-Gourma. This territorial change was the last to affect the Mossi until the end of World War I.[8]

The implementation of full colonial rule among the Mossi was to have a profound effect on their traditional political organization and on the relationship between the people and their chiefs. One of the principal contributing factors was the demand of the French administration that Mossi country not only share in the over-all development of French West Africa, but pay for its own administration as well. The resources of Mossi country were largely limited to agricultural production and stock raising, however, and revenue from these activities was slight. The full weight of administrative expenses thus fell on the Mossi people. Apparently, the first taxation was of a collective nature, for according to the official government report for June 1899, "No regular tax has been levied, but taxes have been collected from the Mogho Naba and the other chiefs."[9]

Decrees of July and November, 1903, authorized "native chiefs to collect taxes, and granted them a commission on the tax yield to arouse their interest in the regular payment of taxes."[10] Accustomed as they were to giving taxes (gifts) to their rulers with the knowledge that subordinate chiefs would extract a share before sending the remainder up the hierarchy, the Mossi were not averse to paying taxes through their traditional rulers to the "new chiefs," the French administration. However, when taxes grew to excessive proportions and chiefs continued to get a percentage, the people accused their rulers of cheating them. The reasons for the Mossi complaints about taxation are described by Tauxier, himself an administrator:

> This tax, light at first, has grown rapidly over the last few years. In 1906 it was 311,000 francs for the territory of Ouagadougou, which had a population of 861,000 inhabitants. In 1907, the tax was raised to 360,000 francs; in 1909, to 555,000 francs; and in 1910, to 656,000 francs. Furthermore, from 1908 onward this tax was exacted with such rigor and on such short notice that it was exactly as though the amount had been tripled. Under the circumstances, the Mossi were compelled to resort to trade in order to obtain the French money they did not have, since the local currency is the cowry and the French administration does not wish to receive it. . . . To meet this difficult situation the Mossi now organize small caravans in the villages, and send the young men to Wanke to sell cattle, sheep, goats, asses, horses, and bolts of cotton. They bring back with them either French money or kola nuts.[11]

Many Mossi had a great deal of difficulty in securing French currency. Mangin, a White Father who arrived in Mossi country in 1904, writes:

> The Europeans who live among the Mossi, including all the riflemen and cercle guards, do not put into circulation a quarter of the five-franc pieces that are required each year from the natives. At first the Mossi were taken by surprise and had to give 10,000 or even 15,000 cowries to obtain this famous coin, this charm which was to free them from all difficulties with the white man. At the official rate of exchange this coin is worth 5,000 cowries.[12]

What Mangin referred to euphemistically as "difficulties with the white man" was, to the Mossi, rather drastic punishment for non-payment of taxes. If a man refused to pay his taxes, the Mossi chief was permitted to sequester his goods and sell them. If the man had neither the taxes nor the goods, the chief had to send him and his wife (or wives) to the administrative post to be punished. Sometimes, a man and his wife would be made to look at the sun from sunrise to sunset while intoning the prayer *Ouennam co mam ligidi* ("God, give me money"). Other times, a man would be made to run around the administrative post with his wife on his back; if he had several wives, he had to take each one in turn. Then his wife or wives had to carry him around. The Mossi claim that a man had to run around the post three times, and his wife four. This is probably an exaggeration, however, because the numbers 3 and 4 are symbolically associated with men and women, respectively.

A further source of difficulty for the Mossi chiefs, and one which became more serious as time went by, was that they were charged by the administration to recruit men for both labor and military service. Initially, the chiefs had to supply men to transport grain for the French-organized agricultural societies from one region to another; later, they were commanded to supply labor for private and public works. Labouret states:

> The initial recruitment, which took place in 1912, was carried out without any difficulty, thanks to the unexpected afflux of volunteers. This was not the case in subsequent years. The reason for this was that the credulous natives of these distant regions, lacking any contact with the world, believed that the Europeans were carrying off their most robust youths to sell them to the Men of the Sea [mythical cannibalistic beings].[13]

The Mossi were alarmed at the high rate of mortality among the young men who went away to work. They had a saying, *Nansara toumde di Mossi* ("White man's work eats [kills] people"), and resisted the recruiting attempts of their chiefs. There was, however, less opposition to recruitment for military service, owing in part to the Mossi tradition of warfare. Many Mossi youths served in France during World War I, and additional hundreds served in an African contingent recruited "by an administrator named d'Arboussier, and with the cooperation of the Mogho Naba, to take possession of northern Togoland."[14]

The manner in which the Mossi chiefs administered their territories before the First World War was conditioned by the colonial administrators even when it was not directly controlled by them. The Mogho Naba had gradually lost most of his power, and he had no authority to act without the specific authorization of the French. He retained most of his ceremonial activities, especially since they were considered interesting "feudal" anachronisms to be shown to visiting officials and travelers. He also retained the power to appoint district chiefs, but the French often vetoed men they disliked and suggested that other candidates be elected. He also lost all control over his provincial administrators. The administrative chain now extended from the cercle commanders, through the provincial ministers and district chiefs, down to the village chiefs. Many provincial ministers, out of loyalty to the traditional system, occasionally briefed the Mogho Naba on the policies the French had ordered them to carry out, and told him about the state of affairs in the districts. This was completely unofficial if not illegal, but it made little difference to the French.

One serious blow to the power of the Mossi chiefs, especially on the district level, was their loss of judicial autonomy. Mossi country was subjected to the Indigénat, a rather harsh code of law for new colonies, which was promulgated by a decree of September 1887. Under this code, administrators could hold summary trials and punish any Moaga, whether chief or commoner. In June 1905, the Mossi chiefs regained some of their judicial power when a supplementary decree established village, district, and cercle courts throughout Haut-Sénégal et Niger.[15] Mossi village chiefs regained their police powers and the right to reconcile disputes among their people, but their decisions could be appealed to a district court. The district chief heard appeals and judged civil and criminal cases, but in all deliberations he was aided by two assessors appointed by the Governor. His judgment could be appealed to a cercle court, which was presided over by a European, who was assisted by two Africans. They heard appeals and judged crimes for which the penalty could be no more than five years. Penalties handed down by this court could be appealed to the Supreme Court of the Federation of French West Africa in Dakar, which judged all major crimes.

Thus the Mossi chiefs did regain part of their judicial power; but because the decree of 1905 did not abolish the Indigénat, local French administrators could easily countermand this power. Moreover, some administrators, dissatisfied with the Mossi courts and possibly resentful at their own loss of judicial power, sent numerous complaints to Dakar about the incompetence of the chiefs and the injustices perpetrated by village and district courts. As a result, a decree of August 1912 abolished the judicial power of the Mossi and of all other African chiefs, and instructed them to refer all litigation to courts at the poste, subdivision, and cercle levels.[16]

During the period before the First World War, the Mossi chiefs lost not only their judicial power but also much of the economic and religious basis of their political power. The French administration abolished slavery and serfdom, and discouraged the various corvées performed by the people for their chiefs on the ground that the chiefs gained sufficient income from tax commissions. What really undermined the economic position of the Mossi chiefs, however, was the abolition of the religio-political practices and ceremonies that provided the rulers with substantial income, while reinforcing the traditional political system. The French permitted Mossi chiefs to celebrate the Basgha, but abolished the Tense with its revenue-producing Soretasgho ritual on the ground that it exploited the local population. The Mossi chiefs could no longer authorize the Tengsobadamba to appropriate sacrificial animals from the villages to propitiate capricious deities. But some chiefs, taking quite seriously the concept that they were the "fathers" of their people, and had been selected for the nam because of their ability to care for their subjects, provided these animals or covertly permitted their servants to seize them and turn them over to the Tengsobadamba.

At the end of World War I, the French administration tried to establish a new policy toward the Mossi chiefs, but new economic programs that were implemented at the same time rendered these plans ineffective and further undermined the old institutions. A new Governor-General of French West Africa, Joost Van Vollenhoven, strongly influenced by one of his predecessors, Merleau-Ponty, and by the policy of *association* between France and her colonies (a policy based on the idea that colonial policy should be determined by the geographic and ethnic characteristics and the level of social development of the regions involved), advocated respect for the chiefs and for strong traditional political systems. Van Vollenhoven stipulated that the chiefs should not be harried by administrators, subjected to corporal punishment, or legally prosecuted without the sanction of higher officials (cercle commanders and lieutenant-governors). They should be granted higher salaries and help for agricultural labor, and should be shown techniques for improving their material well-being. They should also be decorated more often with the Legion of Honor, in order to heighten their prestige and to demonstrate "French generosity." Their relatives should be educated, given prestige and remuneration, and permitted to retain some status.[17]

The colonial economic policy that was to subvert Van Vollenhoven's political concepts and adversely affect the Mossi chiefs was outlined by Albert Sarraut, the postwar French Colonial Minister, who drew up an ingenious plan (*La Mise en valeur des colonies françaises*) to foster the development of railroads, wharves, roads, plantations, and other enterprises in every colony.[18] In contrast to Van Vollenhoven, Sarraut believed that economic development should take precedence over everything else in the colonies. The Mossi were to be directly affected by the policies of both Van Vollenhoven and Sarraut. The colony of Haut-Sénégal et Niger was suppressed in March 1919, and replaced by the new colony of Upper Volta, in which the Mossi were the chief ethnic group. Moreover, Ouagadougou was chosen as the administrative center of this new colony.[19]

The new Governor of the Upper Volta, Edouard Hesling, who arrived in Ouagadougou in November 1919, sympathized with Van Vollenhoven's views, but was even more interested in economic development. He was determined to transform Ouagadougou from a small town with an indigenous population of about 8,000 and some 76 European soldiers, merchants, and missionaries, into a capital worthy of a colony. Shortly after he arrived, he summoned the Mogho Naba and the traditional ministers and had them recruit some 2,000 salaried and unsalaried men to provide enough mud bricks and wooden beams to complete the construction of eleven administrative buildings before the rainy season began the following May.

Hesling and his administrators believed that the Upper Volta, a country "with such diverse products and such a dense population, could attain an exceptional level of development by acquiring those economic elements which ensure prosperity."[20] Cotton was one of those elements. They believed that the Upper Volta "can and should export thousands of tons as soon as an easy and economical way of shipping is established."[21] By 1925, Hesling had constructed 6,000 kilometers of roads in the Upper Volta, about one-eighth the entire road network of French West Africa. Travelers in the Upper Volta at this time wrote of "the enforced enthusiasm with which the natives, under M. E. Hesling, have thrown themselves into agricultural labor and in particular into the planting of cotton."[22]

The administration of the Upper Volta continued to furnish Mossi manpower for the development of the other colonies as well as for the colonial army. In 1922, it was asked to furnish "6,000 workers for the Thies–Kayes railway, renewable every six months; and under the same conditions to furnish 2,000 laborers to build the railways in the Ivory Coast. Similarly, with the consent of the chief administrator of the colony, it was possible to recruit a thousand workers in the regions of Ouagadougou and Bobo-Dioulasso for private business in the Ivory Coast."[23] Londres, who visited the Upper Volta in the late 1920's, reports that Mossi country was known as "a 'reservoir' of manpower."[24] Burthe d'Annelet reports that during this same period, "The Minister of War [took] 45,000 men each year to compensate for the weakness of our metropolitan recruitment, and to cut down the length of service of our draftees as much as possible."[25]

The Governor of the Upper Volta made full use of the Mossi chiefs to develop the colony, and although some chiefs may have objected to the labor imposed on their subjects, others seemingly approved. In commenting upon cotton production in the Upper Volta, Ossendowski writes:

> Cotton is an artificial crop and one the value of which is not entirely clear to the natives. The chiefs with their superior intellect, seeing the profit to be obtained from the plantation of cotton, are continually enlarging the area of the fields, and resort to draft animals, ploughs, manures, and even partial irrigation of the fields; nevertheless, the great mass of the population submit rather unwillingly to those instructions of the administration which aim at the development of cotton cultivation in the colony.[26]

Delavignette's comment on the role of the chiefs in cotton production seems to indicate that they, like their subjects, had to conform to the desires of the French:

> [The French] lived at Ouagadougou in the shade of the great Nabas, and because [the latter] possessed servitors and were at the head of docile provinces, [the French] dignified by the name of "custom," and in any case adjudged convenient, this domestication of the peasants whereby they were forced to work in a common field under the authority of the village chief, and for a salary which was theoretically to be distributed among them afterwards. Sometimes cercle guards were stationed in these fields.[27]

The Governor carried out many of Van Vollenhoven's reforms concerning the Mossi chiefs, and instructed his district administrators to respect the chiefs and to seek their aid in governing the people. De Beauminy, an administrator in the Upper Volta, contrasts the old policy with the new:

> Not without reason, we followed the rule of regarding the great black chiefs as exploiters of their peoples, and this caused us to introduce and to maintain a policy aimed at reducing their authority. Later on we were compelled to abandon this policy in the face of discouraging results. During the past few years we have restored power and prestige to the Mogho Naba and to his vassals, the Mossi chiefs. They are now paid by us, and they administer their kingdoms and territories under our guidance and under the supervision of an extremely small European staff (one official for every 60,000 inhabitants). The rulers are now helping us to restore, on a newer and sounder basis, a political edifice which had once appeared to be on the point of collapse.[28]

An official report also stated that the Mossi chiefs

> understand that the time of their absolute power, and the privileges of their "medieval lordships," are fated to wear away gradually. Certainly, the main-

tenance of their authority and prestige is indispensable, and the local administration is firmly resolved not only to preserve it but even to strengthen it. Henceforth, however, this authority and prestige will be upheld on the basis of principles and methods better suited to the new order of things which has been established.[29]

The administration tried to educate some of the sons of the chiefs "in order to attune them to progress and to the fundamental principles of our policy."[30] It encountered some resistance from chiefs who resented what they considered the "recruitment" of their children for education, and from other chiefs who were afraid that, if educated, their sons might be converted to Catholicism and thus would be unable to perform the traditional religio-political ceremonies. Nevertheless, one official states quite proudly that "Despite some resistance, the results obtained so far are encouraging and of such a nature as to allay our anxiety: 671 sons of chiefs are now attending our schools, among them 52 sons of provincial chiefs and 342 sons of district chiefs."[31] However, very few of these boys even learned French well enough to take part in the government of their society.

Hesling also made an effort to improve the material welfare of the Mossi chiefs. He felt that under the previous administration the chiefs had been "inadequately remunerated," and he considered this bad for their morale. He therefore increased the appropriation for the salaries of chiefs from 86,000 francs in the 1919 budget to 190,000 francs in the 1924 budget, and counted on their receiving an additional 163,260 francs from tax commissions during the year. The Mogho Naba of Ouagadougou, considered the emperor of the Mossi and judged loyal, efficient, and capable by the French, was granted a stipend of 25,000 francs, while the Yatenga Naba, considered his subordinate and judged less capable, was granted only 8,700 francs.[32] Only 276 chiefs out of a total of 497 in the territory received any stipend at all that year, because even an augmented budget was too small to provide funds for the lesser chiefs. These chiefs, in the words of one official, "were often inadequate or incapable, but . . . could not be replaced, either because they had no qualified successors or because the traditional system placed an obstacle in the way."[33] Instead of salaries, they received seeds of new plant species such as mangoes, and they were helped in building dams to irrigate their fields and in sinking deep wells near their compounds. In addition to these material rewards, the Governor increased the prestige of the chiefs by giving them medals and honors.

Despite these increased salaries and honors, and the more important role they now played in the administration of their subjects, the Mossi chiefs did not regain any of their traditional power. They remained auxiliaries of the administration. Taking Mogho Naba Kom as an example, one report states that this "simple, intelligent, compliant man served as news agent and made himself useful to the political administration" until the arrival of Hesling, when he took a livelier interest in the affairs of the colony.[34] Another source says of the same monarch:

> Free of the ancestral traditions that forbade him to leave his palace, and curious about progress and administration, he travels on all the roads and, under our supervision, busies himself with the settlement of administrative problems, to which he lends the weight of his authority. He makes the proposals for the nomination of province and district chiefs; he encourages his subjects to work and produce. Finally, he fulfills with the greatest dignity the representative functions that devolve upon him at his palace and in the official ceremonies.[35]

While it is true that the Mogho Naba made proposals for the nomination of chiefs, he was powerless to prevent their dismissal if they incurred the displeasure of the administration—a frequent occurrence during the Hesling period. For example, when the administration deposed Naba Boulga of Doulougou district for "incompetence" and placed him in "enforced residence" in a neighboring district, the French officials encouraged the election of Bila Kongo primarily because he was a former cercle guard. Bila Kongo was assassinated in 1924, and the Mogho Naba named Mahama Ouedraogo to take his place. This new chief soon had difficulties with the administration, however, and was deposed for exacting unauthorized taxes from his subjects and for abusing his authority. Mogho Naba Kom then appointed Ousmane Ouedraogo, but he was deposed for "incompetence" and exiled to Sao district.

On the other hand, Hesling made few attempts to change the traditional political and administrative structures of the Mossi. One contemporary source says:

> Since its inception the Government of the Upper Volta has made no changes or innovations, or at best very few, in this connection. The native administrative entities in the cercles of Ouagadougou, Ouahigouya, Kaya, and Fada-N'Gourma have remained the same as those which Haut-Sénégal et Niger transferred to the colony in 1919. . . . Only in 1922 did the cercle of Koudougou have its "Gurunsi" districts separated from its "Mossi" districts to form a new province, which was placed under the command of the Leo Naba, a chief of the same Gurunsi race. Tenkodogo, a cercle made up of a large number of small districts ruled by thoroughly inept chiefs, has been the object of a partial internal reorganization since the beginning of 1923. The number of its native *circonscriptions* [districts] has been reduced from 82 to 73.[36]

These were minor changes indeed, but they truncated the power of the Mossi chiefs over the Gurunsi and Busansi, which had been on the increase as recently as the 1880's. Except for these slight changes, however, the Mossi traditional organization remained as it had been since the immediate post-conquest period.

Instead of changing the traditional administrative structure, the Governor introduced a new administrative device, the *Conseil de notables indigènes* (Council of Native Notables) in Ouagadougou in April 1920, and subsequently established similar councils at Ouahigouya, Tenkodogo, Kaya, and Koudougou. By establishing these councils, the administration hoped to provide the Mossi with a better understanding of the ideals and standards of French policy; to place the French administrators in closer contact with the people, who "had been almost totally ignorant of the functioning of [the French] administration"; and to form "an elite who will later be able to contribute in a closer and more personal way to the economic and financial life of the colony."[37] The council at Ouagadougou, which was to serve as a model for Mossi country, was to be presided over by the cercle commanders and to have from ten to sixteen members, including the traditional provincial ministers of the Mossi (with life membership); members of the Moslem community in Ouagadougou; and representatives of foreign groups living in the capital, of French citizens, and of the veterans of World War I. No provision was made to include the Mossi chiefs, but hope was expressed that they would support these councils and work with them.

These councils failed primarily because they turned out to be organs of the French administration and in fact functioned as such, and because their members had varied and often conflicting status. They met two or three times a year at administrative centers and discussed such things as personal taxes, the allocation and execution of prestations, the use of Mossi labor in foreign areas, the licensing and taxation of African traders and merchants, the status of women, the expansion of cultivation, stock breeding, and the collection of shea-butter nuts and kapok pods. None of the Mossi or African representatives had sufficient power or knowledge to challenge the ideas or recommendations of the European members. And the Mossi ministers, while submissive to the Europeans, found it difficult to accept as equals the representatives of non-Mossi peoples who prior to the conquest had lived at Ouagadougou only at the sufferance of the Mogho Naba; nor were they willing to discuss administrative affairs with these people or with the Mossi commoners who represented the war veterans. Ultimately, the councils became rubber stamps for the policies of the administration, and failed to serve as an administrative training ground for either the Mossi ministers or the commoner representatives.[38]

During the Hesling period, the Mossi district chiefs remained in power, but the French, through their African administrative assistants, kept a stricter watch on district affairs. The chiefs regained some of their judicial (or, rather, conciliatory) power in 1921 when the Governor, dissatisfied with the territory's legal system, promulgated a decree reorganizing the courts and giving the Mossi district and village chiefs the right of adjudication in minor cases involving civil and commercial matters.[39] However, they had to send all cases involving serious crimes and all appeals from other cases to higher courts. Because their subjects could appeal to the subdivision courts and because they risked reprimand by administrators when their verdicts were deemed unjust, many Mossi chiefs complied. They tried to do so even when the litigants themselves would have preferred not to deal with the administrators. Often the chiefs overtly told the litigants to go to the administrators but covertly persuaded them not to do so. In this manner they observed all proprieties toward both the French and their subjects.

The village and district courts had to send all criminal offenses such as assault and battery cases and major thefts, as well as appeals against their verdicts, to a "tribunal of the first degree," which was presided over by a subdivision commander and his Mossi assessors. Cases were taken to the tribunal only when the dispute was extremely serious or when people were gravely injured, because Mossi villagers hesitated to take their cases to officials who, when not swamped with work, had little patience with the complexities of Mossi litigation. Moreover, the Mossi feared to subject their fellows to the rigors of the Indigénat, which was still in existence, because, as one official source declares, "If this regime subsists, it is because the Voltaic populations have not yet reached a level of development that would permit the withdrawal of a weapon which is so readily useful to the commanders of administrative units. Besides, when judiciously managed, it does not present any danger in these underdeveloped regions."

Cases which the subdivision commanders considered too serious for their courts were sent to "tribunals of the second degree" at the cercle level. From there, cases were sent to a "colonial court of appeal," which was presided over by the Chief Officer of Political Affairs of the territory and which could sentence a criminal to three to ten years in prison. More serious crimes carrying longer prison terms or the death penalty were sent up to the Supreme Court at Dakar. Owing in part to the lack of communication between the rural districts and the higher courts, the Mossi were seldom able to follow a case higher than the subdivision level. In cases involving long imprisonment or the death penalty, the relatives of the condemned person usually learned about the sentence through rumors from the capital, but seldom through the administration.

One judicial duty which the administration gave the Mossi chiefs and which they had always disliked was the adjudication of domestic cases. They found such cases even more difficult and distasteful after Hesling issued a circular on "The Condition of the Native Woman," which is summarized in a semi-official report as follows:

> [The Governor] is pained to see [the Mossi woman] so often subjected to a special form of slavery which, notably at the time of marriage, reduces her to the role of a domestic animal. Without wishing to interfere with ingrained native traditions, the Governor desires "to prime the desirable evolution by means of judicial decisions." Thus he comes to the decision that in those lawsuits concerning marriage in which formerly the woman was not consulted, she must henceforth be present and must argue the case with her husband. M. Hesling trusts that this procedural reform, which he hopes will give the native woman "a consciousness of her individuality and her rights," will be followed in the courts by further reforms. First of all [the courts] must weaken and then progressively modify those traditions which promote injustice toward women. . . . Questions will no doubt be raised as to whether it is necessary to set up regulations on such matters. However, M. Hesling advises his administrators to adjust [such regulations] to, and apply them with respect for, ancestral traditions. It will be interesting to see the results obtained in this attempt, and to see whether the "moussos" [a malapropism denoting Mossi women] of the Upper Volta will acquire some individuality.[40]

The Mossi chiefs were not told that the Governor's circular recommending a change in the status of women stipulated that traditional practices be taken into account. But even if they had been told, they would not have been impressed, because any fundamental change in the status of women would have placed their whole society in jeopardy. Woman exchange stood at the core of a social, economic, and political nexus that held Mossi society together. True, in pre-conquest times most quarrels and lawsuits were caused by trouble over women, but the marriage system was upheld by all the other institutions. Even after the arrival of the French and the weakening of the chiefs' judicial role, the Mossi could punish violators of the marriage system by imposing social sanctions. They now feared that if the French passed laws giving the women free choice in marriage, and the chiefs had to adjudicate on the basis of these laws, all traditional sanctions would become obsolete. Neither the chiefs nor the Mossi on the Councils of Native Notables nor the elders welcomed any discussion about the status of women. They maintained that the French had conquered the Mossi men, not the women, and that the administration should not interfere with the way in which a Moaga treated his wife. Ironically enough, there was little the administration could do for the Mossi women, since the latter were too timid to approach the Europeans. Most of them continued to react to maltreatment from their husbands by running away, but now they went to the Gold Coast with labor migrants instead of returning to their lineage.

Although the Mossi chiefs had little autonomy in the administration of their subjects, and had to look to the administration for guidance in nearly everything they did, they were not completely powerless. They were the representatives of the colonial administration on the local level, and as such they could control their subjects through the differential allocation of prestations. Those Mossi who had maintained the traditional respect for the chiefs could look forward to less arduous tasks for the administration and to the avoidance of forced labor or army recruitment. Those who by their actions or attitude indicated that they had lost respect for the chiefs were penalized accordingly. Chiefs were also able to retain some control over their subjects because they were still the centers of social, economic, and political relations within their territories. They still received homage and presents from their more loyal or traditionalistic subjects, and with these goods and services they could bind other persons to themselves. Clever chiefs were able to manipulate the colonial administration and use it to enhance their traditional position so successfully that the administration and the missionaries had to take these men into account whenever they wished to establish contact with the population.

The desire of the missionaries to establish missions and schools for the purpose of converting the Mossi to Christianity presented the chiefs with a great challenge because, unlike the administration, the missionaries tried to establish direct contact with the people. The chiefs not only did not like to have Europeans living in their midst, but feared that they would lose control over their subjects who went to live near the missions. However, the chiefs could not refuse to grant the missionaries land on which to build missions and schools. They also provided labor for them, just as they did for the construction of administrative buildings and roads. Similarly, the chiefs recruited children for the mission schools in the same spirit as they recruited students for the schools of the administration. The difference between the Catholic missionaries and the administration with respect to education was that while the former were interested in educating the children of chiefs, they were also interested in children from other backgrounds. Nevertheless, the majority of chiefs continued to send to school only those children whose parents could not prevent them from being sent away. Many of the boys came from serf and commoner families; a few others were the orphan sons or very young sons of chiefs. As a result, few of the chiefs' sons received an education, and thus they were later unable to compete effectively with commoners who had gained a valuable education at the missions.

Acknowledging the average Moaga's refusal to adopt Catholicism as long as his chiefs remained pagan, the missionaries made a valiant attempt to convert the chiefs. Monsignor Socquet reports that when asked why they did not become Catholics most Mossi replied: " 'We are looking to our chief,' that is to say, 'We will follow our chief in conversion as in all other matters. If he is in favor of it, we will not go against his will.' " Socquet concludes: "It is thus easy to understand how important is the conversion of the chiefs, or at least their sympathy for our religion, to the spread of Catholicism."[41] However, the chiefs and their eldest sons were the most difficult to convert because they were responsible for supervising and carrying out the traditional sacrifices to the royal ancestors, without whose help the Mossi people believed that they could not survive.

The attempts of the missionaries to recruit as many girls as possible for education and conversion alienated the chiefs, because it got them involved in the delicate problem of the status of women and struck at one of the few remaining bulwarks of their traditional power. The problem was that many of the girls whom the missionaries wanted as students were or had been betrothed, or were actually living in their husbands' compounds, when they were taken to the mission. Here the girls were educated and, in the words of Sister Marie-André, "wished to abandon those practices" that were "repugnant to them"—i.e., they rejected polygynous marriages and desired to choose their own spouses.[42] Those men who lost fiancées or wives as a result of missionary activities sought redress from their chiefs. But the chiefs were powerless against the missionaries, and after the promulgation of Hesling's circular nothing could be done. Many Mossi chiefs were also parties to the defeated marriage alliances because of their involvement in the pughsiure system. Because their prestige and power were at stake, and because they were unable to combat the Europeans openly, these chiefs often used devious means to spirit away the girls from the missions and to return them to their fiancés or husbands. Such activities angered the missionaries, who through the administrators either punished the guilty chiefs or sought new legislation in this area.

The chiefs, the missions, and the French administration were perpetually embroiled because both the chiefs and the missions wanted Mossi women for their own purposes. The administration was caught in the middle. The Mossi accused the missionaries of being especially anxious to get girls who could become the wives of their converts, and accused them of "stealing" the women. Paradoxically, this charge is supported by a missionary of the White Fathers:

> A Mossi who is unable to acquire a wife by traditional means must either remain unmarried or seduce another man's wife . . . they must choose between celibacy and immorality.
>
> Such a state of affairs creates many problems for the missions, especially since the system is recognized and sanctioned by the colonial authorities. . . . Young native Christians are obviously placed in a very awkward position. Their conversion angers their parents, who refuse to give them a wife; neither will their friends bestow a daughter upon them, because they know that they will not receive one in return, since a Christian may not give a daughter in marriage to a pagan. . . . *Consequently, unless the missionaries help them to find a wife, they must remain unmarried—a very discouraging prospect.* [Italics mine.][43]

The Mossi chiefs objected strongly to these activities of the missionaries on behalf of their converts, for they insisted that marriages could not legally take place outside the traditional pattern of reciprocity in woman exchange. They argued that the priests had no daughters, but that once they had obtained wives for their male converts, the daughters of these converts would in fact be pughsiudse to the priests and would be used by them to obtain further converts. There was some truth in this argument. Some young men, anxious to obtain wives without trouble and hard work, approached the mission girls, only to be told that the missionaries alone could sanction their marriage. The priests asked only that the potential husbands become Catholics. Some young men agreed and became Catholics; others reneged on their promise after they had been baptized and married. When a young man left the Church himself and also forbade his wife to go to church, the missionaries sought help from the district chief. If he did not satisfy them, they asked the district commander to intervene on their behalf. The young man then had to return to the Church with his wife or leave the district. Many men chose the latter course, taking their wives to visit some distant relatives or to the Gold Coast, until the women, burdened by motherhood and reintegrated into the traditional social system, lost all desire to renew their association with the missionaries. Under these circumstances, the missionaries could not summon the couple to the administrative center, because they had not violated any of the tenets of the Governor's circular. Furthermore, most administrators, like the Mossi chiefs, had little interest in such cases.

The Mossi chiefs considered the Catholic missionaries a greater threat to Mossi society and to their own authority than the French administration itself. This was primarily due to the fact that these missionaries, as Frenchmen, were very deeply involved not only in preaching Christianity, but also in changing Mossi society by introducing modern medical practices and education. Moreover, as was later brought out, they did not hesitate to use coercion to gain their ends. In seeking to understand why the number of patients in a maternity clinic had declined from an all-time high in the late 1920's and early 1930's to almost zero in the late 1940's, André Dupont, a Catholic missionary, was told by Mossi women, "We are no longer forced to go." He comments: "Was it the fear of sanction that accounted for the unanimous use of the clinic? Alas! It would seem to be so. The use of force and sanction have made a charitable institution odious. It would have been better if the mothers had only been encouraged to use the clinics. 'These natives do not understand,' I am sometimes told. But how are they expected to understand?"[44]

The American Protestant missionaries did little to challenge the authority of either the Mossi chiefs or the French administration. They were interested only in religious education, and concentrated on teaching the Scripture. The British social critic Geoffrey Gorer, who visited the Mossi during the Hesling period, reports: "There were some American missionaries in this village, a whole family living in a house filled with texts; I do not know what creed they preached or with what success. . . . They spoke with a dispassionate 'none of our business' disapproval of the ill treatment of the negroes, who they said were ruled entirely by fear."[45]

The Moslems, on the other hand, took advantage of the declining power of the Mossi chiefs to spread their doctrines. They pointed out, with little fear of contradiction, that formerly the chiefs had checked the spread of Islam in order to protect their own religion, which supported their political power, but that this power had now been broken by the French. They continued to preach that as soon as all the black people became Moslems the whites would leave, and pointed out that whereas the missionaries had succeeded in getting the administration to attack the marriage customs of the pagan Mossi, they had not interfered with the marriage customs of the Moslem Mossi.[46] Moreover, the Moslems tried to impress upon the chiefs that conversion to Islam brought with it the benefit of being judged according to Koranic principles rather than native law or French statutes. This propaganda was relatively successful, and by the end of the Hesling period the number of Koranic schools and converts among the Mossi had increased eightfold. True to form, however, the Mossi chiefs seldom adopted Islam or permitted their elder sons to do so. But they did allow their younger sons to become Moslems, and soon abandoned their active resistance to Islam.

Hesling did not permit the Mossi chiefs to revive their traditional religio-political rituals and ceremonies such as the Tense, but he continued to tolerate the Basgha. The French banned the Mossi market chiefs, because they believed (with some justification) that these officials used their offices to procure revenue for the chiefs. The difficulty was that the market chiefs were also responsible for arranging sacrifices to the market deities, which in the absence of such sacrifices would not protect the people from quarrels and violence in the market place. Some chiefs covertly retained their market chiefs; others obeyed the administration and remained anxious over the behavior of their subjects in the market. In general, however, most Mossi chiefs tried to adjust to the religious changes that were taking place, and sought to maintain at least surface amicability with all religious groups. Commenting upon the behavior of the Mogho Naba in this regard, Dim Delobson states:

> The Mogho Naba, above all, is a believer in animism like all his subjects, and it is hard to understand how he manages to reconcile his fetishism with the complex dogmas of Islam and with the many interdictions of Christianity. However, the Mogho Naba is quite capable of being a Catholic or a Moslem on appropriate occasions, while at the same time respecting the traditions of his ancestors. Thus, when the Christians are celebrating Christmas, the emperor of the Mossi devoutly attends midnight Mass. Nevertheless, he wears his fez [really the bonnet which is the symbol of his office], just as the bishop wears his miter. He likewise embraces Islam for the three Moslem festivals.[47]

Hesling failed in his attempt to develop the Upper Volta as a viable colony, and many of the chiefs whom he had used as his auxiliaries lost not only a great deal of power but also a great deal of prestige in the eyes of their subjects because of the role they had played vis-à-vis the administration. By 1929 the economy of the Upper Volta was in poor condition: cotton production had declined; taxes (raised from 5,800,000 francs in 1921 to 18,274,000 francs in 1927 and scheduled to be raised to 26,400,000 francs in 1930) were unbearable; many of the roads that were too extensive, too little used, and too difficult to maintain had been abandoned; and more than 46,000 laborers who had worked in the cotton fields and on the roads had fled to the neighboring Gold Coast.[48] The Colonial Minister, Sarraut, ordered that the colony of the Upper Volta be dismembered. He states in his decree of September 1932 that the suppression of the Upper Volta "would permit appreciable savings, and would make the administrative and technical personnel serving in its capital available for general service."[49] But another, more important reason for dismembering the colony was to make available "to the Ivory Coast, a rich and prosperous colony with diversified environments and products, an abundant and disciplined labor force, which alone was lacking to infuse it with hopeful vigor."[50] According to the articles of a decree promulgated in January 1933, the Upper Volta was divided as follows: The cercle of Ouahigouya and part of the cercle of Dedougou, encompassing 52,400 square kilometers and 712,000 people, were attached to the Sudan; the cercle of Fada-N'-Gourma and Dori, with 70,700 square kilometers and 268,000 people, was attached to the Niger; Tenkodogo, Gaoua, Batie, Ouagadougou, Bobo-Dioulasso, and part of Dedougou were given to the Ivory Coast. The Ivory Coast by this change gained some 153,400 square kilometers and 2,019,000 people.

The Mossi chiefs resented the division of the lands conquered by Ouedraogo and Oubri, and while they never ceased to desire the reintegration of Mogho, they were powerless to do or say anything about it at the time. Many young French colonial officials also resented the division of the colony, and were eloquent in their denunciation of what they considered a moribund colonial policy. A member of the Upper Volta administration, Robert Delavignette, says in his obituary of the colony:

> These obscure masses: three million persons. . . . Once they represented a threat, although the thousands of horsemen of the Mogho Naba of Ouagadougou were defeated by the infantry squads of Captain Voulet in 1897. Soon the threat had diminished, but the matchless aggregate of villages remained. It was an alluring challenge to administrators. Let us mention briefly how they dealt with it. The more they pacified it, the more difficult their task became. The more they tried to impose upon it an open economy with a pattern of roads, urban centers, and cotton fields; and the more they tried to discover the vital principle of that economy in order to establish a new harmony between the land and these obscure masses, the more they broke down the old, set, traditional economy. . . . The heartland of the Upper Volta was indeed molded: 6,000 kilometers of roads, 100,000 hectares of collective fields, and a few urban centers built of mudbricks—all or almost all of this done by hand. No original methods or powerful tools were used, no inventiveness or clarity of purpose was shown. This was but a megalomanic copy of old patterns of mercantile exploitation, and [represented], in the heartlands, powerless, joyless work for those obscure masses.[51]

The criticisms of such officials as Delavignette and Henri Labouret persuaded the colonial administration to dispatch to Ouagadougou a higher official, M. Louveau, to relieve the Mossi of excessive prestations and taxation. Louveau cut taxes from 33,000,000 to 24,000,000 francs, a decision which, according to Burthe d'Annelet,

> forward-looking as it was, represented only an amelioration of the past situation. In effect, the natives had exhausted all their reserves, sold their animals dirt cheap, and could not pay their taxes in an honest manner. This represents quite clearly an abuse of taxation. One must conclude from these facts that taxes had been raised too rapidly, and that these excesses had long surpassed the resources of the natives, even though it is the present depression that brings this out.[52]

The administration continued to require the Mossi chiefs to supply laborers, but found that many potential workers were leaving for the Gold Coast instead.

Despite the fact that Abidjan, the capital of the Ivory Coast, is far removed from Mossi country, the administration of the Ivory Coast hesitated at first to maintain an administrative center in Ouagadougou or to return to the Mossi chiefs any of their lost authority for administrative purposes. The situation had become so chaotic by the mid-1930's that Pierre Boisson, the Governor-General of French West Africa, issued a decree making the Ouagadougou region part of an administrative unit called the Upper Ivory Coast. He says:

> In acting thus we wish, on the one hand, to facilitate relations between the Upper and Lower Ivory Coast, and, on the other hand, to ensure for the Mossi population an effective representation of their particular interests, which do not always coincide with those of their neighbors. It also seems to us that in order to ensure this simultaneous liaison and separation, the Governor of the Ivory Coast ought to be seconded by a delegate in Mossi country who would be responsible for coordinating the local interests of [the Mossi] with the general interests of the colony.[53]

Boisson was under increasing pressure from such officials as Delavignette and Labouret to improve the administration of his territories, but when World War II broke out all plans for reform had to be shelved.[54]

The Mossi chiefs, especially the Mogho Naba, swiftly came to the support of France in her hour of need, and several thousand Mossi and other Voltaics were sent to the lines as soon as war broke out. According to Balima:

> In 1940, the old and popular Mogho Naba Kom II, shocked by the spectacle of the French disaster, . . . took his two eldest sons by the hand and declared to the Mossi people in the presence of General Barraud, senior commander of the troops: "Here are my two sons, my eldest sons, to fight for France." Soon afterward this French general was able to recruit more than

10,000 Mossi soldiers, each of whom took this oath like the two princes: "I enlist in the name of God, and I enlist in the name of the Mogho Naba." Throughout the long hostilities, thousands of Mossi sacrificed their lives for France, faithfully and without regret, because all of this was in accordance with the rules of warfare.[55]

France's disaster was so swift and so total, however, that only those Mossi who were in France when the war began took part in the debacle. Many hundreds were killed, and hundreds more were taken prisoners by the Germans.

Boisson's decision to ignore General de Gaulle's appeal to rally to the side of the Free French angered and disappointed Mogho Naba Kom II and his chiefs. Their anger turned to dismay when Boisson allied himself with the Vichy Government. One report states that in West Africa, "Vichy's tenets increased racial discrimination, reinforced the arbitrary features of the Indigénat, and led to elimination of the few existing political and labor organizations and to repression of any movements or individuals favoring General de Gaulle."[56] Vichy replaced the motto of the French Revolution, "Liberty, equality, fraternity," with "Work, country, family." When any administration in French West Africa had work to be done, the Mossi bore the brunt of it. The regime of forced labor, which had been in the process of being ameliorated before the war, grew harsher as the more reactionary groups gained the ascendancy in the Lower Ivory Coast. In addition to providing men for the plantations, the Mossi were forced to double their efforts at home. Because of the war, their territory had to become self-supporting and to provide vegetable fats, cotton, and livestock to other areas as well. Balima reports that what infuriated the Mossi chiefs and the group of young educated Mossi "was that military service was diverted into other channels. In other words, under cover of a vague governmental decision, the massive recruitments of draftees were not transferred to the barracks for shipment to the front, but instead were placed in the hands of the Public Works Department or, worse yet, sent to the plantations of the ubiquitous *colons* of the Ivory Coast." He adds, "This was a psychological mistake which produced dreadful results, and which precipitated the permanent departure of a number of Voltaics to British territories, particularly to the Gold Coast, where compulsory military service was completely unknown and where every deserter was sure to find a well-paid job and shops filled with merchandise."[57]

The Upper Volta, especially Mossi country, came in for a great deal of attention by the Vichyites, not only because its young people fled across the border to the neighboring Gold Coast, but also because agents of the Free

French Forces were present there. The official Vichy radio began broadcasts urging discipline, increased production, and "patriotic cooperation in making the Federation [of French West Africa] a military bastion against the encroachment of its British neighbors."[58] In response, local officials ordered Mossi chiefs to provide laborers to build trenches and fortifications between the two areas. The Free French, for their part, used the Gold Coast as a center for the distribution of anti-Pétain propaganda, and tried to employ returning Mossi labor migrants as couriers. The majority of these young men were not interested in politics, however, and those who were prevailed upon to take propaganda leaflets into Mossi country simply discarded them as soon as they crossed the border.

The pressures, counter-pressures, and anxieties of this period were apparently too much for Mogho Naba Kom II, who died on March 12, 1942. By the next morning, countless rumors to the effect that the Mogho Naba had committed suicide had spread as far as the Gold Coast. The most widespread rumor was that the Mogho Naba's anti-Pétainist views had become clear to the administration. In reprisal, he was "placed under surveillance on Boisson's orders and separated from his subjects. He died solemnly by his own hand after having summoned his son and commanded him not to take office 'until the true French should return.' "[59] Another widely circulated rumor, probably originated by Moslems, was that the Catholic missionaries, freed from the restraints of Paris, had tried to compel the Mogho Naba to divorce his many wives and become monogamous. The Mogho Naba allegedly could not comply with this demand because it would have been a severe violation of Mossi tradition for a royal wife to become the wife of any other man while her husband was still alive. Faced with this dilemma, the rumor said, the Mogho Naba committed suicide.

The official French report on the Mogho Naba's death reveals that the administration was aware of these and other rumors and of their potential influence on the behavior of the Mossi people. The report also shows that the French officials believed, and credited the Mossi with believing, the classical superstition that "The heavens themselves blaze forth the death of princes." The report states:

> Over the last few years, the health of Saidou Congo [Mogho Naba Kom II] has been impaired by heart trouble, and it was a heart attack which carried him off at about 11 P.M. on March 12th.
> The natives have no explanation for sudden deaths, and attribute them either to supernatural intervention or to poison. Besides, two phenomena had occurred just then to strike the imagination: there had been a total eclipse of the moon on the night of March 2d to 3d, which announced,

according to the Mossi, the imminent death of an important chief; secondly, a meteor had passed unexpectedly over Ouagadougou between 8 and 9 P.M. [on March 12th], vividly impressing the Mogho Naba himself.

It is quite possible that the emotions induced by these phenomena aggravated the heart condition that felled him. Certain people have maintained that the Mogho Naba, being opposed to all foreign domination and convinced that serious developments were imminent, voluntarily commited suicide by poison in order to elude them. So far, there is no proof that such a rumor has really been adrift. The matter is under strict investigation.[60]

The Mossi people practiced as best they could the traditional rituals connected with the death of a Mogho Naba. During the interregnum, however, the administration did not permit the usual chaos, ritual or otherwise. One administration report states: "Young people tried to steal things in the market, taking advantage of the old customs, but they were checked."[61] A later report adds that the traditions of the Napoko and the Kourita were honored, and that one hundred persons were arrested for the ritual larceny of small objects.

The traditional Mossi authorities allegedly requested that the deceased Mogho Naba, as one who had worn the Legion of Honor, be given full military honors. This required the placing of his body in a coffin so that the funeral cortege could move through the streets, a fact which introduced a new ritual element in royal funerals. Once this ceremony was over, however, the representatives of the administration withdrew, and the body was buried according to customary rites.

The traditional electoral college then proceeded with the task of choosing a new ruler. The choice was between Issoufou Congo, Kom's eldest son, who was then a lieutenant in the French Colonial Army in the Ivory Coast, and his younger brother, Etienne Congo, chief of the Doulougou district. With the administration's permission, the college elected Issoufou Congo. He took the title "Sagha" (the second Mogho Naba to bear that name), and was installed with traditional ceremonies.

The message Sagha sent to the French High Commissioner bears quoting. Like the traditional speeches of newly elected Mogho Nanamse, it was believed by the Mossi people to contain subtle jibes at enemies, praises to benefactors and friends, and portents of future plans. The Mogho Naba said:

> At the moment when I take command of the Mossi people, I must thank you for having placed me on the throne of my father. I give you assurance of my fidelity toward France in all circumstances. Be assured by this testimony that my father will remain for me an honored person and a guide. I will walk in the footsteps of my father. In these difficult times, my people and I re-

main attached to the French cause. My father is dead, but the soul of Mossi country lives on. I beg you to transmit to Marshal Pétain, Admiral Platon, Governor-General Boisson, and Governor Deschamps the expression of my profound attachment to France and the assurance of my full devotion.[62]

Some contemporary Mossi claim to see the Mogho Naba's appreciation of General de Gaulle, his rejection of the Pétain regime, and his desire to regain power over the Mossi people, in the words, "I will walk in the footsteps of my father. In these difficult times, my people and I remain attached to the French cause. My father is dead, but the soul of Mossi country lives on." No one could be sure that this was indeed the Mogho Naba's true sentiment, but this too is according to custom.

Nine months after Issoufou became Mogho Naba of Ouagadougou, the situation in French West Africa changed radically. The Allied forces invaded North Africa, and, after more than two years of resistance, Governor-General Boisson shifted West African support to the Free French. Forced labor and product requisitions continued, but now the Mogho Naba and his chiefs were told that the aim was to help General de Gaulle. M. Cournarie, who had replaced Boisson as Governor-General in 1943, made no significant changes either in the administration of Mossi country or in its traditional political organization. Nevertheless, the pressures for fundamental changes in European colonial territories were steadily building up throughout the colonial world. De Gaulle, with the foresight he was to show time and again, realized that the prewar colonial system was dead. He attempted to set the stage for the progress of the African peoples by calling a conference of high French colonial officials at Brazzaville in the Moyen-Congo, to open in January 1944. This conference was to effect great changes throughout French Africa and to set the stage for an irrevocable change in the position of the Mossi chiefs.

Visitors to the court of Mogho Naba Sanum salute him in the traditional Mossi manner. From Louis Binger, *Du Niger au Golfe de Guinée par le pays Kong et le Mossi, 1887–1889* (Paris, 1892).

Mogho Naba Sagha II (1942–57), who was instrumental in reuniting the Mossi people into one territory, the Upper Volta.

The Mogho Naba's daughter, the Napoko, impersonates her deceased father at his funeral ceremonies. Note that she wears one of his robes, his slippers,

The musicians of the royal court, the Bendere.

(*Left*) Mogho Naba Kougri and Ouezzain Coulibaly, who became Vice President of the Government Council of the Upper Volta in 1957. (*Center*) Maurice Yaméogo, President of the Republic of Upper Volta. (*Right*) Mogho Naba Kougri (1957–) on his ceremonial horse at his installation.

Mogho Naba Kougri at court. He is flanked on the right by his pages and musicians, and on the left by members of the Moslem community.

Mogho Naba Kougri (*center*) and, from left, the Kambo Naba, the Gounga Naba, the Ouidi Naba, the Larhalle Naba, the Baloum Naba, and the Nemdo Naba.

Mogho Naba Kougri's warriors, many bearing traditional weapons, respond to their sovereign's call for aid against the new French administration.

Mogho Naba Kougri concedes to the administration, and orders his warriors to disband.

XI

CHIEFS AND POLITICIANS

THE MOSSI CHIEFS were neither present nor represented at the Brazzaville Conference, and thus had no voice in the discussions about the postwar political structure of the territories and their place in this structure. The delegates laid the groundwork for the governmental structure, but failed to define the role of the chiefs.[1] Thus, when the first postwar elections were held in August 1945 to select municipal officers (the first elections held in French West Africa outside of Senegal), none of the African chiefs had a role aside from their unofficial influence on their subjects.[2] The Mossi who were in Abidjan, Ivory Coast, and who were qualified to vote took part in the election, but the Mossi in Mogho could not vote because their towns had not yet been granted municipal status.

The first election in which the Mossi and their chiefs voted was the one held in October 1945 to elect delegates from the Ivory Coast (Ouagadougou was then considered the Upper Ivory Coast) to the Constituent Assembly in Paris, which was to establish the Fourth French Republic. Félix Houphouët-Boigny, a Baulé chief, planter, and founder of the African Agricultural Union (Syndicat Agricole Africain), had won the municipal elections in Abidjan, and now sought the support of the Abidjan Mossi for his candidacy to the Assembly. The Mossi spokesman in Abidjan, Zebango Pohi, stated that the Mossi would vote only for a Voltaic, and that the Mogho Naba of Ouagadougou (who because of his father's reputation and his own educational qualifications was now acknowledged as the spokesman for all Mossi chiefs) would decide whom the Mossi would support.[3] Houphouët-Boigny then sought the support of the Mogho Naba, but the ruler was committed to a policy of detaching Mossi country from the Ivory Coast and named one of his own traditional ministers, the Baloum Naba. Houphouët-Boigny and his supporters were reportedly "greatly surprised by the Mogho Naba's choice. They felt that the honest but illiterate Baloum Naba was unqualified for the task, and, moreover, could not hope to gain the support of the coastal Ivory Coast population. There was little they could do about it, however, because 'the decision of the Mogho Naba was irrevocable.' "[4]

The election was hotly contested. The candidates based their campaigns on local issues: taxes, forced labor, the lack of public services, the status of the traditional chiefs, colonialism, racial discrimination, and so on. The Parti Démocratique de la Côte d'Ivoire (PDCI), led by Houphouët-Boigny, stressed the need for combating racial discrimination and exploitation by European planters. The Union pour la Défense des Interêts de la Haute-Volta (UDIHV), formed by the Mogho Naba and a group of mission-educated young men and led by the Baloum Naba, stressed the need to end forced labor, especially among the Mossi, and to place all the Mossi under one territorial government. The UDIHV realized that it had little chance of gaining votes in the south, and therefore concentrated its efforts in the north. However, no credence is to be given to the story that "Whenever [the Baloum Naba] was free from [official] supervision, he told the people, 'Vote for my friend Houphouët. . . . What would I do in Paris, with my forty wives and at my age? I can't speak a blasted word of French.' "[5] Houphouët-Boigny won the election by the surprisingly narrow margin of 12,650 to 11,620.[6]

Houphouët-Boigny played a leading role in persuading the first Constituent Assembly to submit to the voters a number of important liberal colonial reforms. These included the abolition of the Indigénat; the freedom of meeting and association; the bestowal of French citizenship on colonial peoples without affecting their traditional personal status; the use of the French Penal Code in all courts dealing with criminal cases; and the abolition of forced labor.[7]

There was some discussion in the Assembly of what role the traditional chiefs should play in the projected political structure of Overseas France. One group of delegates held that "the structure of the local Assemblies should be tied intimately to the existing structure of the overseas societies. Otherwise, they would be bogus Assemblies whose decisions would serve the interests of only one class in the society, the dominant class."[8] These men felt that while many chiefs were conservatives and might incline to "neo-feudalism," the new elite of young educated Africans who aspired to replace the Europeans were, for the most part, European-trained and out of contact with the rural masses. These delegates believed that only the chiefs could provide adequate popular leadership, and that the French Union could not cohere or develop unless the chiefs had some status vis-à-vis the elite and prestige in the eyes of the people.[9]

Another group held that the chiefs need not be formally associated with the governmental apparatus. A historical precedent was cited: in the early days of colonialism, the chiefs had not become civil servants, and their status had not been impaired. Thus, when a chief collected taxes for the administration, his action was comparable to his former collection of tribute; when he recruited forced labor for the administration and the large plantations, it was similar to the traditional corvée; and when he asked people to plant certain crops, it was like asking them to cultivate his own fields. In a word, as the institution of chieftainship had adjusted to past changes in African societies, so it had the capacity to adjust in the future.[10]

Other delegates, and apparently the French administrators as well, felt that the chiefs should be associated with the administration, but as administrative assistants and not as elected representatives of the masses.[11] Since the position of the chiefs was sacred as well as secular, it was argued, political defeat might impair their position as "the fathers of their people."[12]

The constitution drafted by the first Constituent Assembly (lacking any provisions concerning the traditional chiefs) was finally submitted to the voters in May 1946. Although it won a majority of overseas votes, it was defeated by the French people. The subsequently convened second Constituent Assembly was subjected to a great deal of pressure by a group of colonialists called Etats Généraux de Colonisation, and as a result many of the provisions of the first constitution, among them the single-college provision and various rights of citizenship, were not included in the second. The revised constitution was accepted by the French voters in October 1946.[13] By this time, however, many of the African delegates had become so disillusioned with the French parliamentarians in the National Assembly that they decided to fend for themselves. They met in Bamako in the French Sudan and formed an inter-territorial grouping called the Rassemblement Démocratique Africain (RDA), led by Houphouët-Boigny. Houphouët-Boigny was strongly anti-imperialist, and the party received the active support of the French Communists. It adopted a violently anti-colonial platform, pledging to rally the peoples of Africa to a world-wide struggle against colonial imperialism, and to try to bring all of the emerging political parties in French Africa under its banner in order to achieve the "emancipation of the African masses."[14]

The Mogho Naba and the other Mossi chiefs, noting the anti-colonial posture of the RDA and the hostile reaction of the colonial regime to this group, attempted to take advantage of the situation by advocating the reintegration of the Upper Volta under their more conservative auspices. The Mogho Naba had already taken advantage of the Bastille Day celebration in 1946 to visit and consult with the Yatenga Naba about Mossi reunification, thus ending a centuries-old tradition whereby the two rulers could not meet for fear of death inflicted by the ancestors. Their project was now received with greater interest by the local Europeans, both *colons* and administrators, who were alarmed by Houphouët-Boigny's radicalism and bent on preventing the spread of virulent anti-colonialism among the well-disciplined Voltaic populations.

Shortly after the constitution was approved, the administration announced that elections would be held on December 15 for the Second College of the Ivory Coast's General Council or Territorial Assembly (to be composed of Africans and persons without full French citizenship) and for the other organs of the French Union. Once again Houphouët-Boigny and the RDA, having gained the support of the PDCI and the Parti Progressiste de la Côte d'Ivoire (PPCI), tried to obtain the backing of the Mogho Naba of Ouagadougou and the Mossi-supported UDIHV (shortly to become the Union Voltaïque).[15] Again the Mogho Naba refused. Gabriel D'Arboussier, one of Houphouët-Boigny's lieutenants and an important official of the RDA, later charged that the ruler had been influenced by the Minister of Overseas France, Coste-Floret, who told him that the RDA "was no more democratic than it was African, that it was not an Assembly, and that Africans should rally to an institution that was truly African."[16] In any event, the Mogho Naba and the UDIHV decided to oppose the RDA. They emphasized the common interests of the Upper Volta and championed Voltaic candidates, Mossi and non-Mossi alike.

The electoral law of the territories promulgated in October 1946 did not specifically discriminate against the chiefs, but it was heavily weighted in favor of the educated and urban elite. The electorate was confined to civil servants; soldiers and veterans of the armed forces; chiefs; permanent employees of commercial, industrial, craft, or agricultural establishments; members and former members, for at least two years, of cooperatives, trade unions, and committees of provident societies; holders of official decorations; members of prewar courts and councils including the Chambers of Commerce, Agriculture, and Industry, and agricultural unions; Christian priests and ministers; owners of registered real property; holders of driving or shooting licenses; and persons literate in French or Arabic. Candidates for election to the Territorial Assemblies had to be at least twenty-three years of age, to be registered on the electoral list as residents of the territory, to have a good knowledge of French, and to post a bond of 5,000 CFA (Colonies Françaises d'Afrique) francs, which was forfeited if the candidate received less than 5 per cent of the votes in his election district. Many chiefs were eligible to vote, but, because their fathers had opposed their being educated at mission-sponsored schools, few were qualified to run for office.[17]

More serious for the position of the Mossi chiefs, perhaps, was the fact that many of them either were ill informed about the election or refused to take it seriously. Balima states that a surprisingly large number of Mossi chiefs "could not understand very well the importance of this novelty—which is understandable; had no interest in the formalities, which they nevertheless carried out; and somewhat haphazardly designated as candidates African civil servants to whom they were not even tied by close bonds of friendship."[18] Of course, another reason for this choice of "African civil servants" was that they were among the only persons with the training and education required for candidacy. Nevertheless, the candidates included a few educated members of chiefly families—persons who, not being in the main line of descent or being otherwise ineligible for office in the traditional system, had been "given" to the Europeans to be educated.

The partisans of the Mossi chiefs were victorious in the northern part of the Ivory Coast in an election that saw the emergence of such Voltaic politicians of later fame as Blaise Benon, François Bouda, Zinda Kaboré, Christophe Kalenzaga, Tindougou Ouédraogo, Zebango Pohi, and Maurice Yaméogo. However, the Second College was dominated by Houphouët-Boigny and his RDA colleagues. Despite the Mogho Naba's opposition, RDA delegates set out to ameliorate conditions in the Volta region. For example, the RDA secured the passage of bills to raise the Mogho Naba's salary from 60,000 francs a year, a trifling sum in view of his official and private expenses, to about 500,000 francs a year. Similarly, it ensured that Mossi and other Voltaic students would receive a fair share of the scholarships which France had assigned to colonial students.[19]

These gestures did not dampen the ardor of the Mossi chiefs for the reintegration of the Upper Volta. In April 1947, when French President Auriol, touring the territories to observe the operation of the new political institutions, visited the Upper Volta, the Yatenga Naba, the Tenkodogo Naba, and the head ruler of Fada-N'Gourma met the presidential party at Ouagadougou and pressed their claim for separate territorial status. The French reportedly welcomed this petition because it gave them an opportunity to clip the wings of Houphouët-Boigny, as well as to ensure the aid of the chiefs in procuring adequate manpower for a projected extension of the Abidjan–Bobo-Dioulasso railroad to Ouagadougou. The problem was to convince the National Assembly in Paris that the reunification of the Upper Volta was in the best interests of all concerned.

The French government set up a Parliamentary Commission and sent its chairman, Jean Jacques Duglas, to Ouagadougou and other Voltaic regions to ascertain whether the people desired reunification. Duglas reported his findings to the National Assembly:

> You know as well as I do that the Mossi are proud of their past. Thanks to a political and social organization without peer in West Africa, they have known peace since the Middle Ages, in an Africa ravaged by war and depopulated by the slave trade. . . . This ancient land also desires prosperity and modernization. To achieve this its voice must be heard, not only in the National Assembly but particularly in the Grand Council [the highest consultative body] of French West Africa. The Upper Volta must have its own General Council.[20]

The law authorizing the reconstitution of the Upper Volta as a separate territory was promulgated on September 4, 1947. The non-Mossi populations of the projected territory feared Mossi domination and voiced their opposition in the Assembly, but in the end an accord was reached. The Mossi chiefs next petitioned the French government to pay for the rebuilding and refurbishing of Ouagadougou. François Bouda, one of the few traditional Mossi nakomce to become an elected representative of the Mossi, reminded the members of the Council of the French Union of what had occurred in 1919. He stated that his own father had recruited thousands of men to make bricks for "Bancoville" (an epithet for Ouagadougou; most of its buildings were of sun-dried bricks called *banco*) because Governor Hesling "never considered the possibility of purchasing cement, which was not even expensive. Forced labor was easy to recruit, and no one thought that the day would come when it would be gone."[21] Bouda said that the Government should now help the new territory to modernize the capital.

D'Arboussier, an RDA delegate in the Assembly, declared that he would support the bill, if only because in the past the French government had attempted "to make a crack race horse out of an ordinary horse, and in so doing had made it a decrepit mare."[22] Funds for rebuilding Ouagadougou were finally voted, and the "Bancoville" of French West Africa began to take on a new look with wide avenues, large administrative buildings, official residences, and even a new palace for the Mogho Naba.

With the reconstitution of the Upper Volta, the Mogho Naba and his chiefs attained their highest prestige since the conquest. The chiefs even had strong influence over the Mossi representatives to the organs of the French Union, because of the decisive support they had granted them in the elections. But this increase in prestige was to be short-lived. The chiefs were no longer the sole representatives of their people, and the Mossi were no longer isolated from events in other parts of the Upper Volta, or for that matter from events in French West Africa and the rest of Overseas France. All projects undertaken in the Upper Volta became of interest to the other units of the French Union because the funds to support them had to be voted on by representatives of the whole, including not only local Mossi and non-Mossi, but also Africans in other territories, French colonial populations outside Africa, and the metropolitan French.

The conditions that were to have the greatest effect on the position of Mossi chiefs were created in January 1949, when elections were held to choose the Upper Volta's first General Council. The major parties involved in the election were the Mossi-dominated Union Voltaïque; the Entente Voltaïque, a local section of the RDA representing the interests of such non-Mossi populations as the Lobi, Fulani, Bobo, Senufo, and Gurunsi; and a group of smaller ethnic parties such as the Union Lobie and the Indépendants. The campaign reflected all the tensions and conflicts prevalent among the administration, the RDA, the non-Mossi parties, and the Union Voltaïque. Both the Union Lobie and the Indépendants spoke out against what they feared to be Mossi domination, and accused the Mossi chiefs of "neo-feudalism." The Union Voltaïque accused the RDA of radicalism, of associating with communists, and of hostility to the chiefs. It cited as evidence the deposal of several Agni and Senufo chiefs in the Ivory Coast by partisans of the RDA. The RDA, in turn, charged the Union Voltaïque with supporting reactionary, feudal-minded chiefs, and thus with opposing the true interests of the Mossi and other Voltaic peoples. Furthermore, it accused Masson (Governor Mouragues's executive officer) of encouraging the cercle commanders to fight against the RDA, and of jailing about 300 RDA members at Bobo-Dioulasso.[23]

As expected, the Union Voltaïque won most of the seats in the more populous Mossi section of the Upper Volta, and thus was able to dominate the political institutions created by the administration. Nevertheless, the election produced deep political scars in the Upper Volta, and lasting enmity between the RDA and the Mossi chiefs.

During the years that followed the reunification of the Upper Volta, the Mossi chiefs as such were not accorded any specific status by the administration. Beginning in 1953, bills designed to regularize the status of the chiefs were submitted by Mossi delegates to the Assembly of the French Union and to various other organs of the French Union, but to no effect. The Mossi chiefs meanwhile sought to define their own position. In 1952, under the leadership of the Mogho Naba, they formed an organization called the Union of the Traditional Chiefs of the Upper Volta. Article IV of the statutes which they filed with the territorial administration reads as follows:

The present Union has as its aims:

1. To establish an alliance and effective solidarity among its members, and to defend their material and moral interests in the face of all difficulties;

2. To collaborate closely with the economic and social aims of the French administration;

3. To provide aid to the dependents, wives or minor children, of all deceased members of the society. This aid will be obtained:
   a. by drawing from a special reserve fund;
   b. by contributions from all members; and
   c. by an additional subscription according to the circumstances. The total sum to be granted to each family will be set at the annual meetings of the general assembly.

This organization decided to meet annually in Ouagadougou, Ouahigouya, Tenkodogo, and Koudougou. Member chiefs were to be notified of meetings through the existing traditional political hierarchies. Those chiefs who were unable to attend meetings could send a representative.[24]

Both the politicians and the French administration welcomed the formation of the Union. The politicians saw it as a forum that would support them in elections and to which they could report on their activities on behalf of their constituents. The French officials welcomed the opportunity to meet periodically with the chiefs and to obtain their help and support for official plans and projects.

One of the new administrative policies was to increase the number of administrative units (the cercles, subdivisions, and postes), and to staff them with European civil servants. Mossi country was given one civil servant for every thousand inhabitants. These officials were thus less isolated from the central administration and more directly responsible to their superiors for the areas under their command. Most of them were assisted by young African civil servants, both Mossi and non-Mossi, who kept administrative records, worked in the agricultural extension programs, acted as interpreters and court assessors, and so on. In addition to these administrative assistants, there were usually junior civil servants who were stationed at the homes of the district chiefs. They were called "secretaries," but they actually served as liaison officers between the administrators and the chiefs. Thus the administrators notified the district chiefs through these secretaries that certain taxes were being levied, and would be collected on a specific date; that certain laws affecting them had been passed; that an election would be held on a certain date; or that they should summon the potential draftees in their district to be examined at a certain time.

The postwar administrators did much more than communicate with the district chiefs through their secretaries. They still had considerable authority in local matters, even though the Indigénat had been abolished. They adjudicated minor offenses committed in their territories or referred to them on appeal by the districts and villages. They attempted to settle family quarrels and commercial cases, and ordered that restitution be made in cases of theft. However, they had to send any difficult case or major crime up the hierarchy until it reached the officials authorized to deal with it.

The French administrators also continued to act as intermediaries between the large commercial enterprises in Ouagadougou who wished to recruit men for labor or to buy local produce and enterprises in the larger Mossi towns. Thus, if a private firm in Ouagadougou wanted men to work on the roads, it asked the *chef de poste* (administrator) of a region to tell the district chiefs that its representatives would come to recruit men on a certain date. If a large business was planning to canvass a certain area in order to buy shea nuts, it asked the local administrators to notify the chiefs. No one was ever quite certain whether these activities were legal, but no one questioned them. The *chefs de poste* might simply have been giving the people information that they could not have obtained by any other means.

The Mogho Naba of Ouagadougou, like the supreme chiefs of the other Mossi regions, continued to perform both the administrative role assigned to him by the colonial government and his traditional politico-ceremonial role. He was partly responsible, through his active cooperation with the administration, for the rapidity with which the Upper Volta became a functioning entity. For example, in his anxiety to make his capital worthy of being the territory's administrative center, he gave his full support to the extension of the Abidjan–Bobo-Dioulasso railroad to Ouagadougou. But he always succeeded in giving the impression (to foreigners at least) of detachment and dissociation from the French administration. His behavior was quite different when he functioned as Mogho Naba of the Ouagadougou Mossi. The following is a brief description of a visit he made to one of the districts:

> The Mogho Naba arrived unexpectedly at the district chief's headquarters, where no preparations had been made for his visit. It appears that he was on a tour of his domains to consult with the local chiefs about the forthcoming elections, and had simply dropped in to visit the district chief. However, as soon as his presence became known around the district, important village chiefs and the heads of lineages all put on their robes and appeared to pay homage to him. Meanwhile, he was consulting with his host. But as soon as the conversation was over he came out into the compound, where he was saluted by the chief's Bendere, who praised the royal ancestors by reciting

their genealogies and traditions. The Mogho Naba was pleased by the recitation and thanked the drummer.

Later that day, the Mogho Naba presented himself in the courtyard of the district chief's compound to be saluted by the village chiefs and by the heads of lineages. They came to him in the traditional way, rubbing their palms and bending their foreheads to the ground. He addressed them, and in response they snapped their fingers in the customary manner. Then, one by one, the village chiefs and the lineage elders came to their monarch and gave him presents of money which ranged from 50 to 200 francs. The Mogho Naba paid little attention to the sums given, being more interested in this act of homage and fealty. However, he listened carefully as each donor announced his name and rank within the official hierarchy or village. He later thanked them collectively and departed. This ceremony, while not very elaborate, differed little in detail from those characteristic of the traditional Mossi's relationship to their Mogho Naba. The new element here was that the monarch was traveling around his domain, establishing a close relationship with his chiefs and subjects, whose support he needed for his modern political alliances.[25]

The Mogho Naba continued to hold the morning ceremony at court, even though it was rapidly losing its traditional function and becoming of major interest only to visitors. He also continued to hold those ceremonies associated with individual appointments to the nam and with traditional sacrifices. Unknown to many was the fact that traditional authorities at court still judged legal cases which many Mossi refused to take to the Europeans.

In contrast to the Mogho Naba, the traditional provincial ministers now lost most of the power they had held in the pre-conquest period, and all the duties they had acquired in the immediate post-conquest era. As we have seen, one minister, the Baloum Naba, had entered politics at the suggestion of the Mogho Naba, but even he was now relegated to the entourage that accompanied the Mogho Naba and the European administrators on visits to the ministers' former provinces. The increased number of European administrators had made these ministers superfluous.

The district chiefs retained some prestige after the war. They could still judge legal cases, with the understanding that the litigants were free to go to the Europeans if they so desired and had to be sent there in serious cases. Their major problem was that a more efficient administration was taking a greater interest in district affairs. For the first time since the conquest, officials were visiting some of the more remote villages. No longer were they said to "act as locusts"—that is, to appear periodically to garner supplies and men from the districts and then disappear until the next onslaught. Instead, they appeared regularly to collect taxes and to take censuses, and they were kept informed of almost everything that occurred in the districts by their secretaries and "friends" (usually war veterans who visited the administrative headquarters on business).

Not all the district chiefs accepted with equanimity their gradual loss of power. Many of them had accepted at face value the joyful refrain of the elite and the politicians that the "land was cooling"—i.e., that the rigors of colonialism were over. They welcomed the liberal laws of 1946, and believed that they would regain the power lost by their fathers. Thus, they were among the most surprised persons in the Upper Volta when the easing of colonial rule brought with it more French supervision rather than less. From the standpoint of political power, most district chiefs had been better off in the days of the "locusts." At least the locusts came and went, whereas progressive government slowly but irrevocably eroded their power.

The village chiefs, as those members of the traditional Mossi hierarchy who had the closest contact with the people, felt the postwar administrative changes much more keenly than the other chiefs. They found it increasingly difficult to deal with war veterans, adherents of formal religions, and other people who had lost respect for traditional values and practices.[26] Whereas few Mossi would have refused to visit or to pay allegiance to the Mogho Naba or to their district chief, with whom they had little personal contact, many did refuse to have political relationships with those village chiefs whom they neither liked nor respected.

The rural Mossi, upon whom the position of the Mogho Naba and his chiefs ultimately depended, did not fully comprehend the postwar changes in the Upper Volta, and were initially willing to look to their chiefs for guidance. Most of them referred to their newly won civil rights in the French Union by what they called *soguem minga,* which may be translated as "possession of one's self," "liberty," or "liberation." To the majority of them, however, the reforms meant chiefly the end of forced labor. They were more than willing to leave the new political affairs to their chiefs, despite the assurance of the elite that they could now participate in the governmental processes. Dupont wrote in a romantic vein about the introduction of political reforms in the Upper Volta:

> Can we truly speak of a change for the better in this country? Yes! A page has been turned, the last in a chapter. A new chapter has just begun, and I was the amazed witness of this beginning. . . . One must say, in France's favor, that she did not merely engage in beautiful speeches, but that her liberating decrees deeply modified the life of the natives. Gone is the export of laborers; gone are the uncontrolled prestations; gone the requisitions of produce which the peasants had to buy elsewhere at a higher price and resell at a loss; gone the sales in which the collective price given to the district

chief became ridiculously smaller when distributed among the producers; gone the tolls along the roads. Henceforth, all such services will be duly and individually compensated.

Even in the most remote and least accessible villages, people speak of liberty. The old women who go to the pools for water sit down for a moment near their jars in order to talk about it. Even bush fires spread less rapidly than this news.[27]

Very few Mossi in the rural areas were qualified to vote in the first postwar elections, and those who were qualified voted for the candidates preferred by the chiefs. However, as the franchise was progressively broadened after 1951, and many more Mossi and non-Mossi politicians traveled through the rural areas, the politicians favored by the chiefs found that they had to campaign to maintain their position. Both the chiefs and their politicians resented this. One visitor to the Upper Volta reports: "A highly educated Mossi of the Upper Volta told me, 'Citizenship has unsettled and ruined the people. Everyone has become his own master, and believes himself free to do whatever he wishes.' "[28] Opposition to the chiefs and their friends came from the Moslems, who supported their co-religionists for office, and from a growing group of young Mossi who resented the power of the chiefs. In 1955 one such group in Yatenga, composed of mission-educated youths, war veterans, and former workers, broke away from the Union Voltaïque and formed the Mouvement Démocratique Voltaïque (MDV) under the joint leadership of Gérard Ouédraogo and Michel Dorange, a Frenchman, who had been a captain in the colonial army. The partisans of the MDV often came into violent conflict with the supporters of the chiefs, but the organization itself was not banned by the administration, because its members included many veterans, and because Dorange was one of its leaders.

The appearance of the anti-chief MDV was symptomatic of the problems which the Mossi chiefs were to encounter as the people became free to elect their own representatives. For one thing, the people could now censure their chiefs by voting for their opponents, who appealed to them in terms of release from traditional prestations. But more important, even those Mossi politicians who were still friendly to the chiefs and depended on their support for election were becoming increasingly autonomous. The chiefs were operating in one power structure, the politicians in another and more important one. In Dakar, in Paris, and in the Palace of Versailles (where the Assembly of the French Union met) Mossi politicians dealt not only with local African problems but with problems the chiefs knew nothing about. As the politicians grew skillful at the game of metropolitan politics, their power increasingly eclipsed that of their chiefly benefactors and of local French administrators. For example:

> A local chef de poste summoned the district chiefs to bring their potential draftees for the war in Algeria early in the morning on a specific date to be examined by medical officers. Those chiefs who looked upon any summons with a trepidation born of their past experience with prewar administrators, arrived at the headquarters as early as 5:30 A.M. on the morning in question, bringing their young men with them. Many of these chiefs, whose only means of transportation was their slow-moving ceremonial horse, spent the night en route to be there at dawn. More sophisticated chiefs coming from similar distances left on the same morning and arrived at about 8:00 A.M., the hour when the administrator himself was first seen stirring in his residence. One chief, a war veteran, rode up on his bicycle at about 8:45 A.M. in a most unchiefly manner and became the butt of jokes from the other waiting chiefs. Another district chief, who was an elected representative, did not arrive until about 9:30 A.M., and he was greeted on arrival by the administrator. This man had only about half a mile to travel, and he did so in his car. His colleagues greeted him with a mixture of jokes, feigned awe, and surprise, and some of them addressed him as "Mogho Naba" and "Governor."[29]

Another example of the shift in the balance of power was the relationship that developed between Joseph Conombo and the Mogho Naba of Ouagadougou. The Mogho Naba had nominated and supported Conombo as a candidate for deputy to the National Assembly. He was elected, and later became Secretary of the Interior in the Mendès-France Government of 1954. He thus had access to power undreamed of by the Mogho Naba. Being a Moaga as well as a good politician, he never flaunted his authority before his traditional chief; nor did the Mogho Naba try to exercise his traditional powers over him. But their behavior toward each other clearly demonstrated that they were both aware of the shift in power, even though they were both too wise and too polite to make an issue of it.

Other political forces also jeopardized the position of the chiefs. For example, as head of the Union Voltaïque, Conombo had an honored position within a Paris-based African parliamentary group called the Indépendants d'Outre-Mer (IOM). He would have held an even more important position within this group if he had had wider support among the non-Mossi in the Upper Volta. But his power was limited by the presence and competition of the MDV, which, while Mossi-supported, was anti-chief; the Mouvement Populaire de la Révolution Africaine (MPA), an anti-Mossi and anti-RDA party formed in 1954 by Nazi Boni of the Bobo ethnic group and supported by some officials in the administration; and the Parti Démocratique Voltaïque (PDV), a local branch of a now less radical RDA created out of the defunct Entente Voltaïque. In an attempt to gain the support of these parties and of the young Mossi intellectuals who, while anti-chief, were not yet willing to join the PDV, Conombo officially scrapped the Union Voltaïque in 1955 and formed the Parti Social d'Education des Masses Africaines (PSEMA).[30] The party pledged to promote social reform and the right of Africans to manage their own affairs, and to struggle against family, regional, and racial hatreds. But it did not win the support of the non-Mossi; nor did it attract many young Mossi, who did not believe that it had discarded the mantle of the chiefs. Conombo's readiness to ally himself with anti-chief forces, however, did make it obvious to the chiefs that when politicians were out to gain power, they did not always take the interests of the chiefs into account.

In 1956, when a *loi-cadre* granting almost complete autonomy to the French African territories was approved by the National Assembly, it made no provision for the participation of the traditional chiefs in the projected governmental structure.[31] In fact, as preparations were being made to implement the new reforms, a number of politicians and educated Africans launched an attack on the chiefs which seems to have been a step toward edging them out of power altogether. The newspaper *Afrique Nouvelle*, published in Dakar but read by the educated elite throughout French West Africa, carried a series of articles that proclaimed: "The district chiefs should be given neither a position nor a salary!" "Let us democratize the chieftainship!" and "Let us decapitate the district!" (i.e., let us do away with the district chief). Over a photo showing the traditional chiefs, *Afrique Nouvelle* ran the caption, "Are they still chiefs of the territories?"[32]

The Mossi chiefs, who had retained more power and prestige than any other chiefs in French West Africa, bore the brunt of these attacks and rose to defend the rights of all the chiefs. Their most able spokesman was Bouda, a Councillor of the French Union and a district chief in his own right. He wrote in *Afrique Nouvelle*:

> The Mossi [socio-political] organization, by its simplicity and cohesiveness, aroused the admiration of France, which respected and retained it.
>
> The power of the Mossi chief may be great, but it is not used to oppose the progress which is being made. The Mossi chief is not as much of a conformist as people have a tendency to believe. The social and political revolution which, since 1946, has made Mossi country so different from what it was before the war, is effecting the transition from a society largely encompassed by Nabas possessing real authority, an authority sanctioned by custom, to a more progressive way of life whose essential characteristics are underlined by the growth of towns, the uprooting of a large part of the population, and the triumph of the desire to be on one's own. . . .

The Mossi chiefs indeed understand today that a tradition, no matter how respected, is not immutable. It is susceptible to change and evolution; it will evolve.

In all truth, and with due deference to those who systematically denigrate everything connected with them, the chiefs have borne positive witness to the characteristic spirit of this country, and it is as unfair as it is stupid to deny the important role they have played in certain cases in the cause of tranquility and peace.

As the natural spokesmen for their people, they have been, in many instances, the first to pay a heavy price for the common cause. Without them, demagoguery would have plunged the country into irreparable decadence.
. . .
The demands of the traditional chiefs are justified and deserve to be heeded, because, in the face of the inertia of the Government and the rapid development of events, it is to be feared that the chiefs, although disposed by nature to be patient and to wait quietly, might run rather than walk in the days to come.[33]

In December 1956, the Mossi chiefs, supported by the other traditional chiefs in French West Africa, convoked a Congress of Chiefs at Dakar. This Congress approved a constitution for an organization called the Federal Union of the Syndicates of the Traditional Chiefs, and adopted a proposal on the need for a statute governing the status and material well-being of the chiefs. The Congress did underline the apolitical character of the chieftainship, but asked that the chiefs be given some recognition in the new structures being created by the loi-cadre.

On the local level, the Mossi chiefs convoked a Syndicate of the Traditional Chiefs of the Upper Volta at Tenkodogo a month later. Its president, Etienne Congo, brother of Mogho Naba Sagha II of Ouagadougou, declared:

At this time, when vast changes are under way, it would be inconceivable for us, the traditional chiefs, not to take an active part in the new developments, of whose urgent and precarious nature we are fully aware.

Our position is clear: we are not opposed in any way to this evolution.

As for statutory matters, I wish to express our concern over the fact that at the very moment when the loi-cadre is turning an important page in the history of Africa, our group has been left out.[34]

The Mossi chiefs had indeed been abandoned by the French administration. Although they continued to receive the support of some politicians, it soon became clear that the latter were mainly interested in maneuvering for power under the loi-cadre and in uniting their parties to this end. Conombo, the leader of the PSEMA, was induced by his supporters and by a number of young educated Mossi to merge his party with the PDV-RDA in the hope of gaining a foothold in the Bobo-Dioulasso area and of uniting the Mossi and non-Mossi of the Upper Volta. The two parties did merge in September 1956, becoming the Parti Démocratique Unifié (PDU). The PDU's manifesto roundly condemned the "artificial division of the territory into East and West Volta" and the "classification of the population as Mossi and non-Mossi," and urged all Voltaics to join the new party. In addition, it declared that the Mossi chiefs merited some status in the territory because they had preserved their "political entity throughout African history."[35] The PDU went so far as to make the Mogho Naba its honorary president, and to speculate that he might be made the Governor of an autonomous or independent Upper Volta.

Nevertheless, the merger was to be a greater victory for the opponents of the Mossi chiefs than for their allies in the PSEMA. For one thing, many of the anti-chief Mossi intellectuals now joined the PDU, bringing with them their modernistic views. For another, since former RDA members were running for office in the Upper Volta under the banner of the PDU, the local chiefs had to give up their opposition to these candidates, and the French administration did likewise. This hands-off policy gave all the candidates, even those who were basically hostile to the chiefs, a better chance of being elected.

The PDU won a slight over-all majority and a large Ouagadougou majority in the Upper Volta elections for the Territorial Assembly and the Government Council in March 1957. However, the anti-chief MDV carried the Ouahigouya (Yatenga) area, and an Indépendant candidate, Maurice Yaméogo, defeated a supporter of the Mossi chiefs, Henri Guissou, in the Koudougou area. Of great importance was the election of Ouezzain Coulibaly, one of the early non-Mossi Voltaic supporters of Houphouët-Boigny, who had returned to the Upper Volta after the merger of the PSEMA and the PDV-RDA. Coulibaly was elected on the PDU ticket as a representative for Banfora, a district in the western region.[36]

Unfortunately for the Mossi chiefs, the RDA emerged from the March elections as the strongest party in all the former French West African territories. Because of this, most of the politicians in the Upper Volta sought to establish a modus vivendi with Houphouët-Boigny, the Party's recognized leader. Most of them went to visit him at Yamoussokro, his home in the Ivory Coast, and out of these meetings there emerged a realignment of the MDV and the PDV-RDA wing of the PDU at the expense of Conombo and the PSEMA group. This created a new majority in the Upper Volta, and Coulibaly, an old ally of Houphouët-Boigny long suspected by the

Mossi chiefs of being a modernist, was elected as the first Vice-President of the new government. Not only was the Mogho Naba deprived of the opportunity to become the African head of the Upper Volta, but such stalwart supporters of the chiefs as Conombo and Bouda were left out of the government. Thus, after twelve years of opposition to Houphouët-Boigny, Mogho Naba Sagha and his chiefs were finally defeated. Their defeat was made even more ignominious by the elevation of a non-Mossi commoner to a position of dominance over the Mossi chiefs.[37]

Having lost out in the Upper Volta, the Mossi chiefs had no spokesman when the new Vice-Presidents of the Government Councils of the French West African territories and the European Presidents of these territories met at Dakar to discuss the problems of the truncated French West Africa Federation. No one mentioned the problem of the position of the traditional chiefs. As far as the politicians were concerned, the issue of the chief on the inter-territorial level was dead. It had relevance only in those territories where the chiefs retained some influence.

In an effort to consolidate their hold on the Upper Volta, the PDV-RDA members in the PDU met in September 1957 and sought to convert the PDU into a territorial subsection of the RDA. This move was resisted by the supporters of the chiefs within the PDU, especially by Conombo, who as leader of the PSEMA, an important faction within the PDU, had been completely eclipsed by Coulibaly and the PDV. Conombo resigned from the PDU and announced his intention to rebuild the PSEMA with the support of the Mossi chiefs. On November 12, however, before his plans could be put into action, Mogho Naba Sagha II died in Ouagadougou and political activities in the Upper Volta came to a standstill. A period of national mourning was proclaimed, and politicians from all parties gathered to pay their last respects and to eulogize the monarch.

Sagha's death, like that of all Mossi princes, was ascribed to foul means, although it was clear that he had succumbed to uremia. The people reacted to the interregnum by looting, and the shopkeepers in Ouagadougou and surrounding areas were compelled to close their establishments. "The people of Ouagadougou ran to Saba, but the merchants there were quite diligent, and needed no police force to protect them."[38] It was reported that those wives of the deceased ruler who were not at the palace at the time of his death took off the brass anklets denoting their royal status and became free women. If this actually happened, it was an unprecedented occurrence.

When the Mossi traditional electoral college convened to choose a new Mogho Naba, it reportedly considered the candidacy of both Moussa Congo, Sagha's eldest son, and Etienne Congo, Sagha's brother. Etienne Congo allegedly had the support of some politicians, but he was rejected in favor of Moussa. The new ruler was accepted by the Government Council as the "supreme chief of the Mossi" and was installed in the traditional manner. He indicated in his acceptance speech that he was "like a rock [*kougri*] that nothing can move," and became known as Mogho Naba Kougri. A few days after his installation, he appeared in full regalia before the members of the Territorial Assembly to deliver what was probably the most difficult inauguration speech ever composed by a Mogho Naba. This speech will be quoted in full, because it may well be a eulogy for the Mossi chief:

> Over and above the signs of respect shown to the mortal remains of my father, and later the expressions of keen satisfaction on the people's part for the choice of which I have been the object—over and above all this, I see the great interest that the governmental and administrative authorities attach to the role which my ancestors have always fulfilled, and which I am called upon to fulfill anew. Over and above all of these external manifestations, I see the unfailing love of all the Mossi for the throne I occupy and for the tradition I represent along with my confreres. Because the importance of my position, as well as the honor that befalls me, surpasses the meager reality and the possibilities of one man, it is with conviction, sincerity, and faith that I present myself to all of you to tell you that while I accept with fortitude these responsibilities and these honors for the love of my people, I count upon the cooperation and friendship of all, the faithfulness, devotion, and courage of all the Mossi, to acquit myself worthily and to preside not in a passive but in an active and decisive way over the social and economic evolution of our country.
>
> Although I represent tradition and custom in this country; although I must ensure the survival of venerable customs, concerning which we shall be intransigent; I am aware, nevertheless, that there are customs which adapt themselves with difficulty to the exigencies of the modern times in which we live.
>
> This is why, in addressing myself to all the customary chiefs, and especially to my closest associates, I shall say that we have no right to remain passive observers of the reconstruction of our country and of the multiple transformations of the society over whose destiny we have always presided. We must move along with the tide, but in order not to be swept along at a headlong pace and risk failure before reaching our goal, we must stand in the vanguard of the race and lead it at a vigorous and satisfying pace, but one which does not stifle the weak, for they too have a right to life, to progress, to well-being, and to our protection.
>
> As recently as ten years ago, it was easy to be a chief, just as it was easy to be a cercle commander. It was enough to give orders for everything to run smoothly. But today, the chief must add to his title a real merit, a knowledge of men, a true devotion, an integrity, and, above all, a commitment to the welfare of the people under his jurisdiction. It is under these conditions alone

that the customary chiefs will preserve and extend their influence, and it is our task to extend this influence. For, if the new institutions are meant for the progress and welfare of the Africans, then they must also be meant for that of the chieftainship.

Our intention, then, is not to leave the management of the country to the elected representatives alone, but to remain in close collaboration with them; for, if the elected representatives of yesterday have rights, the representatives of several centuries' standing retain theirs also.

Intent as I mean to be on curbing all the abuses for which the people have customarily blamed the chiefs, I will not cease to remind the Chief of the Territory, the members of the Government Council, and the elected representatives at all levels, that they themselves must remain, before God and man, the ones truly responsible for these abuses. For, while the lot of the civil servant has improved considerably, and that of the elected representative is at the summit of the pyramid, that of the chief has remained quite modest and quite comparable to that of the still miserable peasant—riches for the others, poverty for himself.

Your Excellency the Governor, Honorable Ministers, and Parliamentarians, I am sure that you understand me. I am equally sure that you think of the meager outlook for the territory, but it is necessary that everyone live well during the period of the seven fat cows, and meagerly during that of the seven lean cows. The cooperation of the chieftainship will be granted to you increasingly for the economic and social betterment of our territory. It devolves upon you, as agents of superior authority, to rid the chiefs of the arbitrary vexations to which no civil servant is subjected any longer, and to send them forth, not as mercenaries but as true captains, into the battle which we all have joined against the human misery that weighs so heavily upon our people.

We are all aware of the magnitude of the struggle, and the cooperation of the chiefs, who influence the entire Voltaic population, may be needed to crown it with success.

Moreover, your Excellency the Governor, the chieftainship has always served well—perhaps has served France, or at least its representatives, too well, at the expense of its own interests.

But I will deliberately forget the errors of the past. I shall remember only the true fidelity which my fathers and their associates have always displayed toward France. I shall look only for the gratitude of the Government of the French Republic on their behalf, and for the considerable role they played in transforming our country. I shall think only of that Franco-African friendship which under normal circumstances will lead us to success, happiness, and peace. I know that the times are difficult; I know that men today have numerous reasons for quarrels. I know that vast popular or so-called popular movements sometimes topple all that other men have built with much patience and wisdom. But despite all of these things, it is with words of concord and of peace that I wish to close, hoping that throughout our political battles we shall keep in mind the need for peace, because man is only happy insofar as he enjoys social peace, as well as peace of the heart.[39]

For all its occasional eloquence, the new Mogho Naba's speech was clearly self-serving; moreover, the French officials to whom it was addressed were withdrawing from the territory, and the young Mossi elite had other ideas about the distribution of power. It is no wonder, then, that most of the politicians listened to his speech in respectful silence and then "calmly went ahead with their tasks," confident, it seems, in their new status as the elected representatives of the people.[40]

The new Mogho Naba was faced with a political situation in which he could play only a limited role. His strength now lay exclusively among the more conservative elements of the newly enfranchised rural masses. The political representative of this group was Conombo, who in November 1957 went ahead with his plans to rebuild the PSEMA. In December Conombo saw a chance to embarrass and perhaps defeat the Coulibaly Government when the Territorial Assembly decided to vote on the budget of the Upper Volta; he and his followers withheld their vote of confidence in the Government and tried to force it to resign. But the conditions under which the members of the Territorial Assembly could force a government to resign were not clearly defined by the loi-cadre. The various parliamentary groups appealed in vain to Paris and to Houphouët-Boigny to resolve the problem. Coulibaly broke the impasse by forming a new coalition and giving Maurice Yaméogo, an Indépendant candidate who had been a member of the RDA and later of the MDV but had switched back to the RDA, the important portfolio of Minister of the Interior. Finally, the Assembly, which had been adjourned, reconvened in April 1958 and confirmed Coulibaly in power. In a speech to the Assembly, Coulibaly declared: "It is my imperative task to tell you that each one of you is faced today with a decisive choice. You must choose either a pooling of efforts and good will in the interests of the country, or the pursuit of personal quarrels and partisan rivalries that will undermine the public welfare."[41]

The Mogho Naba and his political allies suffered yet another defeat with the Assembly's approval of the Coulibaly Government. However, Kougri had other strings to his bow. In June 1958, when de Gaulle returned to power, Kougri sought to gain the General's favor, and to raise his own status, by pledging his support and that of the Mossi chiefs. This astute political move infuriated many Voltaics, Mossi and non-Mossi, politicians and non-politicians. Amadou Tamboura, a member of the MDV, replied to the Mogho Naba in the newspaper *Paris-Dakar*. Under the headline, "The Message of the Mogho Naba to General de Gaulle Commits Only Himself," he wrote:

It will be well if the Mogho Naba understands that he owns but the vestige of a past whose hour has irrevocably tolled, and that his message to the President of the Council [de Gaulle] commits no one in the Upper Volta but himself, a mere citizen like the others.

I deplore the discrimination which the message of the Mogho Naba implicitly contains. I should like to say to the Mogho Naba that in the Upper Volta there are no Mossi, Fulani, or Bobo people, but only Black people struggling for their liberty. No Mossi or any other Voltaic would agree to the Mogho Naba's expression of fidelity to France in his name. If this must be done, then the Territorial Assembly and the Government Council alone are qualified to do so.[42]

Despite these attacks and numerous suggestions in the press that the Mogho Naba and the Mossi chiefs were developing a "Touré complex" (i.e., the fear of suffering the same fate as the Fulani chiefs of Fouta Djallon, who had been deposed by Sékou Touré, Vice-President of the Guinea Government Council), the Mossi ruler actively supported acceptance of the constitution of the Fifth French Republic, which promised the colonies full internal self-government within the "French Community." Since the constitution was adopted by the Upper Volta population by an overwhelming favorable vote of 99.1 per cent, no one could estimate how effective the Mogho Naba's support had been.[43]

Coulibaly died just before the referendum, and was replaced on an interim basis by Yaméogo. The parliamentarians accordingly had to choose a new leader, now to be President of the Government Council, as well as to draw up a constitution for the new republic and determine whether it would join any of the regional federations then being considered by several territories. The Territorial Assembly was scheduled to meet in extraordinary session on October 17, 1958, to select a successor to Coulibaly. The Mogho Naba, anticipating dissension and perhaps once again seeking the limelight, sent a message to the representatives on October 15, urging "a government of union and public safety." But the politicians resented what they regarded as his interference in matters that did not concern him; few, if any, took his message seriously, and none replied.

The Mogho Naba therefore decided to force the issue. He summoned his traditional ministers to a conference, and, despite the objections of the Baloum Naba, obtained their permission to order his Tansoba to muster his warriors and lay siege to the Territorial Assembly. Early in the morning of October 17, about 3,000 Mossi warriors, armed with bows and arrows, swords, spears, and ancient flint guns, converged on the Assembly. Later that morning, the Mogho Naba himself, accompanied by his Tansoba, arrived on the scene, dressed in his dark-brown cotton war cloak and his war bonnet, the symbol of his power. The demonstration lasted until 11 A.M., when the French Army undertook to scatter the warriors. Finally, the Ouidi Naba ordered the warriors to return to the palace. Only then did Max Berthet, the High Commissioner, open the Assembly session with an expression of regret for the "unacceptable and incomprehensible" demonstrations.[44]

The Assembly adjourned that afternoon and did not meet again until October 20. In the interim, the parliamentarians took measures to deal with this challenge to their power. On October 18, the Government Council issued a communiqué "stigmatizing Friday's demonstration." The Council regretted that the demonstration had prevented a democratically elected body from sitting, but affirmed that "order and public security, indispensable to everyday life, will be maintained."[45] On the following day a longer communiqué was issued, declaring that a truce had been signed by the authorized representatives of the Union Démocratique (Voltaic section of the RDA) and the Mouvement de Regroupement Africain (Voltaic section of the PRA) after a three-day meeting in Ouagadougou. According to the communiqué, the two groups had agreed that "the unity of the democratic forces of the country" was "the decisive question of the hour."

The Territorial Assembly met in Plenary Session on October 20, and on the basis of the political truce, 68 representatives unanimously elected Maurice Yaméogo as President of the Government Council. The politicians further showed their disdain for the Mogho Naba by adopting the following motion:

> The Territorial Assembly, in the unanimous assurance that it alone has the mandate of the Voltaic people to legislate in their name, solemnly declares that, in the face of all opposition, it will work to give the Voltaic State democratic institutions conforming to the aspirations of the population, within the framework of the constitution which they approved by such a strong majority on September 28. Furthermore, it is insistent in its demands that the authorities responsible for public order do everything in their power to determine the persons responsible for the demonstration and to see what should be done to avoid a recurrence of such an event.[46]

The Mogho Naba soon found to his chagrin that even some of his own vassal chiefs had turned against him. They had been persuaded by the politicians that the French Government would never allow the Mogho Naba to take over the country, and furthermore that he had overstepped his bounds and had thereby endangered further the institution of the chieftainship. The Bureau of the Syndicate of the Traditional Chiefs of the Upper Volta met, discussed "the affair of October 17," and issued a statement dissociating itself from the Mogho Naba's action, reaffirming its desire to collaborate with the established authority, and requesting a clarification of the status of chiefs in the new order. The Government Council of the Upper Volta welcomed this statement, and hastened to reassure the chiefs that their status was not in danger: "It is not a question of damaging the traditional chiefs as a group, but rather of stigmatizing vigorously an act emanating from a superior chief like Mogho Naba Kougri, the consequences of which, unforeseen as they were, could have placed all the Mossi chiefs in a regrettable and irreparable position."[47]

The Mogho Naba had obviously reached a political impasse, and he next turned his attention to creating a new image of the chieftainship. To this end, he married a young Mossi woman in accordance with the civil statutes of the state, thus becoming the first Mogho Naba and the first important Mossi chief to do so. A spokesman at the wedding placed this act in its proper perspective with the following words:

> I should now like to underscore the fact that this date, November 22 [1958], will be inscribed officially in the annals of the Upper Volta. For the first time in the history of our country, an Emperor, the person who best symbolizes tradition, has upset ancestral habits in the interest of progress. For the first time a woman will be given consideration in a royal court where she will be able to feel at her ease. For the first time, the spouse of a traditional chief will have her place near her husband as an equal and steady companion.[48]

The politicians were apparently prepared to recognize the eminence of the chiefs as long as they did not attempt to intervene in the affairs of the state, and a number of them attended the Mogho Naba's wedding. Among those present were the Presidents of both the Government Council and the Territorial Assembly, parliamentarians from various parties, and the mayors of Bobo-Dioulasso and Ouagadougou. On December 10, 1958, the Territorial Assembly confirmed Yaméogo as President of the Government Council. The Assembly also approved his slate of ministers, among them Bouda, the Mossi chief who had once been a strong supporter of the traditional political hierarchy but who now belonged to the UDV-RDA. Then, on December 11, the Assembly decided to adopt the draft of a proposed constitution for the Upper Volta. Articles 2 and 3 of Paragraph I of this constitution state explicitly:

> The Republic of the Upper Volta is one and indivisible, secular, democratic, and social. Its principle is that the government is *of the people, by the people, and for the people*. . . .
> *Sovereignty belongs to the people. No section of the population, and no individual, may usurp it.* [Italics mine.][49]

The proposed constitution thus negated any claims of the traditional chiefs over any section of the Voltaic population. Henceforth, the only leaders of the Voltaic people were to be their elected representatives. The constitution did not even mention the traditional chiefs, and no provision was made to give them a special voice in the government. By its silence on these matters, the constitution had reduced the Mossi chiefs to the status of ordinary citizens. Certain parts of this constitution were later changed, but not the sections dealing with the democratic nature of the emerging state. The power of the chiefs was gone. Yaméogo, who had been a commoner among the Mossi of Koudougou, was given the title of "President of the Republic" by what had now become the National Assembly. It was he who traveled to and from Paris with Houphouët-Boigny and the other members of the Conseil de l'Entente, an organization comprising Dahomey, the Ivory Coast, Niger, and the Upper Volta, to parley for the independence of the Upper Volta; and it was he who traveled around the country explaining his policies. Yaméogo did not belabor the issue of the chiefs, but he declared quite firmly that "the days of devotion to certain little Voltaic saints" were over. "Now must begin the era of the cult of the Upper Volta, next only to that of God."[50]

France finally agreed that the Upper Volta should become independent on August 5, 1960, just 64 years after the conquest. However, sovereignty and power were not to be transferred to those from whom it had been wrested originally. Mogho Naba Kougri was only a spectator at the National Assembly when Yaméogo, praising Houphouët-Boigny and General de Gaulle, announced the coming of independence; and he was only a spectator when the Assembly ratified the independence agreement on July 27, 1960. The President said on that occasion that "Independence is not an end in itself, but a beginning. In effect, from now on we are called upon to assume full responsibility for our destiny."[51] He added that changes in the country would be brought about "in cooperation with the elected representatives, the party [RDA], and the youth organizations." He made no mention of the chiefs, and in fact the only chiefs who played any role during this period did so as politicians. The chiefs were to be honored only on Independence Day, when the President, in a spirit of benevolence, gave thanks to all those who had played a role in recovering the dignity of "Voltaic Man," including not only the French professors, the clergy, the war veterans, and the politicians, but also the "traditional chiefs who safeguarded the integrity of our state against external attack."[52]

The government of the Upper Volta Republic decided to allow the institution of chieftainship to fade away by preventing the election of new chiefs. The Mogho Naba continued to receive a yearly stipend from the government, and local chiefs were still respected by the older people and by the more tradition-minded youths. Nevertheless, the drive toward the elimination of chiefly status in the Upper Volta went on. In January 1962, government decrees prohibited "the wearing of any costume or headgear indicating the status of chief or slave";[53] thus, the remaining Mossi chiefs are to be unrecognizable as such outside their own villages and districts. The chiefs, for their part, seem to have become reconciled to their fate. Many of their young relatives are joining the growing ranks of the new politicians.

XII

EPILOGUE, 1989

Chiefs, Politicians, and Soldiers

NEITHER THE MOSSI chiefs nor the politicians who assumed power and presided over the independence of the Upper Volta were prepared to deal with problems of political economy when their country achieved international sovereignty. They were largely unaware that their country, which had been integrated into the French sector of the world capitalist economy, would have difficulty managing its own affairs and would be more closely integrated into other sectors of that economy as they sought to build a nation-state. Whereas during the colonial period, almost all important decisions affecting life in Upper Volta emanated from Paris, now Ouagadougou emerged as the primate city, the center of economic, political, social, and cultural life of the new republic. In a manner undreamt of by the early Mogho Nanamse, everything was to be directed by the politicians in the capital. Mogho Naba Kougri, having been eclipsed by Maurice Yaméogo, was forbidden to exercise any leadership either over the provincial ministers, who controlled the urban wards, or over the Dimdamba and Kombemba in the rural areas. To all intents and purposes, Mossi society faced a real interregnum. The society was in a liminal state with most of the people not knowing what would emerge. The new ministers of state had to devote most or all of their time to the establishment of operating bureaus and to attending to the problems of representing Upper Volta at the United Nations and in the major world capitals. They did not have the time or energy to deal with the problems of life in the rural areas where most of the Mossi people lived.

Faced with the disruption of their traditional hierarchy and the precipitous departure of the French subdivisional and district officials, the rural Mossi chiefs were apprehensive about their future. With very few exceptions they had followed the lead of deceased Mogho Naba Sagha; and while their fellows on the Council of Chiefs had strong reservations about the new Mogho Naba, Kougri, they were even more concerned with the reported attitude of President Yaméogo toward the traditional leadership. However, there was little that they could do until firm orders came from Ouagadougou. Meanwhile they obeyed the orders of the new African district officers who had been sent out to replace the Europeans. Where, as in the Yatenga region and some parts of the Ouagadougou kingdom, there were local ambitious members of the UDV-RDA, the chiefs were anxious about their status. Nevertheless, so strong was the ideology of the traditional system that most people continued to "look at the chief."

The preoccupation of the government with international and national affairs and the lack of experience in the emerging bureaucracy of the ministry of the interior played into the hands of the Mossi chiefs. Whereas in 1960 they were fearful, and cautious in exercising any power, by the mid-1960s they had taken the measure of the new administration in Ouagadougou. Increasingly the government had to use their services in dealing with rural people, who still revered them. Chiefly control and direction went largely unchallenged because those youth who were potentially rebellious were also the ones who were drawn to Ouagadougou, where they saw the new opportunities.[1]

Ironically, it was also the need of the national government to develop Ouagadougou so that it could serve as an effective capital of the republic, and thereby become the worthy host of international representation, that forced the politicians to deal with some Mossi chiefs, and ultimately with the Mogho Naba. The status of this royal seat of the Mogho Nanamse, capital of the Upper Volta colony, had changed from that of a *commune-mixte* with an administrative-major in 1927, to that of a *commune de moyen exercice* in 1953, to its full status as a *commune de plein exercice* in 1955. It was then given the right to elect its own municipal council and mayor.

During this evolutionary process, the status and roles of the provincial ministers of the Mogho Naba in the emerging municipal wards had been transformed. They had become functionaries of the colonial government, collecting taxes for the commune and performing other duties for the administration. In order to compensate them, the colonial administration had to use the bureaucratic fiction of making them "village chiefs," a status for which there was authorization from Paris.[2] As chiefs, the traditional ministers took care of their wards, distributing land to persons migrating to Ouagadougou and performing those tasks which devolved upon them as servants of the Mogho Naba, as well as quasi-bureaucrats of the French administrative-mayors.

Ouagadougou elected its first mayor, Joseph Ouedraogo, in 1956 as a function of the political changes that were destined to eclipse the traditional Mossi chiefs. He vowed to get rid of the old mud-brick buildings which were "glorious in times past, but today unworthy to serve the population." His new town hall was envisaged as a "Civil Cathedral, a secular basilica, where one works for the people, where the people come to be counseled and helped, and where the people's representatives try their best to secure for their wellbeing, justice and social peace."[3] The mayor said nothing about the chiefs;

but also elected to the Municipal Council were such notables as the Larhalle Naba, the Baloum Naba, and the Ouidi Naba, all provincial ministers. Among the other members of the council were Nakomce (nobles) who were also civil servants of the municipality and of the emerging national government.

Although the politicians in Ouagadougou would have preferred to eliminate the role of the traditional chiefs in urban affairs, they faced the same problems as did the national administration in dealing with rural chiefs, namely, the lack of cadres. The result was that, as in the rural areas, the urban chiefs continued to function, but now combining their traditional roles with that of "councillor." Thus in effect, three political systems operated in Ouagadougou: the national government, the municipal government, and the surviving Mossi political organization. Moreover, while the national government controlled everything, it was really the guest of the municipality, which in turn had to rely upon the traditional system to perform important functions for the people of the town.

The chiefs were permitted to retain control of the land within their wards until the municipality could assume control. They thus had the right to distribute land to the new politicians, the civil servants, as well as to the incoming migrants to town. All these persons became indebted to the chiefs and reciprocated in various ways. Some made outright gifts to them, and others helped by circumventing bureaucratic red tape on behalf of subjects of the chiefs. Second, the municipal government relied upon the chiefs to take censuses because without their help, local taxpayers could not be identified and made to pay. Third, both the state and municipality tolerated the role of the chiefs as judges and conciliators in many disputes among persons who still did not trust the new governmental institutions. Fourth, when the national government requested that the municipality display flags and summon the urban population to greet visiting dignitaries, that organization had to turn to the chiefs of the wards for help. In time, not only the chiefs and their followers appeared at the airport when distinguished notables arrived; Mogho Naba Kougri was also invited to be present. Finally, even the political party that controlled the government found it necessary to hold rallies in the courtyards of the chiefs in the various wards of the town.

The lack of clear boundaries between the various levels of government in Ouagadougou, and the absence of mediating structures between them, made for conflict in the town. Quite aware of the growing unpopularity of President Maurice Yaméogo, the Mossi chiefs increasingly supported a municipal government which itself was unhappy with the president. Matters came to a head in August 1964, when Ouagadougou was flooded because the money which the municipality had asked the French government to allocate for flood control was misappropriated by the national government. Complaints by the mayor not only resulted in the municipality's losing its budget but also in the decision of the president to take away most municipal functions. In a subsequent municipal election the official party claimed victory despite large abstentions by the urban population. A great deal of displeasure was unleashed. Rioting broke out in Ouagadougou at the end of 1964, when labor leaders protesting salary cuts and increased taxes, in collaboration with progressive intellectuals and politicians, stormed the National Assembly and demanded that the army take power. The army "assumed its responsibility," and on 3 January 1963, the chief of staff, Colonel Aboubacar Sangoulé Lamizana, forced the president to resign. The Mossi chiefs finally had their revenge on Yaméogo, but now they had to face a new set of rivals.[4]

Lamizana was a stranger to the Mossi political system since he was of Samogho origin, a small acephalous population in northeast Upper Volta. A Muslim, he had spent a deal of time in the French colonial army, having served in North Africa, Madagascar, and finally as a captain in Indochina. He saw his task as restoring the confidence of the people in their government. To this end, Lamizana formed a broad-based mixed civilian-military administration and started to bring economic sanity to the country. Most important of all for the Mossi were Lamizana's recognition of the continuing role of the chiefs in the changing life of Upper Volta societies and his giving Mogho Naba Kougri a place in the prestigious official and diplomatic ranks in the capital.

Having suffered at the hands of Yaméogo, Mogho Naba Kougri attempted to demonstrate to his subjects that he was serious about modernizing the chieftainship to meet the needs of the times. He had married the daughter of a wealthy Mossi Muslim merchant and insisted that she would appear officially at his side at all public ceremonies. Kougri retained the weekly ceremonies in honor of the royal ancestors but banished from his court a number of practices, including the famous Mossi salutation, which he judged to be old-fashioned, useless, and decadent.[5] In keeping with this change, the Mogho Naba, like a growing number of his chiefs, decided to embrace Islam. What is not clear was whether this was an attempt to fulfill the old prophecy that held that "as soon as all the blacks become Muslims, the whites will leave."[6] Of course there could have been modern political reasons for this act. Regardless of the reason, when he became a Muslim, Kougri was able to appear side by side with President Lamizana as the faithful gathered at the Place d'Armes for prayers during Islamic holy days.

While the Mogho Naba appeared to accept the new political dispensation in the Upper Volta, he apparently was determined to influence the ways in which his people were governed and those persons who governed them. He was not powerful enough to defy the military, but he kept himself informed about the government's plans in 1970 to promulgate a new constitution for the Upper Volta. What Lamizana had in mind was a transitional regime in which he remained in power but in which the political parties were also to be permitted to resume their activities. These parties included the Union Democratique Voltaique-Rassemblement Democratique Africain (UDV-RDA), the Mouvement de Liberation Nationale (MLN), the Parti du Regroupement Africain (PRA), and the Groupe d'Action Populaire (GAP).

Mogho Naba Kougri faced a dilemma. The old UDV-RDA was still strong among the Mossi; but with the fall and imprisonment of Maurice Yaméogo, it lacked a leader. The contenders for this position were Gérard Kango Ouedraogo, of the Mossi royal house of the Yatenga, and Joseph Ouedraogo, who, though of the princely family of Saba district, displayed a great deal of sympathy for the commoners of Ouagadougou. Of course, the people in Ouagadougou wondered where the Mogho Naba stood. Asked to comment upon this issue, President Lamizana allegedly told a visiting newsman that the Mogho Naba, "has the right to his political beliefs, just like anyone else, but he is finally just the guardian of tradition."[7]

The election that took place on 26 December 1970 demonstrated that Kougri was still a force to be reckoned with. He reportedly supported the UDV-RDA which based "its power on the dominant Mossi tribal region where the authority of the King, the Moro Naba, is not to be underrated—as it was by the first President, Maurice Yaméogo."[8] The Mossi traditional political system mobilized itself, and the RDA won 37 seats, an electoral majority. This was attributable to two factors: "the local administration had remained largely as it was in the earlier period of RDA rule; and the support of the chiefs, (especially in the dominant Mossi area)."[9] President Lamizana chose Gérard Kango Ouedraogo as prime minister, over Joseph Ouedraogo. Joseph Conombo, a strong ally of Mogho Naba Kougri and the chiefs, was chosen foreign minister. Several young military officers were also selected for the cabinet. Joseph Ouedraogo was forced to settle for the post of president of the National Assembly.

When Gérard Kango Ouedraogo became prime minister, many Mossi of the Yatenga teased their Ouagadougou neighbors, stating that the Yadese (Mossi of the Yatenga) had finally retrieved the *nam* which their ancestress, Pabre, had taken when she fled from Ouagadougou. The views of Mogho Naba Kougri on the subject are unknown. On the other hand, Joseph Ouedraogo was furious with everybody. Very much the aristocrat, Kango attempted to be conciliatory, but Joseph Ouedraogo ignored the peaceful overtures of the prime minister. This conflict between these two politicians affected the Lamizana government. Matters came to a head when, much to the anger of the young military cabinet ministers, Gérard Kango Ouedraogo supported a "salary allocation for the chiefs." Lamizana had to use all his skills as a conciliator to end the military officers' boycott of his cabinet meetings.

Besides this political crisis, the Upper Volta faced other problems. The

Sahelian region of the country, which had been hard hit by drought, became the theater of a conflict with the neighboring Republic of Mali. Suspecting that minerals and natural gas deposits in their border region would bring them untold riches, the Malians and Voltaics quarreled over the ownership of lands there and finally went to war. The fighting was soon ended through the mediation of heads of neighboring states, even though the dispute was not resolved. Both the Malian and Upper Voltaic armies gained heroes, among whom was a young captain of an Upper Volta parachutist brigade, Thomas Sankara, who would later play an important role in the future of the country.

This Lamizana government fell, finally, because of a rather blatant attempt of Félix Houphouët-Boigny, president of the neighboring Ivory Coast, to retore the civil rights of former-President Yaméogo and return him to power. Mogho Naba Kougri apparently saw an advantage for himself and the Mossi chiefs in this proposal and in December 1973 went to the Ivory Coast with Yaméogo and Joseph Ouedraogo to plot their strategies. Unfortunately for them, the fact of the meeting became known in Ouagadougou. The result was disastrous: the young military officers urged President Lamizana to prevent Houphouët's meddling in Upper Volta affairs; Prime Minister Gérard Kango Ouedraogo, feeling betrayed, sought to embarrass the plotters by releasing from prison a man named Maxine Ouedraogo, a bitter enemy of the former president. Two cabinet ministers, Joseph Conombo and Ali Barraud, were so enraged with the visit of the Mogho Naba and the politicians to Abidjan in the Ivory Coast that they resigned from the government.

To complicate matters, Joseph Ouedraogo in the National Assembly introduced a motion of "no confidence" in the government in an attempt to unseat the administration of Gérard Ouedraogo. This motion won a majority in the assembly, but not the two-thirds votes necessary for passage. With his regime in disarray, President Lamizana dissolved the government, suspended the constitution, banned all political parties and politics, and promised a National Renovation Government. Thus the rivalries and competition between Mossi princes, and between Mossi princes and commoners, now complicated by regional West African factors, had resulted in a political disaster for the Upper Volta republic.

President Lamizana did put his National Renovation Council (CNR) in place and organized a mixed military and civilian government. But the labor unions, which had been the bane of previous governments, clamored for higher wages, and especially for the return to civilian rule. The president ordered the promulgation of a new constitution, which was accepted by the voters in November 1977. Lamizana then dismissed his cabinet, formed a government of national unity composed of sixteen civilians and four army officers to administer the country until elections, and lifted the ban on political parties.

The constitution for Upper Volta's Third Republic sought to avoid unnecessary political conflict by stipulating that only three political parties could participate in the government. The number of deputies was to vary according to the population of each circumscription, and seats were to be allocated on a proportional representative basis. The president was to be elected separately and could not be a member of any political party. Moreover, any military man who chose to run for office had to resign his commission. Most important for the Mossi people was that the constitution

> restored the role which traditional chiefs enjoyed in local government until they were stripped of these functions by Yaméogo just before he fell. Observers saw the move as popular, since the chiefs are an integral part of the country's cultural heritage, and shrewd since Lamizana would be able to count on their support in getting himself elected in the 28 May run-off for the Presidency. All political parties backed this move.[10]

A number of reasons are given for Lamizana's decision to run for the presidency, among them that he loved the job and wanted to be elected to it in his own right and that he was afraid that many military officers were becoming disenchanted with the politicians and might seize power unless one of their own gained the presidency. Nevertheless, it took a great deal of soul-searching and political jockeying for Gérard Kango Ouedraogo, Joseph Conombo, the Mogho Naba, and the leaders of the UDV-RDA to agree to support Lamizana for the presidency. Maurice Yaméogo, still ambitious, but without his civil rights, encouraged his son, Hermann, and a politician named Macaire Ouedraogo to found a new party, the Union Nationale pour la Defense de la Democratie (UNDD). Joseph Ouedraogo split with his erstwhile colleagues in the UDV-RDA to run as an independent candidate. He had become reconciled with Professor Joseph Ki-Zerbo, an old friend whom he had formerly disdained as an "intellectual." Ki-Zerbo scrapped his allegedly radical party, the MLN (National Liberation Movement), and replaced it with a new party, the Union Progressiste Voltaique. Four smaller parties joined the contest, but they had less support.

Despite the support of Mogho Naba Kougri, the urban population of Ouagadougou, increasing losing its respect for the traditional chiefs, failed to give President Lamizana a majority in the election of 15 May 1978. He only slightly edged out Macaire Ouedraogo, the "stand-in" candidate of Maurice Yaméogo. According to observers on the scene:

> The traditional chiefs of the Mossi called on the people (about two-thirds of the population) to vote for Lamizana since they had not forgiven Yaméogo for abolishing some of their privileges; but large numbers were unwilling to vote for a non-Mossi — especially for one who could not even speak their language. In Ouagadougou, heart of the ancient Mossi empire, Lamizana polled only 9,523 votes compared with Ouedraogo's 26,350.[11]

But whereas the urban Mossi and other inhabitants of the town of Ouagadougou could and did ignore the appeal of the Mogho Naba, the rural Mossi chiefs were able to mobilize their followers on behalf of Lamizana. Since both Joseph Ouedraogo and Joseph Ki-Zerbo failed to gain many votes, there was a runoff between the two leading candidates on 29 May 1978. With the massive support of the Mogho Naba and his chiefs and some of the leading Mossi politicians, Lamizana won the runoff.

President Lamizana paid his political debts to the Mossi princes by naming Joseph Conombo as prime minister and by supporting Gérard Kango Ouedraogo to head the National Assembly. Under this new constitution, the right of succession to the presidency of the republic fell to the head of the National Assembly. Fearing the Lamizana might resign before his term ended, thereby placing Gérard Kango Ouedraogo in office, Joseph Ouedraogo and his supporters rejected Gérard as head of the National Assembly president by one important vote (he had 29 votes, and he needed 30 out of the 57 votes in the assembly). The matter was taken to the supreme court, which ruled in favor of those deputies opposed to Gérard Kango Ouedraogo. Faced with the latter's determination to pursue the post, the opposition deputies boycotted the assembly, thereby preventing Lamizana from being sworn in. The president-elect appealed for national unity but hesitated to use his clout, leading many military officers to charge angrily that Lamizana was "insufficiently authoritarian, permitting as he does a multi-party and multi-trade union system, and freedom of speech." Had it not been the fear of many deputies that the army might seize power, they would not have yielded. Finally, the "rejectionists" returned to the assembly, and permitted Lamizana to take office.

Recognizing the support he received from the Mossi people, especially those in the rural areas, Prime Minister Joseph Conombo named such Mossi princes and nobles as François Bouda and Moussa Kargougou to his government. Seeking national unity, Conombo also offered a number of opposition party members seats in his cabinets, but they declined to participate in his government.[12] It soon became clear that the opposition politicians and the trade unions were determined to defeat the government. In February 1979, the three main labor unions, the Confederation Nationale des Travailleurs Voltaiques (CNTV), the Centrale Syndicate Voltaique, (CVS), and the Organisation Voltaique des Syndicate Libres (CVSL), began a campaign of accusing the regime of corruption, nepotism, and favoritism. The unionists called for higher wages, a more equitable distribution of food in the face of continued drought, and the end to real estate speculation in the capital.

These charges led to countercharges by the president and his premier, and the unions decided to call a strike in May 1979, when two of their leaders were arrested. These two men were later released, but the government proposed legislation in late 1979 making all strikes illegal and recommending arbitration councils to control labor disputes. The unions reacted by calling a general strike in January 1980, forcing the government to back down. Then in October 1980, the teachers' union went on strike, demanding higher wages; the return to Ouagadougou of two teachers banished to the countryside; and the censure of the minister of education for having given his wife one of the coveted scholarships to France.

Adding to the malaise in the country and to the disgust of many of the urban population, Mogho Naba Kougri and members of the government became involved in lengthy conflicts over the *nam* in the traditional Mossi districts. The urban populations, increasingly secularized and modernized, failed to appreciate that the rural Mossi were still attached to the chieftainship and that this office could and did yield votes for national politicians. The resulting chaos in the educational system, charges and countercharges of corruption and nepotism, and interminable conflicts over the *nam* infuriated the army. Military officers accused their former comrade, Lamizana, of being like "a dead man when it comes to wielding power. He neither acted, nor reacted, what were the people to do?"[13] Led by Colonel Saye Zerbo, the army seized power on 25 November 1980, thereby ending the Third Republic. Yet another government, which had come to power with the help of the Mogho Naba and the Mossi chiefs in the rural areas, had bitten the dust.

Colonel Saye Zerbo, who like Lamizana had fought for the French in both Indochina and Algeria and was also of Samogho origin, stated that he and his colleagues had seized power because of "the degeneration of social life, and political confusion."[14] The new president placed Lamizana, the army chief of staff, and many members of government under house arrest; suspended the constitution; dissolved the National Assembly; and banned political parties. Saye Zerbo then announced that he would form a 31-member Military Council for Redress and National Recovery (CMRPN) and an 11-member steering committee and would chair both bodies. Then on 8 December 1980, the president formed a 16-member cabinet with nine civilians and seven military officers, none of whom had ever served in a government. Zerbo suggested that none of the infighting in Ouagadougou had helped the rural masses and promised that the new government would emphasize food crop production, and would aim at "moral discipline and spiritual reform, for 'citizens to mobilize themselves around competent leadership, a team determined to work sincerely and selflessly.' "[15] By now the worsening Sahelian drought had started to highlight the parochial problems of the Voltaic people to an increasing concerned world.

Saye Zerbo's problem was that while the labor union leaders in Ouagadougou were sympathetic to the plight of the rural cultivators, they felt an overriding responsibility to the needs of their urban constituencies. During the strikes which led to Lamizana's downfall, the unionists had repeatedly declared that they were not prepared to tighten their belts because of "alibis about the drought." They initially pledged to support Saye Zerbo; but they resented the repeated military coups and really wanted the opportunity to form a government independent of what they considered to be "old-fashioned politicians," backed by "feudal reactionaries," meaning the Mogho Naba and his chiefs. Therefore, when it appeared to the unions that the CMRPN could not promulgate a program of reform, that it continued the state of emergency, that it utilized many of the bureaucrats from the previous regime, and that it was hesitating to try Lamizana and his ministers for corruption, they embarked on a series of strikes. Joseph Ouedraogo, who had taken the leadership of the FPV from Joseph Ki-Zerbo, warned the government that chaos would increase unless the ban on political activities was lifted. In response, President Saye Zerbo declared that his major concern was to avoid the mistakes which in 1970 and 1978 brought men to power who "led the country to the brink of disaster." He denied that the end of civilian government necessarily meant the end of democracy and insisted that elections and a parliament did not necessarily mean democracy.[16]

In response to continued union opposition, President Saye Zerbo vacillated. He banned strikes, lifted the ban, and criticized the urban workers for selfishness in the fact of rural poverty; but he refused to move the country toward civilian rule. This type of vacillation led some persons to accuse the president of fascism. Others claimed that he was being manipulated by Professor Ki-Zerbo, a fellow Samogho, who allegedly had the support of the French Socialist government of François Mitterand. The country's one daily private paper, *L'Observateur*, published a series of articles by Frédéric Guiérma (a Mossi prince turned politician), critical of the government. Then, in what would later be judged an attempt to establish some kind of dialogue with his critics and pacify the young officers in the army, Colonel Saye Zerbo appointed the young hero of the Upper Volta-Malian war, Captain Thomas Sankara, secretary of state at the Presidency in charge of Information.

Saye Zerbo's attempt at reform was apparently too little and too late. On 7 November 1982, Major Jean-Baptiste Ouedraogo, a military doctor, allied with Captain Sankara, seized power. These so-called "Siamese twins" and their young military officer supporters, were said to have led "a really radical coup."[17] The new chief of state lost no time spelling out his intentions. He declared: "Listen to us carefully: There is no possibility of just simply returning to the previous type of government, but there must be a change toward a constitutional government of a new type."[18]

Just one month after this radical coup, on 8 December 1982, the Mossi people and the other inhabitants of the Upper Volta were saddened by the death of Mogho Naba Kougri. The twenty-five-year reign of this 52-year-old monarch was one of the most difficult that any Mogho Naba had encountered. Having been given the *nam* of Ouedraogo and Oubri, the

Capt. Thomas Sankara (far left) is hailed by crowds in Ouagadougou, Burkina Faso. Photo: Bara/AFRICA REPORT. Used with permission.

founders of the Mossi empire, just as the Upper Volta was moving toward international sovereignty, Mogho Naba Kougri was a frustrated monarch. It was reported that

> on the news of the Moro Naba's death on December 8, police closed the central market in Ouagadougou to prevent the scenes of looting which happened in 1957, on the death of Moro Naba Sagha II. The death of an emperor in Mossi tradition marked the end of the established order, hence the traditional looting. Old habits sometimes die hard.[19]

Again, according to tradition, "thousands of people came to the capital to mourn: a total of 333 cattle were slaughtered in sacrifice on December 18, offered by local chiefs and the extended family of the dead emperor." Throughout the realm, ordinary Mossi sacrificed hundreds of sheep, goats, and chickens, as was customary. When the traditional electors met, they chose Ousmane Congo, the eldest son of Kougri, as the new Mogho Naba. He took the name *Baogo*, which means in Moré "marsh or swamp," thereby indicating that in this drought-stricken land, his subjects should look to him for solace as they would for water. President Jean-Baptiste Ouedraogo, the first Mossi head of state since the fall of Yaméogo, and a number of his ministers "attended the funeral ceremonies of the dead Emperor and placed a wreath on the coffin. Apparently Ouedraogo had concluded that to be successful he would have had to work with and to some extent, through the power structures that were still important to the people."[20]

The coincidence of the coup which brought Jean-Baptiste Ouedraogo to power and the installation of Mogho Naba Baogo[21] led a number of traditionalistic Mossi in Ouagadougou to yearn for a return to the erstwhile tranquil rule of the chiefs. A visitor to Ouagadougou was told: "If the new emperor asked every Mossi to bring a sheep to the palace, his courtyard would be inundated the next day. But if the new president asked every citizen to bring an extra 500 francs tax to the Treasury he would be laughed at, or at best, ignored."[22]

Events were soon to demonstrate that neither the president nor his collaborators were prepared to be laughed at or ignored. And while Major Ouedraogo was relatively easygoing, the younger officers, especially Captain Sankara, wanted a clear break with the past. They declared:

> . . . we think that it is necessary to clean up the political behavior, by condemning those who have embezzled public funds, and by then depriving them of their civic rights. It is inadmissible . . . that because of corruption, a politician possesses fifteen villas with each of them rented to foreign ambassadors, at the rate of 300,000 F CFA [African francs], while 15 kilometers from Ouagadougou, people do not have the means to buy even a tube of Nivaquine [antimalarial drug].[23]

The young officers admitted that they were "ideologues," insisting that every political action was based on ideology, but they denied that their ideology was linked to any other existing ones. They declared that they were moved primarily by the need "to reform Voltaic society, to clean it up, and to purify it." This meant, according to them, that they "had no ideology in the sense that they would subscribe to the notion of Karl Marx, of Fidel Castro or of the great capitalist thinkers." They insisted that they were "not the followers of neither [sic] Jerry Rawlings, nor of Mu'ammar al-Qaddafi, nor of any other."[24]

The problem for these young officers who seized power, as for all contemporary revolutionaries, was that the bipolarity in the present international system of nation-states inhibited their development of a unique ideology and prevented others from believing in their claim to having done so. Like most revolutionaries in the formerly colonial world, these young officers were angry about the role that France had played in the conquest and colonization of their country. They were also hostile toward the Western allies of France, especially the powerful United States of America. Therefore, despite their rhetoric, they were drawn to borrow the models of those societies which were in full rebellion against the West.

To the surprise of nobody, President Ouedraogo named Captain Sankara as his prime minister, thereby acknowledging the dominant role the latter had played in the downfall of Saye Zerbo. Many of the other members of the cabinet were allegedly chosen from the Ligue patriotique pour le development (LIPAD), an organization said to be linked to the Parti africain de l'independence (PAI), of reputed Marxist persuasion. Moreover, with the significant exception of Foreign Minister Arba Diallo, who was educated in the United States but who had been very anti-American, most of the relatively young ministers were trained in France, the Soviet Union, and the Eastern bloc. It appeared to many that the Upper Volta had made a generational as well as a radical shift in leadership.

Ouedraogo and Sankara created the Conseil de salut du peuple, or CSP (People's Salvation Council), composed of 120 military men (forty officers, forty noncommissioned officers, and forty privates) as the "supreme governmental body." Its declared task was to "recreate a new man, whose face was resolutely turned toward the future."[25] The new government purged the army of those officers who had played important roles in earlier governments and arrested a number of them who were said to have plotted a countercoup. Also arrested were a number of politicians such as Frédéric Guiérma and Joseph Ouedraogo, who now joined Lamizana, Conombo, and Gérard Kango Ouedraogo, and others waiting to be tried for corruption. There was speculation that had Mogho Naba Kougri not died when he did, he, too, might have been imprisoned.

What alarmed a number of Voltaiques, as well as the international community, were the attempts of the Ouedraogo government, especially of its prime minister, to establish links with some anti-Western forces. Sankara visited Tripoli in February 1983 and reportedly was so impressed with the Libyan Colonel Mu'ammar al-Qaddafi that, much to the concern of President Ouedraogo and the West, he prolonged his visit. His subsequent visit to North Korea and an anti-Western speech he gave at the conference of the nonaligned states in New Delhi, on 7-10 March 1983 allegedly also disturbed the West. What further alarmed France, the Ivory Coast, and the United States, was Sankara's decision to establish close relations with Fight Lieutenant Rawlings of Ghana and with Colonel Mathieu Kerekou of the Benin (formerly Dahomey). Then to the surprise and anger of President Ouedraogo, without saying a word about it, Sankara "sent a secret mission to Cotonou (Benin) [where Qaddafi was visiting] to invite the leader of the Libyan revolution, to stop over at Ouagadougou on his way back to Tripoli."[26]

Prime Minister Sankara's exploits caught the attention of the foreign press and the imagination of the Voltaic people, and he was promptly declared to be a "charismatic" leader. Almost eclipsing the president, he became the center of attention and intrigue and was soon "surrounded by a halo of mystery, embellished by growing myths." Unfortunately for Sankara, his propensity to upstage the president led to his initial downfall as premier. There is also no doubt that the government of François Mitterand disliked Sankara and that many of the senior officers, especially Chief of Staff Colonel Gabriel Yorian Somé had objected to the "aerial bridge" between Tripoli and Ouagadougou. These latter were disturbed that several cargoes of arms had arrived from the Libyan government and that the prime minister had wished to stock these near the Ghanaian border with a parachutist regiment loyal to him.

There was a great deal of speculation about what led President Ouedraogo to dismiss Sankara. According to Sankara's own statement, he was disturbed by the president's failure to move the country forward. He felt that after having promised the Voltaic people on 7 November 1982 to improve conditions in the country, the government was obliged to move clearly toward "democracy, but equally toward the triumph of progressive ideas. That could not be done without entailing some risks, and without dangers." Again, according to Sankara, on 16 May 1983, he went to see the president, naively believing that it was possible to have a frank talk about the prospects of democracy in the country. Sankara added that both of them took firm and clear positions on a number of items and that they "separated themselves from being Siamese twins."[27] In other words, the president and his premier agreed to disagree. Sankara left the president with the understanding that he was to be sent to Paris for further training, and his colleagues were to suffer the same fate. He concluded that all of their plans would be gradually abandoned.

Apparently the French also knew about the disagreement between Ouedraogo and Sankara. What is in dispute is what they planned to do about it. One report is that Mitterand was disgusted with the turn of events in Ouagadougou and planned to send his counselor on Africa, Guy Penne, and his minister of cooperation and development, Christian Nucci, on an official visit to Ouagadougou on 15-16 May to straighten out the mess. Rumor has it that even before Guy Penne left Paris, he had told the press that he was going on a dangerous mission to Upper Volta. What happened when he arrived in Ouagadougou is also in dispute. One report is that he was held at the airport, and another is that he was taken to the French embassy. There he allegedly met Chief of Staff Somé and hatched a plot to arrest Captain Sankara and all the members of the CSP loyal to him. Then on the morning of 16 May army units surrounded both the residences of the president and the premier, and Somé informed Ouedraogo to get rid of Sankara or be deposed. The president then agreed to fire Sankara, and Guy Penne departed for Yamoussoukro, where he reported to Houphouët-Boigny that henceforth there was nothing to worry about in Ouagadougou. He allegedly also sent a telex to the Elysée Palace in Paris, saying, *Mission Accomplished.*

The immediate postmortem over Sankara's initial fall was that his elevation to the premiership, corresponding with similar elevations of relatively young and unknown persons to ministerial positions, disturbed the forces that controlled the Upper Volta, including former politicians. Finally, it was felt that

> wishing to break too quickly with the "old order," Sankara did not understand that the "disinherited masses," were still caught up in the yoke of the ancestral hierarchy. The "working class" who until recently only listened to the emperor of the Mossi, the Moro Naba Ousmane Congo (who succeeded his father, the Moro Naba Kougri, who died on 8 December [1982]), did not know that they needed to be liberated.[28]

There were minor protests in Ouagadougou over the fall of Sankara, especially from the students and trade unionists, but the president rounded up and jailed a number of cabinet ministers and heads of the unions. And when it was rumored that the Libyan *chargé d'affaires* had told some soldiers that his country would effect the release of Sankara through the agency of troops from Ghana if that proved necessary, he was declared persona non grata and given forty-eight hours to leave the country. Meanwhile, Sankara was shipped north to Ouahigouya for safekeeping. There, he said, soldiers who had orders to shoot to kill should he move, continually fired shots over the roof of his cell because "rumors were spread attributing to my magical powers, according to which I was able to transform myself into a ferocious animal, or simply cause myself to disappear."[29] Sankara went on a hunger strike and wrote a letter to the president asking for a frank and public discussion about the future of the country. That letter never left Ouahigouya.

What Sankara did not know was that the precautions that he and his close friends, Captain Henri Zongo, Captain Blaise Compaore, and Major Jean-Baptiste Lingani, had taken in the event of a "palace coup" were in operation. Lingani had been imprisoned in Dori, a town in the north; but Captain Compaore, who was on his way back to the capital when he heard the news, not only escaped arrest but proceeded to Po on the Ghana border to join troops loyal to Sankara. From there Compaore sent an ultimatum to the president and Somé demanding that the arrested officers and officials be released or he would march on Ouagadougou. Somé allegedly sought help from Paris, but the French refused to intervene. He therefore became involved in lengthy negotiations with Compaore. Finally a bargain was struck whereby on 31 May Sankara and those officers and officials who had been incarcerated since the fall of Maurice Yaméogo, including Yaméogo himself, would be freed.[30] Significantly, a large crowd of young persons greeted Sankara when he was released.

President Ouedraogo apparently had long felt that the military had no business in politics and on 27 May had declared that he was disbanding the CSP, sending the troops back to the barracks, releasing all political prisoners, and handing back power to a civilian administration as soon as possible. He also promised to draw up a constitution with the aid of all sections of the country and to submit it to a referendum in six months. Ouedraogo also planned not to run in the presidential elections he planned to organize. He swore that he would honor his pledge to return the country to "normal constitutional life" after two years. Moreover, because he feared the politicization of the armed forces, with the corresponding danger of civil war, the president warned that from then on, any soldier dabbling in politics would be sanctioned. Lastly, Ouedraogo suggested that the old-style politicians were totally discredited in the eyes of the people. He said that he was seeking "patriots" and hoped that "new men with a sense of responsibility and national realities" would come forward. In this he was counting on young people not contaminated with party politics to make a success out of civilian rule.[31]

The president was quite mistaken if he thought that the old politicians would fade away. One of the first to indicate a willingness to return to politics was Mister Maurice, as the first president of Upper Volta was called by his admirers. We are told that "it is certain that every candidate to the next presidential elections must necessarily contend with Maurice Yaméogo." To the surprise of many, Maurice Yaméogo had remained popular after having been excluded from politics for seventeen years.[32] Yaméogo wanted to organize a gigantic march from his fief in Koudougou to the capital in support of the government. After the principal arms depot in Ouagadougou blew up on the night of 16 June, afraid of the consequences of this march, the president called it off less than twenty-four hours before it began.

Capt. Thomas Sankara speaking at press conference at Fespaco, 1985.
Photo: Margaret A. Novicki/AFRICA REPORT. Used with permission.

Meanwhile, other old politicians such as Gérard Kango Ouedraogo, Joseph Ouedraogo, Joseph Conombo, and Joseph Ki-Zerbo all prepared their campaigns in the full expectation of a return to normal constitutional government. The people of Ouagadougou increasingly viewed these events as "the coup of the Cube Maggi," because as with the condiment known as *Maggi*, the attempt was being made to put everything right.[33]

There was, however, a great deal of speculation in Ouagadougou and in the rest of Upper Volta that there might be a coup d'etat either from the right or the left because "none of the protagonists had said the last word." Especially concerned were the young officers who had staged the coup of 7 November 1982, who felt "bitterness and frustration because of the liquidation of the CSP, and the return to the 'affairs' of the right, the feudal regime, and the Church. They are especially bitter that they are aiding the 'rehabilitation' of the anachronic relations which the chiefs daily imposed on their minions."[34]

Shortly after the president had finished his speech on the night of 4 August 1983, commemorating the country's independence, a military column from Po, led by Captain Blaise Compaore, seized the capital. With the capture of the radio station, the now-customary martial music was played, and a curfew was announced. The victorious officers who seized power, named Sankara chairman of the National Revolutionary Council. Sankara also followed the classic pattern of African coups when he declared that the National Revolutionary Council (CNR) was now the supreme organ of the state and appealed to the people in the towns and in the countryside to establish Committees for the Defense of the Revolution (CDRs) in order to participate in the great patriotic battle of rehabilitating the nation. The watchword of Sankara's revolution became: "The Fatherland or Death. We shall win!"

One of Sankara's first acts was to change the colonial name of the country from Upper Volta to Burkina Faso, said to mean a country of "dignified people." He was determined to have a clean and honest government, to exclude all former politicians from power, and finally to deprive the Mossi chiefs, who were survivors of a decadent feudal past, of the power they had held over the centuries.[35]

Sankara's return to power renewed interest in his "charismatic" qualities, and his early life became the source of speculation and analysis. Born in Yako, of humble birth in a district north of Ouagadougou on 21 December 1949, "this Silimi-Mossi (a person born to Fulani and Mossi parents)" spent his childhood in Kaya, a rural district northeast of Ouagadougou, before going to the capital for secondary education. One of his classmates of that period declared: 'Thomas was already convinced that he would be the savior of the Upper Volta.' "[36] After finishing his studies at the military college in the capital, he went off for higher studies in Madagascar, where he received his commission. The legend there was: "He did not smoke, he did not drink, and he did not play around." This kind of behavior was allegedly a great surprise to the Malagasy.

Later trained as a parachutist in France and Morocco, Sankara distinguished himself in the border war with Mali. He was later posted to the town of Po, on the Ghana border, as the head of a paracommando group. There, he spent his spare time playing a guitar in an amateur military orchestra and allegedly also made friends with American Peace Corps volunteers in the region. More important, however, were Sankara's excursions among the peasants in the area. At Po, among the Gourounsi people, he formed the first associations between peasants and military men on the local plantations. We are told that "the populism of Thomas Sankara was born in the millet fields."[37]

In being labelled charismatic, both by his followers and the international media, Sankara was linked spiritually and programmatically to those gifted African leaders such as Kwame Nkrumah, Sekou Touré, Modibo Keita, Jomo Kenyatta, and Patrice Lumumba who had appeared during the 1960s.[38] In an attempt to describe the impact of these men on their contemporaries, David Apter had referred to them as "Robin Hoods," whose roles are "created by patterns of relative grievance, particularly in modernizing societies when older patterns of obligations break down, and by the need for the assertion of new-found rights and obligations to be personal and moral."[39] Apter felt that in its extreme form, "the Robin Hood may lead to charismatic authority."[40] What attracted Apter to Max Weber was, of course, the notion that *"within the sphere of its claims, charismatic authority repudiates the past and is in this sense a specifically revolutionary force"*[41] (emphasis mine). The charismatic figure, we are told, does not accept the legitimacy of existing possessors of authority, whether "on the part of a chief or of socially privileged groups." His only recognizable legitimacy is his ability to satisfy his "followers or disciples." The obvious reason for this, again according to Weber, is that when the charismatic leader appears during periods of suffering or conflict, he "is the greatest revolutionary force" because he provides for a "radical alteration of the central system of attributes and directions of action, with a completely new orientation of all attitudes toward the different problems and structures of the 'world.' "[42]

If, as Weber and Apter believed, the ability of persons to play the role of Robin Hood or the charismatic leader is related to the nature of the "world," or society, it is possible to understand why the early African leaders were fairly successful and contemporary ones may have more difficulty. The early African charismatic leaders were not only brilliant rhetoricians, but they appeared at a propitious time in history when the Cold War made the persisting examples of nineteenth-century imperialism highly costly and unpopular. Thus these men were not only to win acclaim from their local followers but, equally important, they won the approval, or at least the sympathy or understanding, of a larger "world." It has been argued that Europe wanted to get rid of its colonies and gave them to anyone with the nerve or verve to demand power—provided, of course, that certain ground rules were understood. In Africa, even when, as in the case of Algeria and Rhodesia, local colonists proved intractable, decolonization went on apace.

Whether deliberately or not, Thomas Sankara increasingly played the role of a young charismatic leader of a small country, challenging a large, complex, corrupt, and often brutal world. Affectionately known as the PF (president of Faso) and Comrade President, Sankara was handsome, dashing, personable, very much on stage, and sincere. Yet he seemed to lack that frame of reference that might have permitted him to deal effectively with contemporary local, regional, and global political realities.[43] Locally, Sankara appeared determined to revolutionize his country. He immediately championed women's rights and, in an effort to win feminine allegiance, decreed 22 September 1984 as the day for husbands to do family shopping, so that they would know what this task entailed. He banned prostitution and in an unprecedented action, named women to about one-quarter of his ministerial posts. Women not only were in charge of family affairs, health, and culture but also of such key ministries as the environment and the budget. Then in an effort to deal with beggars, that scourge of most African urban centers, Sankara took them off the streets and established "solidarity compounds," where they could be taught trades.

The president was also solicitous of Burkinabe children. Thanks to his efforts, it took only fifteen days to vaccinate more than 3 million children against yellow fever, measles, and meningitis, scourges that had killed many who preceded them. Then, using models borrowed from the Cubans and Nicaraguans, he attempted to curb illiteracy by using the vernacular for primary education. This program failed, however, because many educators felt that such a system would cut the children off from the cultural patrimony of the entire world. The PF's program for changing higher education also failed because the students who initially welcomed the revolutionary effort to build a new society were not prepared to make the necessary sacrifices. They resented the limitations on the number of scholarships for study abroad and the restrictions on programs of studies.

Sankara's early efforts to increase the productivity of civil servants and members of unions were greatly admired, but his more serious attempts to prevent them from battening on the resources of the state generated opposition. He decided that the country could not afford to continue paying out more than 60 percent of its revenue to less than three-tenths of one percent of its population, when famine and drought afflicted the remainder. For him this was a matter of some having "champagne" and the others only "water." He therefore cut the wages of the civil servants, curtailed their allowances for houses and transportation, and called for them to make sacrifices comparable to those of the peasants.

Unlike many African leaders, Sankara did not believe that foreign countries, either Western or Eastern, would help him develop his country. Nevertheless, like previous presidents, he sought financial aid from such bodies as the World Bank to build a railroad from Ouagadougou to Tambao in the northeast, where lay over 10 million tons of high-grade manganese. When Sankara failed to get funding, he launched a "battle of the rails" to build the railroad with the help of local groups. Whether this precarious project will now continue is anyone's guess.

Like many Third World leaders, Sankara resented the low prices which the industrialized countries paid for primary products and complained about the high interests on debts. He therefore took a leaf out of the Chinese book, ordering that all functionaries wear domestically produced cotton dresses, suits, shirts, and burnooses to work. This action struck a patriotic note among many people. It was noted, however, that despite the limitations of the materials and the available colors, many persons attempted to remain in fashion.

While Sankara's views about the nature of external aid were realistic enough, he was nevertheless deeply troubled by the paucity of that aid. His "next best friends," the Soviet Union and Libya, gave less aid than did the United States, and French support declined so drastically that there were unconfirmed rumors that it had become less than that provided by the United States. These facts, more than anything else, diminished the effectiveness of Sankara's criticism of the widespread story that there were as many aid-giving agencies in Ouagadougou as there were "days in the year." He and his minister of development not only railed against such allegations but said that they demonstrated that the activities of organizations such as OXFAM and UNDP were not serious, since they were not solving the country's development problems. The PF was equally cynical about such demonstrations as We Are the World, which allegedly sent no money to Burkina.

Sankara was very much of a pan-Africanist. Nevertheless, he was never quite able to overcome the mistrust of many African leaders, who disliked his initial ideological position. For example, his early declarations that many of his neighboring states needed revolutions and that he was willing to help these take place annoyed the leaders of these countries. Jerry Rawlings of Ghana was the only one of his neighbors with whom he always had good relations. Both Seyni Kountche of Niger and Gnassigbé Eyadema of Togo believed that Sankara was behind attempts to overthrow them.

Relations between the PF and Félix Houphouët-Boigny were never very good. Like most Burkinabe, Sankara resented that previous generations of his people had been used as forced laborers by the French to build up the prosperity of the Ivory Coast. Equally galling to him was that his country continued to depend upon the remittances of Burkinabe who, while doing much of the hard work in the Ivory Coast, were mistrusted and scorned as undesirable criminal "strangers." It was partly for this reason, as well as the suspicion that the Ivory Coast was getting the lion's share from tariffs and custom duties derived from their joint railroad, that Sankara had planned to break the Customs Union. And while the Ivory Coast accepted this decision with equanimity, the Burkinabe functionaries in Abidjan saw this act as a disaster. They and their families did not look forward to returning to possible unemployment and hardship at home.

Sankara allegedly created bitterness between the Burkinabe and the Ivorians, when he embarrassed President Houphouët-Boigny by jailing a former Ivorian minister, Mohammed Diawara, who had defrauded the Community of West African States (CEAO). Houphouët-Boigny, as was his custom, would have preferred to see the malefactor retired and restitution made. Sankara, made of sterner stuff, clapped the official in prison. Partly because of this act, however, Sankara's offers to host the CEAO were frustrated, and his desire to host the 1988 meeting of the Economic Community of West African States (ECOWAS) summarily dismissed.

Nevertheless, it did appear that Sankara was attempting to mend fences with "le Vieux," as Houphouët-Boigny is affectionately called, when to the relief of Burkinabe living in the Ivory Coast, he did join that parade of world leaders who attended the elaborate funeral of Houphouët's sister, Mamie Adjoua, in Yamassoukro early in 1987. Then he sent Captain Blaise Compaore to Abidjan with a personal message to Houphouët on Wednesday, 19 August 1987. The nature of this message could not be divined from the communiqué issued at the end of Compaore's two-hour visit. There was the usual homily about absolute accord between "two fraternal countries which history, economy and culture intimately link. Besides, there is a large Burkinabe community in this country living in perfect harmony with Ivorians whom they consider as brothers, and this sentiment is reciprocated."[44]

Apparently personality differences, as well as competing interests of their respective nation-states, separated Sankara and Moussa Traoré of Mali. The suspicion that there were mineral resources on their joint border had led to an early war between the two states—a war in which Sankara won his spurs. Then in December 1985 war broke out again between the two states when members of Sankara's CDR went to Agacher on the Mali border and seized Malian subjects, sending them back into Faso. Thanks in part to the efforts of the Ivory Coast president, peace was restored between the belligerents. Nevertheless, Sankara's decision to jail an important Malian official, Moussa Diakité, who was also caught raiding the coffers of the CEAO, did embarrass Traoré.

Although many groups outside the West African region appreciated the activities of Sankara, some of his activities did not sit too well with them. For example, thanks to the efforts of earlier governments and the people of Upper Volta/Burkina Faso, who were among the first West Africans to develop an interest in cinematography, Sankara and his government inherited a cinematic festival, called Fespaco. In 1987 thousands of cineasts attended the festival in Ouagadougou, drawn as much by the competition for their films as by the growing renown of Sankara. Most delegates were pleased by their reception by the Burkinabe, but there was a general feeling that the local minister of culture's remark that all art forms, even the cinema, must serve revolutionary purposes, was highly inappropriate meddling. Cineasts, it was held, were among the most iconoclastic persons in the world.

Similarly, while Sankara's initiative to create an Institute of the Black World was hailed by Africans, both on the continent and in the Diaspora, as an important step in rehabilitating the black race, it was clear that the assembled delegates were leery of ideological control. Many speakers emphasized that given the presence of blacks in so many different types of societies, it was necessary to take social and political factors into account before determining what form the organization should take and who should be its members. On balance, however, there was little acrimony, and a consensus was reached that was not achieved by many recent pan-African conferences.

Like many Third World leaders, Sankara was hostile, or at best ambivalent, toward the West, especially France and the United States. He was quoted as stating that "the whites like to shout that AIDS comes from Africa, because for them, everything that is bad comes from Africa." He liked to recall that as a youthful rebel during the waning days of decolonization, he had seized the bicycle of a young French boy, only to be forced by the colonial police to return it. There is, therefore, reason to believe that the mature Sankara probably never forgot the great differences in wealth and status that existed between the colonial French and his people. He was said to believe that the French could never repay Africa and Africans for resources stolen and services involuntarily extorted. He remarked to me: "There is not a Burkinabe who does not remember an uncle or a father who died so that France could be free [from Nazi control]." Sankara was therefore contemptuous of the vaunted Franco-African cooperation and disgusted by "African vassals [who] bring their grievances to the French sovereign, when they go to pay him their respect."

Thus when President François Mitterand visited Ouagadougou in November 1987, during one of his presidential visits to francophone Africa, Sankara ignored the political and economic power of France, broke protocol, and berated his guest about France's foreign policy. The PF was especially caustic about France's policy toward South Africa, its relations with Savimbi, and its activities in Chad. Startled by a man whom he frankly regarded as an *enfant terrible*, Mitterand put aside his prepared remarks and lectured Sankara on the complexity of world affairs. Mitterand could not help reminding Sankara that as a young man, he himself had battled on the side of the early African nationalists, such as Senghor, for African independence. The French president advised Sankara to seek the council of "African elders" (something which Sankara later did). Reflecting on his visit to Ouagadougou, Mitterand later declared:

> President Sankara is a disconcerting man. He titillates you, asks you questions, and prevents you from sleeping in peace. But he ought to know that I am very much like him, with thirty-five years more experience. He has the earnestness and vibrancy of youth and is devoted to his people. But he is too earnest. Yet, if he is not this earnest at thirty-seven years old, would he be not reactionary at seventy years old? I encourage his spirit, but he ought to take it easy.[45]

Sankara was particularly bitter about United States foreign policy under President Ronald Reagan. He felt that an imperialistic United States was supporting reaction in the global system and condemned United States attacks on Grenada and, especially, on Libya. The PF felt that the Reagan administration's policy of constructive engagement toward South Africa was a failure and believed that Reagan could have ended apartheid with the stroke of a pen. Thus when a group of black and white South Africans held an unofficial meeting at Dakar to see whether they could overcome deeply held prejudices, Sankara invited them to Ouagadougou to applaud their efforts.

The PF's attitude toward the United States was made more bitter by one of Sankara's experiences. In 1984, he wanted to visit Atlanta from Cuba, where he had gone to see Fidel Castro; the United States forbade that he land in the Cuban plane at the Atlanta airport. Sankara therefore had to cancel his planned visit to Mayor Andrew Young in Atlanta, Georgia, and flew to Canada before returning to New York to address the General Assembly of the United Nations. While in New York, he was well received by the blacks in Harlem, and later, when asked whether he had visited the White House, he allegedly remarked: "Black Harlem is my White House." Sankara was especially intrigued with the notion that Jesse Jackson wanted to become president of the United States and looked forward to Jackson visiting Ouagadougou.

In retrospect, there is little doubt that Sankara, nicknamed the rebel, won—and was delighted by—the adulation he received from young Burkinabe, and indeed from most young Africans. As one of his admirers wrote in *Jeune Afrique*, "Sankara incarnates African youth. Elevated, poised, incisive. It is the style of the black man of the modern age. After so many cruel deceptions and wounds inflicted on Africans by so-called 'revolutionary' leaders, I cannot help being sympathetic to the style and thoughts of Thomas Sankara."[46] He was not only good copy for visiting reporters, but in the

Capt. Thomas Sankara and President François Mitterand at African Summit in 1983.
Photo: Alain Nogues/Sygma. Used with permission.

spate of two years, 1986 and 1987, had three books written about him and his revolution.[47] Try as he would, Sankara could not help upstaging his elders. Much to the annoyance of President Ibrahim Babingida of Nigeria, when Sankara arrived at Abuja early in 1987 to attend a meeting of ECOWAS, the youth and workers gave him a warmer welcome than that accorded such veteran leaders as Félix Houphouët-Boigny of the Ivory Coast.

What really impressed younger Africans was Sankara's attempt to live within his country's means. He scorned ostentation and reported to a national commission that his assets included an old Renault, one refrigerator, a few guitars and bicycles, $560 in the bank, a weekly salary of $100, and an outstanding mortgage of $2,200 on a house. He was said to be one of the few leaders in contemporary Africa to find himself without cash and to have checks bounced for lack of funds.

Nevertheless, persons who saw Sankara early in 1987 remarked that he was a troubled man. What increasingly disturbed many persons interested in him was the suspicion that his charismatic qualities were very parochial, and inadequate to deal with the realities of economics and power within the global system. Sankara was failing to realize that the different levels in the world system had their own agendas and that a successful leader had to recognize this fact. The Burkinabe economy was not improving, even though the 1987 World Bank's report—not normally a source sympathetic to Burkina Faso—indicated a modest level of economic growth during 1986.[48] And increasingly, people were fearful of what the projected disruption of the railroad accord with the Ivory Coast would do to the Burkinabe economy. Most Burkinabe had already heard that Ivory Coast customs officials on trains traveling from Abidjan to Ouagadougou were seizing the money and goods of returning migrants, on the pretext that the wealth of the Ivory Coast should not be taken out of the country.

Sankara was under increasing pressure to curb the excesses of the CDRs (Committees for the Defense of the Revolution), which he considered to be "the shock troops of the revolution" and which he established throughout all of the country to advance his programs. Convinced that they had the support of Ouagadougou, these organizations often turned rabid. The CDRs often terrorized local opponents, ostensibly in the name of the revolution, but often to settle age-old scores involving family feuds and conflicts over chieftainships. During a 1985 national congress Sankara became alarmed at the reports reaching him about the excesses of the CDRs; he criticized them and vowed to curb their excesses. Nevertheless, he felt that the behavior of the CDRs was only shocking because it was new and concluded that "without the CDRs, we would never have been able to do what we have done."[49]

What Sankara continued to ignore was the growing skepticism about the efficacy of his policies that had grown up among Burkinabe who, after all, had experienced five coups since independence. Many people in Ouagadougou, while appreciating Sankara's attitude toward the past, adopted a wait-and-see attitude. Queried about the changes that have taken place, one unidentified citizen commented:

> In all the wards of Ouagadougou, there are leaders to whom the people listen, more than they do to others. Persons who intervene to deal with all sorts of problems. There exist the traditional ward chiefs, but also the people who are the CDR, and who sometimes live and work properly. Many people respect the Mogho Naba, but I believe that Sankara was right to oblige him to pay his electric bills. After all, if it is not he who pays, then it would be the people who must pay for him, and they do not believe that this is good. We young people cannot live like our parents. Even in the countryside, people do not agree to give their sisters as presents to the Mogho as they did in the past. . . . I will not behave like my father, but I do not yet know how I will behave. I shall wait to see what the future holds for me.[50]

While many of the Mossi in Burkina Faso admired Sankara, they were not all convinced that his attitude toward the Mogho Naba and the chiefs was correct. Many contemporary rural Mossi may not have been willing to give their sisters to the Mogho Naba, but nobility does not easily yield power and prestige. There were reports that in the rural areas, the ranks of the CDRs were being gradually filled with the children of the ancient nobility. In Ouagadougou, visitors were surprised to see that the number of nobles visiting the Mogho Naba and participating in his morning ceremonies had increased and that, in contrast to former times, when such visiting dignitaries were fairly old, these were younger and quite vigorous. At the same time, there was no indication that the traditional nobles were even contemplating challenging Sankara and his government. It was not their style.

While the traditional hierarchy appeared to have been attempting to adapt to the revolutionary climate, Sankara's position increasingly came under attack. It is quite clear, if somewhat trite to say, that Sankara was failing in the attempt to routinize his charisma. The problem involved local power blocs dealing with local political realities, but often acting as though they were affiliated with important actors in the global system. The great quarrel apparently turned over the role of proper role of the CDRs, especially vis-à-vis the powerful trade unions. The Burkinabe trade unions had never forgotten their critical role in the civilian overthrow of the first postcolonial African government.[51] These groups initially welcomed and supported the CNR, but they grew increasingly hostile to the roles given the CDRs. When in 1984, some members of the teachers' union questioned the sacrifices demanded of them and went on strike, they were dismissed. Then when on 27 May 1985 some union leaders, dissatisfied civilians, and military officers were apprehended plotting a coup, seven of the ring leaders, including the unionists, were executed.

The die was cast early in 1987 when the PF declared on the local radio that there were reactionary labor unions in the country which were the creatures of either local or external reactionary forces "directly or indirectly at the service of imperialism." He warned that the government knew who those persons were and that it did not "intend to be gentle with them." In rebuttal, the union leaders declared that they did not intend to subordinate their interests or activities to the CDRs. They became alarmed when at the second conference of the CDRs, held in April 1987, the president, rather than criticizing them as he had done before, reaffirmed the role of the CDRs as the "backbone" of the revolution.[52] These presidential remarks strengthened the hand of Captain Pierre Ouedraogo, the leader of the CDRs, who demanded the execution of two union leaders (Soumane Touré, leader of the Confederation Syndicale Burkinabe, and Salif Kabore of the Patriotic League for Development) who in May 1987 had been arrested for treason. Fortunately for them, Captain Blaise Compaore, in his capacity as minister of justice, not only questioned the arrests of the unionists but firmly opposed their execution. And when the syndicalists appealed to Amnesty International to investigate the torture of their leaders, what had been a local matter became globalized.

Within the CNR there was also pressure on the PF to routinize his governing principles. It was formerly his practice to change his cabinet ministers every year in order to keep them on their toes and to forestall corruption among persons who remained too long in office. In a few instances, cabinet ministers were even sent off to the rural areas to experience the problems of the peasants. Criticized for this practice, Sankara explained:

> The attitude of those who disengage from politics when they are no longer ministers is really deplorable. The only way that one can explain this is to realize that many such persons have the wrong idea of what ministerial positions are. It seems that many militants view ministerial positions as something every successful person hopes to obtain. They are viewed the fruit of a personal victory, a personal accomplishment, and as such a recompense, proof that one has passed an examination and has reached the summit. If that is the way in which a ministerial position is seen, then it is understandable that when one is no longer a minister, one believes that one is lost, and has become decrepit, and has been disavowed, etc. That is not the conception that people should have.[53]

Thus did the PF hope to clarify the dignity of all work in Burkinabe life.

The problem with Sankara's view of ministerial positions was not that it was quite revolutionary — such a practice as the annual turnover being almost unheard of in politics — but that many Burkinabe felt that this view was disingenuous at best, and naive at worst. They wondered aloud why the PF himself did not live up to these principles and surrender his position as chairman of the CNR.

Increasingly, Sankara had difficulty mediating the bitter factionalism of the now avowedly left-wing organizations and tendencies represented with the CNR and other bodies. All of these organizations had their roots in the same stratum of intellectuals, public functionaries, and army officers that had traditionally dominated the country's political life; and while they presumed to speak in the name of the "popular masses," the bulk of the population knew nothing about their political programs.[54] The debates within the inner circles of the CNR, already acrimonious, were fueled by events involving ideology that took place throughout the country. On 2 October 1987 there was a meeting in Tenkodogo between the members of the government, the CDRs, student groups, and many others. The students were particularly incensed, claiming that their analysis of the "national situation and their assessment of the ongoing process of unification," earned them the anger of the CDRs. The students claimed to have discovered a vast plot to liquidate their organizations, to close the university, and to arrest all sincere and honest revolutionaries who wanted a struggle based on principles. They insisted that they foiled this plot by refusing to be drawn into a bloody argument.[55]

Sankara and his ministers allegedly left Tenkodogo and returned to a capital divided into factions and filled with rumors of impending coup attempts. Sankara reportedly remained calm; for like Caesar, he was quite philosophical in the face of rumors that Compaore was planning a coup. He allegedly remarked to a visiting newsman that "the day you learn that Blaise [Compaore] is preparing a coup against me, it won't be worthwhile to try to resist or even warn me. Because by then it will be too late." He knew that Compaore, like Cassius, was made of very stern stuff.

On 8 October 1987, the PF met with Compaore and Lingani, the military members of the CNR, under the chairmanship of Henri Zongo to discuss a "code of revolutionary conduct" that he had decided to present to those organizations that formed the CNR over which he presided: the Union of Communist Fighters — Restructured (ULC-R), the Union of Burkinabe Communists (UCB), the Union of Communist Groups (UGC), and the Organization of Revolutionary Military (OMR). The question to be decided was whether to create a unitary party along Soviet lines or a pluralist avant-garde organization which respected all political tendencies.

While there is controversy as to who was for democracy as against autocracy, there is agreement that the meeting was stormy. Blaise Compaore reported afterward that Sankara even offered him the post of prime minister in a future government as a means of pacifying him. But when agreement could not be reached, Sankara allegedly slammed the door and walked out. This apparently convinced Blaise Compaore, at least, that he was in danger;

EPILOGUE, 1989

and, possibly to avert some dreaded event, he reported to the press that Sankara planned to arrest him and other leaders at a meeting of the ruling National Revolutionary Council scheduled for 8:00 P.M. on 15 October. Compaore came to the conclusion that "it was a question of preempting events by arresting Sankara before the meeting scheduled for 8:00 P.M. during which he wanted to have myself, Lingani and Zongo arrested and executed."[56] Whether Sankara was killed by a grenade even before he left the car which drove him to the Conseil d'Entente or resisted arrest and killed one guard before he himself was gunned down is not now clear. However, his death ended one phase of the Burkina Revolution.

The radio broadcast announcing the execution referred to Sankara as a "renegade," a "traitor to the revolution," "an autocratic mystic," and a "paranoid misogynist." It added that the ex-president's "high treason" was illustrated by his trampling upon all organizational principles, his betrayal of the noble objectives of the democratic and popular revolution, his personalization of power, and by his ambitious use of mysticism to solve the concrete problems of the masses. "This," the broadcast concluded, "was inexorably leading us towards total chaos."[57] When he finally broke his silence, Blaise Compaore, the alleged leader of coup, accused Sankara of "wanting to lead the world revolution."[58]

Oddly enough, Sankara appeared to have had a premonition of the limits of his revolution. On the eve of the celebration of the fourth anniversary of the revolution, which was celebrated on 4 August 1987, a rather pensive leader declared:

> I would like you to remember that the political events that took place in the year now ending, have subjected our revolution to all sorts of contradictory currents. There are certainly contradictions that we have not yet encountered. We have seen other revolutions born, evolve, and sometimes die. Sometimes we think that this only happened to other revolutions. Well, this can also happen to ours.[59]

We will never be sure what thoughts went through Sankara's mind. In a eulogy to his passing, the very perceptive editor of *Jeune Afrique* wrote of Sankara:

> His country was too poor and too small for the revolution which he launched to have been taken seriously. He tried to accomplish a great deal, and he devoted too much time to foreign affairs. But power itself is a school, and Sankara learned quickly. The pity is that he had so little time to prove himself.[60]

At this writing, it is difficult to verify the views of the four leaders, since reports are contradictory, and possibly self-serving. One view is that Sankara opposed the creation of a monolithic party, but that he wanted more coherence among the elements that composed the CNR. He is said to have envisaged elections and had even spoken about a new constitution. In contrast, the three other leaders allegedly felt that this new "brain wave" of the president risked vulgarizing their efforts and drowning them in a mass of anonymous militants, or "Sankarists." Compaore later said in a radio broadcast that the nub of the problem was that "one faction held that democratic debate was the absolutely best means for advancing the August revolution, while the other upheld bureaucratization, militarization, and the assertion of personal power." He insisted that he and the others felt that in spite of Sankara's stubbornness, the solution could have been found in democratic debate. It was apparently then that Compaore decided that "if this proved impossible, all comrades of the front believed that the painful solution was to overthrow him [Sankara] or make him resign of his own will. But that was naive of us; for at the very moment that we were working for a peaceful and revolutionary solution, the bureaucratic wing was plotting— without our knowledge—some brutal, violent, and bloody acts."[61]

Speaking to an obviously hostile group of reporters about Sankara's death, Compaore declared:

> At the end he [Sankara] was not very popular except in certain media, especially Western ones! And the more successful he was in the international press, the more he believed that he could ignore the advice of others. He therefore decided things on his own, and our own role was simply to follow him. I could cite you dozens of examples of this.... His success in the international press had so spoiled him that he found it dishonorable to pull back. He preferred to get rid of us. He played the game. He lost.[62]

Conclusion

The Mossi political organizations, or states, represented here by the kingdom of Ouagadougou, arose at the periphery of the Malian empire; and it is clear that they were influenced by the power of their powerful neighbor. The role of women in the rituals designed to preserve the Mossi political organization bears witness to the role that tradition indicates they played in the early history of these entities. Whether the role of women represents an "African" factor in this organization is not known. But if one were to judge the Mossi political organization by its similarities to the one recorded for medieval Mali, they shared many traits in common. As we have seen, French rule did modify this political organization, as the Mossi chiefs and people attempted to cope with the exigencies of a colonial system which sought to integrate them and their society into a larger economic and political framework. Many thousands of Mossi left their rural districts for work in the Ivory

Coast and Ghana, and taking their political organization with them. This organization still persisted, even though in an attenuated form. Meanwhile at home, the Mogho Naba and his traditional ministers saw their royal seat transformed into urban wards of a colonial capital and then as a municipality which later housed the capital of an independent Upper Volta. In the process, they increasingly melded the roles of chiefs and of functionaries in successive types of government.

The greatest challenge to the Mossi political organization came during the period of decolonization. Faced with the prospect of losing power in a multi-ethnic state, the then-Mogho Naba attempted to seize control of the emerging state. That he was not able to do so demonstrated that the French had more successfully integrated Mossi society into the modern world economy and its corresponding civilization than some Mossi chiefs were willing to admit. The subsequent conflict between the politicians, many of whom were Mossi princes supported by the Mogho Naba, and urban workers, who while largely Mossi were increasingly anti-chief, also indicated that the expansion in scale of Mossi society had sapped the power of the Mossi political organization. Finally, the ability of the Ivory Coast (seen by many as a surrogate of France) to manipulate Mossi chiefs while interfering in the internal affairs of Upper Volta, led a nationalistic military to assume power in the name of all Voltaics.

Thomas Sankara's revolution was designed to uproot most existing institutions in the Upper Volta, especially including those of the Mossi and their chiefs. He attempted to join forces with global actors determined to end Western economic and cultural domination. Very much a charismatic figure, Sankara wished to serve as the vehicle in which the identity of Mossi, which had started to fuse with that of Voltaic, would become that of Burkinabe—a new type of person. But the Committees in Defense of the Revolution (CDRs) which he put in place to foster change often became rivals, competing for traditional power. Meanwhile, a young Mogho Naba appeared to have been in the process of recruiting younger nobles, and possibly waiting for the routinization of Sankara's charisma. At this writing, it is not clear what Sankara's death means for the Mossi traditional political organization. What is clear, however, is that the ability of that political organization to survive and to adapt is not unlimited. Like all human institutions, the Mossi political organization will in time cease to exist because it can no longer adapt. Meanwhile, Sankara's rise and fall has lessons for the emerging leaders of African states.

What Sankara's revolution demonstrates is that while it is understandable why a new generation of African leaders, disgusted and tired of the manner in which the traditional chiefs and earlier politicians dealt with both local and global affairs, would want to chart a new course, these same new leaders must pay attention to the realities of power—locally, nationally, regionally, and globally. In a theoretical sense, Max Weber's cryptic reference to the notion of the "world" as a crucial environment in resurrects the old debate about whether, as in the case of Sankara, it is the hero or the moment that is most important in historical events. Sankara and his collaborators did not pay enough attention to the difficulty of routinizing charisma. Moreover, they appeared to have ignored the changing nature of the world and its effect on the ability of contemporary leaders of small societies (whether charismatic or not) to deal with the realities of power.

Sankara became quite frustrated about the ambivalence of the "world" to his revolution. Commentary in *Jeune Afrique* indicates that it is now clear that "personal impetuosity, insufficiently coordinated initiatives, sudden and often improvised decisions, as well as the spectacular whims of the young *charismatic* Burkinabe leader, ultimately sapped the cohesion of the National Council of the Revolution, supreme organ of the state[63] (emphasis mine). Sankara tried, and did succeed, in making the world "aware" of his revolution. He might have been more successful had he been able to involve the major world actors in his enterprise. But when a possible rapprochement between the major powers enamored by *glasnost'* and *peristroika* is in the air, relative little attention is paid to small states. The result was that when Sankara failed to deal effectively with the realities of power in his own small arena, he was summarily executed. Captain Compaore, his successor, is Mossi; but having participated with Sankara in attempting to produce the Burkinabe, he probably shares many of the same views of the world. What Sankara's execution may well have done is to provide the opportunity for both an interregnum and routinization in which all the people of Burkina Faso learn to build mediating structures among local, national, regional, and global institutions of all types. Failure to do so ends in chaos.

NOTES

Complete authors' names, titles, and publication data are given
in the Bibliography, pp. 263-268.

CHAPTER ONE

1. Murdock states, "The large Gourma and Mossi tribes in the north of the [Voltaic] province have had strong states for at least the past 800 years and have frequently warred with their powerful neighbors on the Niger. . . . Their culture probably reflects fairly closely what that of the Mande must have been prior to the embarkation on a career of empire building and to the advent of the Berbers and Arabs from the north" (p. 78). See also Greenberg, "Negro Kingdoms," p. 130; and Forde p. 206.

2. Binger states, "There does not exist one type general enough to permit one to say: there is a Mossi type. One meets people who resemble the Wolof; others who look like Mandingo from the banks of the Niger; and yet others who resemble the Hausa (2: 491). Tauxier, on the other hand, reports that the nobles' faces were totally different from the Negroes'. According to him, the physiognomies of the nobles were "Semitic" and "truly distinguished" (*Le noir du Soudan*, pp. 578-79). However, judging from the physiognomies of the three most recent Mogho Nanamse, one could make the equally erroneous generalization that the ruling group was the most Negroid of the entire Mossi population.

3. Barth, 3: 202, 643; Dubois, p. 300.
4. Delafosse, *Haut-SenegalNiger*, 1: 115.
5. Greenberg, "Languages," p. 8.
6. See Cardinall; and Rattray, 1: x, xi.
7. Delafosse, *Negroes of Africa*, p. 101.
8. Rattray, 1: xxii, xi.
9. Fortes, "Political System," pp. 255-57.
10. Ibid.
11. Rattray, 1: 343.
12. See Cardinall, pp. 1-14.
13. Dim Delobson claims that this took place toward the end of the tenth century (p. 2). Delafosse (*Haut-Sénégal-Niger*, 1: 306) believes the date to be about A.D. 1030. After comparing the dates of many scholars, Tauxier felt that this event occurred around A.D. 1233 (*Le noir du Yatenga*, p. 672). Most contemporary Mossi believe that it occurred during the eleventh century.

14. According to a belief found among the people of Nobere district, Nedega gave his daughter permission to search for a husband, and she went northward into Busansi country, where an old woman found her a husband named Rialle. Still another tradition states that she became pregnant by an animal and fled north from the anger of her parent. She aborted the child during her flight, and when she arrived in Busansi country she married a hunter called Rialle.

In a version of this tradition given in Delafosse (3: 307), Nyennega is called Poko (a general

Mossi name for "woman"); and it is said that she left her father's house to lead an expedition against the Busansi. Her horse carried her far ahead of her troops and into the forest, past Rialle's hut. The young man caught it and helped her dismount. He told her he was the son of a Malinke (Mali) chief but that he had been deprived of his succession and was now an elephant hunter. Poko was so charmed by his kindness that she decided to remain with him and become his wife.

According to Cardinall (p. 5), the Mamprussi claim descent from a woman warrior named Poko. When she saw her father's troop nearing defeat, she took a stallion and — to the amazement of the men, who believed a woman could not ride — led the troops to victory. Being a woman, however, she could not stop the horse; and it carried her far into Gambaga, where it stopped. Poko dismounted and fell asleep. A Boussanga came upon her sleeping form and, struck by her beauty, had intercourse with her. When she awoke, he confessed his act to her; and in her shame she did not return home but elected to remain with the stranger. The child born as a result of this act was called Widiraogo, after the stallion she had been riding.

Ruelle (p. 675) recounts a tradition that Ouidiraoga was the name of the Dagomba ruler's daughter who fled with a Busansi elephant hunter to Tenkodogo. Here she married the chief of that country, a man called Zangourana, and bore a son called Bougoum. Bougoum pushed his way to Koupela, where he lived with his wives and three sons called Houbri, Nabakere, and Kouda. Houbri conquered Ouagadougou, made it his capital, and forced his brothers to recognize his authority. He then divided the country into provinces, making his brothers *nabas* (chiefs); divided his own fee into provinces, placing his dignitaries as heads; and further divided the provinces into districts, at the heads of which he placed his own relatives.

15. Contemporary Mossi still send a woman's first son back to her patrilineage to live until he has grown to adulthood.

16. Delafosse (*Haut-Sénégal-Niger*, 1: 311-12) states that the people of Fada-N'Gourma have a legend that Diaba Lompo came from the sky while the earth was not yet solid and stood with his wife upon a rock. Lompo then had children who dispersed over the earth and cultivated the soil. In Delafosse's opinion, a comparison of Gurmanche and Mossi genealogies shows that they agree on the date when the Dagomba entered the country.

17. Oubri himself was succeeded by several of his sons. Narimtore (also called Sorba), the eldest, was succeeded by his brothers Naskiemde, Nassebere, and Gningnemdo, all of whom lived at La. This line of succession is of interest since it throws light on the inheritance pattern of the early Mossi. Dim Delobson (p. 290) states that Narimtore had no children and was succeeded by his brother Naskiemde. We know that Naskiemde had sons, because they received districts from him; however, he was succeeded by his brother Nassebere and not by any of his sons. Nassebere had several sons, including Yadega and Koudoumie; but one tradition states that he was succeeded by his brother, Gningnemdo. The latter apparently had no sons, for none of his descendants are heads of districts. There is no way of determining whether he reigned. The interesting point is that there seems to have been an early custom whereby all the sons of a ruler succeeded him before the rule passed to another generation. This custom coincided with one dictating that the ruler must have attained his majority. Because the rule was passed from brother to brother, this latter condition was usually fulfilled without difficulty.

18. See Dim Delobson, pp. 1-12; and Tauxier, *le noir du Yatenga*, pp. 55-75.

19. See Dim Delobson, p. 55. He recognized only four Dimdamba: Boussouma Naba, Conquizitenga Naba, Yako Naba, and Riziam Naba. He specifically states that the Boulsa Naba was not a Dim, and he would not have recognized the claim of such Dimdamba as Mane, Tema, and later, Koupela. At the same time, Dim Delobson took advantage of the ideology of the corporate possession of the *nam* by all the children of Ouedraogo and Oubri to take for himself the title *Dim*. He was in fact a simple Kombere of Sao.

20. Claessen, "Specific Features," in Claessen and Skalnik, eds., *The Study of the State*, pp. 59-86; Cohen, "Evolution, Fission and the Early State," in Claessen and Skalnik, pp. 87-116;

"Oedipus Rex and Regina"; Service, *Origins of the State and Civilization*, and "Classical and Modern Theories on the Origin of Government," in Cohen and Service, eds., *Origins of the State*, pp. 31-34.

21. Lebeuf, "The Role of Women," in Paulme, ed., *Women of Tropical Africa*, pp. 93-119; Lonsdale, "States and Social Processes in Africa."

22. Fried, *The Evolution of Political Society*, p. 231. See also Haas, pp. 53 ff. and passim.

23. Fried, p. 129.

24. Skinner, "The Effect of Co-residence of Sisters' Sons," pp. 471-72.

25. Service, *Origins of the State and Civilization*, passim; Service, "Classical and Modern Theories," pp. 21-34; see also Haas, pp. 53 ff.

26. Cohen, "Evolution, Fission and the Early State," in Claessen and Skalnik, pp. 87-116; Claessen, "Specific Features of the African Early State," in Claessen and Skalnik, pp. 59-86.

27. While my focus is on the role of women in the founding, perpetuation, and expansion of the patrilineal Mossi kingdoms, comparable processes occurred in matrilineal societies. It might also be instructive to look at the role of women in the other polities of West Africa. For example, there were royal women in the Wolof state of Waalo in present-day Senegal who "could even succeed the ruler, and take the title of Bur (ruler)" (Ajayi and Espie, pp. 138-39). There was also Queen Amina of Zaria, who, according to the Kano Chronicles, reigned for more than thirty-four years, conquered such towns as Kwarafa and Nupe and built walled camps all over Hausaland. Ifemesia says of the activities of this semilegendary monarch that "wall-building on this scale implies mass use of corvee labor, substantial military force, intense political centralization, warfare on an imperial scale, slavery, tribute, and technological development" (in Ajayi and Espie, pp. 102-3). However, even this powerful woman was unable to pass on power to female successors.

28. I would like to acknowledge the debt I owe Gwendolyn Mikell of Georgetown University for having pointed out to me the special characteristics of matrilineal systems.

29. See Goody, pp. 61-88.

30. Others might go further to examine how much of this historical pattern of manipulating women's political roles still occurs within modern West African states. It is well known that women have played important roles in the decolonization process leading to the establishment of political parties and the independence of many contemporary African states. As a form of recompense, they are often given ministries in the first governments and have played important roles in the nationalist parties. However, these roles do appear to be temporary, since women are again eclipsed as the power of the state is consolidated; and female politicians tend to become or remain few in number. While competition between political parties, economic instability, and coups add variation to the process of eclipsing female political leaders, the results appear to be the same as in the traditional African states.

31. Wallerstein, pp. 389-415.

32. See Wilks, "The Northern Factor," passim.

33. Al-Sa'di, pp. 16-17. Barth (3: 662-63), who was one of the first Europeans to read *Tarikh es-Sudan*, believed that the Mossi were in Timbuktu ca. 1329. His translation of the pertinent section reads: "The town of Timbuktu having been ransacked and destroyed by fire and sword by the king of Mossi, the garrison of Melle made their escape, and gave up the town. The power of Mossi, which up to this time has always been the successful champion of paganism, is very remarkable at such an early period, but the date is not quite certain within a year or two. If the date given is right, it happened toward the end of the reign of Mansa Musa."

The exact date of the capture of Timbuktu is not known. Nevertheless, the date most usually cited is 1333 or 1334, given by Marc (p. 1354), who argues not only from approximate dates in the *Tarikh* but also from evidence derived from the history of Mali. He believes that the Mossi could have wrested Timbuktu only from a weak ruler and that such a ruler existed in the person of Mansa Magha, who ruled around 1333 or 1334. (What is interesting about Marc's dating is that he used the number 3, as in 1333, which is the symbolic Mossi number for males, in contrast to 4, which is the number for females.) Recent historians have suggested that the sack of Timbuktu was after 1390, during a troubled period following the death of Magha, who had followed Musa. See Oliver, 3: 383.

The identity of the Mossi ruler who captured the city is uncertain. Tauxier (p. 67) believes it was Wemtanango, a younger son of Oubri, who had fought his way north and in the process had carved out for himself a realm which later became the Riziam province. But Delafosse (*Haut-Sénégal-Niger*, 2: 240) believed it was Nasegue (1320-1340) of the Yatenga kingdom. There is a discrepancy of about 200 years between the genealogies of Tauxier and Delafosse. (For a revised chronology of the Mossi invasions, see Levtzion, p. 232 n. 44. For an excellent study of the Mossi of the Yatenga kingdom, see Izard.)

34. Marc, p. 138.
35. Tauxier, *Le noir du Soudan*, p. 459.
36. Tauxier, *Le noir du Yatenga*, p. 554.
37. Binger, 2: 394; Delafosse, *Haut-Sénégal-Niger*, 2: 43-45; Tauxier, *Le noir du Soudan*, pp. 88-91.
38. Tauxier, *Le noir du Soudan*, pp. 621-30.
39. Ibid., p. 609.
40. Marc, p. 17; Barth, 3: 665-66, 671.

CHAPTER TWO

1. See Fortes, "The Structure of Unilineal Descent Groups," pp. 17–41.
2. See Fried, pp. 1–29.
3. Cheron, "Contribution," p. 648.
4. The Mossi also called the Dimdamba by the term *Kyedouende,* which means, literally, "Submit to God alone."
5. See Skinner, "Intergenerational Conflict," pp. 55–60.
6. Cheron, "Contribution," pp. 644–45.
7. *Ibid.,* p. 648.
8. Cf. Mangin, p. 16.
9. Skinner, "The Mossi 'Pogsioure,'" Article 28, pp. 20–22.
10. Archives, Document 1G-316 (1905–1906, Haute Volta).

CHAPTER THREE

1. Dim Delobson, pp. 8–9.
2. Crozat, p. 4849.
3. *Ibid.* The Mossi always use multiples of three in connection with masculine affairs.
4. Archives, Document 15G-190 (1897–98, Haute Volta).
5. Dim Delobson, p. 37. The difficulty here is caused by the Mossi words and their meanings. For example, the words for "God" are Ouennam and Ouende. The words for "sun" are the same. The ethnologists can speculate about whether the Mossi once worshiped the sun or whether a high god has evolved into a supreme deity. But the Mossi do not agree that their use of the same words for God and for the sun implies that they believe God is the sun, or that the sun is their God. It should be pointed out *inter alia* that many African peoples are not awed by their gods and grant them human feelings and attributes. The Mossi regard their supreme being Ouennam as an otiose deity who is not too concerned with human affairs. It is the ancestors who provide the sanctions for good conduct.
6. It seems certain that Ibn Battuta saw a similar salutation in Mali: "The Negroes are of all people the most submissive to their king, and the most abject in their behavior before him. They swear by his name, saying *Mansa Souliman ki* [the Emperor Souliman has commanded]. If he summons any of them while he is holding an audience in his pavilion, the person summoned takes off his clothes and puts on worn garments, removes his turban and dons a dirty skullcap, and enters with his garments and trousers raised knee-high. He goes forward in an attitude of humility and dejection, and knocks the ground hard with his elbows, then stands with bowed head and bent back, listening to what he says. If anyone addresses the king and receives a reply from him, he uncovers his back and throws dust over his head and back, for all the world like a bather splashing himself with water. I used to wonder how it was that they did not blind themselves" (Gibb, p. 327; cf. Mangin, p. 15).

Obviously, Ibn Battuta found this salutation distasteful. Most Europeans feel the same way about the Mossi salute. If a Moaga visited England, he might be equally struck by the sight of a great soldier or statesman kneeling before a *woman ruler* and being touched on the shoulder with a sword.

7. It is interesting to compare this account with Ibn Battuta's description of Mansa Souliman, king of Mali: "On certain days the sultan holds audiences in the palace yard, where there is a platform under a tree, with three steps; this they call the *pempi.* . . . The sultan comes out of a door in the corner of the palace, carrying a bow in his hand and a quiver on his back. On his head he has a golden skullcap bound with a gold band which has narrow ends shaped like knives, more than a span in length. His usual dress is a velvety red tunic, made of the European fabric called *mutanfas.* The sultan is preceded by his musicians, who carry gold and silver guimbris (two-stringed guitars), and behind him come three hundred armed slaves. He walks in a leisurely fashion, affecting a very slow movement, and even stops from time to time. On reaching the *pempi,* he stops and looks round the assembly, then ascends it in the sedate manner of a preacher ascending a mosque pulpit. As he takes his seat, the drums, trumpets, and bugles are sounded" (Gibb, p. 326).

8. It is possible that the Mossi either borrowed this tradition from Mali or shared part of the Mali king complex, for Ibn Battuta reports that a similar rite was held in Mali during the fourteenth century. He says that when the ruler entered the pavilion for the morning ceremony, "two saddled and bridled horses are brought, along with two goats, which they hold to serve as a protection against the evil eye" (Gibb, p. 326).

9. In Dim Delobson's account (p. 60), an unnamed wife of the Mogho Naba ran away, and he allegedly tried to follow her because she was the only person in his household who knew how to cook his favorite food.

It is interesting that the Mossi have a tradition in which their ruler undergoes the same experience as many a Mossi husband, namely, being betrayed by his wife. It is also interesting that Mogho Naba Waraga is the ruler named in this incident. He is the ruler who waged a five-year-long civil war with one of his vassals. It may well be that his ministers devised the myth about his wife in order to prevent him from leaving the capital to fight.

10. The Mossi practice of tasting food before giving it to another person is obviously connected with the fear of poison. The Mossi believe that only a boorish person would give another person something to eat without first tasting it himself.

11. The full significance of this ceremony is unclear, for the Mossi hesitate to talk about it. It is known that the "sacred fire" is linked to the nocturnal visits of the royal ancestors. But the relationship of the fire to another sacred fire kept in Koubri district (about seventeen miles from Ouagadougou) is not known.

Faithful to Mossi tradition or ignorant of the true nature of the ceremony, Dim Delobson says nothing about the ceremony and does not mention the presence of the namtibo. However, he does report that the palace guards would kill anyone who approached the place where the rite was being performed (p. 62).

12. There are several traditions concerning female regents. However, I believe that they may have their basis in the role the Mogho Naba's daughter played during the interregnum.

13. Mossi genealogies show that only in one case in which the nam passed from a Mogho Naba to his brother did the former Mogho Naba's sons receive districts from their uncle, the new ruler. Since it is difficult to believe that the eleven other Mogho Nanamse who were succeeded by their brothers died without issue, it can only be concluded that the descendants of a ruler who did not inherit the nam were ignored by their uncles in power.

14. To this council could be added other men whose experience was valued. For example, the Baloum Naba was called upon in 1942 to give advice about a successor to Kom.

15. Dim Delobson, pp. 130–32.

16. It is interesting that the sheepskin garb of the Mossi pretenders is similar to the dress of the chiefs among the smaller tribal groups of the Voltaic culture area. If we can assume that culture traits characteristic of ritual and ceremonial practices tend to persist longer than most other traits, we might have evidence that the complex Mossi state evolved from the political organizations found among the smaller local groups.

17. The "naming of a name" speech is part of most Mossi *rites de passage*, and is often used to brag about some achievement or to cast aspersions on one's enemies. Most newly elected monarchs pledge good government, brag about their elevation, and vilify their enemies.

In his inaugural speech Naba Kom II said, "When plenty of water falls during the rainy season, the rivers and seas are glad because they are enlarged." "Kom" means "water," and Kom's speech meant that he pledged to bring happiness to all his subjects.

Boukary Koutou insulted his listeners by declaring, "Even if a hundred ghosts join together, they cannot harm an elephant." He was called Mogho Naba Wobogo ("elephant").

18. It is said that if the amulets were stolen during the interregnum, the thief had to be elected Mogho Naba; if they were stolen afterwards, the ruler lost the basis for the mystical quality of leadership and authority he had inherited from his ancestors.

19. There is a curious story among the people of Nobere district that Mogho Naba Mottoba (who reigned in the seventeenth century) was not a Mossi but a Fulani who was given the nam after he chanced upon the installation ceremony and assassinated the newly elected man during the night. This story is denied in Ouagadougou; in fact, it contradicts the genealogical records of the ruling dynasty. However, the genealogy does show that Mottoba's father, Mogho Naba Guiliga, had succeeded his brother, and it is possible that there was dynastic rivalry for the nam between Mottoba and the former Mogho Naba's son.

20. This rite was performed during the installation of the present Mogho Naba of Ouagadougou, although it is hardly recognizable as described in *Newsweek* (December 9, 1957, p. 48): "A man named Moussa Congo assumed the name of Kougri Naba last week and became the 35th Mogho Naba of the Mossi in the capital city of Ouagadougou in the Upper Volta region of French West Africa. Son of Emperor Issoufou Congo, Kougri Naba, as the new Mogho Naba, has one white horse, 200 wives, and 8,000 warriors, who danced around his palace ten times."

21. This practice has apparently lapsed since Mogho Naba Kougri moved into the modern concrete palace built for his father, Mogho Naba Sagha II.

22. Tauxier, *Le Noir du Soudan,* pp. 569–70. Tauxier claims the Mogho Nanamse used the pages for homosexual purposes on Fridays in order to circumvent the Moslem prohibition against intercourse with women on this holy day. Homosexuality is rare among the Mossi, as Tauxier himself admits, and most Mossi deny that the Mogho Nanamse ever resorted to it. However, one respondent did state that he had heard about homosexuality among certain past rulers.

23. Crozat, p. 4849.

24. When Mogho Naba Kom II died under mysterious circumstances in 1942, it was rumored that he had committed suicide rather than reduce the number of his wives as ordered by the administration under the influence of the Catholic missionaries. Kom allegedly held that no one can inherit a sovereign's wife during his lifetime. Therefore, in order to avoid loss of status by seeing his wives go to commoners, he chose death so they would be inherited by nobles.

25. The statement in *Newsweek* (December 9, 1957, p. 48) that Kougri has two hundred wives is untrue.

26. Intermarriage between the Mossi and the Fulani has produced a people known as the Simili-Mossi. Nevertheless, the Mossi are strongly prejudiced against the Fulani, especially against the women, stating that the Moaga who has sexual intercourse with a Fulani woman must bathe in nine different rivers before he becomes clean. The basis of this prejudice appears to be that Fulani women are not cultivators and therefore are unacceptable as Mossi wives.

27. Mossi women know a great deal about the history and traditions of their people. But they never indicate that they do except during such rituals, when they are required to play certain roles.

28. Dim Delobson, p. 96.

29. Dim Delobson (p. 101) states that there are "sacred things" in this village, but I have been unable to substantiate his report.

30. Dim Delobson (p. 104) gives the classic explanation of this nighttime ride. On his ride from Bere to Djiba, the mounted prince must try to touch a certain branch of a certain tree. If he is destined to succeed his father, he will succeed in touching the branch; if he is not, the branch will magically withdraw at his approach.

I visited the area in which this ritual reportedly took place, but the people in the vicinity denied that such a tree existed.

31. *Ibid.,* p. 106.

32. IFAN (Compte Rendu No. 429). There are many other rumors concerning Kom's death. In a book praising the loyalty of the Africans to the Free French Gov-

ernment of Charles de Gaulle, Deveze declares (p. 74): "Moreover, the Mogho Naba, himself king of the Mossi of Ouagadougou, one of the most powerful dynasties of French Africa, who was placed under surveillance by order of Boisson [the local Vichyite commander] and separated from his subjects, committed suicide after calling his son and solemnly commanding him not to take power 'until the true French should return.'" If this is true, the heir to the throne either could not or would not follow his father's advice.

33. Today a girl is usually chosen as Kourita, because it is easier to banish a woman than a man from the capital. Nevertheless, when Mogho Naba Kom II died in 1942, the young girl chosen to be Kourita was hidden by her mother, and as a result the funeral and the investiture of the new ruler were delayed.

34. See Cheron, "La Cour du Boussouma Naba" (pp. 304–12), for a description of the court of the Boussouma Naba, an autonomous provincial ruler.

35. Dim Delobson (p. 8) claims that the Mogho Naba had the right to ratify the nomination of all Dimdamba, and that it was he who gave them their insignia of office.

36. Cheron, "Contribution," p. 651. He also reports (p. 654): "The Boulsa Naba was elected by a special college. In principle, the choice of this college always fell on one of the sons of the deceased, generally the eldest."

37. *Ibid.*, p. 672.

38. Dim Delobson (p. 143) claims that the person who was asked to give a sacrificial animal to the Baloum Naba was thus assured of the nomination. But the Nobere chief with whom I discussed this matter insisted that he and all the other claimants had given sacrificial animals, and that he did not know he had been chosen until he was notified by the Ouidi Naba.

39. Despite a legend which says that a young woman once ruled the Doulougou district as regent for her young son, the choice of district chief was always a man old enough to rule. If a chief's heir was still a boy, the nam was given to another relative and no provision was made for it to return either to the boy or to his descendants. Unless the boy were fortunate, neither he nor his line ever received the nam again.

40. The ingredients used by the Baloum Naba in preparing the namtibo are kept secret. Most people believe that he uses some elements of the royal amulets, blood, and other liquids. It is not known whether the blood used in ancient times was that of a slave or merely of an animal. Most of the district chiefs with whom I discussed this point reacted with horror to the implication of cannibalism, and insisted that the blood was from animals sacrificed the previous day. However, commoners believe that human blood was used.

41. A fact of great importance in understanding Mossi expansion is that the Kouritadamba of the Nobere district chiefs were banished to the Gurunsi region of Gouroungo on the other side of the Red Volta River. The last Kourita from Nobere is now living in that area, where he rules over a Mossi population drawn from Nobere district and Manga district.

42. Cf. Mangin, p. 19.

CHAPTER FOUR

1. Cf. Socquet, p. 62.
2. Barth, III, 643, 648; Binger, II, 479.
3. Crozat, p. 4822.
4. Delafosse, II, 128–29.
5. Tauxier, *Le Noir du Yatenga*, p. 90.
6. *Ibid.*, pp. 93, 100.
7. Crozat, p. 4849.
8. Delafosse, II, 29.
9. Mangin, pp. 12 ff.
10. Cheron, "Contribution," pp. 673–74.
11. *Ibid.*, pp. 654–55, 657–58.
12. *Ibid.*, p. 680.
13. *Ibid.*, p. 670.
14. *Ibid.*, pp. 685–86.

15. *Ibid.*, p. 673.
17. Binger, II, 502.
19. *Ibid.*, p. 4822.
16. Delafosse, II, 128–29.
18. Crozat, p. 4849.

20. The structure of the Mossi kingdoms and their relationship with the autonomous principalities make it difficult to determine the exact number of districts within each unit. For example, the Mossi people always claimed that the Mogho Naba of Ouagadougou was sovereign over "333" chiefs (cf. Binger, I, 502). However, since the Mossi always associate the number 3 with males, any number giving a multiple of threes is suspect. Binger stated that some of the chiefs referred to as part of the 333 were no more than village chiefs. However, Tauxier (*Le Noir du Soudan*, p. 567), describing the kingdom of Ouagadougou, states, "At the top of this hierarchy is the king, the Mogho Naba, paramount chief of the Mossi, residing at Ouagadougou. To give at least an idea of the relative importance of this empire, without going further than, say, the cercle of Ouagadougou, there were eight provinces comprising 300 *cantons* [districts], 5,000 villages or small towns, and 861,700 inhabitants."

While voicing the myth that the Mogho Naba had "under his control 333 chiefs or Nabas," Dim Delobson actually gives only about 150 chiefs in his list of district and other chiefs (pp. 46, 288–97). It was impossible for me to get any idea of the number of chiefs, because the Mossi hierarchy has changed radically since 1905.

21. Dim Delobson, p. 63.
22. Cheron, "Contribution," p. 651.
23. The Mossi did not acknowledge the defeat of Mogho Naba Wobogo by the French until the Ouidi Naba surrendered to the invaders and installed a ruler they had chosen.
24. Archives, Document 1G-334. Lambert describes Karfo as "a curious figure who unfortunately is not well known."
25. Binger, I, 465.
26. Dim Delobson, pp. 15–45, *passim*.

27. It appears that the monarchs found fault with their district chiefs most readily when they had sons or other relatives in need of districts to govern. Since a possessor of the nam could not be deprived of it while alive, he had to be accused of some crime and executed. Koabga was replaced as Doulougou Naba by Lassanne Congo (called Naba Kouliga), a son of the Mogho Naba. On the other hand, when Naba Pusha of Nobere district fled rather than commit suicide or start a civil war, he was replaced by his own brother, who became Naba Soulougou.

28. Dim Delobson, p. 44.
29. Cheron, "Contribution," p. 655.

CHAPTER FIVE

1. Mangin, p. 25.
2. Mangin does not discuss rape, but reported that an "abductor" was beaten and put in irons. The girl was returned to her family, and if she gave birth to a child, it was killed (pp. 26–27).
3. Dim Delobson, p. 55.
4. Most of my informants state quite clearly that the district chiefs did not have the right to impose the death penalty, but could do so if they were discreet about it and did not take advantage of their subjects. But Dim Delobson states: "Contrary to what people generally believe, the Kombere—the chief of the *canton* [district]—also had the power of life and death over his subjects. How many persons have been put to death only because they were wealthy? How many village chiefs have been killed by the district chiefs in their territories without the Mogho Naba's intervention?" (pp. 55–56).
5. Dim Delobson (p. 56) insists that justice was free of charge, but added that

plaintiffs gave the chiefs the traditional presents of a white cock and a sack containing from 200 to 1,000 cowries.

6. Mangin declares: "Most of the troubles which arise between one Mossi and another derive from their wives and from their debts; yet it may not be said, as a general rule, that women are unhappy or ill treated" (p. 39; see also p. 33). But cf. Dim Delobson, pp. 182, 185.

7. Mangin states that in Koupela a recidivous thief was "led to the market place with a rope around his neck; he was supplied with an abundance of meat and beer, and then clubbed to death at the foot of a tree" (p. 25). I doubt whether this practice was very widespread, because the Mossi were afraid to anger the market Tengkouga (earth spirits) by spilling blood in the market place.

8. Cf. Ruelle, pp. 679 ff.
9. Binger, I, 462.
10. But cf. Marc, p. 134.

CHAPTER SIX

1. Sa'di, pp. 45–46. The date of this battle and the location of Benka are unknown. However, Delafosse (II, 141) believes that it was located in the Massina region on the shores of Lake Debo.
2. Sa'di, pp. 112–13.
3. *Ibid.*, pp. 114–15.
4. *Ibid.*, pp. 121–23. The chronicle also states (p. 168) that these Mossi captives were installed in a special ward of Askia's capital, a practice apparently followed by all victorious Sudanese groups including the Mossi.
5. *Ibid.*, p. 173.
6. See Delafosse, II, 143–45, and Tauxier, *Le Noir du Yatenga,* pp. 88–91.
7. Crozat, p. 4822.
8. Binger, I, 502.
9. Almamy Samory Touré was the last empire-builder in the western Sudan. He was defeated by the French in 1898 and exiled to Gabon, where he died in 1900. See Binger, I, 84ff.
10. Crozat, p. 4837.
11. *Ibid.*, p. 4849.
12. Archives, Document 1G-315 (1903–1904).
13. Crozat, p. 4849.
14. Tauxier, *Le Noir du Soudan,* p. 463.
15. Mangin, p. 13.
16. Cheron, "Contribution," pp. 655, 675–76.
17. *Ibid.*, p. 673.
18. *Ibid.*, p. 676.
19. *Ibid.*, p. 654.
20. *Ibid.*, pp. 685–86.
21. *Ibid.*, p. 674.
22. Ruelle, p. 686.
23. Mangin, p. 62.
24. Binger, I, 473.
25. Cheron, "Contribution," p. 660.
26. Crozat, p. 4849.
27. Mangin, p. 12.
28. For example, when Mogho Naba Sanum's army attacked Boussouma, it made "such a rapid retreat" that Ligidi, the Boussouma Dim, could only counterattack the army's rear guard (Cheron, "Contribution," p. 676).
29. Archives, Document 15G-190 (1897–98).
30. Mangin, p. 12.
31. *Ibid.*
32. Dim Delobson, p. 21.
33. *Ibid.*, p. 29.
34. Cf. Southall (pp. 246–60) for a discussion of the "segmentary" state in Africa.

CHAPTER SEVEN

1. Dim Delobson, pp. 153ff.
2. *Ibid.*, pp. 251–54.
3. Cheron, "Contribution," p. 674.
4. Crozat, p. 4849.
5. *Ibid.*
6. Skinner, "Trade and Markets," pp. 237–78.
7. Barth, III, 644–49.
8. *Ibid.*, pp. 202–4.
9. Dubois, pp. 282–92, 300.
10. Great Britain, Parliamentary papers: Cd. 788–27, No. 357, Acc. Papers, Vol. LXIV (1902).
11. Marc, p. 178.
12. Binger, I, 467.
13. Crozat, p. 4849.
14. Binger, I, 465.
15. Mangin, p. 23.
16. Dim Delobson, pp. 85–86.
17. Ruelle, p. 679.
18. Bovill, p. 244.
19. Gautier, p. 139; cf. Mangin, p. 112.
20. Cf. Sa'di, p. 168.
21. The chief of the Kamboinse was the only Mossi "chief" to possess a stool, which is indicative of an Akan origin. The Akan origin of this group is further supported by Koelle's evidence: a Mossi informant told him that the Mossi called the Ashanti "Kamboinse" (Koelle, p. 6).
22. Skinner, "The Mossi 'Pogsioure,' " pp. 20–22.
23. Cf. Ouédraogo and Prost, pp. 16–18.
24. Dim Delobson, p. 25.
25. Binger, I, 470.
26. *Ibid.*, pp. 502–4.
27. *Ibid.*, pp. 504–5.
28. *Ibid.*, p. 456.
29. *Ibid.*, p. 502.

CHAPTER EIGHT

1. Cf. Dim Delobson, p. 156. He speculates that the Mogho Naba himself sacrificed the animals in the presence of his senior wife and courtiers.
2. *Ibid.*, p. 157.
3. Tauxier (*Le Noir du Yatenga,* p. 379) reports that a comparable ceremony among the Yatenga Mossi was called the "Bega," and that in reality it was a Fulse ceremony "adopted by the Mossi." According to him, both the Fulse and the Mossi held this festival in order to obtain good harvests the following year, and made sacrifices to "the ancestors, to the Earth, and to God."
4. Tauxier, *Le Noir du Soudan*, p. 588.
5. Dim Delobson's description (pp. 148 ff) of the Tense differs somewhat from that given to me by my respondents. According to his version, the Tansoba played the role I have ascribed to the Larhalle Naba. Furthermore, he states that the Tense was held on Friday, an impossible fact since Saturday is the Mossi "day of the dead." In any case, all of my respondents insisted that Saturday, and not Friday, was the day on which the Tense was held. It is possible that Dim Delobson mistook the eve of the festival for its beginning, in which case his error is understandable. In most other respects our descriptions are not too different.
6. *Ibid.*, p. 152.
7. There is a widespread tradition in Mossi country that the Tenkodogo Naba made and still makes similar sacrifices at Kouroungoutenga and Sansabloga, two important earth shrines. There is a controversy about whether human sacrifices were ever offered there. The missionaries in the region claim they were. The Mossi deny this and accuse the missionaries of slander.

8. Cf. Marc, p. 156.
9. Cf. Fortes, pp. 258–71.
10. Skinner, "The Diffusion of Islam," pp. 659–69.
11. Tauxier, *Le Noir du Soudan*, pp. 585–86.
12. Dim Delobson, p. 205.
13. Crozat, p. 4820.
14. *Ibid.*, p. 4822.
15. *Ibid.*, p. 4835.
16. Binger, I, 452.
17. *Ibid.*, p. 456.
18. *Ibid.*, pp. 452–56.
19. Archives, Document 15G-190 (1897–98). Instructions left to Captain Scal by Destenave, June 1897.

CHAPTER NINE

1. Marc, p. 17.
2. Barth, III, 595. Although it is possible that the Wolof prince Bemoy did hear about the Mossi, he was mistaken about the name of their ruler. Interestingly enough, the title "Ogane" is not too dissimilar from Hogon, the title of head men among the Dogon (Habe or Kado) whom the Mossi had pushed into the hills of Bandiagara. Cf. Bascom, p. 24.
3. Barth, III, 606.
4. Bowdich, p. 180.
5. Dupuis, Appendix CVII.
6. Clapperton, II, 323.
7. Barth, III, 643–49. As cited earlier, Barth states that the Portuguese got reports about the Mossi in the year 1533 "from the wrong side, namely from Benin." This may not have been altogether "the wrong side," however, for Barth gives us data on caravans from Mossi country to Sansane Mango in Togoland that indicate how news about the Mossi might have traveled from the interior to Benin city in Nigeria.
8. Koelle, p. 6. Dixon, who seems to have been one of the few captured Mossi sold to the West, reports: "Mose is west of Gurma, east of Andemtenga, where a different language is spoken. Mose is also two days journey from Butmera, where the same language is spoken; four days from Bulega [Bolga tanga], the language still the same, and confederate with Kambonse, i.e. Asante; two days from Yaongo, with still the same language; six days from Bosanse which is at enmity with Mose and where people bore their lips, and often tie them together with grass, and whose language is different from Mose; four days from Busma also a different language, and in which country there is a very high mountain (Tanga) from which those who ascend never come back again [probably a reference to Plimpikou, the Mossi holy mountain]; three or four weeks from Kambonse, i.e. Asante. Kupeala is four days from Wardyga [Ouagadougou] the Mossi capital, whither the king of Asante often sent presents; and one month from Salak [Salaga], an Asante town, where they bring kola nuts."
9. Marc, p. 30.
10. Great Britain, Parliamentary papers xlvi, 1882.
11. The people of Nobere, Manga, and other districts surrounding Bere have traditions about Krause, who is remembered as the first white-skinned person ever seen in those parts. The color of his skin was attributed to the fact that, "like the fish," he had come out of the sea.
12. Krause, pp. 92 ff. Although there is no evidence to this effect in the literature, it appears certain that Mossi government officials knew of Krause's visit. They treated most travelers in the following manner: "After entering a town the party is given in charge of a man usually termed 'housemaster.' It is his duty to exercise surveillance over the action of the stranger and to report the result to the authorities. . . . The trader conducts his business through his 'housemaster,' who usually makes a handsome gain by acting as middleman (G. E. Ferguson, quoted in Wolfson, p. 199).

13. Binger, I, 18, 440.
15. *Ibid.*, pp. 469–70.
17. *Ibid.*, p. 467.
19. Marc, p. 36.
21. *Ibid.*, p. 4835.
23. *Ibid.*, p. 4836.
25. *Ibid.*
27. *Ibid.*, p. 4850.
14. *Ibid.*, p. 450.
16. *Ibid.*, p. 460.
18. Von François, p. 143 ff.
20. Crozat, p. 4820.
22. *Ibid.*
24. *Ibid.*
26. *Ibid.*, p. 4849.

28. Marc, p. 38. He attempts to maintain historical veracity: "Contrary to what Crozat believed, the Mogho Naba was able to assemble thousands of horsemen with which to confront the French."

29. Monteil, p. 163.

30. He gives an account of the northern region of Ghana in a secret report quoted in Wolfson, p. 199.

31. "Les Missions Françaises dans La Boucle du Niger," *Bull. du Comité de L'Afrique Française*, VII (1897), 108–9.

32. *Ibid.*

33. *Bull. du Comité de L'Afrique Française*, V (1895), 276. The people of Nobere say that Alby went to the ruler's son at Djiba and asked to be taken to Ouagadougou because he had presents for the Mogho Naba. But the prince, noting the soldiers with the European, secretly went to his father and told him about the mission. Mogho Naba Wobogo then called his ministers together and asked them whether the visitor should be received. They told him that they feared this visit was a trick to capture the country, and told the Djiba Naba to tell his guest that Mogho Naba Wobogo did not want any Europeans in his kingdom.

34. Marc, pp. 35–38. See "Les Missions Françaises dans La Boucle du Niger," *Bull. du Comité de L'Afrique Française*, VII (1897), 107–12, for a discussion of the controversy between the European powers for control of these territories.

35. Tauxier, *Le Noir du Yatenga*, p. 109.

36. Barry, p. 131.

37. Tauxier, *Le Noir du Yatenga*, p. 111.

38. Noll, p. 257. The Mossi were a bit chagrined that a relatively small force conquered them. This force consisted of Lt. Voulet, his adjutant Lt. Chanoine, Sergeants Laury and Le Geriel, 29 Senegalese infantrymen, 10 spahis, 180 Sudanese infantrymen armed with European weapons, 40 Sudanese horsemen, and 250 porters. The Mossi now insist that although this force was small, it had more fire-power than they had ever encountered, and that they had only flint guns aside from their traditional weapons. They say that if they had had rifles, no one would ever have entered their country.

39. Archives, Document 15G-190 (June 1897).

40. Noll, p. 257.
42. *Ibid.*, p. 39 ff.
41. Dim Delobson, p. 38.
43. Randau, p. 433.

44. It is not clear whether Mazi was poisoned (as the French claim), or whether he died a natural death. Despite French claims to the contrary, the Mossi insist that Mazi was never ruler of Ouagadougou, and they do not include him in their genealogies. The present chief of Nobere insists that Mazi was never Mogho Naba and that he died a natural death. Dim Delobson also declares that although Mazi was Wobogo's sworn enemy, and would have liked to become Mogho Naba, he was ill when Voulet called upon him and died before acceding to power. (Dim Delobson, pp. 41–42.)

45. Lambert, p. 73.

46. Archives, Doc. 15G-190 (May 1897). The Nobere people deny that they supported the French, but official documents of the period report that it was the Nobere Naba who informed the French of Boukary Koutou's activities. The people of Nobere

declare that they supported Boukary Koutou all along, but that he was defeated because he had lost the confidence of the country.
47. Great Britain, Colonial Report, 1900.
48. Lambert, p. 73.
49. Great Britain, Colonial Report, 1903.
50. Dim Delobson, p. 45.

CHAPTER TEN

1. Arnaud and Meray, pp. 1–32. See also Roberts, I, 89–102.
2. IFAN.
3. Archives, Doc. 15G-190 (1877–78).
4. *Ibid.*
5. *Bull. d'information et de Renseignements Coloniaux* (hereinafter cited as *Rens. Coloniaux*), XLVIII (Aug. 25, 1938), 307.
6. *Ibid.*
7. De Beauminy, "Une Féodalité," p. 24. During this period and for many years afterward, the neighboring acephalous Lobi and Gurunsi groups refused to pay taxes (*L'Afrique Française* [Feb.–Mar. 1910], pp. 77, 341).
8. Mahaut, pp. 20–27.
9. IFAN.
10. Mahaut, p. 31.
11. Tauxier, *Le Noir du Soudan*, p. 538.
12. Mangin, pp. 61–62.
13. *L'Afrique Française*, XLVIII (1938), 20.
14. Burthe d'Annelet, I, 291.
15. Mahaut, pp. 36–39.
16. Buell, I, 1006.
17. *L'Afrique Française,* XIX (1909), 348–49; see also Van Vollenhoven, pp. 187 ff.
18. Sarraut, pp. 1–12 *passim.*
19. The Europeans in Mossi country received this news with mixed feelings, and according to one source their opinions were based "principally on questions of pure interests" (*Rens. Coloniaux,* XXXI [1921], 6). De Beauminy stated that "the principal riches actually utilizable in Mossi country are its numerous laborers" (De Beauminy, "Le Pays de la Boucle," pp. 71–78). See also Ledange, pp. 133–36.
20. *Rens. Coloniaux*, XXXI (1921), 4–5.
21. *Ibid.*
22. Ossendowski, p. 272.
23. Ledange, pp. 133–36.
24. Londres, pp. 126 ff.
25. Burthe d'Annelet, I, 204.
26. Ossendowski, p. 276.
27. *L'Afrique Française*, XLII (1932), 520.
28. De Beauminy, "Une Féodalité," p. 24.
29. *Rens. Coloniaux*, XXXI (1921), 4.
30. *Rens. Coloniaux*, XXXIII (1923), 439.
31. *La Haute Volta*, p. 55.
32. Burthe d'Annelet, I, 292.
33. *Rens. Coloniaux*, XXXIII (1923), 441.
34. *Ibid.*
35. *La Haute Volta*, p. 54.
36. *Rens. Coloniaux*, XXXIII (1923), 439.
37. *Journal Officiel de la République Française* (circular of June 16, 1919), p. 410.
38. Cowan (p. 117) states that in French West Africa, "It was almost universally admitted that the *conseils de notables* served little, if any, useful purpose." The fol-

lowing comment applies most aptly to the situation in Mossi country: "Perhaps the most serious defect in the *conseils de notables* lay in the fact that, consisting as they did usually of older, and often illiterate, members who were without a knowledge of modern administration, they were unprepared to offer any opinion on a matter of technical nature even if the administrator were prepared to consult them." It should be added, however, that there were hardly any western-educated Mossi in the country at this time, and the officials in and around Ouagadougou were not willing to listen to the local people. Cf. Buell, I, 998–1000.

39. Buell, I, 1007.
40. *L'Afrique Française*, XXX (1920), 299.
41. Socquet, p. 62.
42. Soeur Marie-André, p. 236. Her propaganda in favor of ameliorating the status of the African woman led to the Mandel decree of June 1939, which forbade the marriage of preadolescent girls and instituted other reforms.
43. Bouniol, p. 60.
44. Dupont, p. 4.
45. Gorer, p. 149.
46. Cf. Tauxier, *Le Noir du Soudan*, p. 203.
47. Dim Delobson, p. 203.
48. Burthe d'Annelet, I, 288.
49. *Journal Officiel de la République Française* (Sept. 10, 1932), p. 9927.
50. Burthe d'Annelet, I, 299.
51. *L'Afrique Française*, XLII (1932), 523–33.
52. Burthe d'Annelet, I, 301–2.
53. *L'Afrique Française*, XLVIII (1938), 21.
54. *Ibid.*, XLIX (1939), 136–39.
55. Balima, p. 36.
56. Thompson and Adloff, p. 29.
57. Balima, pp. 36–37.
58. Thompson and Adloff, p. 29.
59. Deveze, pp. 184–85.
60. IFAN (Compte Rendu No. 429).
61. *Ibid.*
62. *Ibid.*

CHAPTER ELEVEN

1. The text of the recommendations and of other documents from the Brazzaville Conference can be found in "La Conférence Africaine Française, Brazzaville, 1944," in *Renaissance* (Paris, 1944).
2. Thompson and Adloff, pp. 206–7, and Cowan, pp. 175 ff.
3. Thompson and Adloff, p. 122.
4. Amon d'Aby, pp. 55–56.
5. Hodgkin and Schachter, p. 405.
6. Thompson and Adloff, p. 124.
7. *Ibid.*, pp. 33–35.
8. Gonidec, p. 328.
9. *Ibid.*, p. 331.
10. *Journal Officiel, Débats de la République Française* (April–Dec. 1955), p. 2534.
11. Gonidec, pp. 333–34.
12. Holleaux, pp. 18 ff.
13. Wright, pp. 148–49, 178–79, 227.
14. "Manifeste du Rassemblement Démocratique Africain," *Le RDA dans la Lutte Anti-impérialiste* (Paris, 1948), p. 23.
15. Amon d'Aby, pp. 55–56.
16. *Journal Officiel, Débats de l'Assemblée de l'Union Française* (June 22, 1949), p. 769.
17. Cowan, pp. 98–99.
18. Balima, pp. 42–43.

19. *Journal Officiel, Débats de l'Assemblée de l'Union Française* (June 22, 1949), p. 749.
20. *Journal Officiel, Débats de l'Assemblée Nationale* (Mar. 1, 1948), p. 1881.
21. *Journal Officiel, Débats de l'Assemblée de l'Union Française* (June 22, 1949), p. 749.
22. *Ibid.*, p. 767.
23. *Ibid.*, p. 768.
24. Balima, p. 41.
25. Taken from my field notes.
26. Skinner, "Labour Migration," pp. 393–94.
27. Dupont, pp. 2327–28.
28. Soeur Marie-André, p. 490.
29. Taken from my field notes.
30. *L'Afrique Française*, LXIV (1955), 63.
31. For the provisions of the loi-cadre, see "Political Evolution in the French Overseas Territories," *African Affairs*, Bull. 14A, Ambassade de France, Service de Presse et d'Information (New York, August 1956).
32. See Mathias Moriba in *Afrique Nouvelle* (Nov. 12, 1957), p. 1; see also *ibid.* (Oct. 15, 1957), p. 1, and (Feb. 19, 1957), p. 2.
33. *Ibid.* (Nov. 5, 1956), p. 6.
34. *Ibid.* (Feb. 5, 1957), p. 3.
35. "Party alignments in Afrique Occidentale Française," *West Africa* (London), Nov. 17, 1956, p. 920. See also Siriex, p. 110.
36. *Afrique Nouvelle* (April 2, 1957), p. 6.
37. Dugue, p. 25.
38. *Afrique Nouvelle* (Nov. 26, 1957), p. 3. For an account of Mogho Naba Kougri's installation, see *ibid.* (Dec. 3, 1957), p. 2.
39. *Ibid.* (Feb. 21, 1958), p. 1.
40. *Marchés Tropicaux du Monde* (Paris), No. 847 (Feb. 3, 1962), 227.
41. Dugue, p. 34.
42. Balima, pp. 44–46.
43. "Birth of a new community of free peoples," *French Affairs*, Bull. 71, Ambassade de France, Service de Presse et d'Information (New York, Oct. 1958).
44. *Ibid.*
45. *Ibid.*; see also *Le Monde* (Paris), Oct. 23, 1958.
46. *Ibid.*
47. *Ibid.*
48. *Bull. Quotidien d'Information*, Distribué par le service de l'information de la République de Haute-Volta (Nov. 23, 1958), p. 2.
49. Lajus, p. 3.
50. *Carrefour Africain* (Ouagadougou), Dec. 4, 1960, p. 3.
51. *Bull. Quotidien d'Information*, Distribué par le service de l'information de la République de Haute-Volta (June 20, 1960), p. 1.
52. *Afrique Nouvelle* (Aug. 10, 1960), p. 8.
53. *Marchés Tropicaux du Monde* (Paris), No. 847 (Feb. 3, 1962), 227.

CHAPTER TWELVE

1. Skinner, "'Paradox,'" 199-201; see also Kabore, pp. 12-16.
2. Skinner, *African Urban Life*, pp. 405 ff.
3. Ibid.
4. Skinner, "Political Conflict," 1208-17.
5. Balima, *Genese*, pp. 112 ff.
6. There is a possibly apocryphal story that the Mogho Naba sought to have the Catholic Church support the *nam* by receiving the blessings of the priests. The latter attempted to avoid the issue by asking Kougri to become monogamous, something they did not believe he would do. When, to their surprise, the king accepted the offer, they convinced him that their blessing his bonnet would have the same effect. If this is indeed what happened, Kougri was not completely satisfied with this gesture, and he also sought the help of the Muslims.
7. Borders, p. 14.
8. Legum and Drysdale, eds., *Africa Contemporary Record*, Annual Survey and Documents, 1972-1973, p. B744.
9. Legum and Drysdale, ibid., 1970-1971, p. B459.
10. Ibid., 1978-1979, p. B790.
11. Ibid., p. B791.
12. Maïga, "*Haute Volta: Une tache,*" 26 July 1978, p. 26.
13. Diallo, "*Haute Volta: Un putsch,*" pp. 55 ff.; *Africa Contemporary Record*, 1980-1981, pp. B627 ff.
14. Diallo, "*Haute Volta: Un putsch,*" pp. 50 ff.
15. Ibid.
16. "Upper Volta: The Soldiers' Brief Honeymoon," p. B565.
17. Ibid., pp. B565 ff.; *Jeune Afrique*, 22 December 1982, pp. 50 ff.
18. Diallo, "*Haute Volta: Qui sont les nouveaux dirigeants?*", pp. 55 ff.
19. "Death of the Moro Naba," pp. 326 ff.; "The Mossi and the Military," p. 18.
20. "The Mossi and the Military," p. 18.
21. The practice of the Mogho Nanamse taking a name by which they rule is an old one among the Mossi. While his father took the name *Kougri*, which meant "rock," Ousmane Congo preferred a name comparable to that of his grandfather, who was known as *Mogho Naba Sagha*, meaning "rain."
22. "The Mossi and the Military," p. 18.
23. Diallo, *"Qui sont les nouveaux dirigeants?"*, p. 52.
24. Ibid.
25. Diallo, *"Haute-Volta: Les marxistes s'installent,"* pp. 34-35.
26. Diallo, *"La chute de l'aigle,"* p. 29.
27. Maïga, *"Haute-Volta: Douze heures avec Thomas Sankara,"* p. 18.
28. Ibid., p. 19.
29. Ibid., p. 20.
30. "Upper Volta: Postponing Marxism?", p. 7.
31. "Upper Volta: Ouedraogo Goes It Alone," p. 21.
32. Diallo, *"Monsieur Maurice' est de retour,"* p. 38.
33. Maïga, *"Ouaga sur le qui vive,"* p. 28.
34. Had many commentators known the history of Mogho Naba Motaba, a Fulani who allegedly seized the throne during the interregnum following the death of Mogho Naba Oubi, to whom he had become an indispensable councillor, they might not have dismissed Sankara as quickly as they did. A few perceptive observers felt that as "a good Marxist attentive to the lessons of history, he should meditate on the sad experiences of Rawlings, if he would like, as the Ghananian to return to power one day" (ibid., p. 28).

35. Balima, pp. 21 ff.
36. Andriamirado, "Thomas Sankara," p. 30. There are reports that it was Sankara's grandfather, not his father, who was a Fulani and a servant of a Mossi prince. This prince gave his Fulani a wife; and their children, including Thomas's father, bore the surname *Ouedraogo*. It was allegedly Thomas's decision to change his last name from Ouedraogo to Sankara, in honor of his Fulani grandfather.
37. Andriamirado, p. 30.
38. Apter wrote, "Around the slogans and demands, around the green, white, and red of the CPP banners, around the almost mythical person of Kwame Nkrumah there slowly emerged a faithful flock, shepherded by the leader into paths of nationalism and independence. We shall call Nkrumah a *charismatic leader*" (his emphasis; p. 174). Auma-Osolo also hypothesized that the "more Africans produced charismatic leadership, the more they intensified their resistance to the colonial discriminatory policy" (p. 138).
39. Apter, p. 174.
40. Ibid.
41. Weber, pp. 358-73.
42. Ibid.
43. Sankara had asked me to call upon him during his visit to New York in 1984, and during a long conversation he sought to assure me that many of the persons I knew in Ouagadougou, including former members of the government, were safe. He did not reveal until my visit to Ouagadougou in 1986 as a delegate to a meeting of the Institute of the Black World that as a young cadet at the military school in Ouagadougou he had visited my embassy to receive a prize he had won in a contest held by the United States Information Agency. I remarked to Donald Easum (also a former United States ambassador to Upper Volta), who had overheard the conversation, that it was wise for United States ambassadors to meet all types of persons, even students. I had private interviews with Sankara after that period and became increasingly troubled by his moralistic views of foreign relations. I had also sensed during visits to Ouagadougou that he was losing some support. These forebodings led me to write to the program committee of the ASA meeting from Abidjan, Ivory Coast, on 30 April 1987, that my contribution to the Denver African Studies Association (ASA) meeting in November of that year would be entitled "Sankara and the Revolution in Burkina Faso: The Limits of Charisma." By the time of that meeting, Sankara himself was dead and his revolution called into question.
44. *"Blaise Compaoré (Burkina Faso) reçu hier par le President."*
45. *Jeune Afrique*, 28 October 1987, p. 35.
46. James Brooke, p. 8.
47. These books are Bamouni's *Burkina Faso*; Ziegler's *Sankara*; and Andriamirado's *Sankara le rebelle*.
48. "Coup in Burkina Faso," p. 5.
49. Bailley, *"Interview Exclusive,"* p. 9.
50. Maiga, *"Ouaga sur le qui vive,"* pp. 26 ff.
51. Skinner, "Political Conflict," passim.
52. Foreign Broadcast Information Service (FBIS-AFR-87-199), West Africa, 15 October 1987, p. 9.
53. Sankara, *"Mon dernier message,"* p. 9.
54. Harsch, p. 36.
55. FBIS-AFR-87-201, West Africa, 19 October 1987, p. 24.
56. "Compaoré Takes Over," in *West Africa*, 26 October 1987, p. 2104.
57. "Dateline Africa," in *West Africa*, 26 October 1987, p. 2133.
58. "For Better or Worse?" in *West Africa*, 2 November 1987, p. 2148.
59. Sankara, p. 11.
60. Béchir Ben Yahmed (editor), *Jeune Afrique*, 28 October 1987, p. 4.

61. FBIS-AFR-87-202, 20 October 1987, p. 24.
62. *"Compaoré se defend d'avoir fait tuer son ami,"* p. 23.
63. Diallo and Thibout, p. 25. Sankara's death is still being mourned by Africans both on the continent and in the Diaspora. An editorial in *African Connection* declared: "Thomas Sankara, your works, dedication and commitment have put you forever among the legends of modern Africa. You have transformed a little known country, Burkina Faso, into an emerging political influence on the continent" (1[6]: 2).

GLOSSARY

BABISSI. Literally, "fathers' brothers." A large extended family (minimal lineage) composed of people who had a common ancestor three, four, or five generations back.
BAGLERE. A group of bondsmen believed to be descended from the Fulani or from war captives.
BALOUM NABA. A provincial minister and the chief steward of the royal household.
BASGHA. Annual feast of the royal ancestors.
BENDERE NABA. A bard or minstrel who is often called upon to recite the ruler's genealogy at royal functions.
BOODKASMA (pl. BOODKASEMDAMBA). Head of a lineage or lineage segment.
COGANAMARSE. Stones on which dignitaries are seated during court ceremonies.
DAPORE. A group of bondsmen believed to be descended from war captives.
DIM (pl. DIMDAMBA). Literally, "submit only to God." King or king's son.
DOGUNBA. Literally, "keepers of the household." The younger wives of the ruler.
FADO. An inheritance tax.
GANDE NABA. An official charged with performing sacrifices on the ruler's behalf and with distributing gifts from the ruler to the royal officials and the royal household.
GOUNGA NABA. A provincial minister.
KAMBOINSE. Guards of the royal household.
KAMBO NABA. Head guard of the royal household.
KAMSAOGHO NABA. A provincial minister. He is also a eunuch.
KEEMA (pl. KEEMSE). Ancestral spirit; also, a deceased person.
KOMBERE or KOMBERE NABA (pl. KOMBEMBA NANAMSE). A district chief.
KOS NABA. Collector of taxes on general merchandise sold in the market.
KOURITA (pl. KOURITADAMBA). A young son of a deceased Mogho Naba chosen to represent his father on earth. He is banned from the capital, and forbidden to see the new Mogho Naba under pain of death.
LARHALLE NABA. A provincial minister. He was also responsible for offering sacrifices to the royal ancestors.
MABISSI. Literally, "sons of the same mother." All the children of one woman.
MOAGA (pl. MOSSI). A member of the Mossi group or nation.
MOGHO. Literally, "the world." The country of the Mossi.
MOGHO NABA. Literally, "ruler of the world." The title of the ruler of the Ouagadougou kingdom.
NABA (pl. NANAMSE). Chief, ruler, or official.
NABA ZID OUENDE. Literally, "sun king." God.
NAB'YIRI. House of the chief or ruler.

NAB'YURE. Literally, "king's name." No child born during his reign could bear the ruler's name, and those persons who already bore it when a new ruler was chosen called themselves Nab'yure.

NAKOMCE (sing. NABIGA). Children of the Naba; people of the ruling or noble class.

NAM. Sovereignty, which was conceived of by the Mossi as "that force of God which permits one man to control another."

NAMTIBO. The royal amulets, or any substance or object embodying the nam.

NAPOKO. Literally, "female ruler." The eldest daughter of a Mogho Naba. She ritually impersonates her deceased father during the interregnum.

NEMDO NABA. Collector of taxes on meat sold in the market, and the person responsible for distributing meat within the royal household.

NINISI, see TINGUIMBISSI.

OUAGADOUGOU NABA. The earth priest (Tengsoba) who had ritual control of the capital district.

OUEDRANGE NABA. Head groom of the royal stables.

OUIDI NABA. An official of the ruler. In Ouagadougou, he was both a provincial minister and the prime minister.

POGOPOSSUM. Premarital gift from a man's family to his wife's family.

PUGHSIUDSE. Women whom the chief received from his subjects and whom he subsequently gave out as wives on condition that their husbands give him their eldest daughters as future pughsiudse.

PUGHTIEMA. Head wife of a ruler.

PWE NABA. A religious practitioner in a ruler's household; he is responsible for the virtue of the ruler's wives and pages.

RAGA NABA. Official in charge of the market.

SAKA (pl. SAGHSE). A section of a village.

SAKAKASMA (pl. SAKAKASMADAMBA). Head of a village section; usually the senior man of the senior lineage segment in the village.

SAMANDE (pl. SAMANDE-KAMBA). A servant in the royal household or the chief's household.

SAMANDE KASMA. Head retainer in a ruler's household.

SAMANDE NABA. Official in charge of palace retainers.

SEKA (pl. SEGHSE). Compulsory labor performed for a ruler by his subjects.

SIMILI-MOSSI. An ethnic group formed through the intermarriage of the Fulani and the Mossi.

SOGHONE (pl. SOGHONDAMBA). A page in the ruler's household.

SOGHONE-KASANGA. Head page.

SOLEM. Kingdom or area ruled by the Mogho Naba.

SOSOGHA (pl. SOSOSE). Voluntary labor performed for a ruler by his subjects.

TANSOBA. War minister.

TENGA (pl. TENSE). Generalized female earth deity. Tenga had local manifestations called Tengkouga, or earth shrines. The Mossi talk about these shrines as though they are deities in their own right.

TENGKOUGA (sing. TENGKOUGRE). Earth shrines, including mountains, rivers, clumps of trees, etc. See TENGA.

TENGKOM. Civil war between villages or districts.

TENGSOBA (pl. TENGSOBADAMBA). Earth priest.

TINGUIMBISSI. Literally, "sons of the earth." The autochthonous population of Mossi country; also called Ninisi.

WEOGHO (pl. WEOTO). Wasteland or uncultivated land.

YAGENGA (pl. YAGENSE). Literally, sister's son. The son or grandchild of a female lineage member.

GLOSSARY

YIRI (pl. YIYA). A Mossi household.
YIRISOBA (pl. YIRISOBADAMBA). Head of a household.
YUMA (pl. YUMBA). Herald or musician.
ZAKA (pl. ZAGHSE). Interior courtyard of a compound.
ZOM KOM. A beverage made with millet flour and water. Sometimes honey is added.
ZONGAGONGO. War drum.
ZONGO. Reception hall of a ruler.
ZUSOABA KASANGA. Head eunuch.

BIBLIOGRAPHY

Ajayi, J.F. Ade, and Espie, Ian. *A Thousand Years of West African History*. Ibadan, Nigeria: University of Ibadan Press, 1965.
Amon d'Aby, F.J. *La Côte d'Ivoire dans la cité africaine*. Paris, Larose, 1951.
Andriamado, Sennen. *Sankara le rebelle*. Paris: Jeune Afrique Livres, 1987.
———. *"Thomas Sankara entre Rawlings et Kaddafi," Jeune Afrique*, 1 June 1983, pp. 30-32.
Apter, David. *Ghana in Transition*. New York: Atheneum, 1968.
Archives of the Gouverneur Général de l'Afrique Occidentale Française. Dakar, Senegal. Unpublished documents.
Arhim, Kwame. "The Role of Akan Women." In *Female and Male in West Africa*. Edited by Christine Oppong. London: Allen & Unwin, 1983.
Arnaud, A., and Meray, H. *Les Colonies françaises: Organisation administrative, judicaire, politique, et financière*. Paris: Larose, 1900.
Auma-Osolo, Agola. *Cause-Effects of Modern African Nationalism on the World Market*. Lantham, Maryland; New York; and London: University Press of America, 1983.
Bailly, D. *"Interview Exclusive: Sankara m'a dit . . ." Ivoire Dimanche*, 5 July 1987, pp. 4-15.
Balima, Albert S. *Genese de la Haute Volta*. Ougadougou: Presses Africaines, 1970.
———. *Notes sur l'organisation de l'empire mossi*. Unpublished manuscript, n.d.
Bamouni, Babou Paulin. *Burkina Faso: Processus de la Revolution*. Paris: Points de vue L'Harmattan, 1986.
Barry, J. *Histoire de l'Afrique occidentale française*. Paris: Hatier, 1949.
Barth, Henry. *Travels and Discoveries in North and Central Africa*. New York: Harper & Bros., 1859.
Bascom, William. *"Les Premiers Fondements historiques de l'urbanisme Yoruba." Présence Africaine* 23 (Dec. 1958-Jan. 1959): 24.
Betts, Raymond F. *Assimilation and Association in French Colonial Theory, 1890-1914*. New York: AMS Press, 1960, 1971.
Binger, Louis. *Du Niger au Golfe de Guinée par le pays Kong et le Mossi, 1887-1889*. 2 vols. Paris: Hachette, 1892. *"Blaise Compaore (Burkina Faso) recu hier par le President." Fraternité Matin/Jeudi*, 20 August 1987, p. 24.
Borders, William. "In Upper Volta, No One Fears the Tribal Sun King Anymore." *New York Times*, 17 August 1971, p. 14.
Bouniol, Joseph. *The White Fathers and Their Missions*. London: Sands, 1929.
Bovill, E.W. *The Golden Trade of the Moors*. London: Oxford University Press, 1958.

Bowdich, T. Edward. *Mission from Cape Coast to Ashantee.* 1819. 3d ed. London: Frank Cass, 1966.
Brooke, James. "Young Voice in Africa: Sports and Clean Living." *New York Times,* 7 September 1987, p. 8.
Buell, Raymond L. *The Native Problem in Africa.* 2 vols. New York: Macmillan, 1928.
Burthe d'Annelet, J.C. *A travers l'Afrique francaise.* 2 vols. Paris, 1939.
Busia, K.A. *The Position of the Chief in the Modern Political System of Ashanti.* London: Oxford University Press, 1951.
Cardinall, A.W. *The Natives of the Northern Territories of the Gold Coast.* London: Routledge, 1925.
Cheron, Georges. *"Contribution á l'histoire du Mossi: Traditions relatives au cercle du Kaya (Haute-Volta)." Bull. du Comite d'Etudes Historiques et Scientifiques de l'Afrique Occidentale Francaise* 7 (1925): 648.
_____. *"La cour du Boussouma Naba." Bull. du Comité d'Etudes Historiques et Scientifiques de l'Afrique Occidentale Française* 8 (1925): 304-12.
Claessen, Henri J.M. "Specific Features of the African Early State." In Claessen and Skalnik, pp. 59-86.
Claessen, Henri J.M., and Skalnik, Peter, eds. *The Study of the State.* The Hague: Mouton, 1980.
Clapperton, Hugh. *Journal of a Second Expedition into the Interior of Africa.* London: Lea and Carey, 1829.
Cohen, Ronald. Evalution, Fission and the Early State." In Claessen and Skalnik, pp. 87-116.
"Compaore se defende d'avoir fait tuer son ami." Jeune Afrique, 4 November 1987, p. 23.
"Compare Takes Over." *West Africa,* 19 October 1987, p. 2104.
Coronel, Patricia Crane. "Aowin Terracotta Sculpture." *African Arts* 13, no. 1 (November 1979): 28-35, 97-98.
"Coup in Burkina Faso." *West Africa,* 26 October 1987, p. 5.
Cowan, L. Gray. *Local Government in West Africa.* New York: Columbia University Press, 1958.
Crozat, Dr. *"Rapport sur une mission au Mossi (1890)."* "Journal Officiel de la Republique Française, 5-9 October 1891, pp. 4820-50.
"Dateline AFRICA." *West Africa,* 26 October 1987, p. 2133.
"Death of the Moro Naba." *West Africa,* 20 December 1982, pp. 326 ff.
De Beauminy, André. *"Une Féodalité en Afrique occidentale française.*
"Bull. d'Information et de Renseignements Coloniaux 35 (1925): 24.
_____.*"Le Pays de la boucle du Niger, étude économique."Revue Géographique et Commerciale de Bordeaux* 6 (1919): 71-78.
Delafosse, Maurice. *Essai de manuel de langue Agni.* Paris: Presses Universitaires de France, 1900.
_____. *Le Pays, les peuples, les langues, l'histoire, les civilisations du Haute-Sénégal-Niger.* 3 vols. Paris: Larose, 1912.
_____. *Negroes of Africa.* Washington, DC: Associated Publishing, 1931.
Deveze, Michel. *La France d'outre-mer.* Paris: Hachette, 1948.
Diallo, Siradiou. *"La chute de l'aigle." Jeune Afrique,* 1 June 1983, pp. 28-29.
_____. *"Haute-Volta: Les marxistes s'installent." Jeune Afrique,* 6 April 1983, pp. 34-35.
_____. *"Haute-Volta — Un putsch presque banal." Jeune Afrique,* 3 December 1980, p. 31.

———. "Haute-Volta: Qui sont les nouveaux dirigeants?" *Jeune Afrique*, 22 December 1982, pp. 50 ff.
———. "Monsieur Maurice est de retour." *Jeaune Afrique*, 15 June 1983, p. 38.
Diallo, Siradiou, and Thibout, Monique. "Burkina: Compaore est-il en train de reussir?" *Jeune Afrique*, 2 March 1988, p. 25.
Dim Delobson, A.A. *L'Empire du Mogho Naba*. Paris: Donat-Montchrestier, 1932.
Dubois, Felix. *Tomboctou le mystérieux*. Paris: E. Flammarion, 1899.
Dugue, Gil. *Vers les Etats-Unis d'Afrique*. Dakar: Editions "Lettres africaines," 1960.
Dupont, André. "La rapide evolution des Africans dans la Haute-Volta." *Marchés Coloniaux* 163 (25 December 1948): 2327-28.
Dupuis, Joseph. *Journal of a Residence in Ashantee*. London: F. Cass, 1824.
"Editorial." *African Connection*, 28 November 1987, p. 2.
"For Better or Worse?" *West Africa*, 2 November 1987, p. 2148.
Forde, Daryll. "The Cultural Map of West Africa." *Transactions of the New York Academy of Science* 15 (April 1954): 206-18.
Foreign Broadcast Information Service. FBIS-AFR-87-199, 15 October 1987, p. 9; FBIS-AFR-87-201, 19 October 1987, p. 24; FBIS-AFR-87-202, 20 October 1987, p. 24.
Fortes, Meyer. "The Political System of the Tallensi of the Northern Territories of the Gold Coast." In *African Political Systems*. Edited by Meyer Fortes and E.E. Evans-Pritchard. London: Oxford University Press, 1940.
———. "The Structure of Unilineal Descent Groups." *American Anthropologist* 55 (1953): 17-41.
———. "The Submerged Descent Line within Ashanti." In *Studies in Kinship and Marriage*. Edited by I. Schapera. London: RAIGE, 1963.
Fried, Morton. "The Classification of Corporate Unilineal Descent Groups." *Journal of the Royal Anthropological Institute* 87 (1957): 1-29.
———. *The Evolution of Political Society: An Essay in Political Anthropology*. New York: Random House, 1967.
Gautier, E.F. *L'Afrique noire occidentale*. Paris, 1935.
Gibb, H.A.R. *Ibn Battuta: Travels in Asia and Africa, 1325-1354*. New York: A.M. Kelley, 1969.
Gonidec, P.F. "Les Assemblées locales des territoires d'outre-mer." *Revue Juridique et Politique de l'Union Française* 7 (1952): 328.
Goody, Jack. "The Mother's Brother and the Sister's Son in West Africa." *Journal of the Royal Anthropological Institute* 89 (1959): 61-88.
Gorer, Geoffry. *Africa Dances*. New York: Knopf, 1935.
Great Britain. Colonial Report (Annual), 1900, No. 239. Gold Coast, C9046-17.
———. Colonial Report (Annual), 1903. Gold Coast, Cd. 2238-6.
———. Parliamentary papers 46, 1882. (C. 3386, #42, enc. 2).
———. Parliamentary papers: Cd. 788-27, No. 357, Acc. and Papers, vol 64, 1902.
Greenberg, Joseph H. "The Languages of Africa." *International Journal of American Linguistics* 29 (January 1963): 8.
———. "The Negro Kingdoms of the Sudan." *Transactions of the New York Academy of Science* 11 (February 1949): 126-34.

Haas, Jonathan. *Evolution of the Prehistoric State*. New York: Columbia University Press, 1982.
Harsch, Ernest. "Burkina Special Report: A Revolution Derailed." *Africa Report* 33, no. 1 (1988): 36.
La Haute Volta. Report prepared for the Exposition Coloniale Internationale de 1931 by the Gouverneur Général de l'Afrique Occidentale Française.
Hodgkin, Thomas, and Schachter, Ruth. "French-speaking West Africa in Transition." *Bulletin of International Conciliation*, no. 528 (February 1961).
Holleaux, Andre. "Les Elections aux assemblées des territoires d'outre-mer." *Revue Juridique et Politique de l'Union Française* 10 (1956): 18 ff.
IFAN (Institute Français d'Afrique Noire). Unpublished documents. Ouagadougou, Burkina Faso.
Ifemesia, G.C. "States of the Central Sudan." In Ajayi and Espie, pp. 72-112.
Izard, Michel. *Gens du pouvoir, gens de la terre*. Cambridge: Cambridge University Press, Editions de la Maison des sciences de l'homme, 1985.
Kabore, Victor G. "*Organisation traditionelle et evolution politique des Mossi de Ouagadougou. Rechérches voltaique* C.V.R.S. (1966), pp. 12-16.
Koelle, Sigismund. *Polyglotta Africana*. London: Unveranderte Nachdnick der Ausgabe London, 1854.
Krause, Dr. "Krause's Reise." *Peterman's Mittheilungen* (Berlin), 1887-1888, pp. 42ff.
Lajus, Michel. *"La République Voltaique."* *Le Revue Française*, November 1959, pp. 22-28.
Lambert, Capt. *"Le Pays Mossi."* *Bulletin de la Societé Géographique de l'Afrique Occidentale Française*, June 1908, pp. 60-70.
Lebeuf, Annie, M.D. "The Role of Women in the Political Organization of African Societies." In *Women of Tropical Africa*, pp. 93-120. Edited by Denise Paulme. Berkeley: University of California Press, 1963.
Ledange, Paul-Louis. *"Une colonie nouvelle: La Haute-Volta."* *La Revue Indigéne* 17 (1922): 133-36.
Legum, Colin, and Drysdale, John. *African Contemporary Record*. Annual Survey and Documents. Exeter: Africa Research, 1970.
Levtzion, N. *Ancient Ghana and Mali*. London: Metheun, 1973.
Londres, Albert. *Terre d'ébène*. Paris: Albin Michel, 1929.
Lonsdale, John. "States and Social Processes in Africa: A Historiographical Survey." *African Studies Review* 24, nos. 2-3 (June-September 1981): 139-225.
Mahaut, Charles. *La Colonie du Haut-Sénégal et Niger*. Paris, 1910.
Maïga, Mohamed. *"Haute-Volta: Douze heures avec Thomas Sankara."* *Afrique-Asie*, 26 September-9 October 1983, pp. 18 ff.
_____. *"Haute Volta: Une tache ardue pour le Premier Ministre."* *Jeune Afrique*, 27 February, 17 April, 24 April, and 26 July 1978.
Mangin, Eugene. *Les Mossi*. Paris: Challamel, 1921. (Rpt. from *Anthropos*, 1916). Translated by Ariane Brunel and Elliott Skinner and reissued by Human Relations Area Files, New Haven, CT: 1959.
Manoukian, Madeline. *Akan and Ga-Adangbe Peoples of the Gold Coast*. London: Oxford University Press, 1950.
Marc, Lucien, *Le pays mossi*. Paris: Larose, 1909.
Meyerowitz, Eva L.R. *Akan Traditions of Origin*. London: Faber & Faber, 1952.

Mikell, Gwendolyn. *Akan Funerary Terracottas and Ethno-Historical Change.* Washington, DC: Smithsonian Institution Museum of African Art Research Report, 1982.
──────. "Filiation, Economic Crisis, and the Status of Women in Rural Ghana." *Canadian Journal of African Studies* 18 (1948): 195-218.
Monteil, Lt.-Col. P.L. *De Saint-Louis à Tripoli par le Tchad.* Paris: F. Alcan, 1894.
"The Mossi and the Military." *West Africa,* 24 January 1983, p. 18.
Murdock, George P. *Africa: Its Peoples and Their Culture History.* New York: McGraw-Hill, 1959.
Noll, Ned. *"Le Mossi: La Mission du Lt. Voulet."* La Tour du Monde 33 (14 August 1897): 257.
"Oedipus Rex and Regina." *Africa* 47 (1977): 14-30.
Oliver, Roland. *The Cambridge History of Africa.* Cambridge: Cambridge University Press, 1977.
Ossendowski, Ferdinand. *Slaves of the Sun.* New York: E.P. Dutton, 1928.
Ouedraogo, Joseph, and Prost, André. *"Le Proprieté foncière chez les Mossi."* Notes Africaines 38 (1948): 16-18.
Posnansky, Merrick. "Archaeology and the Origins of Akan Society. In *Ghana Talks.* Edited by M. Dodds. Washington, DC: Three Continents, 1976.
──────. "Dating Ghana's Earliest Art." *African Arts* 13, no. 1 (1979): 52-53.
Randau, Robert. *"Au pays mossi."* Bulletin de la Societé de Géographie d'Alger et d'Afrique du Nord 39 (1934): 433 ff.
Rattray, R.S. *The Tribes of the Ashanti Hinterland.* 2 vols. Oxford: Oxford University Press, 1932.
Roberts, Stephen H. *History of French Colonial Policy, 1870-1925.* 2 vols. London: P.S. King & Son, 1929.
Ruelle, E. *"Notes anthropologiques, ethnographiques, et sociologiques sur quelques populations noires du 2° territoire de l'Afrique occidentale française."* L'Anthropologie 15 (1904).
al-Sa'di, Abderrahman (also as es Sadi). *Tarikh es-Sudan.* Translated by O. Houdas. Paris, 1900.
Sankara, Thomas. *"Mon dernier message: La tolerance."* Jeune Afrique, 4 November 1987, pp. 4-11.
Sarraut, Albert. *La Mise en valeur des colonies françaises.* Paris: Payot & Cie, 1923.
Service, Elman. "Classical and Modern Theories on the Origin of Government." In *Origins of the State,* pp. 21-34. Edited by Ronald Cohen and Elman Service. Philadelphia: Institute for the Study of Human Issues, 1978.
──────. *Origins of the State and Civilization.* New York: W.W. Norton, 1975.
Siriex, Paul-Henri. *Une nouvelle Afrique.* Paris, 1957.
Skinner, Elliott P. "The Diffusion of Islam in an African Society." *Annals of the New York Academy of Sciences* 96 (20 January 1962): 659-67.
──────. "The Effect of Co-residence of Sisters' Sons of African Corporate Patrilineal Descent Groups." *Cahiers d'etudes africaines* 16 (1964): 467-78.
──────. "Intergenerational Conflict among the Mossi: Father and Son." *Journal of Conflict Resolution* 5 (March 1961): 55-60.
──────. "Labour Migration and Its Relationship to Socio-Cultural Change in Mossi Society." *Africa* 30 (October 1960): 393-94.
──────. "The Mossi 'Pogisoure.'" *Man* 60 (February 1960): 20-23.

———. "The 'Paradox' of Rural Leadership: A Comment." *Journal of Modern African Studies* 6, no. 2 (1970): 199-201.

———. "Political Conflict and Revolution in an African Town." *American Anthropologist* 74 (1972): 1208-24.

———. "Trade and Markets among the Mossi People." In *Markets in Africa*, pp. 237-78. Edited by Paul Bohannan and George Dalton. Evanston, IL: Northwestern University Press, 1962.

Socquet, Msgr. "*L'eglise catholique en Afrique noire.*" *Magazine de l'AOF* 15 (August 1956): 62.

Southall, Alain. *Alur Society*. Cambridge: Cambridge University Press, 1956.

Tauxier, Louis. *Le noir du Soudan*. Paris: Larose, 1912.

———. *Le noir du Yatenga*. Paris: Larose, 1917.

Thompson, Virginia, and Adloff, Richard. *French West Africa*. Stanford, CA: Stanford University Press, 1958.

"Upper Volta: Postponing Marxism?" *Africa Confidential*, 8 June 1983, p. 7.

"Upper Volta: Ouedraogo Goes It Alone." *Africa Now*, July 1983, p. 2.

"Upper Volta: The Soldiers' Brief Honeymoon." *Africa Contemporary Records*, 1981, p. B565.

Van Vollenhoven, Joost. *Une Ame de chef*. Paris, 1920.

Von François, P. "*Voyage à Salaga et au Mossi.*" *Mittheilungen von Forschungsreisen den und Gelehrten aus den Deutschen Schutzgebieten* (1888): 143.

Wallerstein, Immanuel. "The Rise and Future Demise of the World Capitalist System: Concepts for Comparative Analysis." *Comparative Studies in Society and History* 16, no. 4 (October 1974): 389-415.

Weber, Max. *The Theory of Social and Economic Organization*. New York: Oxford University Press, 1947.

Wieskel, Timothy C. *French Colonial Rule and the Baule People: Resistance and Collaboration*. Oxford: Clarendon Press, 1980.

Wilks, Ivor. *Asante in the Nineteenth Century*. Cambridge: Cambridge University Press, 1975.

———. "Ashanti Government." In *West African Kingdoms of the Nineteenth Century*. Edited by D. Forde and P. Kaberry. Oxford: Oxford University Press, 1967, pp. 206-38.

———. "The Northern Factor in Ashanti History." Institute of African Studies, University College of Ghana, 1961.

Wolfson, Freda. *Pageant of Ghana*. London: Oxford University Press, 1959.

Wright, Gordon. *The Reshaping of French Democracy*. 1948. Rpt. Boston: Beacon Press, 1970.

Ziegler, Jean. *Sankara: Un nouveau pouvoir africain*. Paris: editions Pierre-Marcel Favre, 1986.

INDEX

Abidjan, 176, 181, 211, 227, 231
Abuja, 231
Adjoua, Mamie, 227
Adultery, 43, 86-87, 91, 94. *See also* Wives; Women
African Agricultural Union, 181
Afrique Nouvelle, 194
Agriculture, 2, 14, 163, 214
   revenues from, 109-11, 118-20
ben-Ahmad, Amin, 95
Ahmadou, 150
AIDS, 228
Alby, 149
Algeria, 214, 225
Amnesty International, 233
Amulets, royal. *See* Namtibo
Ancestors,
   veneration of, 5, 62, 128-35
Animals
   domestic, 4, 8, 92, 112, 113, 114-15, 122
   wild, 4, 5, 119
Apter, David, 224
Armies, 104-8. *See also* Tansoba
Asantehene, 142
Ashanti, 2, 11, 12, 99, 119, 143
Askia Daoud, 14, 97
Askia-El-Hadj-Mohammed (Askia the Great), 14, 96-97
Atlanta, Georgia, 229
Auriol, Vincent, 185

Baba. *See* Ouidi Naba
Babingida, Ibrahim, 231
Babissi, 20-21, 29, 55. *See also* Lineages
Baganda, 10
Bagare, 50, 152
Baglere, 6-7, 29, 116-17
Baglere Naba, 20, 91, 94

Balima, Albert S., 176-77, 185
Baloum Naba, 181, 182, 208
   administration of district of, 70-71, 75, 76
   ceremonial duties of, 37, 129, 130, 131, 137
   and election of district chief, 55, 56, 57, 58
   and election of Mogho Naba, 40, 41
   sources of revenue, 118
   and war, 105
Bambara, 14, 97
Bandiagara, 8, 9
Banditry, and district chiefs, 122-23
Baongo, Mogho Naba, 115-16
Baongo Naba, 150
Baogo. *See* Ousmane Congo, Moro Naba
Barkago, 29-31, 135
Barkago Naba, 61
Barraud, Ali, 211
Barraud, General (French), 176
Barth, Henry, 4, 14, 62, 112-13, 141, 142-43
Basgha, 121, 129-32;
   in colonial period, 162, 174
   defined, 111
Batie, 175
Baulé, 181
Bendere, 34
Bendere Naba, 56, 110
   historical and musical duties of, 35, 37, 41, 43, 130-31
Benin, the, 219
Bergo, 5
Berlin Conference (1884-85), 143
Berthet, Max, 202
Bilbalgo ward, 110
Biligo, Naba, 17-18
   descendants and followers of, 27-31
Binger, Louis, 137, 146
   and Boukary Koutou, 123, 144-45, 154
   on Mossi political strengths, 98, 127

and Naba Sanum, 63, 67, 71, 98, 114, 126-27, 144-45
on Ramadan, 138-40
on slave raids, 103-4, 211
on taxes, 115
Birifo, 5
Black Volta River, 3, 5, 9
Bobo, 5
Bobo-Dioulasso, 175, 185, 203
Boisson, Pierre, 176
Bondsmen. *See* Baglere; Dapore
Boni, Nazi, 193
Boodkasma (pl. Boodkasemdamba), 20-24, 81, 124
Boodoo, 15, 20-22
Bornu, 1
Bouda, François, 185, 186, 194-95, 203, 213
Boukary Koutou. *See* Binger, Louis; Wobogo
Boulga Naba, 56, 166
Boulsa, 9, 10, 16, 18, 101, 102, 104, 106, 107
Boussouma, 2-3, 9, 10, 65-66, 100, 101, 102, 152
Bowdich, T.E., 142
Brazzaville Conference (January 1944), 178-79
Burkina Faso, name change to, 2, 223
Busansi, 8, 9, 13, 29, 143, 167
as slaves, 103, 115
Burthe d'Annelet, J.C., 176

Canada, 229
Caravan routes, 5, 112-15, 143
Catholicism, 165, 171-174
Castro, Fidel, 218, 229
CDRs. *See* Committees for the Defense of the Revolutions
Centrale Syndicate Voltaïque (CVS), 213
Cercles, 158, 166
Charismatic leadership
Sankara's, 219, 223-25, 231-32, 238
theory on, 224
Cheron, Georges, 18, 54, 69
Christianity, 141, 165, 170-74
Cinematography, Burkinabe festival of, 228
Claessen, Henri J.M., 11
Clans. *See* Boodoo
Clapperton, Hugh, 142
CMRPN. *See* Military Council for Redress and National Recovery

CNR (National Revolutionary Council)
under Sankara, 223, 233, 234
Cohen, Ronald, 11
Committees for the Defense of the Revolution (CDRs), 223, 227
and Sankara's downfall, 234, 237
and terrorism, 231
and trade unions, 232-33
Compaore, Blaise, 221, 223, 227, 238
and coup against Sankara, 234-35
and labor unions, 233
"The Condition of the Native Woman" (Hesling), 169
Confederation Nationale des Travailleurs Voltaiques (CNTV), 213
Confederation Syndicale Burkinara, 233
Congo, Etienne, 179, 195, 198
Congo, Issoufou. *See* Sagha II
Congo, Moussa. *See* Kougri, Mogho Naba
Congo, Ousmane. *See* Ousname Congo
Conquizitenga, 10
Conombo, Joseph, 193-97, 200, 210, 211, 212, 213, 218, 223
Conseil de l'Entente, 204
Conseils de notables indigènes (Council of Native Notables), 167-69
Conseil de salut du peuple (CSP). *See* CSP
Constituent Assembly, 18, 182, 183
Cotton, 4, 47, 113, 115, 163, 226
Cotonou, 219
Coulibaly, Ouezzain, 196-97, 200, 201
Council of Chiefs (rural Mossi), 206-7
Courts, 82-92, 121
under French, 161, 168-69
of Mogho Naba, 43, 92-93
Crimes, 80-90, 93-94
Crops, 3-5, 113, 114, 118-19, 185. *See also* by name, e.g., Cotton; Indigo
Crown Prince. *See* Djiba Naba
Crozat, Dr., 97, 98, 99, 105, 107
and Moslems, 137
on political organization, 63, 67-68
and taxes, 111-12, 114
and Wobogo, 34, 45, 64, 146-48
CSP (Conseil de salut du peuple), 218, 220, 221, 223
"Cube Maggi," coup of, 223
Customs Union, 227

Dabili, 131
Daga Naba, 120

Dagari, 5
Dagoumba, 5, 6, 7, 8, 99
Dahomey, 5, 219
Dakar, 229
Dapore, 29, 116
Dapore Naba, 20, 43, 91, 94
Dapoya, 110, 116
D'Arboussier, Gabriel, 160, 184, 186
Dawoema, Mogho Naba, 64
Death and funeral rites, 51-53, 58, 61
Debere River, 3
De Beauminy, André, 164
Dedougou, 175
De Gaulle, Charles, 177, 180, 200-201, 204, 206
Delafosse, Maurice, 5, 63, 67
Delavignette, Robert, 164, 175, 176
Delobson, Dim. See Dim Delobson
Destenave, Cdr., 150, 156
Diaba Lompo, 8, 9, 208
Diakité, Moussa, 227
Diallo, Arba, 218
Diawara, Mohammed, 227
Dim (pl. Dimdamba), 10, 18, 58, 59, 102, 128, 206
 and election of Mogho Naba, 54
 and Mogho Naba, 16, 66-68, 100, 111
Dim Delobson, 34, 46, 174
 on capture of Ouagadougou, 151-52
 and Djiba Naba, 48, 50
 and revenues, 122
Dimvousse, 42
District chiefs. See Kombere
Districts, 16-17, 26, 68-73
Dixon, Andrew, 143
Djenne, 10, 13, 14
Djiba, 26, 47-48, 49
Djiba Naba, 47-53, 111
Dogon, 5, 8
Dogunba, 46-47. See also Wives
Dorange, Michel, 192
Dori, 113, 175, 221
Doulougou district, 17
Doulougou, Mogho Naba, 64-66, 99, 105, 137
Dry season, 3-4
 and warfare, 107-8
Dubois, Félix, 113
Duglas, Jean Jacques, 185-86
Dupont, André, 173, 191-92
Dupuis, Joseph, 142

Earth deities and shrines. See Tengkouga
Economic Community of West African States (ECOWAS), 227, 231
Education, 165, 170, 171, 225
Egypt, 1, 10
Electoral colleges, 54, 179, 197-98
Electoral law, 184
Entente Voltaïque, 187, 194
Eunuchs, 43, 45, 88, 116. See also Kamsaogho Naba
The Evolution of Political Society (Fried), 10
"On the Evolution of Social Stratification and the State" (Fried), 10
Executions, 20, 43, 90-93
Eyadema, Gnassigbe, 226

Fada-N'Gourma, 2, 8, 9, 33, 158, 175
 relationship to Mogho Naba, 62, 98
 and Mogho Naba, 62, 98
 war with Boulsa, 106, 107
Fado, 60, 111, 112, 118. See also Taxes
Federal Union of the Syndicates of the Traditional Chiefs, 195, 202
Ferguson, George Ekem, 149, 154
Fespaco, 228
Fortes, Meyer, 6, 7
Foulse, 8
Fouta-Djalon, 14
Fouta-Toro, 14
FPV, 212, 215
France, 2, 12, 178-91, 200, 204, 206, 207, 208
 assimilation policy of, 156
 conquest of Mossi, 100, 104, 105, 106, 150-154
 economic policy, 163-66, 175-76
 effects of World War II on colonial policy of, 176-78
 Lamizana and Saye Kerbo in army of, 208, 214
 Missions to Mossi, 144-49
 and Mossi political organization, 156-62, 167, 168
 and religion, 171-73
 and Sankara, 220, 221, 224, 226, 228
 and young officers, 218, 221, 226, 228
Free French Forces, 177-78
French Union, 186, 187, 192
French West Africa, 159, 177, 187, 197
Fried, Morton H., 10-11, 12
Fruit trees, 118-19
Fulani, 14, 29, 102, 223

Fulbe, 14
Fulse, 5
Gambaga, 7, 8, 14
Gandago, 9
Gande Naba, 43, 131, 134
Gaoua, 175
Germany, 144, 149
Ghana, 1, 5, 6, 7
  Burkinabe workers in, 237
  and Sankara, 219, 220, 221, 224, 226
Ghanata, 10
Gifts, 60, 71, 86, 112, 117
Godin, 29, 30, 31
Gold Coast, 113, 149, 172, 174, 176, 177
Gorer, Geoffrey, 173
Gounga Naba
  administration of, 69, 72
  and Crown Prince election, 48-49
  and district chief election, 55
  and Mogho Naba election, 39
  and war, 105
Gourcy, 9, 150
Gourma, 5, 9, 13
Gourounsi, 244
Great Britain, 143, 145, 149, 154. *See also* Talensi
Grenada, 229
Group d'Action Populaire (GAP), 210
Guiérma, Frédéric, 215, 218
Guilingou, 8, 9
Gurmanche, 5
Gur languages, 5
Gurunsi, 5, 8, 17, 154, 166-67
  as slaves, 29, 103, 115

Habe, 8
Harlem, Sankara on, 229
Harmattan, 3
Hausa, 1, 5, 44, 142
Haut-Sénégal et Niger, 158, 161, 163
Hesling, Edouard, 163, 165, 166, 168, 169, 171, 173, 174, 186
Houphouët-Boigny, Félix, 181-85, 196, 200, 204
  and end of Lamizana administration, 211
  and young officers and Sankara, 220, 226-27, 231

Illiteracy reforms, Sankara's, 225
Imam, 35, 44, 49, 136-40
Incest, 80
Indépendants d'Outre-Mer (IOM), 193

Indigénat, 161, 168, 177, 182, 189
Indigo, 4, 113
Indochina, 209, 214
Inheritance law, 85-86
Interregnum, periods and rites, 51-53, 70, 124
Institute of the Black World, 228
Islam, 4, 12, 13, 14, 96-98, 136-40, 167, 173-74, 209. *See also* Imam
Ivory Coast, 5, 163, 175, 176, 177, 179, 180, 181, 182, 211, 231
  and Burkinabe residents and workers in, 227, 236-37
  Sankara, 226-27
  and young officers, 219

Jackson, Jesse, 229
Jeune Afrique, 229, 235, 238
John II (King, Portugal), 14, 141

Kabore, Salif, 233
Kaglere, Naba, 27, 88, 89, 153
Kam Naba, 110
Kambo Naba, 43
Kamboinse, 117
Kamsaogho Naba
  administration of, 69
  and election of Mogho Naba, 39
  and the French, 157
  and Kourita, 53
  source of revenue, 112, 116, 118
  and war, 105
Kanem, 1
Kango Naba, 63-64
Kaoko, 42
Kankam Moussa, 13
Karfo, Mogho Naba, 70, 102
Kargougou, Moussa, 213
Kasena, 8
Kasko, 42
Kaya, 223
Keemse, 128. *See also* Ancestors, veneration of
Keita, Modibo, 224
Kenyatta, Jomo, 224
Kerekou, Col. Mathieu, 219
Kiba Naba, 65, 100
Kibisi, 9
Ki-basgha. *See* Basgha
Killing, accidental and homicidal, 89-91
Kinship. *See* Lineages
Kipirsi mountain range, 2, 8, 9

Ki-Zerbo, Professor Joseph, 212, 213, 215, 223
Koabga, 74, 152
Koelle, Sigismund, 143
Kombemba, 206
Kom Naba, 65-66, 101
Kom II, Mogho Naba, 46, 157-58, 166, 176, 179
  death of, 178-79
  in World War II, 176-77
Kombere (pl. Kombemba), 16, 20, 72-77, 118-22
  under French, 190-91
Kongo, Bila, 166
Konkomba, 5
Kongo lineage, 30
Kos Naba, 44, 114-15, 120
Koudougou, 9-10, 212
Koudoumie, Mogho Naba, 9-10, 18, 128
Kougri, Mogho Naba, 40, 46, 197-205, 206, 207, 208, 212, 213, 214
  death of, 215, 217, 218, 220
  and Islam, in Lamizana administration, 209-10
  Ivory Coast trip of (1973), 211
  Mossi wedding of, 203
Kouliga, 30
Koulougbagha, 7
Kountche, Seyni, 226
Kourita, 16, 53, 94, 128, 179
Koutou, Boukary. *See* Binger, Louis; Wobogo, Mogho Naba
Koutou, Kouta, 74
Koutou, Mogho Naba, 101, 145, 155
Krause, Dr., 129, 144
Kuna'aba, 6
Kurugu, 7
Kwaga, Basgha, 37, 129

La, 9
Labor, forced, 177, 180, 186
Labor unions. *See* Trade unions
Labouret, Henri, 160, 176
Lalle Naba, 107-8
Lambert, Capt., 70
Lamizana, Aboubacar Sangoulé
  administration of, 209-11, 212, 213
  downfall of, 214
  post-coup, 215, 218
Land, Mossi attitude toward, 32, 109
Languages, Niger-Congo family, 5
Larhalle Naba

administration of, 69, 208
and election of Mogho Naba, 39
and the French, 157
religious duties of, 129, 132-34
sources of revenue, 118
and war, 105
Libya, 219, 220, 226, 229. *See also* al-Quaddafi, Mu'ammar; Tripoli
Ligue patriotique pour le development (LIPAD), 218
Ligidi, Naba, 65, 100-101
Lingani, Maj. Jean-Baptiste, 221, 234, 235
Lineages, 15-24
  administrative, 69
  of Barkago, 29-31
  and nam, 30-32, 60
LIPAD. *See* Ligue patriotique . . .
Lobi, 5
Loi-cadre, 194, 200
Londres, Albert, 163
Lonsdale, Capt. R. La T., 143
Louveau, M., 176
Lovedu, 10
Lower Ivory Coast, 176, 177
Lumbila, 9
Lumumba, Patrice, 224

Mabissi, 28
Madagascar, 209, 223
Mali, 1, 2, 5, 8, 13, 14, 95, 141, 211
  and Sankara and 1985 war, 224, 227
Mamprusi, 5, 6, 7, 98-99
Mandingo-Dioula, 14
Mane, 10, 16, 101, 115, 152
Mangin, Eugène, 80, 107, 159-60
  on slaves, 103, 115
Mansa, Souliman, 13
Marabout, 114, 139
Marc, Lucien, 13, 92, 114, 141, 145-46, 148
Marie-André, Sister, 171
Markets, 43-44
  chiefs of, 174
  taxes, 114-15, 120
Marriage, 24-26, 46, 172
Marx, Karl, 218
Mazi, 135, 153
M'barengma, 129
Mecca, 13
Metals, 4
Millet, 72, 120, 127

Military Council for Redress and
    National Recovery (CMRPN), 214,
    215
Ministers
    administration of, 69-73
    ceremonial duties of, 35-38, 129-35
    and Crown Prince, 48-50
    and death of Mogho Naba, 51-53
    of districts, 75-76
    and election of district chief, 55-57
    and election of Mogho Naba, 39-42
    and the French, 157
    sources of revenue, 110, 112, 116, 118
    and war, 104-8
Missionaries, 170-73
Mitterand, François, 215, 219, 220,
    228-29
MLN, 212, 214
Mogho
    defined, 2
    features of area, 3-5
Mogho Naba, 9, 20, 31-43, 92-93, 174
    administration of, 62-68, 70-72
    court of, 43-51
    death of, 51-53
    Dimdamba, 16, 66-68
    and district chief, 55, 58, 73-74
    and French, 160-61, 165, 168, 183-95,
        200, 204-5
    historical, 105
    sources of revenue, 109-17, 121, 126-27
Monteil, Lt. Col., 148
Moré, 217
Moro Naba. See Mogho Naba
Morocco, 13, 224
Moshi-Gurunshi languages, 5
Moslems. See Islam
Mossi. See also Fada N'Gourma;
    Ouagoudougou; Tenkodogo;
    Yatenga; Rural Mossi; Urban Mossi
    cash crops and farming of, 3-4, 5
    geography and geology of, 2-4
    myth of origin of, 7-10
    political organization, 6-7, 125-27,
        156-59
    and Sankara, 217, 223, 238
    social structure, 1-2
    trade by, in Barth, 5
Mottoba, Mogho Naba, 212
Moumde, 17
Mour-Salih-Djaaura, 96-97
Mouvement Democratique Voltaïque
    (MDV), 192-96

Mouvement de Liberation Nationale
    (MLN), 210
Mouvement de Regroupement Africain,
    202
Mouvement Populaire de la Revolution
    Africaine (MPA), 193
Municipal Council (Ouagadougou), 208
Muslims. *See* Islam

Na (also Nab, Naba), 5, 19, 33, 43
Na'asira, 96-97
Nab'yiri, 27
Nab'yure, 41
Nakomce, 18, 20, 52, 208
Naleregu, 7
Nam, 15, 54, 63, 128
    and kin group, 22
    and Kombere, 58-59
    and Mogho Naba, 38-39, 47-48
    and Mogho Naba Kougri, 215
    1980 conflict over, 214
    and village chief, 82
Namenda Naba, 16, 18
Namoos lineages, 6, 7
Namtibo (royal amulets), 9-10, 16, 37,
    40, 41, 42, 55, 131
    "drinking" of, 40, 42, 56, 136
    sacrifices to, 55, 130
Nankana, 7
Naouri mountains, 3
Napoko, 41, 51-53, 179
Narila, 30
Natenga, 29
National Assembly, 186, 209, 210, 211,
    213, 214
National Council of the Revolution, 238
National Renovation Council (CNR),
    211, 223
National Revolutionary Council (CNR),
    223-35
Nedege Naba, 7, 8
Nemdo Naba, 44, 114
New York, Sankara in, 229
Ngado, 27, 30
Niger (nation), 226
Niger area, 10, 13, 95, 113, 158
Niger-Congo languages, 5
Nigeria, 231
Ninisi, 5, 8, 9, 14, 17, 31, 119, 134
Nkrumah, Kwame, 224
Nobere, 17, 26-29, 48, 75-77
Nobere Naba, 57-59

Nobila, 58-59
Nobili, 77
Nobles, 76, 82, 89, 91
  and commoners, 12, 28, 125
Noll, Ned, 149, 151
Nunuma, 8
Nyennega, 7, 13, 128, 133, 140
  as Mossi progenitrix, 8, 99
Nucci, Christian, 220

L'Observateur, 215
Omar, El Hadj, 2, 98, 127
Organisation Voltaique des Syndicate
  Libres (CVSL), 213
Organization of Revolutionary Military
  (OMR), 234
Ouagadougou, 11, 25, 33, 113
  administration of, 68-69
  as capital of post-1955 republic, 206, 207
  and the French, 151-52, 158
  kingdom of, 2, 8-10, 13, 14, 236
  political systems in, post-1955, 208
  riots of 1964 in, 209
  and Yatenga, 99-100, 112, 128
Ouahigouya, 8, 9, 13, 158, 220
Ouaraga, Mogho Naba, 66
Ouayougya, 100-101
Oubri, 8, 9, 15-20, 107, 175
  and governors, 69
  line of descent, 33, 100, 128
  nam of, and Mogho Naba Kougri, 215
  and Tense, 132-33
Oubritenga, 9
Oubya, Mogho Naba, 66
Ouedrango Naba, 43
Ouedraogo (Stallion),
  as progenitor of Mossi, 8, 9, 10, 15, 20, 133, 175
  line of descent, 33, 100, 128
  nam of, and Mogho Naba Kougri, 215
Ouedraogo, Gérard Kango, 192, 210, 211, 212
  as head of National Assembly, 213
  post-coup, 218, 223
Ouedraogo, Jean-Baptiste
  coup by, and Sankara, 215
  as Mossi, 217
  1983 coup removing, 223
  relationship with Sankara, 219-20, 221
Ouedraogo, Joseph, 223
  arrest by young officers, 218
  as first mayor of Ouagadougou, 207

  as FPV leader, 215
  under Lamizana, 210
  and G.K. Ouedraogo, 211
Ouedraogo, Macaire, 212
Ouedraogo, Maxine, 211
Ouedraogo, Capt. Pierre, 233
Ouende, 128
Ouennam, 128
Ouidi Naba, 208
  administration of, 69-70, 73, 75-76
  as Baba, 70
  and Crown Prince, 49-50
  and election of district chief, 55
  and election of Mogho Naba, 38-41
  and revenues, 110, 118
  and war, 105
Ousmane Congo
  Moro Naba, 220, 232, 237
  made Mogho Naba, 217
Overseas France, 182, 187
OXFAM, 226

Pabre, myth of, 9-10, 128, 210
Pacts, ritual Mossi, 98-100
Pages, 43-45, 51-52, 58, 117
Pan-Africanism, 226, 228
Paris, 219, 220, 221
Paris-Dakar, 200
Parti africain de l'independence (PAI), 218
Parti Démocratique de la Côte d'Ivoire (PDCI), 182, 184
Parti Démocratique Unifié (PDU), 196
Parti Démocratique Voltaïque (PDV), 193
Parti du Regroupement Africain (PRA), 210
Parti Social d'Education des Masses
  Africaines (PSEMA), 194-97, 200
Paspanga, 42
Patriotic League for Development, 233
Peace Corps, 224
Penne, Guy, 220
People's Salvation Council. See Conseil de Salut du Peuple
Petain, Marshal, 178, 180
Peulh Fulani, 14
PF (President of Faso). See Sankara
Piga Naba, 64-66, 101
Pinchon, 98-99
Place d'Armes, 209
Plants, in Mossi territory, 3, 107. See also
  Agriculture; Crops

INDEX

Plimpikou, 2
Poison, 107
Po, 221, 223, 224
Poko, 36, 126
Portugal, 14, 74, 141
Postes, 158
Poughtoenga, 8, 132
Pougoula, 66
Pouitenga, 5
Pouriketa, 8
Provinces, government of, 68-73
Pughsiudse, 25, 45, 116
Pughsiure system, 117, 171-72
Pughtiema, 45, 84, 129-32
Punishments, 80-91
Pwe Naba, 43, 84

al-Qaddafi, Mu'ammar, 218, 219

Raga Naba, 43, 44, 114
Railroads, 163, 189, 226, 231
Rainfall, 3
Ramadan, 138-39
Raogo tales, 126
Rape, 81-82
Rassemblement Démocratique Africain (RDA), 183, 187, 193, 197, 202
Rattray, Robert Sutherland, 6, 7
Rawa, 8, 9, 10
Rawlings, Jerry, 218
  and Sankara, 219, 226
Reagan, Ronald, 229
Red Volta River, 3, 5, 26
Refugees, 19, 28
Republic of the Upper Volta, name change to Burkina Faso, 2, 223
Rhodesia, 225
Rialle, 7-10, 128
Riziam, 10, 101
Robin Hoods theory, Apter's 224
Ruelle, E., 103
Rural Mossi, post-1955 political power of, 206, 207-10, 212, 214, 217, 232
  effect of French on, 236-37
  and Sankara, 223

Saba district, 210
Sacrifices, 30, 43, 48, 132-35
  for dead Mogho Naba, 53, 55, 61
al-Sa'di, Abderrahman (also es-Sadi), 13
Sagha I, Mogho Naba, 27, 42, 58
Sagha II, Mogho Naba, 40, 179-80, 195, 197, 206

looting on death of, 217
Sahel, drought in, 211
Saka (pl. saghse), 27, 78
Sakakasma. *See* Village chief
Sakhaboutenga, 136, 139
Saksobadamba, 78
Samande Naba, 43, 105
Samande Nabila, 40, 43
Samande-kamba, 43, 56, 61, 84
Samogho population, 209
Saye Zerbo of, 214, 215
Sana, Mogho Naba, 10
Sankara, Thomas
  books on, 231
  as charismatic leader, 219, 223, 224-25, 232, 238
  coup against, and death, 234-35
  development and reform policies of, 217-18, 219, 224-26, 231, 233
  in Mali-Upper Volta conflict, 211
  pan-Africanism and populism of, 224, 226
  relationship with Jean-Baptiste Ouedraogo, 215, 219-21, 237
Sanum, Mogho Naba, 39, 46, 64-67, 77, 94, 121
  Binger on, 63, 71, 98, 114, 126-27, 144-45
  and Ligidi, 100-101
  and Tanga, 74, 108
Sarafere, 10
Sarraut, Albert, 162-63, 174-75
Savimbi, 228
Scal, Capt., 154, 156
Seabrooks, 164
Sebogo Naba, 102
Seghse, 118
Segou, 14
Senghor, Léopold Sédar, 229
Senufo, 5
Sere, 9
Serfs. *See* Baglere; Dapore
"Siamese twins," coup by, 215, 219. *See also* Ouedraogo, J.-B.; Sankara
Siamse, 28
Sighiri, Mogho Naba, 153-54, 157
Sighiri Naba, 101
Simili-Mossi, 14, 29
  Sankara as, 223
Sisala, 8
Slaves and slavery, 20, 73, 84, 103-4
  abolished by French, 161-62
  revenue from 115-16

Socquet, Msgr., 171
Somba, 5
Somé, Gabriel Yorian, 219, 220, 221
Songhai, 1, 13, 14, 44, 95-97
Soninke Moslems, 14
Sonni-Ali, 96, 127
Sore Naba, 110
Soretasgho ritual, 109, 162
Sosogha, 110, 120, 123
Sourou River, 3
South Africa, 228, 229
Soviet Union, 218, 226
Sudan, 3-4, 12, 62, 127, 139, 143, 158, 175
Swazi, 10

Taleland, 7
Tallensi, 5, 6, 7
Tambao, 226
Tamboura, Amadou, 200-201
Tanga, 74, 102, 108
Tankourou, 8
Tansoba
  and death of Mogho Naba, 52
  of district, 75-76
  and election of Mogho Naba, 39, 42
  and war, 104
Tarikh es-Sudan, 13, 95-96
Tauxier, Louis, 13-14, 132, 150, 159
Taxes, 44, 63, 120, 188
  fado, 60, 111, 112, 118
  by French, 158-60, 176
Tedego, 17
Tema, 10
Ten, 5
Tena, 5
Teng, 5
Tenga, 5, 40, 132, 135
Tenga Naba, 59, 61
Tengkom, 102-3
Tengkouga, 17, 110, 120, 128
Tengsoba (pl. Tengosobadamba), 5, 8, 30, 59, 61, 119, 131
  under French, 162
  and Mogho Naba, 52, 135-36
  and Tense, 134
Tenkodogo, 2, 8, 9, 52, 62, 69, 100, 156, 175
  decline of, 33
Tense, 121, 162, 174
  ritual of, 132-35
Territorial Assembly, 184, 201-2
Theft, 80, 88, 168

Third Republic
  constitution of, 212
  1980 overthrow of, 214
Timbuktu, 10, 13, 14, 95, 113, 141
Tinguimbissi, 8
Tiraonogo, 18
Toese, 7, 26
Togo, 226
Togoland, 113
Tombo, 8
Tongo area, 6
Torture, 91
Totebaldo Naba, 64
Totoabo, 66, 102
Tougouri Naba, 64
Touré, Samory, 2, 98, 127, 224
Touré, Sekou, 201, 224
Touré, Soumane, 233
Trade, 4, 112-14
Trade unions, 211
  and Sankara, 220, 232-33
  strike of May 1979, 213
  strikes of 1980, 214-15
Traoré, Mobessa, 227
Treason, 94
Trentinian, Lt. Col., 150
Tripoli, Sankara in, 219

UDV-RDA, 202, 203, 207
  Kougri support of, 210
  and Lamizana, 212
UNDP, 226
Union of Burkinabe Communists (UCB), 234
Union of Communist Fighters— Restructured (ULC-R), 234
Union of Communist Groups (UGC), 234
Union Démocratique Voltaïque-Rassemblement Démocratique Africain. *See* UDV-RDA
Union Nationale pour la Defense de la Démocratie (UNDD), 212
Union Progressiste Voltaïque (FPV), 212
Union of the Traditional Chiefs of the Upper Volta, 187-88
Union Voltaïque (UDIHV), 182, 184, 187, 192
United Nations, 206
  Sankara's General Assembly speech, 229
United States
  aid, 226

Sankara's view on, 228, 229
   and young officers, 218, 219
Upper Ivory Coast, 176
Upper Volta, 2, 5, 163-64, 174-75,
      183-87, 191
   constitution under Lamizana, 209, 211
   elections (1970, 1978), 210, 212-13
   independence of, 204
   international sovereignty of, 206, 207,
      209, 217
   Lamizana administration of, 210-11
   name change of, to Burkina Faso, 2,
      223
   post-1955 political parties, 210, 211, 212
   restoration of, 100
   Third Republic (1977), 211-12, 214
   and Vichy government, 177-78
   and young officers, 211, 217-23
Urban Mossi, post-1955, 212, 214

Van Vollenhoven, Joos, 162-64
Venewende, 65-66
Vichy government, 177-78
le Vieux. *See* Houphouët-Boigny, Félix
Village chief, 76-79, 82
   election of, 54-55, 59-61
   under French, 189
   source of revenue, 123-24
Villages, 18, 21, 68
   law in, 81
   of Nobere, 26-29
   revenue to district chief, 119-22
   wars between, 102-3
Voltaic culture area, 5
Von François, P., 145
Vooko district, 58-59, 77
Voulet, Lt., 150-54, 175

Walata, 10, 13
Waraga, Mogho Naba, 36, 44, 107
Waregoumga, 9
We, 5
We Are the World, 226
Weber, Max, 224, 238
Weogho, 119, 123
White Volta River, 3, 5, 57
Witchcraft, 90
Wives, 51, 80-82, 110
   and Crown Prince, 47
   of Kombere, 58
   of Mogho Naba, 43-47
   and punishment, 160
   as vote incentive, 60

Woboto, Mogho Naba (Boukary
      Koutou), 45, 50, 74, 103, 123, 127,
      135.
   and administration, 64-66
   and Binger, 144-45
   and Crozat, 146-48
   deposed, 154-55
   election of, 34, 39-40
   and Moslems, 138-40
   taxes, 114
   and warfare, 64, 99, 105, 107
Women, 24-26, 51, 83, 102. *See also*
      Pughsiudse; Wives
   and court cases, 86-87
   and French, 169-72
   Hesling on, 169
   role of, 51, 167, 169, 170, 236
   under Sankara, 225
   in state development theory, 10-12, 132
World, Weber concept of, and new
      republic, 206-7, 237-38
   and Robin Hoods theory, 224-25
World Bank, 226, 231
World War I, Mossi service for France
      in, 160, 167
World War II, Mossi service for France
      in, 176-78
   and Sankara, 228

Yadega, 9-10, 128
Yadese. *See* Yatenga
Yagenga, 80-82
Yako, 5, 9, 10, 63-64, 68, 99, 223
Yamassoukro, 227
Yaméogo, Hermann, 212
Yaméogo, Maurice (M. Maurice), 196,
      200-204, 206, 208, 212
   forced resignation of (1964), 209, 210
   Houphouët-Boigny, 211
   as Mossi head of state, 217
   prison term, end of, 221
Yange, 13
Yarse, 14, 29, 112
Yatenga, 2, 10, 13, 68, 95, 128, 158, 207,
      210
Yatenga Naba, 10, 33, 62, 111-12, 165
Yemde Naba, 65-67, 94, 100
Yemse, 115-16
Yirisoba, 24, 80, 124-25
Yiya (sing. yiri), 27
Young, Andrew, 229
Young officers
   anti-Western links of, 219

break of, 219-20
coup of 1982, 223

Zabo, 66
Zande Naba, 65, 77
Zandoma, 8, 9, 10

Zende Naba, 102
Zerbo, Colonel Say, 214, 218
Ziri, 8, 9
Zombere, Mogho Naba, 48
Zongo, Capt. Henry, 221, 234, 235
Zoungourana, 8-9, 133